LEARNING TO 1
FOREIGN LANGUAGES
IN THE SECONDARY
SCHOOL

This new, fourth edition has been comprehensively updated to take account of recent policy and curriculum changes, and now covers a range of relevant statutory frameworks. Fully revised chapters cover the key knowledge and skills essential for becoming a foreign language teacher:

- What can we learn from research into language teaching and learning?
- Teaching methods and learning strategies
- Creating a meaningful learning environment
- Transition from Primary to Secondary
- The role of digital technologies
- Teaching in the target language
- Receptive skills and productive skills
- Teaching and learning grammar
- Planning and reflecting on classroom practice
- Pupil differences and differentiation
- Assessment for and of learning.

It includes many examples of how to analyse practice to ensure pupil learning is maximised, together with activities and tasks to support you as you analyse your own learning and performance.

Learning to Teach Foreign Languages in the Secondary School provides practical help and support for many of the situations and potential challenges you are faced with in school. It is an essential purchase for every aspiring Secondary foreign languages school teacher.

Norbert Pachler is Professor of Education at the Institute of Education, University of London.

Michael Evans is Reader in Education at the University of Cambridge.

Ana Redondo is Senior Lecturer in Education and Subject Leader of a Secondary PGCE in Modern Languages at the University of Bedfordshire.

Linda Fisher is Senior Lecturer in Education at the Faculty of Education, University of Cambridge.

LEARNING TO TEACH SUBJECTS IN THE SECONDARY SCHOOL SERIES

Series editors: Susan Capel, Marilyn Leask and Tony Turner

Designed for all students learning to teach in Secondary schools, and particularly those on school-based initial teacher training courses, the books in this series complement *Learning to Teach in the Secondary School* and its companion, *Starting to Teach in the Secondary School*. Each book in the series applies underpinning theory and addresses practical issues to support student teachers in school and in the training institution in learning how to teach a particular subject.

Learning to Teach in the Secondary School, 6th edition
Edited by Susan Capel, Marilyn Leask and Tony Turner

Learning to Teach Art and Design in the Secondary School,
2nd edition
Edited by Nicholas Addison and Lesley Burgess

Learning to Teach Citizenship in the Secondary School, 2nd edition
Edited by Liam Gearon

Learning to Teach Design and Technology in the Secondary School, 2nd edition
Edited by Gwyneth Owen-Jackson

Learning to Teach English in the Secondary School, 3rd edition
Edited by Jon Davison and Jane Dowson

Learning to Teach Geography in the Secondary School,
2nd edition
David Lambert and David Balderstone

Learning to Teach History in the Secondary School, 3rd edition
Edited by Terry Haydn, James Arthur, Martin Hunt and Alison Stephen

Learning to Teach ICT in the Secondary School
Edited by Steve Kennewell, John Parkinson and Howard Tanner

Learning to Teach Mathematics in the Secondary School, 3rd edition
Edited by Sue Johnston-Wilder, Peter Johnston-Wilder, David Pimm and Clare Lee

Learning to Teach Foreign Languages in the Secondary School,
4th edition
Norbert Pachler, Michael Evans, Ana Redondo and Linda Fisher

Learning to Teach Music in the Secondary School, 2nd edition
Edited by Chris Philpott and Gary Spruce

Learning to Teach Physical Education in the Secondary School,
3rd edition
Edited by Susan Capel

Learning to Teach Religious Education in the Secondary School, 2nd edition
Edited by L. Philip Barnes, Andrew Wright and Ann-Marie Brandom

Learning to Teach Science in the Secondary School, 3rd edition
Edited by Jenny Frost

Learning to Teach Using ICT in the Secondary School, 3rd edition
Edited by Marilyn Leask and Norbert Pachler

Starting to Teach in the Secondary School, 2nd edition
Edited by Susan Capel, Ruth Heilbronn, Marilyn Leask and Tony Turner

LEARNING TO TEACH FOREIGN LANGUAGES IN THE SECONDARY SCHOOL

A companion to school experience

4th Edition

**Norbert Pachler,
Michael Evans,
Ana Redondo and
Linda Fisher**

Routledge
Taylor & Francis Group

LONDON AND NEW YORK

Fourth edition published 2014
by Routledge
2 Park Square, Milton Park, Abingdon, Oxon OX14 4RN

and by Routledge
711 Third Avenue, New York, NY 10017

Routledge is an imprint of the Taylor & Francis Group, an informa business

First edition published by RoutledgeFalmer 2001
Third edition published by Routledge 2009

British Library Cataloguing in Publication Data
A catalogue record for this book is available from the British Library

Library of Congress Cataloging in Publication Data
  Pachler, Norbert.
  [Learning to teach modern foreign languages in the secondary school]
  Learning to teach foreign languages in the secondary school: a companion
  to school experience/Norbert Pachler, Michael Evans, Ana Redondo,
  Linda Fisher. – Fourth Edition.
  pages cm – (Learning to teach subjects in the secondary school series)
  Previously published as: Learning to teach modern foreign languages in
  the secondary school, 3rd ed, 2009.
  1. Languages, Modern – Study and teaching (Secondary) I. Title.
  PB35.P13 2014
  418.0071'2–dc23
  2013026065

ISBN: 978-0-415-68994-6 (hbk)
ISBN: 978-0-415-68996-0 (pbk)
ISBN: 978-0-203-18192-8 (ebk)

Typeset in Times New Roman and Helvetica Neue
by Florence Production Ltd, Stoodleigh, Devon, UK

CONTENTS

ILLUSTRATIONS

FIGURES

TABLES

TASKS

TASKS ▨ ▨ ▤ ▪

INTRODUCTION

Foreign Languages (FLs) teaching can be very rewarding. Trying to broaden the horizons of young people and provide them with an opportunity to engage positively with one of the key challenges of modern life, namely linguistic and cultural diversity, can be fulfilling. A FLs teacher can be the catalyst for a life-long curiosity in young people and contribute to their personal, social, cultural, interpersonal, cognitive and intellectual development. FL learning can also be seen to make a significant contribution to wider society in that it fosters plurilingualism, social cohesion and intercultural understanding. For an interesting account of demand and supply of the language skills in the UK, see e.g. Tinsley, 2013.

However, there are a number of challenges facing FLs teachers, which you need to be aware of on starting out on your professional trajectory as these can have a profound impact on your work. They include:

- the ongoing struggle for recognition of the teaching profession compared to other professions;
- the influence of external stakeholders, in particular politicians, in relation to the ability for decision-making at a local level;
- the status of FLs other than English given the dominance of English as a lingua franca across the world;
- the perception among pupils, parents and other stakeholders of FLs being a difficult subject;
- the direct and indirect (e.g. in relation to the European Union, the euro, etc.) coverage of FLs and cultures in the media;
- the understanding by colleagues, parents and other stakeholders and decision makers of the educational value of FLs;
- the lack of availability of curriculum time as well as time and support for extra-curricular activities required to achieve the challenging aims around intermediate and advanced levels of proficiency;
- the relative importance of certain aspects of learning such as memorisation and recall compared with other subjects;
- the comparative limit of opportunities for real-life application of FLs skills at school and in the wider community;

- the highly conceptual nature of the subject matter;
- the use of the target language (TL) as main means of classroom instruction and interaction;
- the constraints in terms of communicative range and complexity resulting from pupils' invariably limited linguistic repertoire (vocabulary size, knowledge of grammatical structures) in the TL compared with their mother tongue.

Some will have a greater or lesser impact on you personally and they will often be beyond your control, such as events taking place at national and/or international level. This includes how FLs are prioritised in relation to economic and cultural developments in the world, e.g. the perceived importance of Mandarin compared with that of German or the increased popularity of Spanish, learning more than one FL, the inclusion of FLs at Primary level, etc. It is important that you keep abreast of such developments and understand their interrelationship with educational policies concerning the teaching and learning of FLs and are able to examine them critically.

Among many other things, as FLs teacher you need to be determined, imaginative, creative, patient, outgoing, enthusiastic and very well organised in order to be successful. You need to have a clear sense of purpose, have a vision about FLs education and high standards about your expectations of yourself and your pupils. At the same time you need to be versatile and sensitive to the needs of your learners and to contextual factors. Teaching is a highly complex task characterised by an increasing degree of accountability to a wide range of stakeholders. It requires, among other things, good subject knowledge (across linguistic, metalinguistic and cultural domains) and an ability to empathise with perceived difficulties of that knowledge for learners; the management of learning, the classroom and resources; interpersonal skills; an ability to make complex subject matter learnable; the ability to empathise with, and relate to young people. You need to plan well; be willing to try out new ideas; implement policy requirements at local level; cater for the needs of and differences in individual pupils; make learning challenging and enjoyable; assess pupils' learning regularly and effectively; evaluate your actions constantly and adapt to an ever-changing educational context.

Task 0.1 YOUR VISION ABOUT FL EDUCATION

Spend some time before the start of your programme of teacher education articulating your vision for FLs education and your personal values as a FLs student teacher. What attracts you to the teaching profession? What do you hope to achieve as a FLs teacher for yourself personally, the pupils you teach, the wider community, etc.? What are your core beliefs about FLs teaching? Keep a careful record of this personal philosophical statement.

At the end of the programme, revisit your original statement. What is still the same? What has changed? And what have you learnt? What 'critical incidents' did you encounter and how have they shaped your outlook? What were the key formative influences?

Becoming and continuing to be an effective FLs teacher requires a commitment to keeping up with developments in the field as well as a willingness to engage in continuing professional development. It also requires challenging sometimes deeply held personal views on what constitutes effective FLs teaching and learning.

ABOUT THIS BOOK

Our perspective on FLs teaching and learning is based on our own experience of working with pupils, students and student teachers; research and scholarship we are engaged in; curriculum development undertaken; professional development work undertaken, planned and provided; dialogue with FLs teachers, teacher educators, researchers and policy makers nationally and internationally as well as reflections on the ideas expressed in the scholarly work of practitioners and researchers. Consequently, the aim of the book is to support your development as a professional by providing stimuli for discussion, reflection and evaluation of a wide range of practice.

In this book we address the perceived tension between theory and practice. We hope to show that theory and practice go hand in hand. Each would be poorer without the other as a wealth of literature shows. The relationship is not unidirectional – that is, from theory to practice – but reciprocal: practice informs theory and vice versa. There are various types and levels of theorising, and systematic reflection on personal practice with reference to external points of reference including relevant academic and professional literature is a type of theorising we want to foster through the approach taken here. The book is not intended as a prescriptive set of rules on how to teach FLs, nor as a collection of 'tips for teachers' but instead as a framework for FLs teaching based on an understanding of pertinent theoretical issues, possible approaches, strategies and examples to help you learn to teach FLs effectively.

The book is primarily aimed at FLs student teachers on a programme of teacher education, irrespective of the type of programme, and it is underpinned by one main premise, namely the need for an aspiring FLs teacher to develop a personal approach to FLs teaching. With the proliferation of different routes into teaching and different types of provision, certainly in England, a range of terms is being used to refer to participants on such programmes. We use the term 'student teacher' rather than 'trainee teacher' here on the one hand as we consider it to have wider international currency but also because we recognise the importance of both, practical experience as well as the conceptual and theoretical framing afforded by universities supporting engagement with practice. The focus is on beginner and intermediate level FL learning contexts with an important reference point being Secondary schools in the UK. Nevertheless, we have tried to make our discussion sufficiently generic to make the book a valuable read for student teachers irrespective of their location and draw on a range of reference points from across Continental Europe, the United States and Australia. While the content of FLs teaching is prescribed in many ways and differently in different jurisdictions and contexts, the 'art' of FLs teaching lies in choosing the most effective and appropriate methods to develop in pupils the relevant knowledge, skills and understanding about the TL and culture(s) and to maximise their learning. This is why the ability in FLs student teachers to make personal professional judgements is so important. FLs student teachers learn a lot from observing and working with FLs teachers in schools and/or teacher educators during the course of their programme of teacher education. This book aims to support this learning process.

We hope that the book will also be useful to mentors and tutors, i.e. school and university-based staff who work with FLs student teachers and provide an overview for them of some of the most important issues FLs student teachers engage with during their programme of teacher education.

The text is designed to allow the reader to 'pick and choose' chapters and refer to specific topics at any one time rather than read the book from cover to cover. Individual chapters features the following sections:

1   introduction with reference to current debates in the literature;
2   objectives: which identify what the reader should know, understand and/or be able to do having read the chapter and carried out the activities in it;
3   discussion: the most important theoretical, conceptual and practical issues of a topic are investigated with reference to their application in the classroom, and activities inviting the reader to reflect on the content of the chapter and relate it to her work in school are included. Wherever possible, you should record your work on the reflection activities in a personal 'journal' or blog as these reflections can yield very useful evidence of your personal learning and development. Wherever practicable, you should try to discuss findings with peers, your mentor and other colleagues as well as your tutors;
4   summary: providing a reminder of the key points in a chapter.

Individual examples in the book are given in one foreign language, in French, German or Spanish. Most of the examples, we hope, are transferable to other languages.

While it is intended that the content of the book applies across the range of FLs taught, it is primarily concerned with general methodological considerations. No systematic discussion of pertinent, language-specific issues can be provided in the space available, for example how to address the possible difficulties pupils may have with the correlation of the spoken and the written word in French, the inflectional tendencies of the German language and its comparatively flexible word order or differences in scripts/alphabets/writing systems. These issues may occasionally be touched upon in the practical examples given. For language specific issues, other resources and publications need to be consulted.

There is a separate book accompanying the current title called *A Practical Guide to Teaching Foreign Languages in the Secondary School*, also published by Routledge and currently in its second edition, which offers a number of practical examples that complement and extend our discussion here.

Because of the many differences, particularly in teaching methods, the issues involved in advanced level FLs teaching cannot be dealt with in any detail here. Our primary concern in this book, therefore, is with the teaching of FLs at beginners and intermediate level as part of compulsory schooling. Again, a separate, complementary book is available, edited by the lead author of the current title, entitled *Teaching Modern Foreign Languages at Advanced Level*, also published by Routledge.

In order not to make the style of the book too unwieldy and to avoid formulations such as 's/he' or 'his/her', we tend to use the feminine form generically when referring back to – what could be called – the 'natural' gender of nouns like 'the pupil', 'the teacher' or 'the mentor'. Only the term 'FLs department' is used in this book when referring to teams of FLs teachers, although schools may also be organised on a faculty basis, etc.

4th edition

In this 4th edition of *Learning to Teach Foreign Languages in the Secondary School* we take account of important changes, particularly at the policy level, and we take account of key research findings available since the book was last published.

Importantly, rather than referring to the statutory framework of one specific context, England, we have tried to make reference to a range of such frameworks to enable the reader to make comparisons about different approaches and to reflect critically and analytically on your own context. References to statutory requirements tend to be used for contextualisation and exemplification purposes of generic principles and frameworks.

We have restructured some of the content of the book and all the chapters have been significantly updated in the light of recent developments and research. In part, the revisions made reflect a change in authorship. Kit Field, at the time of writing Dean of the School of Education and Professor of Education at the University of Wolverhampton, thought his own professional trajectory since the publication of the first issue no longer warranted his inclusion as author – we want to gratefully acknowledge his significant contribution to the text here. Readers will be saddened to hear that since the publication of the 3rd edition, Ann Barnes sadly died after a long illness; her untimely death is a significant loss to the FLs teaching profession and teacher education in the UK and we want to dedicate this edition to her memory.

All websites cited in the book were available as of 1 May 2013.

PART

1

CONTEXT RELATED

FOREIGN LANGUAGES IN THE SECONDARY SCHOOL CURRICULUM

INTRODUCTION

The teaching and learning of foreign languages (FLs) as part of compulsory education, certainly in the UK, remains subject to regular policy swings. This includes not only the question of whether or not FLs should be included in the curriculum and, if so, the age at which the formal study of FLs should start but also which FLs should be offered (European, Modern, Ancient, etc.), how many and how they best be taught.

These swings manifest themselves in the form of frequent changes to the curriculum with new governments and new ministers often wanting to make their mark on the school curriculum. Of late, this has tended to happen in the context of an increasing politicisation of school education as its outcomes have become measures of international competitiveness, for example in relation to the OECD Programme for International Student Assessment (PISA). The 'National' Curriculum (NC) in England is a particular case in point. It applies only to England and at the time of writing it is not compulsory for all types of schools. Excluded are in particular those favoured and promoted by government policy in effect at the time of writing such as free schools and academies as well as private schools. The school curriculum reflects particular views of society and what knowledge, skills and understanding it considers important for the next generation (see e.g. Pachler *et al.*, 2007).

Education researchers and Second Language Acquisition (SLA) and Foreign Language Learning (FLL) specialists have offered varied insights into curriculum design, the processes governing FL learning and have suggested implications for approaches to teaching (see Chapter 3). It is arguably incumbent upon FL professionals to be familiar with at least the most salient findings in these fields *inter alia* in order to be able to make sense of national guidelines locally or make informed choices about coursebooks and examination specifications and their inherent methodological approaches.

For example, in early 2012, in the context of the consultation around the 2014 National Curriculum, 100 academics took it upon themselves to criticise the Secretary of State's curriculum proposals in an open letter to the press warning that, if implemented, the strong emphasis on memorisation and rote learning of facts and cramming for the test would be detrimental to educational standards and that much of the proposals, in their view, were too narrow and demanded too much too soon. For the Secretary of State, supported by his Chief Inspector of Schools, such criticism was 'bad academia', ideological baggage as well as a manifestation of low expectations and a lack of ambition. As key stakeholders, the outcomes of such debates invariably impact significantly on teachers' everyday personal professional practice and we consider it important for teacher education programmes to provide ample opportunity to discuss the precepts underpinning curriculum design.

Another example concerns the introduction of languages in Primary education (see Chapter 4), where seemingly common-sense positions ('the earlier, the better') appear to drive policy making. Research on the optimum age to start to learn a foreign language is inconclusive and research findings depend on the setting, i.e. whether the focus is on naturalistic or instructed settings, what the first language of the learners is, what research methods are used and which aspects of the language are researched. In the case of instructed settings, key variables can be seen to be curricular aims, the time available, the number of pupils in the class, the content knowledge and pedagogical content knowledge of teachers and the level of cognitive development of learners. We would argue that Primary language teachers need to be familiar with relevant research findings and possible curriculum models concerning primary languages in order to be able to make the best possible pedagogical decisions taking into account local requirements and conditions.

Changes in the education system bring greater freedoms for certain types of schools, and greater knowledge about FLs education and the evidence that underpins it can impact on your ability to make decisions about FLs and its role in the curriculum.

Over the years, certain teaching methods have enjoyed varying degrees of popularity – consider, for example, the role of explicit grammar teaching (see Chapter 11) or the use of the target language as a medium for instruction and interaction (see Chapter 8) – and there have been considerable innovations in the field of educational technologies, the affordances of which continue to develop apace (see Chapter 6). The recent normalisation of mobile devices in everyday life and the growth of significance of social networking tools as part of everyday communication as well as the proliferation of applications of mobile devices for language learning are a case in point. These developments can be seen to have significant impact not only on how we communicate but also on the language and related skills we and our pupils need as a prerequisite and they pose questions about the role of formal education and the curriculum in preparing young people for a world dominated by such cultural practices.

In addition, changes occurring in the wider educational context, including legislative requirements and entitlements as well as the nature of education and purpose of schools in society – such as the recent political shift away from education as a public service towards a conception of education as a commodity – are impacting on the curriculum and its role.

After a period of extensive use of supplements to curriculum orders in England in the form of so-called National Strategies, which provided support material for teachers but importantly also prescribed in some detail what and how to teach, such as the National Language Strategy for England (NLSfE) (DfES, 2002), the pendulum has swung the other direction. With some exceptions, such as the teaching of phonics where the government believes a particular approach, namely the systematic teaching of synthetic phonics, is the best way of 'driving up standards', guidance documentation has all but disappeared. Even curriculum orders are trimmed right back in a political attempt to seek to reduce 'red tape' and create freedom for teachers. The potential importance of such curricular 'supplements' in the working lives of teachers must not be underestimated. The NLSfE, for example, contained far-reaching decisions about the future of FL teaching and learning by making its study in Key Stage 2 (for pupils aged 7–11) an entitlement as well as by discontinuing the requirement for pupils to study a foreign language at Key Stage 4 (for pupils aged 14–16). It is important, therefore, to be familiar not only with the core curriculum requirements but also to keep abreast with debates about educational policy more generally. Daily newspapers as well as the educational press tend to offer useful summaries of and commentaries on current debates.

In this chapter we consider the rationale behind teaching and learning FLs (in the Secondary school) and discuss some examples of FL curricula with a focus on England but also going beyond.

OBJECTIVES

By the end of this chapter you should:

■ be aware of the rationale and purposes of FL teaching and learning in the Secondary school curriculum over time;

■ have an understanding of some curricular requirements.

FLs in the Secondary school curriculum – rationale and purposes

One significant reason for the study of FLs is the recognition that it has an important role to play in terms of contributing to the personal, social, cultural and general linguistic development of pupils in preparation for their adult lives, both for work and leisure. This is explicitly reflected, for example, in the 1999 version of the MFL NC Orders for England:

> For example, MFL provides opportunities to promote:
>
> ■ *spiritual development*, through stimulating pupils' interest and fascination in the phenomenon of language and the meanings and feelings it can transmit
>
> ■ *moral development*, through helping pupils formulate and express opinions in the target language about issues of right and wrong

■ *social development*, through exploring different social conventions, such as forms of address, through developing pupils' ability to communicate with others, particularly speakers of foreign languages, in an appropriate, sympathetic and tolerant manner, and through fostering the spirit of cooperation when using a foreign language to communicate with other people, whether other learners or native speakers

■ *cultural development*, through providing pupils with insights into cultural differences and opportunities to relate these to their own experience and to consider different cultural and linguistic traditions, attitudes and behaviours.

(DfEE/QCA, 1999: 8)

The draft programme of study for languages of the National Curriculum published for consultation in early 2013 reflects such general aims to some extent when it identifies the following purpose for the study of languages as follows: 'Learning a foreign language is a liberation from insularity and provides an opening to other cultures' (DfE, 2013: 173). However, what follows is a rather less educational and more utilitarian perspective (see e.g. Williams, 1991: 247):

A high-quality languages education should foster pupils' curiosity and deepen their understanding of the world. The teaching should enable pupils to express their ideas and thoughts in another language and to understand and respond to its speakers, both in speech and in writing. It should also provide opportunities for them to communicate for practical purposes, learn new ways of thinking and read great literature in the original language. Language teaching should provide the foundation for learning further languages, equipping pupils to study and work in other countries.

(DfE, 2013: 173)

Remaining very important, in our view, is the provision of what Eric Hawkins called an 'apprenticeship in foreign language learning' (Hawkins, 1987: 282), the development of a foundation in pupils for future FL learning by arousing in them a curiosity for and an interest in learning (about) FLs and cultures. As such, the study of FLs 'exposes learners to new experiences and enables them to make connections in a way which would not otherwise be possible, and this in itself deepens their understanding of their mother tongue' (DES/Welsh Office, 1990: 3).

In addition, FL learning, like other subjects of the Secondary curriculum, can be very valuable in teaching young people important transferable skills such as working with reference material, e.g. dictionaries, and other skills such as (inter)personal skills, study skills or problem solving, equipping them for their working lives and providing them with the skills base required by employers. Indeed, the 1999 version of the MFL NC Orders listed a number of opportunities for promoting so-called key skills through MFL:

For example, MFL provides opportunities for pupils to develop the key skills of:

■ *communication*, through developing their awareness of the way language is structured and how it can be manipulated to meet a range of needs, and through reinforcing learning in specific areas such as listening, reading for gist and detail, and using grammar correctly

- *application of number*, through talking and writing about the time and measures in the target language, and carrying out conversions about distances and currency
- *IT*, through using audio, video, satellite television and the internet to access and communicate information, and through selecting and using a range of ICT resources to create presentations for different audiences and purposes
- *working with others*, through developing their ability to participate in group conversations and discussions
- *improving own learning and performance*, through developing their ability to rehearse and redraft work to improve accuracy and presentation, and through developing learning strategies such as memorising, dealing with the unpredictable, and using reference materials
- *problem solving*, through developing their ability to apply and adapt their knowledge of the target language for specific communication purposes.

(DfEE/QCA, 1999: 8)

To an extent, FL learning can be seen to be instrumental in preparing pupils for life in multicultural and multilingual societies and, indeed, in the world in an age of increasing globalisation. FLs have a valuable contribution to make to the wider school curriculum in terms of cross-curricular perspectives but also as a focus for extra-curricular activities. The former is exemplified again in the 1999 version of the MFL NC Orders:

For example, MFL provides opportunities to promote:

thinking skills, through developing pupils' ability to draw inferences from unfamiliar language and unexpected responses, through enabling pupils to reflect on the links between languages, and through developing pupils' creative use of language and expression of their own ideas, attitudes and opinions

(DfEE/QCA, 1999: 9)

From a national economic point of view, the argument has repeatedly been put forward that – in the current context of competitive international economic activity – the UK, as a trading nation, urgently needs a workforce with competence in FLs (see e.g. DES/Welsh Office, 1990: 4). When wanting to sell goods to customers abroad, the fact that English is the international lingua franca is insufficient. The business world is in the process of globalisation both in terms of national businesses increasingly operating in an international context and in terms of multinational companies establishing themselves firmly on the national scene. Pupils might well find themselves in work situations requiring them to operate in a FL. It could, indeed, be argued that it is this national economic concern that has become dominant at times in justifying the place of FLs in the school curriculum. The global market is forever evolving, however, and accurately pinpointing which *language* will be economically valuable for pupils personally and the country's economy is rather difficult. It could be argued that it is primarily the successful learning of a FL or of FLs, where the learner develops confidence in FL learning and competence in language learning strategies that is the key, enabling the learner in the future to use these attributes when learning a language needed for specific purposes. Learning Mandarin or German now does not necessarily mean that it will be that language, which is required by a particular pupil in later life. Equally, the fact that revenue from tourism makes a major contribution to the country's gross national product is also mentioned by some as an important incentive to study FLs. The 2013 National Curriculum consultation document is not taking an overtly utilitarian approach. Indeed, the explicit inclusion of Latin and Ancient Greek in the list of eligible languages indicates a shift back to a more educational rationale. It is worth noting that European language policy, with its goal that every European citizen can speak at least two languages other than his/her mother tongue, is not reflected.

Another interesting reference point, which implies other important reasons for including FL education in the curriculum, particularly between the ages of 7 and 11, are the 12 curriculum aims proposed by The Cambridge Primary Review (p. 19 in www.primaryreview.org.uk/downloads/CPR_revised_booklet.pdf). Here we focus in particular on the cluster of aims entitled 'self, others and the wider world'.

The individual
Well-being
Engagement
Empowerment
Autonomy

Self, others and the wider world
Encouraging respect and reciprocity: promote respect for self, for peers and adults, for other generations, for diversity and difference, for ideas and values, and for common courtesy. Respect between child and adult should be mutual, for learning and human relations are built upon reciprocity.
Promoting interdependence and sustainability: develop children's under-standing of humanity's dependence for well-being and survival on equitable relationships between individuals, groups, communities and nations, and on a sustainable relationship with the natural world and help children to move from understanding to positive action.
Empowering local, global and national citizenship: enable children to become active citizens by encouraging their full participation in decision-making within the classroom and school, and advancing their understanding of human rights, conflict resolution and social justice. They should develop a sense that human interdependence and the fragility of the world order require a concept of citizenship which is global as well as local and national.
Celebrating culture and community: every school should aim to become a centre of community life, culture and thought to help counter the loss of com-munity outside the school. 'Education is a major embodiment of a culture's way of life, not just a preparation for it', as Jerome Bruner said.

Learning, knowing and doing
Exploring, knowing, understanding and making sense
Fostering skill
Exciting imagination
Enacting dialogue

This set of aims takes full account of the increasing interconnectedness of the modern world and identifies associated challenges, many of which will manifest themselves in aspects of interpersonal communication in the everyday and working lives of learners as adults. Arguably, FL education has an important role in preparing young people for this.

In the field of FL research the importance of the role of culture is enjoying increasing attention. Indeed, the relationship between language and culture has been the focus of inquiry for some time (see e.g. Byram and Morgan *et al.*,1994). What is more recent is a growing focus on intercultural (communicative) competence, a term that tries to reflect the growing cultural and linguistic diversity of the contexts in which communication takes place and the attendant encounters of people from different cultural backgrounds and their linguistic and cultural capital for communication purposes. These contextual factors have implications for the FL curriculum and raise questions about the extent to which prevailing frames and conceptualisations help prepare young people to communicate effectively in an increasingly complex world.

In 2005 the DfES published a document on how to develop the global dimension in the school curriculum, which provides useful guidance across subjects and age groups. It sets out the following eight concepts (DfES, 2005: 12–13) through which a global dimension can be understood:

- *global citizenship*: gaining the knowledge, skills and understanding of concepts and institutions necessary to become informed, active, responsible citizens;
- *conflict resolution*: understanding the nature of conflicts, their impact on development and why there is a need for their resolution and the promotion of harmony;
- *social justice*: understanding the importance of social justice as an element in both sustainable development and the improved welfare of all people;
- *values and perceptions*: developing a critical evaluation of representations of global issues and an appreciation of the effect these have on people's attitudes and values;
- *sustainable development*: understanding the need to maintain and improve the quality of life now without damaging the planet for future generations;
- *interdependence*: understanding how people, places, economies and environments are all inextricably interrelated, and that choices and events have repercussions on a global scale;
- *human rights*: knowing about human rights including the UN Convention on the Rights of the Child;
- *diversity*: understanding and respecting differences and relating these to our common humanity.

Task 1.1 **AIMS OF FL LEARNING**

What are your own personal aims in teaching FL? How do you envisage turning these aims into reality when teaching your learners?

Task 1.2 **PRODUCING A DISPLAY FOR A YEAR 9 OPTIONS EVENING**

Imagine your placement school is in the process of organising an Options Evening for Year 9 (13 year old) pupils and their parents making decisions about further language study. The head of languages wants to produce a digital presentation for pupils and parents pointing out the benefits that can be gained from the continued study of a FL. What arguments would you include in the display that could appeal to pupils and parents?

Task 1.3 **EXPLORING LINKS TO OTHER CURRICULUM AREAS**

Examine the curriculum requirements for other subjects such as English, Geography, History or Citizenship and explore what links to the FLs curriculum are possible, for example in relation to the linguistic and cultural domains. Discuss with relevant colleagues from these disciplines in what ways work in your respective subjects can be linked and how.

Languages in the 2013 National Curriculum proposal for England

As has already been indicated, the 2013 curriculum proposals (DfE, 2013: 173–176) are rather shorter than previous versions and adhere to a different structure. Importantly, they also cover primary languages that will be compulsory. Where previously the levels of attainment have set out what pupils were expected to achieve in different skills areas and in what sequence, the 2013 proposals only contain a programme of study setting out, for Key Stage 2 and Key Stage 3 subject matter, skills and processes.

At KS2, pupils should be taught to:

- listen attentively to spoken language and show understanding by joining in and responding;
- explore the patterns and sounds of language through songs and rhymes and link the spelling, sound and meaning of words;
- engage in conversations; ask and answer questions; express opinions and respond to those of others; seek clarification and help;
- speak in sentences, using familiar vocabulary, phrases and basic language structures;
- develop accurate pronunciation and intonation so that others understand when they are reading aloud or using familiar words and phrases;
- present ideas and information orally to a range of audiences;
- read carefully and show understanding of words, phrases and simple writing;

- appreciate stories, songs, poems and rhymes in the language;
- broaden their vocabulary and develop their ability to understand new words that are introduced into familiar written material, including through using a dictionary;
- write phrases from memory, and adapt these to create new sentences, to express ideas clearly;
- describe people, places, things and actions orally and in writing;
- understand basic grammar appropriate to the language being studied, such as (where relevant): feminine, masculine and neuter forms and the conjugation of high-frequency verbs; key features and patterns of the language; how to apply these, for instance, to build sentences; and how these differ from or are similar to English.

At Key Stage 3, the requirements are separated into two sections, one on grammar and vocabulary, and another on linguistic competence.

Grammar and vocabulary
Pupils should be taught to:
- identify and use tenses or other structures that convey the present, past, and future as appropriate to the language being studied;
- use and manipulate a variety of key grammatical structures and patterns, including voices and moods, as appropriate;
- develop and use a wide-ranging and deepening vocabulary that goes beyond their immediate needs and interests, allowing them to give and justify opinions and take part in discussion about wider issues;
- use accurate grammar, spelling and punctuation.

Linguistic competence
Pupils should be taught to:
- listen to a variety of forms of spoken language to obtain information and respond appropriately;
- transcribe words and short sentences that they hear with increasing accuracy;
- initiate and develop conversations, coping with unfamiliar language and unexpected responses, making use of important social conventions such as formal modes of address;
- express and develop ideas clearly and with increasing accuracy, both orally and in writing;
- speak coherently and confidently, with increasingly accurate pronunciation and intonation;
- read and show comprehension of original and adapted materials from a range of different sources, understanding the purpose, important ideas and details, and provide an accurate English translation of short, suitable material;
- read literary texts in the language, such as stories, songs, poems and letters, to stimulate ideas, develop creative expression and expand understanding of the language and culture;
- write prose using an increasingly wide range of grammar and vocabulary, write creatively to express their own ideas and opinions, and translate short written text accurately into the foreign language.

The strong focus on grammar and translation as well as the emphasis on literary texts mark a noticeable departure from previous curricular requirements at this level and resonate with the stronger educational rationale diagnosed above. Of particular note is also the inclusion of 'transcription', which appears to imply a desire on the part of the Secretary of State to bring back dictations and can be seen to link to phonics-related work at Primary level.

Task 1.4 CARRYING OUT LESSON OBSERVATIONS RELATING TO THE NC PROPOSALS FOR ENGLAND

Observe a number of FL lessons of a class of your choice focusing on the coverage of the subject matter, skills and processes set out above. Choose a number of the statements and observe through which activities they are covered.

Task 1.5 PRIMARY SCHOOL VISIT

It is customary for student teachers in the Secondary phase to visit a Primary school for a few days in order to understand issues around the transition from the Primary to the Secondary phase better.

How are FLs taught in Primary schools? What similarities and differences in terms of methodology can you delineate compared with your main placement school? How is the developmental stage of the children being catered for?

Also, ask to observe some phonics teaching. How do the approaches to mother tongue teaching of reading and writing compare with those in FLs?

Teaching FLs at Key Stage 4

FLs are not a *statutory requirement* subject at KS4 (pupils aged 14–16), although they feature as an option on the so-called English Baccalaureate (Ebacc) subject list, which is why the National Curriculum proposals do not cover it. Instead, at the time of writing, teaching at this level is governed by the GCSE subject criteria (Ofqual, 2011) on the basis of which awarding bodies develop their GCSE examinations. These criteria set out the aims underpinning the examination as well as the intended learning outcomes and subject content together with assessment objectives and grade descriptions. In an appendix, they also detail the grammar requirements for the examination. At the time of writing, examinations at school leaving age are a hotly contested topic with the coalition government considering a range of changes to address a perceived lack of standards. For details about qualifications at Key Stage 4, see www.education.gov.uk/schools/teachingandlearning/qualifications/gcses.

The 2011 criteria set out the following grade description for Grade C (Ofqual, 2011: 7):

Candidates show understanding of different types of spoken language that contain a variety of structures. The spoken material relates to a range of contexts, including some that may be unfamiliar, and may relate to past and future events. They can identify main points, details and opinions.

They take part in conversations and simple discussions and present information. They express points of view and show an ability to deal with some unpredictable elements. Their spoken language contains a variety of structures and may relate to past and future events. Their pronunciation and intonation are more accurate than inaccurate. They convey a clear message but there may be some errors.

They show understanding of different types of written texts that contain a variety of structures. The written material relates to a range of contexts, including some that may be unfamiliar and may relate to past and future events. They can identify main points, extract details and recognise opinions.

They write for different contexts that may be real or imaginary. They communicate information and express points of view. They use a variety of structures and may include different tenses or time frames. The style is basic. They convey a clear message but there may be some errors.

Grade descriptions for Grades A and F are also available.

Task 1.6 FAMILIARISE YOURSELF WITH THE GCSE CRITERIA AND GCSE SPECIFICATIONS

Obtain a copy of the GCSE specification used by your placement school. In your opinion, how well does it test the requirements in the NC proposals?

The GCSE Criteria allow some flexibility of weighting for the four assessment objectives (AO). Each AO can now count for between 20 and 30 per cent.

Assessment objectives:

AO1 understand spoken language
AO2 communicate in speech
AO3 understand written language
AO4 communicate in writing

At least 10 per cent of the total marks for AO2 and AO4 must be allocated to knowledge and accurate application of the grammar and structures of the language prescribed in the specification.

The curriculum requirements for England are clearly not the only conceptualisation possible. For a useful discussion of subject breadth in international jurisdictions, see e.g. DfE, 2011a.

In a recent paper, Richards (2013: 5) distinguishes three approaches to curriculum design: forward, central and backward design. The first starts with syllabus planning (e.g. input based on corpus research), followed by methodology and finishes with assessment of learning outcomes. The second starts with classroom processes and methodology (e.g. task-based instruction) and develops a syllabus and learning outcomes as part of the implementation process. The third begins with the specification of learning outcomes (e.g. CERF); decisions about methodology and syllabus are developed from learning outcomes. He concludes that there is no best approach to curriculum design.

Graves (2008: 149), in another interesting paper that ultimately sets out to discuss the concept of curriculum enactment, notes that despite hierarchical approaches such as National Curricula, which might make them appear top-down, a curriculum is 'a plan for WHAT is to be taught and teachers, through instruction, implement the plan'. Graves goes on to discuss problems with a 'specialist' approach such as a potential lack of coherence with different discourses underpinned by different beliefs and assumptions prevailing at different levels (policy making versus school and classroom) as well as a lack of agency on the part of practitioners.

THE COMMON EUROPEAN FRAMEWORK OF REFERENCE FOR LANGUAGES: LEARNING, TEACHING, ASSESSMENT (CEFR)

The CEFR is not a curriculum; instead, it is intended to provide 'a common basis for the elaboration of language syllabuses, curriculum guidelines, examinations, textbooks, etc. across Europe' (Council of Europe, 2001: 1). The framework sets out six levels of language proficiency from C2 to A1 each described with a set of competence-based descriptors combined with contextual information. The CEFR identified the following Common Reference Levels (Figure 1.1).

Figueras (2012), who offers a useful discussion of the impact of CEFR some ten years after its publication, points out that the CEFR level descriptors are not objectives or outcomes; they merely state what is observable in a learner at a certain level. By comparison, Figueras argues, a learning outcome needs to state what the learner will have learnt and will be able to do at the end of a course of study.

It is interesting to note that the 2013 National Curriculum proposals make no explicit reference to the CEFR. However, the common reference levels resemble the grade descriptors at GCSE level. This is particularly interesting in the context of a foreword by the Secretary of State for Education to a recent paper by Tim Oates (2012), the chairman of the Curriculum Review expert group, in which the former claims that the 'best-performing education nations deliberately set out to compare themselves against international benchmarks' (p. 121).

THE US NATIONAL STANDARDS FOR FOREIGN LANGUAGE LEARNING IN THE 21ST CENTURY

Although also not a curriculum guide, the US National Standards, developed by the American Council on the Teaching of Foreign Languages, the American Association of Teachers of French, the American Association of Teachers of German and the American Association of Teachers of Spanish and Portuguese as part of the America 2000 education initiative and first published in 1996 for the K-12 context (pupils aged 4–19), do imply a range of curricular experiences as well as a sequence of study. They, too, represent a particular conceptualisation of the field of languages

Proficient user	C2	Can understand with ease virtually everything heard or read. Can summarise information from different spoken and written sources, reconstructing arguments and accounts in a coherent presentation. Can express him/herself spontaneously, very fluently and precisely, differentiating finer shades of meaning even in more complex situations.
	C1	Can understand a wide range of demanding, longer texts, and recognise implicit meaning. Can express him/herself fluently and spontaneously without much obvious searching for expressions. Can use language flexibly and effectively for social, academic and professional purposes. Can produce clear, well-structured, detailed text on complex subjects, showing controlled use of organisational patterns, connectors and cohesive devices.
Independent user	B2	Can understand the main ideas of complex text on both concrete and abstract topics, including technical discussions in his/her field of specialisation. Can interact with a degree of fluency and spontaneity that makes regular interaction with native speakers quite possible without strain for either party. Can produce clear, detailed text on a wide range of subjects and explain a viewpoint on a topical issue giving the advantages and disadvantages of various options.
	B1	Can understand the main points of clear standard input on familiar matters regularly encountered in work, school, leisure, etc. Can deal with most situations likely to arise while travelling in an area where the language is spoken. Can produce simple connected text on topics which are familiar or of personal interest. Can describe experiences and events, dreams, hopes and ambitions and briefly give reasons and explanations for opinions and plans.
Basic user	A2	Can understand sentences and frequently used expressions related to areas of most immediate relevance (e.g. very basic personal and family information, shopping, local geography, employment). Can communicate in simple and routine tasks requiring a simple and direct exchange of information on familiar and routine matters. Can describe in simple terms aspects of his/her background, immediate environment and matters in areas of immediate need.
	A1	Can understand and use familiar everyday expressions and very basic phrases aimed at the satisfaction of needs of a concrete type. Can introduce him/herself and others and can ask and answer questions about personal details such as where he/she lives, people he/she knows and things he/she has. Can interact in a simple way provided the other person talks slowly and clearly and is prepared to help.

■ **Figure 1.1** CEFR Common Reference Levels

Source: Council of Europe, 2001: 24.

and offer a set of processes across five so-called goal areas: communication, cultures, connections, comparisons and communities. They are a deliberate attempt to move away from a focus on the how (grammar) to say what (vocabulary) and focus on the organising principle of the why (communication) with reference to whom and when, thereby foregrounding the ability to communicate meaningfully and in appropriate ways with others (see pp. 2–3 of www.actfl.org/publications/all/national-standards-foreign-language-education):

COMMUNICATION

Communicate in Languages Other Than English

Standard 1.1: Students engage in conversations, provide and obtain information, express feelings and emotions, and exchange opinions.

Standard 1.2: Students understand and interpret written and spoken language on a variety of topics.

Standard 1.3: Students present information, concepts, and ideas to an audience of listeners or readers on a variety of topics.

CULTURES

Gain Knowledge and Understanding of Other Cultures

Standard 2.1: Students demonstrate an understanding of the relationship between the practices and perspectives of the culture studied.

Standard 2.2: Students demonstrate an understanding of the relationship between the products and perspectives of the culture studied.

CONNECTIONS

Connect with Other Disciplines and Acquire Information

Standard 3.1: Students reinforce and further their knowledge of other disciplines through the foreign language.

Standard 3.2: Students acquire information and recognize the distinctive viewpoints that are only available through the foreign language and its cultures.

COMPARISONS

Develop Insight into the Nature of Language and Culture

Standard 4.1: Students demonstrate understanding of the nature of language through comparisons of the language studied and their own.

Standard 4.2: Students demonstrate understanding of the concept of culture through comparisons of the cultures studied and their own.

COMMUNITIES

Participate in Multilingual Communities at Home and Around the World

Standard 5.1: Students use the language both within and beyond the school setting.

Standard 5.2: Students show evidence of becoming life-long learners by using the language for personal enjoyment and enrichment.

Task 1.7 **COMPARING DIFFERENT CONCEPTUALISATIONS OF LANGUAGE LEARNING REQUIREMENTS**

Having read through the Common European Framework for Reference and the US National Standards, what do you consider to be the defining features of each approach? What are their respective strengths and weaknesses?

SUMMARY

In this chapter we discussed a number of diverse educational, economic, vocational and linguistic reasons for including the study of FLs in the school curriculum. The aims and objectives governing the study of FLs have changed over the years as has the composition of pupils and the organisation of their learning. These developments go hand in hand with changes in society and are a reflection of changes in national educational policy and its links to international developments.

In this chapter, the advantages of a broad national FLs skills base have been discussed. A brief examination of aspects of FL policy and associated initiatives as well as curricular requirements has introduced some frameworks governing current FL curriculum planning, teaching and assessment.

FURTHER READING

Pachler, N., Evans, M. and Lawes, S. (2007) *Modern Foreign Languages: Teaching School Subjects 11–19*. London: Routledge.
This book sets out to engage critically, but constructively, with the orthodoxies in the field of foreign language teaching and learning with specific reference to UK Secondary schools. It promotes a principled and evidence-informed approach to foreign language pedagogy and sets out essential areas of professional foreign language teacher knowledge.

CHAPTER 2

ON BECOMING A FOREIGN LANGUAGES TEACHER

INTRODUCTION

In recent years the work of student teachers and the nature of teacher education programmes in the UK have been subject to a number of fundamental changes. New QTS (Qualified Teacher Status) Standards apply since September 2012 and this chapter will introduce you to their requirements in the context of a broader discussion about subject/content knowledge and pedagogical content knowledge. The 2012 Teachers' Standards represent a noticeable departure from previous iterations in terms of structure, content and application. They reflect the Coalition Government's perspective on good teaching and set out the minimum level of practice expected. They are intended to be applied with reference to contextual factors, in particular the level of experience of a teacher, and they also form the basis of judgements made as part of teacher appraisal.

As we have already noted in Chapter 1, the year 2010 saw the publication of a Government White Paper on the importance of teaching (DfE, 2010), which – among other things – set out a new paradigm for teacher education (or rather teacher 'training') in the form of School Direct, which seeks to place the main responsibility for teacher preparation with schools and envisages only a supporting role for universities. A range of financial support mechanisms are on offer for students, such as salaried training places, to incentivise this paradigm shift. The main idea behind this policy is to strengthen the practical skills focus of teacher preparation and to reduce the role of theory and research. The opportunity for sustained practice in schools and the ability to develop personal practical repertoires through sustained contact with teachers and pupils is welcome. The increase in practical experience has also created and/or reinforced certain tensions. It remains to be seen whether the particular type of engagement with practice valorised by current teacher education policy will be effective in delivering the intended improvements in the quality of teaching espoused by the government.

In this chapter we discuss aspects of subject/content knowledge and pedagogical content knowledge as well as some key processes involved in developing them. We affirm the importance of practice in the process of learning to teach FLs and we introduce a number of types of engagement suggested by the literature which we consider to be useful for you and your mentors irrespective of which route into teaching you are on. The approaches we advocate here have a number of features in common: in addition to focusing on practice, they recognise the importance of theory and research as well as the centrality of a partnership approach between key stakeholders including teachers, learners and tutors.

OBJECTIVES

By the end of this chapter you should:

■ be familiar with different approaches to teaching standards, including those pertaining to FL teaching in England;
■ understand the nature and importance of subject knowledge and subject application, i.e. pedagogical content knowledge, and their implications on your practice;
■ recognise the desirability of a symbiotic relationship between theory and practice and be familiar with possible approaches to achieving it;
■ be aware of possible stages of your development as a student teacher;
■ appreciate the nature of your work in schools.

TOWARDS A MULTIDISCIPLINARY APPROACH TO FL TEACHING

A main aim of FL teaching is to enable pupils to communicate in the target language (TL) and one important measure of your efficacy as a teacher is pupil learning. Quality of teaching is widely considered to be a, if not *the* key factor in pupil learning. In order to be an effective FLs teacher requires a range of skills and knowledge. We argue here that there is no one single way of FL teaching that is more effective or desirable than any other and that it is important for you as a FLs student teacher to develop a personal approach to FL teaching that takes into account your personal strengths and development needs as well as the respective statutory requirements and other contextual factors that govern your practice. We also strongly recommend that you take into account what is known from research (see Chapter 3). There are many different source disciplines that potentially inform FL teaching:

> As an applied discipline, language learning obviously needs to be informed by a 'conceptual framework': i.e. by a body of knowledge, drawn from various areas, which both helps to render the teaching experience coherent and provides a basis for evaluating its effectiveness. Without such a body of knowledge, refined into principles for classroom practice, there simply exist no criteria – beyond the weight of custom or fashion – for deciding what is or is not pedagogically effective.
>
> (Roberts, 1992: 6)

This observation identifies two key concerns: that FL teaching is an applied discipline and as such inextricably linked to a number of source disciplines; and that these disciplines provide a wealth of knowledge, which allows a better understanding of the teaching process. This body of background knowledge is important but is not sufficient to ensure effective FL teaching. In addition, there is no single 'recipe' which will work for each group of learners in each specific context at a specific time. All methodological ideas and recommendations have to be adapted in the light of circumstances.

Gerhard Neuner and Hans Hunfeld (1993) draw attention to a number of disciplines and factors, which continue to yield important information in this context (translated loosely here from German, p. 9):

- findings from the field of psychology;
- pedagogical knowledge and research into teaching;
- findings from the field of (applied) linguistics;
- conceptions about the foreign country;
- individual differences of learners;
- previous experience of FL learning;
- conceptions about work with (literary) texts;
- specific objectives of learners;
- traditions of teaching methodology; as well as
- methods of mother tongue teaching.

To become knowledgeable about, and keep abreast with, this wide range of considerations requires commitment and enthusiasm. It is, we would argue, an exciting if career-long quest to expand your methodological repertoire. As we have already noted, research, in our estimation, has a very important role to play in contributing to the knowledge base of FLs teachers, and it is to this end that we have included a chapter summarising and presenting an overview of relevant insights to be gained from research in this book (see Chapter 3). This is also recognised by the 2012 Teachers' Standards, which expect teachers to 'demonstrate a critical understanding of developments in the subject and curriculum areas, and promote the value of scholarship' (DfE, 2012: 7).

THE IMPORTANCE OF SUBJECT KNOWLEDGE

Subject knowledge is an important consideration for all FLs teachers. For a detailed discussion, see Pachler *et al.*, 2007. Again, this is reflected in the 2012 Teachers' Standards, which expect teachers to 'have a secure knowledge of the relevant subject(s) and curriculum areas, foster and maintain pupils' interest in the subject, and address misunderstandings' (DfE, 2012: 7). The UK standards are by far not the only ones to recognise the importance of subject knowledge and, arguably, not the best at conceptualising it. The US InTasc Model Core Teaching Standards (CCSSO, 2011) in our view offer a more useful resource in this respect. Not only do they differentiate subject/content knowledge from its application but also go on to discuss each in relation to three components: performances, essential knowledge and critical dispositions. For subject/content knowledge, Standard 4, defined as 'the teacher understands the central concepts, tools of inquiry, and structures of the discipline(s) he or she teaches and creates learning experiences that make these aspects of the discipline accessible and meaningful for learners to assure mastery of the content' (CCSSO, 2011: 13) the following explication is offered:

PERFORMANCES

4(a) The teacher effectively uses multiple representations and explanations that capture key ideas in the discipline, guide learners through learning progressions, and promote each learner's achievement of content standards.

4(b) The teacher engages students in learning experiences in the discipline(s) that encourage learners to understand, question, and analyse ideas from diverse perspectives so that they master the content.

4(c) The teacher engages learners in applying methods of inquiry and standards of evidence used in the discipline.

4(d) The teacher stimulates learner reflection on prior content knowledge, links new concepts to familiar concepts, and makes connections to learners' experiences.

4(e) The teacher recognizes learner misconceptions in a discipline that interfere with learning, and creates experiences to build accurate conceptual understanding.

4(f) The teacher evaluates and modifies instructional resources and curriculum materials for their comprehensiveness, accuracy for representing particular concepts in the discipline, and appropriateness for his/her learners.

4(g) The teacher uses supplementary resources and technologies effectively to ensure accessibility and relevance for all learners.

4(h) The teacher creates opportunities for students to learn, practice, and master academic language in their content.

4(i) The teacher accesses school and/or district-based resources to evaluate the learner's content knowledge in their primary language.

ESSENTIAL KNOWLEDGE

4(j) The teacher understands major concepts, assumptions, debates, processes of inquiry, and ways of knowing that are central to the discipline(s) s/he teaches.

4(k) The teacher understands common misconceptions in learning the discipline and how to guide learners to accurate conceptual understanding.

4(l) The teacher knows and uses the academic language of the discipline and knows how to make it accessible to learners.

4(m) The teacher knows how to integrate culturally relevant content to build on learners' background knowledge.

4(n) The teacher has a deep knowledge of student content standards and learning progressions in the discipline(s) s/he teaches.

CRITICAL DISPOSITIONS

4(o) The teacher realizes that content knowledge is not a fixed body of facts but is complex, culturally situated, and ever evolving. S/he keeps abreast of new ideas and understandings in the field.

4(p) The teacher appreciates multiple perspectives within the discipline and facilitates learners' critical analysis of these perspectives.

4(q) The teacher recognizes the potential of bias in his/her representation of the discipline and seeks to appropriately address problems of bias.

4(r) The teacher is committed to work towards each learner's mastery of disciplinary content and skills.

As already noted, the application of subject/content knowledge is discussed in similar detail in a separate standard, to which we will turn below.

In the case of FL teaching, subject/content knowledge (including its application) can be considered to be a high level of proficiency in the TL, good structural knowledge as well as the ability to make effective use of the TL, wide-ranging awareness of the culture(s) of the countries where the TL is spoken, some knowledge of the linguistic theories underpinning the language learning/acquisition process as well as a familiarity with the respective statutory framework and related documents. It also comprises knowledge of the affordances of digital technologies for FL teaching and learning and to be able to *apply* them appropriately to the benefit of learners.

For so-called native speakers of the language they teach, particular issues need to be considered. While not unproblematical, the distinction between native and non-native speaker teachers can be useful in highlighting some difference in teaching behaviours attributable to divergent language backgrounds of FLs teachers (see e.g. Medgyes, 2001: 429–430). The terms are problematic, for one because it is difficult to define what 'native' means, particularly in today's multilingual and plurilingual world, and how best to define it. Medgyes (2001) attempts the definition of who a native speaker teacher is with reference to linguistic and sociolinguistic criteria, but also from an educational perspective linked to the goals of language education and the arguably unattainable goal of near-native proficiency as well as the difficulties around the feasibility of measuring it. 'Native speakerhood', Medgyes (2001: 433) notes with reference to English, 'is an intricate concept, which includes birth, education, the environment in which the individual is exposed to English, the sequence in which languages are learned, levels of proficiency, self-confidence, cultural affiliation, self-identification, and political allegiance'. Native speaker teachers may need to pay particular attention to the adaptation of the use of the TL in terms of complexity, speed of delivery, register and tone if pupils are to understand and respond appropriately. Medgyes (2001: 434–435) also reports on a questionnaire-based self-reporting survey he conducted among 325 teachers from 11 countries, of whom 86 per cent classified themselves as 'non-native', which suggests that differences in pedagogical approaches between the two groups do exist and that non-native speakers tend to be more preoccupied with accuracy and formal linguistic features, the printed word and formal registers. He found they also reported lacking fluency, possess less insight into intricacies of meaning, have doubts about appropriate language use, are less familiar with colloquial expressions and have a restricted knowledge of context, all of which tends to lead them to be reluctant to 'let go' and operate more controlled and cautious pedagogic approaches. Medgyes (2001: 436) goes on to suggest that conversely, non-native speakers can:

- provide a better learner model;
- teach language-learning strategies more effectively;
- supply more information about the language;
- better anticipate and prevent language difficulty;
- be more sensitive to their students;
- benefit from their ability to use the students' mother tongue.

There is often only little time to focus on personal proficiency in the TL or cultural awareness during the course of teacher education. As is the case throughout a teaching career, the onus is on the *individual* to maintain a high level of subject/content knowledge, including up-to-date linguistic competence and cultural understanding. A starting point for this process tends to be a subject/content knowledge audit you are asked to complete, where you keep a record of your personal achievements and potential 'gaps' in your subject/content knowledge. Any such gaps in knowledge need to be rectified as early as possible, e.g. a specific grammatical construction, pronunciation issue, etc. You are one of the main linguistic models for your learners and the model you provide needs to be as accurate as possible. This is also the case with structuring lessons, creating resources, etc; your accuracy in these areas is paramount.

Task 2.1 **YOU AS A LINGUIST**

Create a brief 'pen portrait' of yourself as a linguist. Include both your first foreign language and your second foreign language, if you have one. If you consider yourself to be a native speaker, adjust the list accordingly (e.g. for your second foreign language and/or how you will make language accessible). Be as honest as you can in analysing your strengths and weaknesses in the following areas:

- grammar 'rules';
- accuracy (grammar application);
- pronunciation;
- range of language;
- cultural knowledge.

Work out some initial strategies for how you might address these areas.

Task 2.2 **FLs SUBJECT/CONTENT KNOWLEDGE**

Obtain a copy of an examination specification at GCSE and, where appropriate, A level used by the FLs department at your placement school for your main FL(s). Reflect on how well you feel your first degree course or equivalent has prepared you for meeting the requirements of the specifications in terms of your subject/content knowledge. Use Figure 2.1 to record your reflections.

Requirement	Degree course content	GCSE requirement	A/AS level requirement
Cultural knowledge			
Structural knowledge of language			
Non-literary topics			
Literary topics			
Phonetics			
Translation			
Other (specify)			

■ **Figure 2.1** Mapping personal subject knowledge against examination requirements

SUBJECT APPLICATION

We have already noted that subject/content knowledge is essential but not in and of itself enough to being an effective teacher. You need to be able to teach pupils subject/content knowledge and relevant skills in *appropriate* ways. You need to acquire knowledge in a wide range of fields to be able to do so effectively. You need to apply and use your own subject/content knowledge, and make it accessible and 'learnable' for the pupils. Having the 'knowledge' yourself and trying to 'transmit' it is not enough.

Shulman's (1987: 8) seven categories of knowledge clearly underline the complexity of the teaching process. They are adapted in Figure 2.2 and related to the process of learning to teach FLs (although they were not devised for any specific subject).

There is much to be learnt in the course of teacher education and often only little time is available to focus on subject/content knowledge. As Shulman's categories indicate, the onus is on application, what he calls pedagogical content knowledge, and the development of an ability in student teachers to develop in pupils FLs-related knowledge, skills and understanding.

There are, of course, other and more recent conceptualisations and models – for example, by Banks *et al.* (1999) who discuss the professional knowledge of English teachers. At the centre of their model is the personal subject construct of the teacher, i.e. their view of the subject domain informed by their biography and personal experience. Around it are what they call 'subject knowledge' and in other literature is sometimes called 'domain knowledge', which in the case of FLs would comprise things such as (meta)linguistic and (inter)cultural competence, etc.; 'pedagogic knowledge', including things like knowledge about the methods of grammar teaching or effective target language use or possible approaches of working with texts or using translation, foreign language learning/second language acquisition/applied linguistics research; and 'school knowledge' relating to the subject domain, such as knowledge about the content of language curricular requirements and specifications.

The InTASC Core Teaching Standards (CCSSO, 2011: 14) define application of content, Standard 5, as follows: 'The teacher understands how to connect concepts and uses differing perspectives to engage learners in critical thinking, creativity, and collaborative problem solving related to authentic local and global issues.'

No.	Category	FL relevance
1	*Content knowledge*	Need to update linguistic competence, cultural awareness/intercultural (communicative) competence and technological competence on a regular basis.
2	*General pedagogical knowledge*, with special reference to those broad principles and strategies of classroom management and organization that appear to transcend subject matter	Need for an understanding of adolescent development and the relationship between language and learning in general.
3	*Curriculum knowledge*, with particular grasp of the materials and programmes that serve as 'tools of the trade' for teachers	Growing familiarity with the content and application of the statutory framework and specifications as well as commonly used resources including digital technologies.
4	*Pedagogical content knowledge*, that special amalgam of content and pedagogy that is uniquely the province of teachers, their own special form of professional understanding	Knowledge of, and a willingness to experiment with and evaluate different approaches to FL teaching including digital technologies; awareness of relevant background reading and research. Need to expand relevant methodological repertoire which engages various groups of/individual learners.
5	*Knowledge of learners and their characteristics*	Awareness of the existing language skills of learners and of what motivates the individuals within a class; awareness of how current approaches to FL teaching and learning relate to learning theories.
6	*Knowledge of educational contexts*, ranging from the workings of the group or classroom, the governance and financing of school districts, to the character to communities and cultures	Knowledge of the institutional, local and national context of FL teaching including policy matters and inspection findings.
7	*Knowledge of educational ends, purposes and values, and philosophical and historical grounds*	Knowledge of how current approaches to FL teaching and learning have evolved; awareness of the rationale and purposes of FL teaching and learning how they relate to the wider Secondary school curriculum.

■ **Figure 2.2** Lee Shulman's seven categories of teacher knowledge

PERFORMANCES

5(a) The teacher develops and implements projects that guide learners in analysing the complexities of an issue or question using perspectives from varied disciplines and cross-disciplinary skills (e.g. a water quality study that draws upon biology and chemistry to look at factual information and social studies to examine policy implications).

5(b) The teacher engages learners in applying content knowledge to real world problems through the lens of interdisciplinary themes (e.g. financial literacy, environmental literacy).

5(c) The teacher facilitates learners' use of current tools and resources to maximize content learning in varied contexts.

5(d) The teacher engages learners in questioning and challenging assumptions and approaches in order to foster innovation and problem solving in local and global contexts.

5(e) The teacher develops learners' communication skills in disciplinary and interdisciplinary contexts by creating meaningful opportunities to employ a variety of forms of communication that address varied audiences and purposes.

5(f) The teacher engages learners in generating and evaluating new ideas and novel approaches, seeking inventive solutions to problems, and developing original work.

5(g) The teacher facilitates learners' ability to develop diverse social and cultural perspectives that expand their understanding of local and global issues and create novel approaches to solving problems.

5(h) The teacher develops and implements supports for learner literacy development across content areas.

ESSENTIAL KNOWLEDGE

5(i) The teacher understands the ways of knowing in his/her discipline how it relates to other disciplinary approaches to inquiry, and the strengths and limitations of each approach in addressing problems, issues, and concerns.

5(j) The teacher understands how current interdisciplinary themes (e.g. civic literacy, health literacy, global awareness) connect to the core subjects and knows how to weave those themes into meaningful learning experiences.

5(k) The teacher understands the demands of accessing and managing information as well as how to evaluate issues of ethics and quality related to information and its use.

5(l) The teacher understands how to use digital and interactive technologies for efficiently and effectively achieving specific learning goals.

5(m) The teacher understands critical thinking processes and knows how to help learners develop high level questioning skills to promote their independent learning.

5(n) The teacher understands communication modes and skills as vehicles for learning (e.g. information gathering and processing) across disciplines as well as vehicles for expressing learning.

5(o)   The teacher understands creative thinking processes and how to engage learners in producing original work.

5(p)   The teacher knows where and how to access resources to build global awareness and understanding, and how to integrate them into the curriculum.

CRITICAL DISPOSITIONS

5(q)   The teacher is constantly exploring how to use disciplinary knowledge as a lens to address local and global issues.

5(r)   The teacher values knowledge outside his/her own content area and how such knowledge enhances student learning.

5(s)   The teacher values flexible learning environments that encourage learner exploration, discovery, and expression across content areas.

This conceptualisation of subject/content knowledge application stresses the importance of a project-based, interdisciplinary approach that enables learners to communicate about, and make links across, topics and subjects. It implies the use of digital technologies and emphasises the importance of perceived notions of relevance, i.e. the importance of linkages to real world problems for learners.

COURSE EXPECTATIONS: THE STUDENT TEACHERS' POINT OF VIEW

There is a wide range of student teachers who opt to learn to teach FLs. Many of them will elect to train to teach directly after completion of their undergraduate studies or shortly thereafter. Others may have followed one or more careers in areas other than education and, for a variety of reasons, have decided that the time is now appropriate for them to retrain. Many others are native speakers of the target language, who may have worked as foreign language assistants (FLAs). In this chapter, with permission of the writers, we present two authentic case studies of FLs student teachers. They are drawn from accounts written during a PGCE course. The views expressed are invariably personal and specific to individual circumstances but, nevertheless, illustrate a number of general issues about the process of student teachers' development. The case studies are divided into two sections: an initial statement giving reasons for wanting to become a teacher written before the start of the PGCE course, which are included in this section, and a concluding statement on completion of the course, which can be found at the end of this chapter.

THEORY AND PRACTICE IN (FLs) TEACHER EDUCATION

As we have seen, teacher education courses are required to assess you as a FLs student teacher against a set of standards, i.e. your ability to display certain observable types of behaviour to enable pupils to learn effectively. In order to be able to demonstrate the standards (DfE, 2012: 8–9) of:

1   setting high expectations which inspire, motivate and challenge pupils;

2   promoting good progress and outcomes by pupils;

Case Study 1 **INITIAL STATEMENT**

From the age of 13, pupils are encouraged to investigate career choices, or rather that was the case in my educational experience. At this time, no other career option appealed to me in the same way as teaching and the situation has not changed in ten years. When I ask myself what I wanted from a successful and satisfying career, teaching fulfils most of my requirements. Teaching allows me to continue to work with my subject interests. I want to work in a team but also with the public, a combination that demands good communication and diplomacy skills. I see teaching as an immense challenge because the potential for rewards, satisfaction and excellence is infinite, but on the other hand failure is unacceptable. I want to be able to bring or even drag out the best in my future pupils and I am fully aware that that does not mean expecting them all to achieve grade A.

My desire to be a teacher has been reinforced by teaching both English and French (to small groups and individuals) and by the satisfaction that these experiences have brought me. I discovered that I have confidence, discipline and organisational skills that enabled me to teach a language and to engage my pupils' interest. I feel I am able to relate to the educational, personal and social needs of young people and to deal with them within the teaching environment.

I am aware of the conflict between teaching a modern foreign language to enable pupils to pass an exam and teaching it to prepare pupils for using a specific language in and outside of the countries where it is spoken.

I am also concerned about the behaviour of today's pupils and the lack of respect they seem to have for each other and for adults. Any improvement, however small, I can make to this situation during my career will give me great satisfaction.

Case Study 2 **INITIAL STATEMENT**

Unlike a lot of people on this course who seem to have wanted to teach all their lives, the one thing I knew that I was not going to do when I graduated was teach. This was mainly due to my father recommending that teaching was not a profession to go into. As he is himself a teacher, I figured he must know what he was talking about, so I took his advice. I went on to work in a variety of mainly PA, research, and sales and marketing roles, none of which ever seemed particularly satisfying or rewarding. I finally decided I had to re-examine what I was after in a career. The result pointed to the fact that I had been avoiding a profession which I secretly thought I might enjoy.

I have not forgotten my own experiences in Secondary school, sometimes sitting in a (language) classroom feeling incredibly stupid and panicking because I had not understood what the teacher had been explaining and was too scared to ask. Of course this is a very naive thing to say, but I would like to think that I could persuade pupils in my class not to be afraid to make clear that they have not understood what I have tried to explain. I believe this to be a crucial point in beginning to build a sound working relationship with a class. I am of the opinion that as long as a pupil is making an effort to understand, that pupil deserves the best effort that I can make to help her. I also believe that if that pupil is not making the effort, it is my job to give her a reason to make that effort.

As far as teaching my particular subject is concerned, I am convinced that my enthusiasm for what I have to teach is of prime importance in helping me do my job well. I want to be able to impart this enthusiasm to my pupils, but I can see that this is where the difficulties are most likely to occur. The reason for this is because I have, for the majority of my life, been taught using very conservative and academic methods. It is all I know and it is what I am most comfortable with at present. To complicate matters further, I am naturally a quite reserved character. So when I see videos of teachers using 'radical' communicative methods, I think 'brilliant!' and then I think 'but I can't do that'. I believe the methods are effective, I can see how they would work, but I am not sure that I am capable of applying them myself. Ideas on how to teach MFL have changed drastically since I was at school, and although it is a change that I approve of, it is also one that I will have to make an effort to adapt to successfully.

On a more general level, classroom management is my greatest worry at the moment, particularly after having seen some classes during my induction week in school. I am aware that with the best lesson plan in the world, if the class is not managed correctly the pupils are not going to learn as effectively as they could.

Planning my work I do not as yet see as a big problem. I am fairly confident of being able to get straight in my own mind the objectives of a lesson and being able to get from there in terms of suitable activities to meet these objectives.

Task 2.3 COMPARING PERSONAL AND COURSE EXPECTATIONS

The discussion in this chapter so far has highlighted the complexity of FL teaching and has shown how much there is to be learnt by a student teacher. This task aims to help you decide priorities for your professional development.

1   Reflect on and note down how the discussion so far in this chapter relates to your personal expectations concerning your teacher education programme. In your opinion, what knowledge and skills does an effective FLs teacher need? Also, what characterises a good FLs teacher? What types of behaviour do you think are best avoided by a FLs teacher?
2   What expectations did the two student teachers have initially about teaching? How do their expectations relate to your own?
3   Then, carefully study your course documentation. What expectations are stated in the documents? How do they compare to your expectations?
4   What issues arise from this comparison? What will your priorities be?

Task 2.4 PUPIL EXPECTATIONS

When you have the opportunity, carry out a small survey among pupils at your placement school, asking them what characteristics they wish to see in a FLs teacher. Note down positive and negative responses. Are there any differences in your own and the pupils' perceptions?

3   demonstrating good subject and curriculum knowledge;
4   planning and teaching well-structured lessons;
5   adapting teaching to respond to the strengths and needs of all pupils;
6   making accurate and productive use of assessment;
7   managing behaviour effectively to ensure a good and safe learning environment;
8   fulfilling wider professional responsibilities.

and to ensure that pupils learn as a result of your actions, you need to develop professional judgement and an ability to reflect, among other things, on your own professional practice and its effectiveness in bringing about learning. This, we argue, requires practical as well as theoretical knowledge. The relationship between theory and practice is, therefore, an important issue. Indeed, reflection and theorising have long been viewed in the literature as central features underpinning student teachers' development and as catalysts in moving student teachers from dependency to autonomy (see e.g. Furlong *et al.*, 1996: 32).

To find time for reflection as part of a busy schedule is not necessarily easy. However, you do need to ensure that you evaluate your teaching and pupils' learning regularly. You should do so by focusing first and foremost on pupils' learning, progress and understanding. In addition, you should look at aspects of your teaching, such as your position in the classroom or the modulation of your voice – elements that can have a significant impact on pupil learning. Ask yourself questions such as:

▓   How well did pupils learn what you intended them to learn?
▓   What may have impeded/boosted their learning?
▓   How well did they understand new concepts you introduced?
▓   Did they make progress from previous learning?
▓   Which groups/individuals were particularly successful/less successful? Why?

The ability to analyse the processes of your classroom is central to your work as a student teacher and reference to external sources, such as relevant literature, can provide welcome support:

> The most useful role of theory for the practitioner is to offer a strong constructivist foundation for their activity, and to provide a basis upon which to question the leading fads and rhetoric of the field. . . . The role of researchers, then, is to provide comprehensible input for practitioners, and the role of practitioners is to provide rational interpretation of those ideas for researchers to ponder. Both are locked into a symbiotic relationship that eventually propels the field and advances knowledge.
>
> (Bialystok and Hakuta, 1995: 218)

However,

> 'Theory as intellectual process' . . . is inadequate; what should be offered is theoretical knowledge which may be tentative and to be questioned, but which

is also specifically believed 'to be of practical value' and usefully assimilated into the professional development of student teachers.

(Dunne, 1993: 105)

FL teaching, we believe, requires a systematic engagement with practical knowledge, including – but going beyond – reflection on what can be observed – that is, practical knowledge, which is predicated on conceptual and theoretical understanding enabling teachers to make deliberate choices at various stages of the teaching process. Recent literature on teacher education has a number of recommendations on how this can be achieved and we will look at some of them briefly here.

Before we do so, let us have a brief look at the purposes of reflection. Roberts (1998: 54–58) distinguishes eleven different purposes for, or types of reflection to:

1   raise awareness of personal images of teaching;
2   raise awareness of one's personal theories, values and beliefs;
3   reflect on one's own language learning style;
4   raise awareness of one's current performance as a learner;
5   develop the ability to analyse teaching situations;
6   recall and analyse new and recent learning experiences;
7   review and access one's own actions in class;
8   raise awareness of one's routines and their rationale;
9   test the consistency between classroom events and educational theories;
10 become able to reframe interpretations of one's practice;
11 become aware of the social and political significance of one's work.

Reflection can offer a very useful means of integrating theory and practice and of enabling you to deepen your understanding of your own personal and professional development. However, awareness of the multifaceted nature of the term and the concept is important to ensure the appropriate type of reflection is used for a specific purpose.

For Yaxley (1994: 26) the process of reflection consists in the first instance of the description of good practice, leading to articulating of the principles, which underpin this practice. This, in turn, leads to the sharing of ideas through open discussion, whether orally or in written form, followed by a process of challenging and justifying professional decisions. The final phase of reflective practice in this model is the close scrutiny and questioning of practice as an independent professional. From our perspective, sustained reference to relevant conceptual and theoretical frameworks gained, for example, through discussion with peers, teachers and tutors or engagement with professional and academic literature, is essential in the process (see also Calvert, 2014).

Task 2.5 **REFLECTING ON PRACTICE**

When reflecting on your work on the course (for example, when discussing an observed lesson, or when evaluating pupils' learning), refer to Roberts's types of reflection as well as the research chapter at the end of the book.

What type of reflection do you tend to engage in? Why?

At certain stages of your teacher education programme, you might find it difficult to relate what you are taught at university and/or what you read about to what you observe in school. For Grenfell, this potential tension in subject methodology is important in so far as it requires student teachers 'to decide *for themselves*' (1998: 171) and respond practically, intellectually and emotionally. Teachers 'who are simply told what to do and what not to do' are less likely to develop the 'multitude of senses, knowledges and ways of acting . . . required in schools and in classrooms' (1998: 178).

Grenfell (1998: 131–144) outlines 13 problem areas, or dichotomies, which some of his student teachers experienced:

1 the incongruity between personal views of teaching and those presented on the course;
2 past experience, which has proved to be successful versus a new approach which has not;
3 the choice to be made between trusting what I know about teaching and learning from and trusting what others tell me to do;
4 the need to respond personally to the pedagogic approach versus the need to fulfil the course requirement;
5 the ability to criticise versus the ability to do better oneself;
6 to teach by technique versus to teach through individual personality;
7 the need to attend to personal security versus the need to attend to the pedagogic needs of the pupils;
8 how can I be a teacher versus how can I be myself?;
9 'I want everything planned so that I know what I am doing' versus 'I want flexibility to take pupils' response into account';
10 how far to bring the approach to the particular class versus how far to bring the particular class to the approach?;
11 do I use the target language or English?;
12 to teach grammar versus to teach through the target language;
13 who do I turn to with problems?

Task 2.6 TENSIONS FREQUENTLY EXPERIENCED BY STUDENT TEACHERS

Consider Grenfell's dichotomies. To what extent are they representative of problem areas you have encountered and are facing? Have you been able to resolve them? What strategies did you use? It may be useful to consider these dichotomies at various stages in your programme.

Grenfell also emphasises the importance of the personal theories of school-based mentors. Rather than viewing their practice as behaviours to be modelled and copied, regarding what teachers say and how they teach as being in some ways theoretical 'allows student teachers to be explicit about what they think, and in so doing, objectifying it' (1998: 148). This, Grenfell argues, allows student teachers to change and discuss change as well as 'to develop ways of thinking and acting which allow them to become competent as a teacher in a range of contexts' (1998: 148).

Pickering *et al.* (2007: 5–6) identify three design elements for teacher development programs, which we also consider to have merit in teacher education contexts:

- shared practice, i.e. more than just an exchange of practice but one that leads proactively into changes in practice. This contains the potential for all teachers to be agents for change, and is not best practice, 'delivered' as a top-down model by experts;
- collaborative . . . professional development, which draws on the strengths of learning networks that are most effective when they are classroom-focused, and, where possible, cross-phase, cross-subject, cross-experience, i.e. not hierarchical;
- scholarly reflection on practice, which regards the fusion of theory and practice as being what teaching is about. . .

In many ways this mirrors Grenfell's findings about the need for student teachers to take a critical stance and contest practices observed. It also adds an important new perspective – namely, the importance of sharing and collaboration and encourages student teachers to develop dispositions of openness to feedback from others as well as a willingness to offer contributions. Digital technologies, in particular social networking tools and services, have considerable potential for teachers wanting to work as part of a community of practice.

One interesting type of engagement with practice discussed in the recent literature is that of 'pedagogies of enactment' or 'approximation of practice' (Grossman and McDonald, 2008: 190). Grossman and McDonald promote these concepts in an attempt to go beyond reflective practice by promoting 'an expanded view of teaching that focuses on teaching as a practice that encompasses cognition, craft, and affect' (2008: 185). This refers in particular to opportunities to practise elements of interactive teaching in settings of reduced complexity with the nature of the simplification being key. Replacing real pupils with fellow student teachers, which happens typically in university-based microteaching contexts, is thought not to be as conducive to learning about practice as working with actual pupils. Nevertheless, one instantiation of the approximation of practice, which is frequently used on university-based courses, often at the beginning of, or prior to student teachers going out on their teaching practice, is microteaching. Zhang and Cheng (2011) describe a model of microteaching that is practicum-based and their study finds that it can provide student teachers with 'opportunities for interactive learning practices, for rehearsal, revision, and retrial, and for manageable chunking of professional practices' (pp. 355–356). Grossman and McDonald (2008: 190) argue that approximation of practice also addresses the gap between practices advocated by university-based teacher education courses and what they are likely to see in typical school settings. Culturally relevant practice is a term coined by Ladson-Billings who defines it as 'a pedagogy that empowers students intellectually, socially and emotionally, and politically by using cultural referents to impart knowledge, skills, and attitudes' (1994: 17–18). The concept promotes the importance of teachers needing to learn about the cultural knowledge of learners and to reflect that knowledge in their pedagogical practice.

Another key notion promoted by the literature is that of 'high-leverage' practices. These, according to Grossman *et al.* (2009: 277) are practices that

- occur with high frequency in teaching;
- novices can enact in classrooms across different curricula or instructional approaches;
- novices can actually begin to master;
- allow novices to learn more about students and about teaching;
- preserve the integrity and complexity of teaching;
- are research-based and have the potential to improve student achievement.

The authors suggest that the organisation of the teacher education curriculum is not around knowledge domains but around high-leverage practices.

We briefly also want to mention 'lesson study' in this section, which originated in Japan and has come to the UK via the US. According to Lewis *et al.* (2012), lesson study is an 'inquiry cycle' which is conducted by a team of teachers and is centred around what they call a 'research lesson', by which they mean an actual lesson which has been designed to 'investigate and improve the teaching of a particular topic' (p. 368). The lesson is observed by team members and data is gathered, which is then presented and discussed in a post-lesson discussion in which team members formulate implications for future teaching of the topic in hand.

Finally, and very briefly, we also want to mention practitioner research as an important strategy of a systematic engagement with practice. Practitioner research is much discussed in the literature, sometimes under the label of 'action research', and it has become an integral part of many teacher education programmes. In essence, it involves the formulation of specific questions about personal practice, the design of particular interventions over a period of time, the collection and analysis of data about the intervention, and replanning on the basis of the findings. One useful resource to support the planning and execution of practitioner research is Wilson (2012). Borg (2010: 402–403), in his review of relevant literature, identifies a number of claims about the potential of teacher research, such as: the development of autonomous professional judgement; the lessening of a dependency on external drivers; an increase in reflexivity; criticality; an analytical orientation towards personal professional practice; and a problem-solving mindset as well as of pedagogical decision-making.

STAGES IN THE DEVELOPMENT OF STUDENT TEACHERS

Different levels of theorising, to be addressed at different stages of (student) teachers' development and by different partners in the teacher education process can be identified. In the course of teacher education, learning takes place at different rates. FLs student teachers undergo a developmental process, which is governed by individual personal differences. One change most FLs student teachers undergo is the gradual shift from a concern with themselves as teachers, as lesson planners and 'deliverers' of subject matter, towards an increasing concern for pupils as learners with individual traits and specific needs.

No.	Stage	Summary
1	Early idealism	Student teachers often come to the course with an educational philosophy based on good or bad examples from their own 'careers' as pupils.
2	Personal survival	Student teachers can feel quite overwhelmed by their first experience of teaching; they tend to feel insecure and want the pupils to accept them as teachers; they use strategies such as copying the mentor, appraising their initial idealistic view of themselves as teachers, and working at gaining and maintaining classroom control.
3	Dealing with difficulties	Student teachers start to appreciate the complexities of teaching and gain a basic understanding of certain aspects of the job; many look to pupils for feedback and judge their own effectiveness by how well pupils like them; teaching strategies and classroom organisation become increasingly important, and student teachers often try to assimilate the teaching style and methods used by their mentor.
4	Hitting a plateau	While having gained certain basic competences, many student teachers can lack real understanding; they can often act like teachers but not really think like teachers at this stage.
5	Moving on	Student teachers start to think of themselves as professional educators.

■ **Figure 2.3** Stages in the development of student teachers

Based on their work with Primary PGCE student teachers, Furlong and Maynard (1995: 73–97) suggest that there are a number of different broad stages of development. These stages are summarised in Figure 2.3. None of these developmental models can be seen as inevitable or linear, however. Student teachers develop at different rates of progress according to a variety of circumstances and characteristics. See Barnes (2006) for a discussion of FL student teachers' concerns, demonstrating that they are indeed concerned with, for example, subject/content knowledge issues from an early stage in their programmes and that the stages are much less linear than may be implied by some models.

DEVELOPING A PERSONAL APPROACH TO FL TEACHING AND LEARNING

Gradually, as FLs student teachers become more familiar with the processes of classroom organisation and more confident in interacting with pupils, they begin to develop their own personal teaching style. You need to determine your personal approach to FL teaching and learning on the basis of:

■ the statutory requirements and their methodological implications;
■ the individual differences and needs of pupils;
■ personal preferences concerning teaching styles;

■ the policies and practice prevalent in placement schools;

■ good practice described in relevant literature/lectures or observed in FLs classrooms.

The last few decades have witnessed a wide range of approaches to FL teaching and learning, none of which provided a panacea. In an appendix to his book *Designing Tasks for the Communicative Classroom*, Nunan (1989: 194–196) provides an interesting overview of important language teaching methods. His matrix provides a useful tool for analysing personal preferences concerning FL teaching and learning.

Many student teachers tend to start to teach in a way they have been, or would like to be taught. Below are two activities intended to broaden your perspective and to encourage you to consider other strategies to meet the needs and preferences of pupils in your classroom.

Task 2.7 features a questionnaire (Figure 2.4), which is based on Nunan's matrix. It also builds on Kolb *et al.*'s (1974) learning styles inventory. The purpose of this task is to guide you towards an understanding of your own preferred learning style and at the same time to make you aware of the principle features of other styles.

In Task 2.8 you can then apply the understanding of learning styles gained in Task 2.7 and start to develop your own approach to FL teaching.

Task 2.7 **IDENTIFYING PREFERRED LEARNING STYLES**

1 Read through the questions and statements in Figure 2.4. For each question/ statement there are four contrasting views. There are no 'right' or 'wrong' responses. You are asked to respond to each question/statement in terms of how it best corresponds to your own personal views. Do not think too hard before responding. Allocate 2 points to the response closest to your views, 1 point to the one ranked second; give –1 point to your third favourite response and –2 points to the response you agree with the least.

2 Transfer your points into the table in Figure 2.5. For the time being disregard the acronyms at the top of each column.

3 Then, plot your scores on the grid in Figure 2.6 and join them to a geometrical form. You should end up with a drawing in the shape of a kite. Your preferred learning style is represented by the quadrant, in which the majority of your kite shape can be found. It is defined by combining two of the descriptions in Figure 2.7, which account for the two axes. The graph shows your preferences and strength of feeling.

■ ■ ■ ■ ON BECOMING A FOREIGN LANGUAGES TEACHER

No.	Questions	Score
1	**Do you believe that language is essentially:**	
a	a set of rule-governed structures?	- 2
b	a system that has developed to convey meaning?	2
c	composed of a unique rhythm and spirit based around the culture of the country where the language is spoken?	1
d	built around correct, grammatical concepts?	- 1
2	**A modern foreign language is best learnt by:**	
a	memorisation and forming good language habits;	- 2
b	listening, reading and then practising;	- 1
c	undertaking realistic tasks, achievable only by use of the TL;	✗ 1
d	acquisition through constant exposure to and immersion in the TL and culture.	2
3	**The primary aim of learning a FL is:**	
a	to achieve a practical command of speaking, listening, reading, writing;	- 1
b	to achieve functional and linguistic objectives;	- 2
c	to provide basic communicative skills as well as essential academic learning skills;	2
d	to provide enjoyment and stimulation through access to a foreign culture.	1
4	**A FLs course should be structured so that language presented:**	
a	is graded in forms of ever-increasing levels of difficulty;	1
b	is determined by the learner's individual needs;	2
c	is based around grammatical items and associated vocabulary;	- 2
d	consists of excerpts from cultural texts.	- 1
5	**The purpose of classroom activities is:**	
a	to practise and reinforce correct forms of language;	1
b	to engage the learner in communicative tasks;	2
c	to allow the learner to respond to commands, questions and clues in her own way;	- 2
d	to build upon structures and language forms learnt previously.	- 1
6	**The learner's chief responsibility is:**	
a	to listen, repeat and to respond;	- 1
b	to negotiate objectives and to respond accordingly;	1
c	to move towards independence, autonomy and responsibility;	2
d	to maintain passive and to allow the materials and activities to determine the nature of learning.	- 2

■ **Figure 2.4** Questionnaire

No.	Questions	Score
7	**The teacher's place in the teaching/learning process is:**	
a	to act as a model of good TL use and to orchestrate drill practice;	−1
b	to facilitate through presentation, advice and the provision of authentic, realistic tasks;	1
c	to provide comprehensible input and orchestrate a variety of related activities;	2
d	to teach, test and to reinforce accurate language forms.	−2
8	**In the main, the following materials should be used by the teacher:**	
a	a coursebook and visual aides;	1
b	audio tapes and transcripts;	−2
c	authentic, realistic materials;	−1
d	structured examples and related exercises.	2

■ **Figure 2.4** *continued*

No.	OBH	LMPU	ERP	SGA
1	a = −2	b = 2	c = 1	d = −1
2	a = −1	c = 1	d = 2	b = −1
3	a = −1	b = −2	d = 1	c = 2
4	a = 1	b = 2	d = −1	c = −2
5	a = 1	b = 2	c = −2	d = −1
6	a = −1	b = 1	d = −2	c = 2
7	a = −1	c = 2	b = 1	d = −2
8	a = 1	c = −1	b = −2	d = 2
Total	−3	7	−2	−1

■ **Figure 2.5** Scoring table

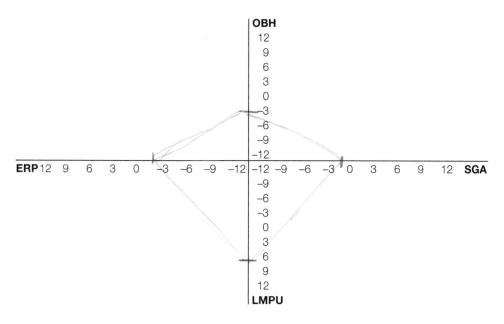

■ **Figure 2.6** Plotting grid

Off-by-heart language learning (OBH)	Learning to manipulate language for personal use (LMPU)	Exposure, repetition and practice (ERP)	Structured grammar approach (SGA)
The content of a course is defined within strict topic areas. Set phrases and key vocabulary are learnt irrespective of their grammatical complexity in order to meet perceived needs and corresponding usefulness in given situations. Learning 'parrot fashion' enables a task to be completed.	Language is learnt through the personalisation and manipulation of language forms presented. Motivation is achieved through realistic and successful communication. The learner is personally involved and takes considerable responsibility for her own learning.	The process of learning is through immersion in the language. Unstructured practice is reinforced through the reactions of others. The learner learns which parts of language work in which situations, thereby identifying and developing positive linguistic habits for herself.	The explanation of grammatical concepts in a logical sequence and the structured application of this knowledge lead to a sound understanding of language structures. This understanding facilitates a sound mastery of linguistic systems.

■ **Figure 2.7** Description of learning styles

Task 2.8 **DEVELOPING YOUR PERSONAL APPROACH TO FL TEACHING**

1   Having identified a preferred learning style, reflect upon the types of learning activities associated with it. What are the implications for your FL teaching?
2   Then consider activities, which will suit other learning styles, for instance by talking to other student teachers. What are the implications for your FL teaching?

When planning FLs lessons, try to account for the full range of learning styles. It will certainly not work for your learners if all your lessons are wonderfully tailored to suit you and your learning style.

SCHOOLS' EXPECTATIONS AND THE MENTOR'S POINT OF VIEW

Schools can have a number of roles in the teacher education process. Traditionally, they have offered practical experience placements for student teachers. Over time, they grew into full partners of higher education institutions contributing to the selection of candidates, contributing to the design of the teacher education programmes as well as making some contributions to the teaching on the course, mostly in the form of professional studies sessions on the broader professional issues such as information about the pastoral system, inclusion, equal opportunities, special needs, PSHE, contractual and legal responsibilities, etc. The 2010 White Paper has started to change the landscape for teacher education significantly. Through the School Direct initiative an increasing number of schools are able to bid to the relevant government agency, at the time of writing the National College for Teaching and Leadership, for student teachers directly, and they can apply for Teaching School designation to assume a leading role in the training and professional development of teachers. One key element of this role concerns the selection of candidates.

Irrespective of the type of teacher education programme you are on, you will be working with an experienced colleague acting as your mentor whose role it is to seek to help you to progress through the stages in Figure 2.3. In order to maximise the effectiveness of the mentor's experience and advice, you need to establish a good working relationship with your mentor and with other staff at the school. In order to be able to do so it is important for you to gain some awareness of schools' expectations. This section offers some advice and guidance from the point of view of mentors. This includes induction, support in organisational matters, observation of practical teaching, the giving of advice, guidance and diagnostic feedback, the provision of input on methodology and appropriate approaches as well as, importantly, assessment of practical teaching and target setting.

Why schools and mentors get involved in teacher education

Schools and departmental teams agree to get involved in, or even lead on teacher education and to take student teachers for a whole host of reasons. A study carried

Benefits	Subject mentors
Professional development	90
Job satisfaction	81
Management skills	76
Curriculum innovation	64
Morale	54
New teaching methods	45
Addition of new resources	42
Support with extra curricular activities	36
Career prospects	26
Pupil motivation	20
School status	12

■ **Figure 2.8** Perception of the level of benefit in per cent (non FLs-specific)

out by researchers at the University of Warwick (Barker *et al*., 1996: 57) for the Association for Teachers and Lecturers (ATL) among a representative sample of teacher education courses running at the time found that subject mentors saw a number of benefits arising from participation in a partnership scheme and receiving student teachers (see Figure 2.8).

You need to realise, though, that these benefits to mentors come at a certain cost, for instance, an increased demand on time, workload and administration as often work with student teachers is carried out without receiving any financial rewards or time off in lieu. Having an additional person in the team has a number of implications for the work of a department. This you need to be aware of while on a school placement.

The role of your mentor

It is important for you to appreciate that established channels of communication need to be observed. These vary from course to course and from school to school. Your course handbook as well as the staff and departmental handbooks provided by your school(s) should contain all the relevant information with which you need to familiarise yourself. At the same time there tends to be a co-ordinating mentor/ professional tutor (usually a senior teacher or deputy head) with overall responsibility for student teachers, who works in tandem with subject mentors.

In each department there is usually a named individual, the so-called subject mentor, who has undergone a training programme with the respective HEI and who is your main point of contact during your attachment to the placement school. The responsibilities of subject mentors can vary. However, they typically include liaison with relevant colleagues in the partnership, observing lessons, giving regular advice and feedback regarding your progress and performance against the standards as well as contributing to your assessment. Subject mentors tend to carry out their duties in consultation with all members of staff in the FLs department, who work with you as well as with colleagues involved in running the teacher education programme such as link tutors, university tutors or specialist leaders of education.

It is important for you to be clear from the very beginning what you can realistically expect from your mentor; for instance, how often and when you will be able to meet with her. At the same time you need to be fully aware of your responsibilities. For instance, in terms of personal organisation you need to appreciate that any necessary equipment and resources in the school or department required for teaching need to be booked well in advance. Failure to do so might result in you being unable to proceed with a lesson according to plan and cause disruption.

Building a professional relationship with members of staff at your school

Usually you will be asked to observe and work with a number of experienced teachers with the aim of gaining as wide a range of experiences of teaching styles and pupils' responses to them as possible. This is an important part of your learning experience. It is important that you establish a good working relationship with all members of staff, not just with your mentor.

Working closely with more than one FLs teacher can, on occasion, create certain tensions: you might experience uncertainty as to what teaching styles and strategies to adopt or reject and sometimes advice given by different teachers might seem inconsistent or even irreconcilable to you. You should follow up specific observations made in lessons, which will trigger questions, and seek clarification as the reasons for using particular teaching strategies are not always obvious to an observer. In many instances there is more than meets the eye to the way teachers manage their lessons and relate to pupils who they know well. If any doubt still persists as to why a staff member may have behaved as she did, issues can be raised with your mentor and/or tutor without necessarily personalising them. When seeking clarification in this way you engage in the important process of reflection on practice. This can provide you with an increased understanding of individual pupils and their behaviour as well as teachers' approaches to dealing with them. However, you need to display a professional attitude throughout this process. You need to be acutely aware that some questions you may want to ask might be sensitive.

Any worries or problems need to be resolved in a mature and professional manner by following the correct procedures normally outlined in the course handbook. Remember that not all professional relationships necessarily turn into personal friendships. In the event of a personality clash, which can occur occasionally, mediation through a third party can help to resolve possible tensions.

Learning from members of staff

You will normally be expected to work within the agreed policies of both the department you work in and the school more generally, which may well be linked to policies of a wider group of schools if your school is part of an alliance, group or network of schools. Where asked to do so, you need to follow the routines set by members of staff for different groups as pupils can benefit from experiencing continuity of practice and consistency. Often certain variations to set routines are possible but they need to be discussed with, and approved by, the member of staff responsible for a given class. Innovation and exploration of new approaches to teaching are exciting, desirable and commendable in a student teacher and, as can be seen in Figure 2.8, perceived as a benefit by mentors. They must, however, not upset pupils' well-established routines, which can serve them well in maximising their learning.

Appreciating the range of responsibilities of members of staff at your placement school

To ensure high quality in collaborative teaching, there is a need for frequent information exchange and discussions between the student teacher and the relevant member of staff. You will soon become aware that, beside teaching, a typical day of an FLs teacher may include: tidying up the classroom and getting ready in between lessons, doing duties, attending meetings (at lunchtime or after school sometimes on several days in the week), liaising with colleagues, invigilating detentions (at breaktime or after school), meeting visitors, discussing work with pupils outside lesson time, running lunchtime or after-school clubs, photocopying, dealing with and responding to e-mails, marking pupils' work or making and receiving phone calls, etc. Importantly, they also need time for breaks, their lunch and for socialising with colleagues. Subject mentors often have other responsibilities, apart from those for student teachers. You need to respect the busy schedule of teachers and observe arranged meeting times.

In the light of these demands and in order to obtain an accurate picture from the beginning of what teaching entails, student teachers need to play a full part in school life. This will probably include you staying on after school for staff and departmental meetings, being attached to a form group for registrations, pastoral and guidance time, attending assemblies, attending parents' evenings, performing break duties, contributing to extra-curricular activities or assisting in fund-raising activities.

Task 2.9 **FINDING OUT ABOUT YOUR SUBJECT MENTOR'S DAILY ROUTINE**

Ask your subject mentor whether you can shadow her for a whole teaching day (including break, lunchtime and any free periods) and after school to become familiar with her daily responsibilities and duties.

1   In the course of the day list all her duties and responsibilities, note the time of occurrence and their duration.
2   Then discuss with your mentor how representative the day was and which other responsibilities and duties she has on a regular basis.

The student teacher as a role model

From the very start you need to see yourself as an educator, not merely as a subject specialist. You need to take on the wider brief of teachers, which includes concern for your pupils' spiritual, moral, social and cultural development. One way of taking on the full role of a teacher is by displaying a responsible and caring attitude towards pupils. You will often be perceived as a (role) model by pupils just as members of staff are and need to gain pupils' trust and respect both inside and, importantly also, outside the classroom. You need to be acutely aware that pupils observe the behaviour and conduct of those around them carefully and can be duly influenced in their behaviour and/or attitudes towards the subject. When working with pupils, you must never underestimate the formative influence you might have on them.

Accepting and acting upon advice

There is a lot to be learnt from the experience and knowledge of (FLs) teachers at your placement school. Part of their role is to share their practice with you and to advise you on your development as a student teacher and set targets. It is your responsibility to take this advice on board and act upon it. You need to learn from members of staff at your placement school as well as learn to work with them. In all your interactions with pupils, colleagues and the school, personal and professional integrity are essential. When something goes wrong, you need to try, together with your mentor, to identify contributory factors and devise possible strategies for improvement.

Invariably, many things will not work out the first time round during your programme of teacher education. Qualified practitioners strive every day to improve their teaching. No less is expected from those new to the profession. A genuine desire to contribute to a positive learning experience about the ways people from other cultures communicate and live is what is required. For a detailed review of literature in language mentoring, see Delaney (2012).

Task 2.10 **WHAT IS YOUR MENTOR TO YOU?**

In evaluating your own performance and in planning your own future development, you need to consider the place and role of your mentor.

Identify words from the list below which:

■   represent the role you wish your mentor to take on;
■   do not describe the relationship you want with your mentor;
■   need discussion with your mentor;
■   are missing and you wish to raise with your mentor.

colleague	guide	appraiser
protector	motivator	teacher
consultant	assessor	listener
helper	diagnoser	trusted guide
reviewer	facilitator	counsellor
expert	challenger	critical friend

Discuss with your mentor the ways in which she can respond to your needs and promote your development.

(Source: Turner et al., 1997: 33)

BECOMING A FLs TEACHER – THE STUDENT TEACHERS' POINT OF VIEW

Case Study 1 **CONCLUDING STATEMENT**

Being a teacher turned out to be much different than I expected or rather much more than I expected. I find being a teacher overwhelming as well as being very challenging. Over this year I have developed not only many skills but also as a person. My previous experiences of teaching really did not prepare me for the 'whole school experience'.

After the time spent at my first placement school I felt that I was ready to be a 'real' teacher and that the rest of the course was simply a formality but beginning again at the second placement brought me back down to earth. For the first few days I felt that I was back at the start of the course again, which was rather unnerving. The factor which struck me the most was the different ethos between the schools of my first and second placements. The 'feel' of the two schools is amazingly different. In my second school placement I experienced a pastoral system based on 'Houses' rather than 'Years'.

Throughout this year I have developed in all the competence areas. I have built up a wide range of resources from my first placement for all years which I use to supplement the coursebooks and to add an element of fun to my lessons. My planning and preparation overall has become more efficient and I am more aware of how to approach teaching points and more able to pinpoint areas of teaching which need more attention. My record keeping has become more organised and consistent.

I have now developed my own classroom routines which I intend to improve on when I have my own classes and classrooms. I have drawn these routines and practices from observations made at both placement schools. Throughout my practices I have built up my use of pair and group work which has helped me to forge better relationships within my groups. My relationships with both pupils and staff have developed well in both placements.

I have chosen five personal targets as an NQT (newly qualified teacher): displays, authentic materials, special needs, differentiation and extra-curricular activities. Not having my own classroom as a student teacher I am unable to provide my pupils with adequate and appropriate visual aids around the room. Next year I intend to make my classroom educationally stimulating as well as attractive and inviting. I am looking forward to developing in all of these areas next September.

Case Study 2 **CONCLUDING STATEMENT**

Like most people on the course, I suspect, I feel this year has gone surprisingly quickly. The overall impression I am left with, as the end approaches, is not simply of how much progress I have made, but rather of the realisation of how much more there is to teaching than just 'teaching'! This impression has roller-coasted as I started my practice at my second school, was offered a job there and shown what opportunities are available.

I found combining deadlines for college assignments and teaching quite taxing, partly due to the amount of time which has elapsed since doing my degree, allowing me to get out of practice where essays etc. are concerned. This did get easier as I became more familiar with the criteria and got used to writing again. More specifically to do with teaching, looking back at my initial statement, I see that certain of my fears did not materialise, while others did in a slightly different shape to that which I had imagined.

My concerns over planning and preparation, for example, proved to be unfounded. Similarly, where classroom management and discipline were concerned, I found I had very few problems, and was if anything occasionally too strict – and this in turn brought about a problem which I had not foreseen, that of being so strict (wanting to keep too much control) that I was very distant from the pupils I was teaching, even to my tutor group. After Christmas, and even more so after Easter I found that my own self-confidence allowed me to relax and concentrate more on how much pupils were learning, rather than how well they were behaving.

Being aware of pupils' academic abilities not only allowed me to plan more effectively, it also helped me to avoid problems with pupils who would find certain tasks either too easy or too difficult.

Task 2.11 FLs STUDENT TEACHERS' POINT OF VIEW

Having read the two case studies, consider the following: did the student teachers' perception about teaching change in the course of their programme of teacher education? Can these changes be accounted for by the stages of development described in Figure 2.8?

SUMMARY

This chapter has shown that teacher education has witnessed a number of important changes in the recent past. Certain issues, such as the perceived dichotomy between theory and practice, and the importance of subject knowledge in the teacher education process, continue to evolve in the light of changing contexts.

FL teaching is a highly complex profession requiring an understanding of a number of related disciplines. Learning to teach FLs in the Secondary school often features a steep initial learning curve followed by a long process of discovery going beyond the period of teacher education into continuing professional development. Teaching FLs is very complex but it can be a very rewarding career. Above all, it requires an on-going commitment on your part and a willingness to keep abreast with developments in and across a range of areas.

FURTHER READING

Moore, A. (2004) *'The Good Teacher': Dominant Discourses in Teacher Education*. London: Routledge.
    This book explores the question 'What makes a good teacher' from a range of perspectives and it unpacks and critiques prevailing perspectives on what constitutes good practice.

CHAPTER 3

FOREIGN LANGUAGE LEARNING AND SECOND LANGUAGE ACQUISITION RESEARCH

Some implications for foreign language teaching and learning

INTRODUCTION AND SOME WORDS OF CAUTION

The increasing concern with evidence-informed, rather than judgement-based policy making in the UK (for a detailed discussion see e.g. Pachler, 2003) can be seen to have afforded greater importance to research findings in FL teaching. The concern is with 'what works'. Only, for complex reasons, the ability of research to advise on 'what works' is limited (see e.g. Davies *et al.*, 2000). Moreover, the trend towards aligning (parts of) teacher education with Master's level criteria has led to an increased emphasis on research-orientated approaches.

Out of these developments a number of questions arise, such as: what types of evidence are considered valid and what research methods are fit-for-purpose? For example, research into the foundation disciplines of education, such as psychology, sociology or the history of education? Subject-specific research from the fields of Foreign Language Learning (FLL) and Second Language Acquisition (SLA)? Large-scale, longitudinal, quantitative studies carried out by academics or small-scale, short-term, qualitative enquiries by (practitioner) researchers? What is the role of FLs teachers in research? Increasingly, professional enquiry carried out by teachers (supported by university tutors) is being advocated (see e.g. Lamb and Simpson 2003, or Macaro 2003a and 2003b) and it is argued that educational research literacy, i.e. the ability to carry out educational research, is an important part of a teacher's professionality. Against a background characterised by growing account-ability for pupil attainment, some schools and teachers are increasingly interested in research findings and even in engaging in practitioner research and its dissemination.

As space is limited, and as guidance on how to become educationally research literate abounds (see above and Pachler *et al.*, 2007), we will focus here on the findings of recent research into FLL and SLA and consider possible implications for teaching. It is worth noting that, in addition to empirical studies per se, this chapter also draws on literature reviews as well as more scholarly, i.e. conceptual rather than necessarily empirical pieces.

By and large we draw on work carried out by researchers, rather than teachers, not because we don't recognise the significance of practitioner knowledge but because it is not always easily available in published form due to the fact that, for a host of reasons, it remains largely restricted to the educational settings in which it is generated.

We want to stress the dangers of unrealistic expectations in relation to research and its ability to offer clear-cut answers. In engaging with research, particularly educational research and more specifically research in the fields of FLL and SLA, readers of research reports have to bear in mind that education and FLs learning and teaching are highly complex fields influenced by many contextual factors and variables. Classrooms and schools are complex environments, or 'ecological' systems, where factors such as the physical environment, the time of day, the number of learners, the personal characteristics of the teacher and the learners, the profici-ency of the learners, their ages, their motivation, the time available, the teaching resources used, the status of languages in the educational institution and the society more widely, etc. all have a potentially important impact on the learning experiences of pupils. It is very difficult, and often impossible to control these variables in a way that allows researchers to draw hard-and-fast conclusions, which are transferable and generalisable to other contexts. Research findings, therefore, remain 'fuzzy' and the old adage 'apply with caution' (Hatch, 1978) invariably applies.

Caution is particularly important in respect of the summary of key research findings presented in this chapter as necessarily, in order to be able to provide an overview of a range of studies across a number of topics, it is not possible to offer any meaningful background information, context and (methodological) detail about the individual studies from which the recommendations presented here have been drawn. It is not possible, therefore, to validate the interpretations of the data made by researchers of the studies featured and in the literature reviews summarised. In our view, this does not, however, invalidate our attempt to provide an overview of some of the key research that exists and what relevance it might have for the foreign language classroom, provided the reader is fully aware of the limitations that exist, particularly as it is meant primarily as a springboard for readers to follow up the work presented and examine the details themselves.

With Grabe (2004: 59–60) we argue that, while there is unlikely to be a 'definitive research study', there is a danger in relying on the notion of 'doing what works' in that it can limit progress. We concur that reliable evidence in support of instructional practices, even if it is invariably not perfect, can help minimise some of the negative consequences of relying on 'best practice' and allows teachers to test new ideas in their search for more effective outcomes: 'The ideal . . . is a merging of practitioner knowledge and persuasive research support: both are needed for effective instruction' (Grabe, 2004: 60). Lightbown (2003: 10) similarly argues that SLA research is an important source of ideas and 'can help shape teachers' expectations of themselves and their students, and provide valuable clues to effective pedagogical practice'. And she rightly asserts that 'pedagogical innovations must be implemented and adapted according to local conditions including the strengths of individual teachers and students, the available resources, the age of the learners, and the time available for teaching'.

The discipline of applied linguistics, within which both FLL and SLA are located, also deals with mother tongue (L1) research; important considerations, therefore, when examining the usefulness of research, in particular in terms of its transferability to classroom situations, among others are whether or not it has been carried out with L1 or L2 learners, whether it concerns itself with language use in or outside the classroom, whether the language concerned is English as a Foreign/Second Language or another language, the relationship between L1 and L2 and what the age of the subjects was.

OBJECTIVES

By the end of this chapter you should:

■ be aware of findings of recent research into FLL and SLA and possible implications for FL teaching;

■ have realistic expectations in relation to what (FLL and SLA) research is available and its ability to offer answers (for pedagogical practice);

■ have a heightened awareness of what types of evidence can be considered valid, what research methods are fit-for-purpose and what the role of teachers can be in research.

TEACHER KNOWLEDGE AND TEACHER COGNITION AND LEARNING TO TEACH

Prior to our review of FLL and SLA research, we want to address the questions of how teachers learn (about) the content and practices of teaching.

In his review article tracing the conceptualisations of the above over time, Freeman (2002: 4) rightly reminds his readers that learning to teach is more than mastering specific content and methodologies for transmitting that content. Not only can, and should, content not be seen as fixed and given, but as constantly evolving and as being constructed by those involved in the teaching and learning process, but also does such a view not take into account the centrality of the multilayered sociocultural context at macro (national educational policy), meso (school policies) and micro level (factors pertaining to specific classes and pupils, and individual teachers and their educational and experiential histories) in which learning to teach takes place:

> the theory–practice gap is no longer an issue of lack of relevance or of faulty transfer of skills; rather it is one of connecting and integrating the social contexts of professional education with those of the classroom and the school.
>
> (Freeman, 2002: 7)

In addition to the recognition of the importance of context, teacher thinking and decision-making, as cognitive as well as socially embedded and public activities, and the meta-level knowledge of teachers of their practical experience have become central (see Pachler *et al.*, 2008). For Freeman (2002: 11), and we agree with him, the continued attempt of trying to find meaning in personal professional experience as well as that of more experienced teachers is key.

Borg (2003: 81) defines the term 'teacher cognition' as 'the unobservable cognitive dimension of teaching – what teachers know, believe, and think' – and he posits that research into teacher cognition shows that

> teachers are active, thinking decision-makers who make instructional choices by drawing on complex, practically-oriented, personalised, and context-sensitive networks of knowledge, thoughts, and belief.

A key issue for student teachers is to what extent their programme of teacher education is able to influence their cognition and to what extent prior beliefs remain dominant. With reference to research carried out with PGCE student teachers, Borg argues that extant factors from student teachers' own schooling are a strong influence on their practice but that a teacher education programme can and does promote some change at least at the structural level, i.e. it leads to a clearer organisation – reordering, relabelling and sometimes reversal – of personal theories into thematic clusters of ideas, and he recommends that student teachers should have opportunities early on in their course to confront their existing beliefs (2003: 90). We would strongly recommend to you to reflect on your own beliefs about learning, teaching and learning to teach from the start of your course.

Richards (1998: 117–118) notes that experienced teachers used more improvisation than inexperienced teachers which, according to him, suggests that they draw less on 'preactive decision making', by which he means planning, and more on 'interactive decision making'.

In a piece with Li and Tang, Richards (1998 in Borg 2003: 95) identifies four areas of language teaching in which less experienced teachers differ from more experienced colleagues:

1   thinking about the subject matter from the learner's perspective;
2   having a deep understanding of the subject matter;
3   knowing how to present subject matter in appropriate ways;
4   knowing how to integrate language learning with broader curricular goals.

In our view, you need to be aware of this gap and you are strongly encouraged to try to bridge it as you work through the course.

SOME GENERALISATIONS AND HYPOTHESES FROM FLL AND SLA RESEARCH

We start the review of FLL and SLA research findings with a number of generalisations drawn from recent research. Three commentators in particular have tried to extract a number of such generalisations from available research: Lightbown (2003), Ellis (2005) and Chapelle (1998).

Lightbown starts off by asserting that adults and adolescents can 'acquire' a second language, i.e. that while it is true that learners learn things that were never the subject of explicit teaching, instruction can enhance language acquisition. The fact that FL instruction is not necessarily a futile endeavour seems to us to be a reassuring starting point. Another generalisation Lightbown makes is that the developmental stages of learners' language learning, their so-called 'interlanguages', are often characterised by systematic errors children make when learning the language as an L1 as well as others, which are based on the learners' own L1. According to Lightbown, research shows that there are predictable sequences in L2 acquisition, i.e. that some structures have to be acquired before others. Grammar teaching, or 'form-focused instruction' as it tends to be called in the research literature, may speed up learners' progress through a sequence; the sequence itself, however, is not significantly changed by it. This suggests that learners can only be taught what they are ready to learn. It also makes it clear that progress cannot simply be equated with greater accuracy: 'the developmental stages through which learners pass on their way to higher levels of proficiency include stages in which their performance, while systematic, is still far from target-like' (p. 5). Lightbown warns against the conclusion that teachers should plan according to developmental sequences as there are only few detailed descriptions of such sequences in a small number of languages and as it is not feasible to determine the level of all pupils in a class. Even if these difficulties could be overcome, she sees a danger in teaching focusing too much on language features in isolation, which has been discredited by research. The main conclusion that Lightbown recommends to teachers from the developmental sequence generalisation is the realisation that progress need not necessarily manifest itself in terms of an increase in accuracy. Lightbown's next generalisation is that pattern practice and drill in isolation from meaningful language use does not make perfect. She also posits that knowing a language rule does not mean that one will be able to use it in communicative interaction. Research suggests that learners do benefit from instruction that focuses their attention explicitly on language form (although that need not be rule learning); and learners need to notice certain features before they can acquire them and instruction may increase the likelihood for learners to notice how the target language (TL) works. Lightbown also states that isolated explicit error correction is usually ineffective in changing language behaviour. She does note, though, that error feedback can be an effective approach to grammar teaching if it is focused on something the learner is capable of learning, if the learner is able to distinguish between feedback that is confirmatory of the content and feedback that provides information about linguistic accuracy or pragmatic appropriateness, and if it is sustained over time. Furthermore, Lightbown posits that, in instructional settings, the age at which learners start to learn a language is less important than the quality and intensity of instruction and the adequacy of time available. Lightbown also reminds us of the enormity of the task in hand for language learners in view of the complexity of language in terms of vocabulary, morphology, syntax and pronunciation as well as pragmatic and sociolinguistic features of language use, even for learners with high levels of aptitude, i.e. individual learner's strengths in the cognitive abilities required for language learning compared with other learners. Lightbown's final generalisation states that the learners' ability to understand language in a meaningful context is greater than their ability to comprehend decontextualised language and to produce language of comparable complexity and accuracy; in other words, learners' receptive language use will invariably exceed their productive ability, and presentation of language and language use in context is important.

Ellis (2005) is particularly concerned with the teaching of grammar and points out that there is no agreement among researchers whether the focus should be on the systematic teaching of grammatical features or on attention to linguistic features in the context of communicative activities or tasks. Like Lightbown, Ellis also identifies ten generalisations.

First of all, he stresses the need for teachers to ensure that learners develop both a rich repertoire of formulaic expressions and rule-based competence as research evidence shows that learners first internalise prefabricated patterns and chunks of language which they later break down and analyse. Zimmer (2010), in a *New York Times* language blog, discusses the role of chunking in language learning, particularly to learn ritualised moments of everyday communication such as fixed idioms, conventional speech routines or collocations. Zimmer argues that it is the knowledge of such chunks that allows non-native speakers to approximate native-like fluency. He does note, though, with reference to personal correspondence with Michael Swan, that there is a danger that formulaic expressions can get more attention than they deserve at the expense of more generative approaches. The role of formulaic language is also at the heart of a study by Myles *et al.* (1998) which showed that learners gradually 'unpacked' chunks, which they define as 'multi-morphemic units memorised and recalled as a whole, rather than generated from individual items based on linguistic rules' (p. 325), they had been taught as beginners as well as used constituent parts productively in language generation, suggesting to the authors that rote-learning of formulas and rule construction interact.

Second, Ellis reminds his readers that teachers need to ensure that learners focus predominantly on meaning. Two types of meaning can be distinguished, semantic meaning, i.e. the meanings of lexical items or grammatical structures, and pragmatic meaning, i.e. the contextualised meanings that arise in communication. To be able to cater for the latter, Ellis argues, a task-based approach to language teaching is required which views language as a tool for communication whereas for the former, language can be treated as an object of study.

Third, Ellis stresses that teachers need to ensure that learners also focus on form, according to some researchers in particular on form-function mapping, i.e. the correlation between specific forms and the meaning(s) they realise in communication.

Fourth, Ellis reminds teachers to direct instruction predominantly at developing implicit knowledge of the L2, which is procedural and held unconsciously and available for use in real-time, while not neglecting explicit, declarative knowledge, which tends to include rules as well as metalanguage, i.e. terminology to label knowledge about grammar and other aspects of language. Ellis contends that 'explicit knowledge is arguably only of value if it can be shown that learners are able to utilize this type of knowledge in actual performance' (p. 215). It can do that, among other things, by facilitating the development of implicit knowledge. He also reports that explicit grammatical knowledge can be seen to make it more likely that learners attend to the structure in the input and make comparisons with their respective interlanguage. Depending on what role teachers afford to explicit knowledge, very different approaches to language teaching flow. If one takes the view that explicit knowledge is of no or little value, one is likely to adopt a 'zero grammar' approach. If, on the other hand, one takes the view that it is of value, one is likely to adopt the explicit presentation in a PPP model. If, however, one adopts a middle position of affording explicit grammar teaching some importance, this can provide the basis of a consciousness-raising approach. It is the latter that Ellis sees best supported by research findings.

Fifth, Ellis points out that teachers need to take into account a learner's 'built-in syllabus', i.e. the 'natural' order and sequence of acquisition followed by learners in learning grammar as implicit knowledge (but see Lightbown's point above). Research suggests that the order and sequence of acquisition is the same for instructed and natural learners, but that instructed learners generally achieve higher levels of grammatical competence. Teachers can, therefore, take into account Ellis' fifth generalisation by a) adopting a zero grammar approach, b) ensuring that learners are developmentally ready to acquire a specific grammar point and/or c) focusing in their teaching on explicit rather than implicit knowledge as, according to Ellis, explicit knowledge is not 'subject to the same developmental constraints' as implicit knowledge.

Sixth, Ellis posits that successful FL learning requires extensive TL input; only with exposure to TL input that is 'comprehensible', i.e. that has been modified or is contextually supported, can learners acquire language. This can be achieved by optimising the use of the TL in the classroom and making it the medium as well as the object of teaching. As we have also seen already, teachers can create opportunities for exposure to the TL outside the classroom, in particular in countries where the TL is spoken.

Seventh, Ellis reminds us that successful language learning also requires opportunities for output as it, among other things, requires learners to engage in syntactic processing and to test out hypotheses as well as to automatise existing knowledge and to develop discourse skills. Task-based learning (TBL) can be seen to be a particularly advisable approach in this context for Ellis; it focuses on activities that require learners to use language with an emphasis on meaning to obtain certain objectives (see Skehan, 2003) and it will be discussed in more detail below.

Ellis' eighth generalisation asserts that the opportunity to interact in the TL is central to developing proficiency in it. Among other things, interaction allows for the negotiation of meaning, which is considered to be a key process in language learning. Teachers, according to Ellis with reference to relevant research findings, therefore, should try to create contexts of language use where pupils have a reason to attend to language; they should provide opportunities for learners to express their own personal meanings in the TL; they should help pupils participate in activities that are just beyond their current level of proficiency, and they should offer a wide range of contexts. These key requirements for acquisition-rich classroom interaction are said to be more likely to occur in less rigid academic task and social participation structures, i.e. by less tightly sequenced subject matter and by less prescriptive allocation of roles and responsibilities of interactants. Again, Ellis views this as evidence in support of the use of tasks, as opposed to exercises, but recognises that a looser approach to interaction in the classroom is not easily achieved as teachers have to ensure classroom discourse is orderly. Because of classroom management considerations, Ellis argues, the so-called IRF (initiation-respond-feedback/follow-up; see also below) approach to controlling discourse topics is so widely used where the teacher initiates, the pupils respond and the teacher provides feedback. This highly structured approach, however, does not appear to provide ideal conditions for interaction in the TL, which is why small group work, in which pupils interact among themselves, is so important. Once again, in order to be effective, small group work needs to be characterised by certain features and the avoidance of excessive use of the mother tongue in mainly monolingual groups is an important one. (For a detailed and very useful discussion of tasked-based learning, see Ellis, 2003.)

Generalisation nine suggests that teachers need to take account of individual differences in learners, in particular their aptitude and motivation. Again, Ellis acknowledges the practical difficulties of identifying individual differences of all learners in large classes and he therefore suggests the adoption of a flexible approach to teaching which involves a variety of learning activities. He also points out the need to make pupils more aware of their own approaches to learning as well as to develop an awareness of alternative approaches. In particular, it is suggested that a balance is struck between analytical as well as experiential approaches. We will discuss the importance of learner and learning strategies and motivation from a research perspective later in this chapter.

Finally, Ellis reminds us that it is important to focus on free as well as controlled language production in assessing learners' TL proficiency.

Chapelle (1998) sets out a model of SLA which is based on the notion that TL input is the key to successful language learning and attempts to describe, with reference to cognitive processes, what makes input comprehensible and how it is processed; the model delineates the following process from input to output: apperception (the noticing of salient features of input), comprehension (the understanding of semantic and syntactic features of input), intake (comprehended language) and integration (the development of learners' linguistic system). On the basis of this model, which notably excludes the social dimension of language learners, Chapelle formulates seven hypotheses about ideal conditions for language learning (with particular reference to computer-assisted contexts).

First of all she notes that teachers need to make the linguistic characteristics of TL input noticeable. Then she posits that learners need to receive support in comprehending semantic and syntactic aspects of linguistic input. She stresses the need for learners to have opportunities to produce TL output and to notice errors in their own output. She also suggests that learners need to correct their linguistic output. Furthermore, she believes that learners need to engage in TL interaction whose structure can be modified for negotiation of meaning. And, finally, she thinks that learners should engage in L2 tasks designed to maximise opportunities for good interaction.

In exploring the notion of 'good interaction' she draws on research which, among other things, sets out a number of task characteristics around the roles and relationships of participants in relation to each other and the information to be exchanged as well as requirements in terms of information exchange.

HOW TO MOTIVATE LANGUAGE LEARNERS

Dörnyei, in a number of publications, notably 1998 (with K. Csizér) and 2001, takes the view that motivation is one of the most important factors in determining the rate and success of FL attainment:

> Without sufficient motivation, even individuals with the most remarkable abilities cannot accomplish long-term goals, and neither are appropriate curricula and good teaching enough to ensure student achievement. . . . high motivation can make up for considerable deficiencies both in one's language aptitude and learning conditions.
>
> (Dörnyei and Csizér, 1998: 203–204)

Yet, as Macaro rightly points out (2003a: 89), motivation does not have obvious direct causes and it is even difficult to discern what the concept encompasses. He identifies the following 'determinants' for motivation, i.e. whether someone will be motivated to learn a FL (p. 91):

■ the usefulness of speaking another language;
■ the influence of significant others such as parents or friends;
■ the difficulty of the subject;
■ its status compared to other subject on the curriculum;
■ world events;
■ its 'genderedness';
■ one's social and cultural background;
■ contact with the target culture.

Dörnyei developed a framework that categorises motivational components into three main dimensions: language level (ethnolinguistic, cultural-affective and intellectual components and pragmatic values and attitudes), learner level (personality traits) and learning situation (course-, teacher and group-specific components). On the basis of empirical work with Csizér he (Dörnyei and Csizér, 1998: 215) formulates the following 'ten commandments' for motivating language learners (but is keen to stress that degree of complexity involved in trying to conceptualise motivation):

1 Set a personal example with your own behaviour.
2 Create a pleasant, relaxed atmosphere in the classroom.
3 Present tasks properly.
4 Develop a good relationship with the learners.
5 Increase the learners' linguistic self-confidence.
6 Make the language classes interesting.
7 Promote learner autonomy.
8 Personalise the learning process.

9   Increase the learners' goal-orientedness.
10   Familiarise learners with the TL culture.

By discussing an identity-, rather than achievement-orientated dimension of motivation, Ushioda (2011) provides an interesting additional dimension by emphasising how L2 motivation is linked with identity, reflecting the learner's self and the social world. She refers to van Lier (2007) and his view that learning a new language necessitates the construction of new ways of linking the self to new worlds and words by 'forging new identities and new ways of expressing our identities' (Ushioda, 2011: 202). Motivation in language learning, from this point of view, is linked to the envisioning of 'possible future selves' and their relationship with 'current selves'. Communication in the FL becomes direct engagement with 'possible future selves'. From a pedagogical perspective this suggests the desirability of the use of the TL for self-expression and self-development (p. 204). And, in this context, Ushioda points to the relevance of the work of Richards (2006) which distinguishes three aspects of identity: situated (conferred by context), discourse (interactional roles) and transportable (latent or implicit).

The issue of motivation, or rather lack of it, to learn FLs has dogged FL education for some time. One solution to lack of motivation suggested by the research literature is an emphasis on learning strategies and it is to these that we turn next.

LEARNING STRATEGIES

In his review of learning strategies and use, Macaro (2006: 320–321) reports, among others, the following claims based on evidence-informed scholarship:

1   Strategy use appears to correlate with various aspects of language learning success although there is a lack of consensus about whether the range, frequency and/or the nature of strategy use/strategies is the determinant factor.
2   There are group differences and individual differences in strategy use.
3   Strategy instruction/training appears to be effective in promoting successful learning if it is carried out over lengthy periods of time and if it includes a focus on metacognition, i.e. learning about learning.

Macaro also points out a number of problems in relation to learning strategies and use (2006: 325), not least the fact that there is no consensus about what learner strategies are, whether they consist of knowledge, intention, action or all three. He then goes on to describe and define learner strategies in terms of a goal, situation and mental action, and asserts that strategies are the raw material of conscious cognitive processing and need to be distinguished from subconscious activity and processes.

Chamot (2005), in her research review, defines learning strategies as 'procedures that facilitate a learning task' (p. 112). In her view, strategies are often conscious but, through repeated use, can become automatised to some extent. She posits that learning strategies are important for two main reasons:

1   because they allow us to gain insights into the (meta)cognitive, social and affective processes involved in language learning;

2 learning strategy instruction can help pupils become better language learners.

Learning strategies are sensitive to the learning context as well as learner characteristics and their effectiveness depends as much on the frequency of use as it depends how they are used (p. 115). Good language learners can be said to be better at matching strategies to task requirements, something less successful learners appear to lack (p. 116). Chamot (p. 115) reports various learning strategy research studies which identify the good language learner as someone who

- ■   is mentally active;
- ■   monitors language comprehension and production;
- ■   practises communicating in the language;
- ■   makes use of prior linguistic and general knowledge;
- ■   uses various memorisation techniques;
- ■   asks questions for clarification.

On the basis of her overview of research studies in the field of learning strategies, Chamot reports that the development of pupils' metacognition, i.e. 'their ability to understand and regulate their own thinking and learning' (p. 124), is an aspect that language teachers should consider very carefully. Metacognition, she also notes, can be considered to encompass both declarative as well as procedural knowledge, i.e. self-knowledge, world knowledge, task knowledge and strategy knowledge, as well as knowledge how to plan for, monitor and evaluate learning. In terms of strategy training she proposes a recursive metacognitive model for learning in which teachers select learning strategies in the areas of planning, monitoring, problem-solving and evaluating on the basis of perceived need rather than covering them in a sequential manner (p. 125).

A recent study focusing on psychological as well as sociocultural perspectives by Grenfell and Harris (2013) suggests that strategy instruction seems to have a significant role in determining the progress of 12–13-year-old FLs learners and suggests that learning how to learn languages may well be an effective pedagogical approach in encouraging learners to stick with FLs.

THE IMPORTANCE OF PRONUNCIATION

Despite the importance afforded to the teaching of pronunciation in some research, this aspect of FL teaching remains rather neglected. Derwing and Munro (2005) remind their readers that foreign accents are a normal result of second/ foreign language learning characteristic of most people starting to learn a second/ foreign language after early childhood. Pronunciation research, they argue, can help teachers and learners to set realistic goals of which improved intelligibility should be the most important. In order to be able to set pedagogical priorities, they argue, an accurate understanding of the phonological system of the TL is necessary. Derwing and Munro note that while a foreign accent does signal the potential need of modified input, it may also lead to negative social evaluation. Listener reactions, they also note, can be understood at the following levels:

(a)   the extent to which the speaker's intended utterance is actually understood by a listener (intelligibility);

(b)   the listener's perception of the degree of difficulty encountered when trying to understand an utterance (comprehensibility);

(c)   how much an L2 accent differs from the variety . . . commonly spoken in the community (accentedness).

(p. 385)

In terms of choice of pedagogical interventions, they argue that noticing is of central concern, as is the relationship between perception and production, namely that production difficulties result from perception and that perceptual training can lead to improvement.

Jenkins (2004) notes that pronunciation teaching typically covers consonant and vowel sounds in isolation (segmental features) and in connected speech, word stress patterns, rhythm and intonation (suprasegmental features). She also reminds her readers of the importance of pronunciation in speakers' success or failure in communication in terms of conveying meaning in specific contexts, its links with a speaker's sense of identity, its contribution of signalling group membership, etc. Jenkins reports the moving away from an emphasis on native-like goals towards a stronger listener perspective in terms of intelligibility and comprehension of non-native speech. Setter and Jenkins (2005: 2) note that when a pronunciation feature gets in the way of the intelligibility of a word, non-native speakers (NNSs) are particularly affected, as they tend to focus on the acoustic signal rather than use contextual cues to resolve ambiguity. They suggest that teachers should consider replacing the notion of correctness with one of appropriateness. Jenkins (2004) also notes the concept of 'accent reduction', which regards learners as subjects for speech pathology by trying to get them to lose all traces of their mother tongue accent, and suggests that the concept of 'accent addition' be promoted. Jenkins (2000: 209–210) identifies the following five stages of pronunciation learning (for English as an International Language):

1   addition of core items to the learner's productive and receptive repertoire;

2   addition of a range of L2 TL accents to the learner's receptive repertoire;

3   addition of accommodation skills;

4   addition of non-core items to the learner's receptive repertoire;

5   addition of a range of L1 TL accents to the learner's receptive repertoire.

She estimates that learners, who wish to acquire an accent that enables them both to preserve their mother tongue identity in their pronunciation of the TL and use intelligible pronunciation to NNSs, will restrict themselves to stages 1–3. If they also want to be able to understand the pronunciation of various native speaker (NS) accents, they are likely to go for all five stages. An important implication for FL teaching is the need to increase the availability of NNS renditions in listening activities.

It seems also relevant to point out the potential of digital technologies in terms of the identification and production of phonemes; of particular relevance in this context is voice recognition for independent pronunciation practice, i.e. learners listening to and repeating words and sequences, recording and listening to themselves and comparing themselves to the input provided, etc., although there remain some issues around the ability of the software to deal effectively with NNS input (see e.g. Pachler, 2002).

Jenkins (2004) stresses the importance of pronunciation in terms of learners' identities and notes the fact that accent tends to lead to linguistic insecurity. Research suggests that pronunciation relates significantly to social identity and the construction of self and other, particularly in international rather than national contexts of language use.

Setter and Jenkins (2005) report that while contrastive analysis was once thought to provide conclusive insights into what was difficult in TL compared with mother tongue pronunciation, research has shown that the syllable is a 'unit of immense importance' and the context of sounds in syllable need to be borne in mind. In line with the development of the notion of a constantly developing interlanguage, researchers promote the idea of an interlanguage phonology according to which interference from the mother tongue is more prevalent in the initial stages of phonological acquisition to be replaced in importance over time by developmental factors similar to L1 phonological acquisition processes.

In terms of implications for pronunciation teaching, Setter and Jenkins (2005) conclude that, while pronunciation practice should be incorporated as early as possible, pronunciation should not be treated in isolation but instead as part of communication and discourse, i.e. on meaning making in communicative situations.

Macaro (2003b: 136) re-enforces the importance of phonology as being important and as being a desirable teaching focus particularly in relation to helping learners understand the relationships between the sounds of the TL and the written form. He advises teachers to encourage beginners to sound out phonemes and phonological units as a precursor to reading comprehension as it lessens the cognitive burden during reading (see the section on reading below). He also notes that by not focusing on pronunciation, language teachers not only deprive learners of sounding authentic but also of the ability to access reading texts by sounding out the phonemes of unknown words (p. 209).

Foote *et al.* (2013) note that the question of how pronunciation should be taught in L2 classrooms has received little research attention but that there was some evidence of certain types of perception training leading to improvements in pronunciation accuracy. They note that some studies have found that training in which learners are exposed to multiple speakers leads to perceptual learning but these have tended to be carried out in controlled laboratory rather than classroom settings. Others indicate that repetition can lead to improved pronunciation accuracy. The best researched area, according to Foote *et al.*, is that of corrective feedback where in particular recasts, i.e. the repetition of learner utterances without the errors made by them, tended to lead to pronunciation repair. This, in combination with form-focused tasks could be seen to have a positive effect. In their own research they found a lack of pre-planned pronunciation episodes in lessons as well as a complete absence of suprasegmental instruction, i.e. a focus on vocal effects extending over more than one sound segment (pitch/intonation, stress, tone). This has clear implications for planning.

LEARNING AND TEACHING VOCABULARY

Knowledge of words and their meaning(s) is important, as words are central components of language production and use. For Carter (1987: 3) some of the key questions pertain to what the FL learner's mental lexicon looks like and how it differs from that of a monolingual native speaker. Is it best to view both lexica as an undifferentiated whole? What makes certain FL words more difficult than others and how does this relate to the L1? Carter asserts that there are phonological, semantic and associational links between both mental lexica. He reports research that suggests that the more words are perceived as infrequent, irregular, semantically or structurally opaque, etc., i.e. psycholinguistically marked, the less likely is their transfer from one language to another. Other issues arising for him include the relationship of learnability and teachability of core words and decisions about the relative importance of semantic texture of polysemous words.

Groot points out that learning a word is an 'incremental process that gradually develops with repeated exposure' and he distinguishes three stages of word acquisition (2000: 64):

1   Notice of the various properties of the new word: morphological and phonological, syntactic, semantic, stylistic, collocational, and so forth.
2   Storage in the internal lexicon in networks of relationships that correspond to the properties described in (1).
3   Consolidation of the storage described in (2) by means of further exposure to the word in a variety of contexts that illustrate its various properties. This results in a firmer embedding in the memory needed for long-term retention.

In order to be able to use vocabulary effectively in receptive and productive use, Groot argues (p. 65), these three stages need to be implemented adequately. Also, he posits what he calls a 'stringent relationship' (p. 65) between retention of vocabulary and the extent to which the various properties of words have been processed, i.e. the better the knowledge of the various properties of a new word the better it will be remembered. From that he concludes that it is preferable to expose learners to new words in context rather than in isolation as only the context will enable the learner to fully understand the properties of a word. He concludes that it is better to ask learners to infer the meaning of new words from context rather than giving them the meaning, as deducing meaning requires greater cognitive effort. He does note, though, (p. 64) that it is essential to have a thorough understanding of the context in order to be able to deduce the meaning of an unknown word.

One distinction frequently made in research on vocabulary learning is that between 'incidental' and 'intentional' learning and the consensus appears to be that while 'incidental' vocabulary learning as a by-product of learning activities or of extensive reading certainly takes place, the systematic learning of vocabulary is also required, particularly in FL learning contexts where there is limited exposure to the TL not least as extensive reading is not a very prominent activity in typical FL classrooms in the UK.

Bruton *et al.* (2011) take issue with the term 'incidental L2 vocabulary learning' and, instead, propose the notion of 'induced vocabulary salience', which they define as follows (p. 765);

> Induced vocabulary salience is where either specific vocabulary items in the linguistic discourse input, or the expected linguistic discourse output, are intentionally made more salient or prominent for the language learner by other parties, especially teachers and/or materials.

One of their key arguments is that just because vocabulary learning may be a by-product of some other activity – one of the recurring definitions of 'incidental' in the literature – does not mean that there needn't be a conscious intention to learn vocabulary.

Read (2004) points out that learners are normally conscious about the fact that lack of vocabulary knowledge can and does hamper effective communication in the TL. This is because 'lexical items carry the basic information load of the meaning (learners) wish to comprehend and express' (p. 146). He also argues that FL teachers are often unsure about how best to teach vocabulary. And he suggests that the tendency within communicative approaches to FL teaching to assume that vocabulary learning will take care of itself provided there is sufficient access to comprehensible input is not supported by research.

According to Hulstijn (2001: 275), 'it is the quality and frequency of the information processing activities (i.e. elaboration on aspects of a word's form and meaning, plus rehearsal) that determine retention of new information'. He suggests that both 'incidental' and 'intentional' learning should be promoted. Considering the implications of Hulstijn's work, Read identifies two important implications for teaching: 1) the need to return to approaches such as regular rehearsal of words, rote learning, automatic word recognition, and 2) the grading of learning tasks according to their potential for vocabulary learning; here Read (2004: 148) identifies the following three factors: 'the learners' *need* to achieve, a requirement that they *search* for information on the meaning or form of the word, and *evaluation* of how the information obtained applied to the particular use of the word in question'.

Research on word frequency suggests that there is value in focusing on the relatively small proportion of words that are highly used, bearing in mind there are differences across writing and speaking. Read notes that studies suggest that in English around 2,000 word families (rather than individual words) account for at least 80 per cent of running words in writing and for 95–99 per cent in speech. Other studies suggest 3,000 word families are needed for being able to deal effectively with everyday conversation. Some studies suggest that 80 per cent was the minimum threshold but that 98 per cent was required to be able to read independently. 'Thus, . . ., it appears that the vocabulary learning goals for minimum levels of both listening and reading comprehension need to be set somewhat higher than the 95 per cent coverage that has been widely recommended until now' (Read, 2004: 150). Macaro (2003b: 65) reports Nation's work (2001), which suggests that reading for pleasure in the TL requires understanding of 98 per cent of tokens in the text which, he rightly points out, has serious pedagogical implications in terms of the selection of texts. Groot (2000) also offers a very useful discussion of issues concerning word frequency. In his discussion, Read draws attention to what happens when learners engage with specific purpose vocabulary such as in academic writing where an academic word list combined with 'general purpose' vocabulary can make a significant difference in the percentage of the running words (up to 95 per cent in written texts), which suggests that there is value in explicit coverage of specialist terminology. Another valuable source on the size of word families required is Schmitt, 2008. Macaro also points out that to some extent so-called receptive skills, i.e. listening and reading, will require a higher amount of vocabulary than the productive skills of speaking and writing, and that an over-emphasis on oral interaction in FL teaching may result in lower vocabulary gain as spoken texts feature a higher percentage of high-frequency words.

Pedagogical approaches suggested are for learners to compile learner or discipline-specific dictionaries, glossing, and the selection and recording of their own vocabulary based on individual needs or interest (although learners tend not always to choose suitable words); some electronic tools allow for the easy compilation and distribution of such custom-made dictionaries (see e.g. Pachler, 2001). Based on his review of available research, Read concludes that little research is available reporting on methods of presenting and practising vocabulary in the classroom.

One important question that Macaro raises in his discussion of vocabulary teaching and learning is that of what it actually means to 'know' lexical items. He reports 'vocabulary knowledge criteria' from Paribakht and Wesche (1993) who, among others, identify the following criteria:

1   The word is not familiar at all.
2   The word is familiar but the meaning is not known.
3   Learner gives correct synonym or translation.
4   Learner uses word with semantic appropriateness in a sentence.
5   Learner uses word with semantic appropriateness and grammatical accuracy in a sentence.

McCarten (2007: 18), drawing inter alia on Nation (2001), addresses the issue by asking what things learners need to know about a word before they can say they have 'learned' it:

- The meaning(s) of the word.
- Its spoken and written forms.
- What 'word parts' it has (e.g. any prefix, suffix and 'root' form).
- Its grammatical behaviour (e.g. its word class, typical grammatical patterns it occurs in).
- Its collocations.
- Its register.
- What associations it has (e.g. words that are similar or opposite in meaning).
- What connotations it has.
- Its frequency.

While different criteria can be found in the literature, these lists go to show that 'knowing' a word is far from straightforward and that it is important to be aware of different meanings individual words might have in different contexts. Schmitt (2008: 333) refers to the importance of depth of vocabulary knowledge, which he considers to be as great as vocabulary size. Macaro (2003b) suggests that FL teachers should look not only for in-depth knowledge of vocabulary, but also in particular increasingly sophisticated uses of function words, as well as topic coverage when considering notions of progression.

Barcroft (2004: 203) identifies the following five principles of effective L2 vocabulary instruction:

■ **Table 3.1** More and less effective vocabulary learning tasks

The more effective task	The less effective task
Meaning selected from several options	Meaning explained by synonym
Meaning looked up in a dictionary	Reading with/without guessing
Meaning looked up in a dictionary	Meaning provided in a marginal gloss
Meaning negotiated	Meaning not negotiated
Negotiated input	Pre-modified input
Used in original sentences	Used in non-original sentences
Used in a composition (L1-L2 look up)	Encountered in a reading task (L2-L1 look up)
Interactionally modified output	Interactionally modified input
Reading and a series of vocabulary exercises	Reading only (and inferring meaning)
Reading, words looked up in a dictionary	Reading only, words not looked up

Source: Schmitt, 2008: 340.

1 present new words frequently and repeatedly in the input;
2 use meaning-bearing comprehensible input when presenting new words;
3 limit forced output during the early stages of learning new words;
4 limit forced semantic elaboration during the initial stages of learning new words;
5 progress from less demanding to more demanding vocabulary-related activities.

According to Barcroft, these principles stress the importance of lexical input processing as a framework for understanding L2 vocabulary acquisition.

Schmitt (2008) raises a number of issues of pedagogical relevance in vocabulary acquisition. The first is the need to establish an initial from-meaning link. He explains that the developmental sharpening attendant to becoming attuned to features and regularities of L1 input can get in the way in the L2, particularly if phonemes and graphemes and their combinations are different. Schmitt goes on to suggest a role for the L1 in second language learning, specifically in establishing an initial form meaning link and particularly for less proficient learners. Also, he makes the case for learner engagement: 'the more attention given to an item, and the more manipulation involved with the item, the greater the chances it will be remembered' (p. 339). He includes the table above about more and less effective vocabulary learning tasks (p. 340).

Schmitt concludes his piece by quoting Hunt and Beglar's (1998) seven principles of vocabulary learning as a good starting point:

Principle 1 Provide opportunities for the incidental learning of vocabulary.
Principle 2 Diagnose which of the 3,000 most common words learners need to study.
Principle 3 Provide opportunities for the intentional learning of vocabulary.

Principle 4   Provide opportunities for elaborating word knowledge.
Principle 5   Provide opportunities for developing fluency with known vocabulary.
Principle 6   Experiment with guessing from context.
Principle 7   Examine different types of dictionaries and teach students how to use them.

LEARNING AND TEACHING LISTENING

Vandergrift (2004: 3) notes that listening is no longer considered to be a passive skill but an active one. According to him, approaches to listening instruction have evolved from 'listen to repeat' via 'question and answer' to 'real life listening in real time'. He also posits that listening instruction is expanding from 'listening to learn', with a focus on the product, to 'learning to listen', with a focus on the process.

In a systematic literature review, Macaro *et al.* (2005) stress the role of listening not just in formal education in general, but also in FL learning in particular. They point out that listening plays an important part in what they call 'interaction-based acquisition' (p. 6), by which they mean that, among other things, it is by listening to the TL that new vocabulary and the rule system are acquired. In their review, the authors report on research that suggests that both top-down and bottom-up processing are important, even if it is still unclear what the best balance between the two might be:

> Top-down processing is when *schemata* (or prior knowledge of a topic), as well as other strategies (logic, other knowledge of the world, such as speaking conventions), are applied to the incoming speech stream in order to offset the tendency to listen to every word, a virtual impossibility with fast flowing text. Bottom-up processing involves cognitive strategies for *perceiving* (for example, developing phonemic awareness) and *parsing* (segmenting the speech stream) of the linguistic input. This bottom-up processing is essential not only to identify key vocabulary and syntactical elements in the speech stream but also in order to confirm the initial conclusions made by the application of prior knowledge.
>
> (Macaro *et al.*, 2005: 7)

In their section on findings (pp. 46–48), Macaro *et al.* explore the complex relationship between prior knowledge and comprehension in listening and conclude that there is a difference between prior knowledge facilitating listening comprehension and improving it.

Vandergrift (2004: 4–6) notes that beginners have limited prior language knowledge, can only process a limited amount automatically and have a limited working memory; instead, they need to focus on detail and use compensatory strategies. He advocates the use of advance organisers provided they do not distract from the main focus of the text.

Based on Lund (1991), Macaro (2003b: 154) argues that there are a number of major differences between reading and listening:

■   the complete text is not available;
■   the text exists in time not in space;

- ■ the listener cannot control the pace of the text;
- ■ listeners tend to try to integrate information from multiple sources simultaneously (parallel distributed processing);
- ■ the sound system of the L2 can pose a significant problem;
- ■ gaps in speech are different to gaps in writing;
- ■ cognates may sound different in continuous speech;
- ■ spoken texts have intonation, stress, regional accents, background noise and other variations of acoustic features.

In listening, more cognitive effort has to be placed on the decoding of a text in terms of noticing and then processing of acoustic information compared with reading where decoding tends to be an issue only where a word-recognition problem exists.

In addition to making allowances for the cognitive difficulties involved in listening, Macaro (2003b: 158–159) points to Lund's suggestion that listening to a spoken text twice allows the learner to create context, generate hypotheses and identify gaps to focus on during the first exposure, whereas during the second listening learners can infer meaning, confirm discarded hypotheses and fill gaps in detail missed the first time round. He also stresses the importance of prosodic features and clues, in particular intonation and stress.

For teaching and learning purposes Macaro also emphasises the distinction between 'listening alone' or 'one-way listening' (2003b: 152), i.e. where the listener has not got the opportunity to interrupt the speaker, and 'listening as interaction' or 'two-way listening' (2003b: 171f.), where negotiation of meaning takes place between the speaker and the listener with a view to coming to a shared understanding of what is said and/or to have a satisfactory conversation. Interruptions, according to Long (1981), can be classified as

- ■ confirmation checks, where the listener is trying to ensure they have understood correctly;
- ■ clarification requests, where the listener is asking for help with understanding what was said;
- ■ comprehension checks, where the speaker tries to assure herself that the listener has understood.

This reinforces the importance of the quality of the input, not the quantity of it; the focus should not be on talking at the learners, but on talking with them (Macaro, 2003b: 253).

Macaro also offers a very useful set of questions in relation to 'mediated listening' (2003b: 176), in particular, in relation to the use of the pause button, with the help of which, he argues (2003b: 177), one-way listening can be turned into two-way listening. These include:

- ■ breaking down a long text into manageable chunks;
- ■ allowing the hearer to ask for repetition;
- ■ allowing the hearer to build hypotheses about what is to come;
- ■ structuring listening texts into component parts, etc.

He also strongly supports the use of video and video captions in the TL (2003b: 180) and endorses Chambers's recommendation (1996) to use predictive pre-listening activities as well as while-listening and post-listening activities, focusing on different aspects of the listening process.

Vandergrift (2004: 9–10) draws a number of conclusions for listening instruction based on the review of some qualitative studies:

1   Limitations of working memory dictate that supports provided to the listener should relate directly to the text and the listening task. . . .

2   Captions, annotations, and computer programs to slow down speech may be useful for developing word recognition skills and learning vocabulary. . . .

3   Visual supports that are natural to the listening situation can provide important contextual information to help the listener. . . .

4   . . . context is important to listening. . . .

5   A strategies-based approach to listening instruction with beginner-level listeners builds confidence, raises awareness of the process of listening, and helps listeners to use effective combinations of metacognitive and cognitive strategies to understand texts in real time.

He also notes (2004: 10) that listening is too often associated with testing. Being asked to focus on the right answer creates high levels of anxiety, which negatively affects the learner's attention while it does not tell the teacher anything about the process of how learners came to formulate their answers, which is what they need to know in order to be able to help learners discover effective listening strategies.

In 2007, Vandergrift carried out a review of literature of listening comprehension research in recent years, which reiterates a number of the findings of his 2004 piece. He provides an overview of listening processes and explains how listeners prefer top-down processes when they use context and prior knowledge to build a conceptual framework for comprehension; they use bottom-up processes when they construct meaning. The type of processes used depends on the purpose for listening, learner characteristics, e.g. proficiency and context. He also notes that strategic use of compensatory mechanisms such as contextual, visual or paralinguistic information, world knowledge, cultural information and common sense are very important in determining success in listening. He cites his own work, which shows that skilled listeners reported greater use of metacognitive strategies such as comprehension monitoring and questioning elaboration than less skilled listeners who reported greater use of online translation. Indeed, he argues that skilled L2 listening is a question of skilful orchestration of metacognitive and cognitive strategies.

He reports findings by Anderson (1995), which provide useful insights into reported difficulties with listening:

During the perceptual processing phase (segmenting phonemes from the speech stream) listeners reported the following difficulties: 1) not recognizing words, 2) neglecting what follows, 3) not chunking the stream of speech, 4) missing the beginning of the text, and 5) concentration problems. During the parsing phase (segmenting words and constructing a meaningful representation of the meaning), listening difficulties included: 1) quickly forgetting what is heard, 2) an inability to form a mental representation from words heard, and 3) not understanding subsequent parts because of what was missed earlier. During the utilization phase (using information sources in long-term memory to interpret the intended meaning), listening difficulties reported were: 1) understanding the words but not the message, and 2) confusion because of seeming incongruencies in the message.

(Vandergrift, 2007: 193–194)

This list of difficulties provides a useful stimulus for targeted support by the teacher. In addition to cognitive processes, Vandergrift (2007) also stresses the importance of affective factors, i.e. the social and psychological dimensions, in order to be able to make the correct inferences and understand implied meaning.

In relation to the parsing of linguistic input to foster word recognition, Vandergrift (2007) references Hulstijn's (2003) six-step procedure:

1   listen to the recording;
2   ask yourself whether you have understood what you heard;
3   replay the recording as often as necessary;
4   consult the written text to read what you have just heard;
5   recognize what you should have understood;
6   replay the recording as often as necessary to understand all of the oral text without written support.

It is clearly important that listening practice is not constantly linked to assessment to enable greater awareness of relevant processes to develop.

LEARNING AND TEACHING SPEAKING

In their review of recent research in the teaching of speaking, McCarthy and O'Keeffe (2004: 27) note the shift away from native speakers as the dominant model for speaking. They also point out (p. 29) that the value of scripted dialogues for enhancing conversation skills has been challenged as they don't really reflect the unpredictability, features and structures, such as discourse markers, incomplete utterances, vague language, ellipses and hedges, of real-life conversations and, therefore, offer learners only limited opportunities. With reference to Burns (2001), they note that two-part question-and-answer sequences, which often feature in coursebooks, are not very common in real conversations where replies to questions are usually followed up with a routine phrase. They also refer to Slade (1997), who found that social conversations are dominated by narrative genres such as narratives, anecdotes, exempla and recounts, all of which are rarely presented in language learning material and teaching contexts.

McCarthy and O'Keeffe (2004: 30) also examine the value of the so-called 'IRF routine', which is the dominant interactional pattern in language classes, and point out that according to Kasper (2001) it fails to provide opportunities for addressing the complex demands of everyday conversations – for example, as the learners often remain in a passive and the teacher in an active role.

Rather than relying on exchange structure analysis (IRF), which appears to be more beneficial for developing listening skills, McCarthy and O'Keeffe's review suggests the use of pre-task planning, (critical) discourse analysis ((C)DA) and conversation analysis (CA) as a productive way forward (2004: 30–32). They quote Burns (2001) who suggests that language tasks can be developed by a focus on turn-taking, i.e. a discussion of speaker roles, rights to turns, etc., and turn types, i.e. an exploration of more or less preferred responses, repair strategies and reformulation. Such focus on the 'microstructures' of conversations, according to Burns (2001)

> can offer teachers the opportunity to highlight for students the appropriate-ness of utterances, how speakers negotiate certain situations . . . as well as providing a framework for the performance of speech acts.
>
> (McCarthy and O'Keeffe 2004: 33)

Burns *et al.* (1997; in McCarthy and O'Keeffe 2004: 33) suggest the following analytical framework for teachers:

1 transcribe the recording;
2 give the background information to the text;
3 analyse the text using an analytical approach;
4 identify the significant teaching points that arise from the analysis.

Based on a review of literature on DA and CA, Dörnyei and Thurrell (1994) suggest the following headings for the selection of aspects of spoken language for teaching purposes (in McCarthy and O'Keeffe, 2004: 34):

■ conversational rules and structure (e.g. opening, topic shifting and closing);
■ conversational strategies (e.g. paraphrase, asking for repetition and clarification);
■ functions and meaning in conversation (e.g. illocutionary functions);
■ social and cultural contexts (e.g. social norms and appropriateness).

Macaro (2003b) stresses the dual function of speaking, i.e. to communicate meaning but also as a tool to think and organise (p. 191).

Fluent speech is predicated on the speaker's ability to proceduralise declarative knowledge, i.e. to have overcome the need to explicitly and consciously focus on form. Macaro's reading of the available research evidence (pp. 186f.) suggests that input that is modified through interaction leads to improved oral production with there being more emphasis on the acquisition of lexis than grammatical patterns. Interaction and the production of output also give the learner an opportunity to 'notice' linguistic features, i.e. attend to them cognitively and establish connections with the long-term memory. However, there is a need for a balance between message and medium-focused interaction and, for pragmatic reasons such as large class sizes, the quality of teacher–whole-class interaction is very important to compensate for lack of one-to-one interactions between the teacher and individual learners as well as of learner talk. Alternatively, Macaro argues, an emphasis can be placed on learner–learner interaction with research showing that lower-proficiency learners can gain a lot from working with higher-proficiency learners without the latter being disadvantaged (p. 192). In relation to learner–learner activities, such as pair and group work, he particularly draws attention to the need for clear structuring of the language as well as the task: the language to be used by pupils needs to be clearly defined, as should the pathways leading to completion of the task (p. 193). Related questions are whether, when and how the teacher should intervene. Lynch (1997) argues that rather than intervening by correcting when monitoring, or at least to go for quality rather than quantity of corrections, or changing the focus or direction of the interaction, the teacher should intervene as late as possible to allow learners to attempt their own communication repair and focus on initiating the process of negotiation of meaning and supporting the confirmation of clarification requests.

In her analysis of the quality of teacher-fronted interaction, Antón (1999) distinguishes co-constructed or dialogic approach and a transmission-based approach to knowledge with the former comprising the following four features:

- ■ eliciting problems and solutions when focusing on grammatical patterns; consciousness-raising of grammatical forms;
- ■ feedback (to error) through awareness raising;
- ■ turn allocation according to individual bidding;
- ■ encouragement of learners to identify and articulate their learning difficulties and to attempt new learning styles and strategies.

Another study demonstrating the importance of the quality, rather than the quantity of teacher interaction is Walsh (2002), who identifies a number of facilitative and obstructive features for learning potential. Positive teacher moves, he suggests, include direct error correction through explicit recasts, a personal dimension in content feedback, confirmation checks and the encouragement of clarification requests, extended waiting times, scaffolding and avoidance of teacher dominance in turn-taking. Obstructive features, on the other hand, include teachers completing turn for or interrupting pupils as well as the use of IRF exchanges. The three-part IRF exchange (Sinclair and Coulthard, 1975) is reported to account for as much as 70 per cent of all classroom talk (Wells, 1993), and is considered to be constitutive of classroom discourse. Macaro (2003b) also points to the pejorative effect of 'teacher echo' (p. 199).

Thomas's recent review article (2012) takes a classroom discourse perspective and starts out with a review of language learning from a sociocultural perspective, arguing that discursive practices in the classroom context are intimately tied to language learning; in other words, how learners interact with each other and their teacher, i.e. classroom talk matters, in particular as it not only provides much of the input received but also represents much of the mediation provided by others (other-regulation) with the latter being 'largely responsible for development, or the ability to accomplish actions on one's own, and recognize and generalize these actions, linguistic or otherwise, across analogous contexts' (p. 10).

Thomas (2012) goes on to discuss a range of studies exploring the triadic dialogue sequence dominant in FLs classrooms: initiation–response–evaluation (IRE), initiation–response–follow-up/feedback (IRF). Thomas argues that, although similar, there are importance differences between IRE and IRF. In IRE the teacher initiates the interaction with the learner providing a response and the teacher evaluating the response. This frames the teacher as the expert and responsible for guiding the interaction as well as judging the accuracy of the response. Also, it controls and sanctions the amount and type of interaction taking place in the process, often restricting students' spoken output by limiting topic choice, elaboration, managing turn-taking, negotiating directionality, etc. In short, it 'maximizes teacher talk and minimizes student talk' (p. 12). Evaluation, even if intended as an attempt to build a positive classroom climate, tended to limit students' participation. IRF, on the other hand, focuses on non-evaluative feedback/follow-up and can foster a comparatively greater degree of learner participation by adhering better to inherent pragmatic conventions of conversations. Thomas (2012: 18) also reports research that shows that prosodic cues, i.e. aspects of rhythm, stress and intonation, can be very important, particularly at the third stage of the sequence, and could affect how students responded to whole-class discourse.

With reference to Hall (2004), Thomas notes that research shows that speaking practice dominated by 'listing and labeling of objects and concepts' and 'lexical chaining' limits cognitive engagement and linguistic skill. Instead, he (2012: 15) advocates thoughtful and meaningful teacher questions, drawing on the six functions of scaffolding delineated by Wood *et al.* (1976):

1   recruitment (i.e. the expert 'enlists the problem solver's interest in and adherence to the requirements of the task);

2   reduction in degrees of freedom (i.e. the expert makes adjustments to the task to reduce the number of actions needed by the novice to solve the problem);

3   direction maintenance (i.e. the expert keeps the novice on task by motivating the novice to achieve the task objective);

4   marking critical features (i.e. the expert provides cues or 'accentuates certain features of the task that are relevant');

5   frustration control (i.e. the expert encourages the novice whenever the novice makes an error while working on the task);

6   demonstration (i.e, the expert models solutions to the task).

Finally, for our current purpose, Thomas (2012: 18) reports research by Waring (2009), which stresses the importance of student questions posed in the silent gaps between teacher initiated sequences, so-called 'pivot questions', which could result in a more student-led classroom discussion and fostered consideration of more complex issues.

LEARNING AND TEACHING READING

Macaro (2003b: 118–119), rightly in our view, draws attention to the fact that compared with the other 'core' skills of foreign language learning, listening, speaking and writing, reading proficiency and overall text comprehension is comparatively difficult to gauge. He explains the reading process as one whereby the reader engages in phonemic 'recoding', i.e. the sounding out of words, if she does not recognise a word and its meaning directly. At a whole-text level, rather than advocating either a bottom-up (decoding of meaning by the reader encoded by the writer) or a top-down model (the inference of meaning on the basis of activating prior semantic, pragmatic, syntactic and discourse knowledge), he promotes an interactive model in which reading is a process which draws on various knowledge sources allowing for the fact that meaning does not reside in the text alone but is a co-construction of the writer's text and the reader's interpretation. Here there is a constant interaction between the surface structure of the text and the reader's own knowledge of the topic which that text is attempting to communicate. This model involves the reader in elaborating on the meaning of the text, inferring meaning but also at times stopping to pause and ponder over individual words and syntactic patterns and their relationships with other words and phrases in order to confirm hypotheses, strengthen connections and build up layers of interpretation.

(pp. 120–121)

Macaro points to the importance of contextual and prior knowledge as a combination of all clues surrounding the text, including schemata (individual constructs) or scripts (knowledge shared by certain socio-cultural contexts) (2003b: 122) which help in text comprehension and 'fill in the gaps' even if the meaning of individual words is not clear; these include titles, pictures, etc. He also stresses the importance of the need for effective strategies to make contextual and prior knowledge count. This clearly raises interesting questions for FL teachers around whether the emphasis on reading instruction should be on the teaching of lexical and syntactic knowledge, on so-called world knowledge, on strategy training or on a combination of them.

Another important aspect of reading discussed by Macaro (2003b: 143) is the role of mental translations. He refers to a study by Kern (1994) which suggests that a certain critical threshold of language development needs to be crossed before they can be minimised and, thereby, reading rates can be increased. In his study, Kern identifies a number of benefits of mental translation including:

■ support with the consolidation of meaning and clarification of contextual information;
■ provision of an 'affective boost';
■ help in the maintenance of concentration and in not losing track;
■ clarification of the syntactic role of certain lexical items.

These findings suggest that up to a certain level of proficiency there is a role to be played for mental translation.

Grabe (2004: 46) outlines ten instructional implications for L2 reading instruction and curriculum design in his review of research:

1 Ensure word recognition fluency.
2 Emphasize vocabulary learning and create a vocabulary-rich environment.
3 Activate background knowledge in appropriate ways.
4 Ensure effective language knowledge and general comprehension skills.
5 Teach text structures and discourse organisation.
6 Promote the strategic reader rather than teach individual strategies.
7 Build reading fluency rate.
8 Promote extensive reading.
9 Develop intrinsic motivation for reading.
10 Plan a coherent curriculum for student learning.

In relation to text comprehension, Grabe (2004: 51) recommends the following individual comprehension strategies:

- prior knowledge activation;
- mental imagery;
- graphic organizers;
- text structure awareness;
- comprehension monitoring;
- question answering;
- question generating;
- mnemonic support practice;
- summarization.

Grabe (2004: 52) notes the importance of what he calls 'signalling systems', i.e. discourse structures, of texts, e.g. pronominal systems, other antecedent referencing, thematic signalling, transition words and structures, and syntactic foregrounding and backgrounding, which have functional purposes that need to be recognised by readers.

In terms of reading strategies he recommends the promotion of the strategic reader, rather than to teach individual reading strategies and lists the following ten approaches as an effective combination (pp. 53–54):

1 KWL: Know, Want to know, Learned
2 ETR: Experience–Text–Relate
3 QAR: Question–Answer–Response
4 DR-TA: Directed Reading and Thinking Activities
5 Reciprocal Teaching
6 Collaborative Strategic Reading (CSR)
7 Direct Explanation
8 Questioning the Author
9 Transactional Strategies Instruction (TSI)
10 Concept-Oriented Reading Instruction (CORI)

LEARNING AND TEACHING WRITING

In her review article on writing in a foreign language, O'Brien (2004: 2) refers to Kern's (2000: 172) arguments in support of writing:

it develops learners' ability to think explicitly about how to organise and express thoughts, feelings and ideas in ways compatible with imagined readers' expectations; it provides a platform for readers to text hypotheses about the new language; it provides time for learners to process meaning, reducing the anxiety often felt in oral production; it provides opportunities for creativity. . .

With reference to the literature, she reminds her readers that L2 processing is different from L1 processing and that, therefore, a specific pedagogical approach to the teaching of L2 reading and writing are required (2004: 6).

O'Brien (2004: 3) reports on a number of studies that aim to describe the processes of writing and enumerates planning, translating and formulating into language, revising as well as linguistic processes (grammatical, lexical, morphological, graphemic). In terms of process-based pedagogic approaches, awareness of successful writing strategy use and feedback from the teacher or peers are mentioned, as are purpose- and reader-specific tasks, as well as focusing on meaning before accuracy and allowing sufficient time for drafting and redrafting (p. 7). She notes that the perceived benefits from teacher and peer feedback vary: some pupils report that they gained a greater sense of ownership and audience from peers and a better grasp of macro-level organisation from the teacher (p. 10). In terms of teacher feedback, the effectiveness of grammar correction is questioned and teachers are encouraged to give more explicit and positive comments as well as train pupils how to benefit from feedback by some researchers (pp. 11–13).

Way *et al.* (2000) investigated the difference between three writing task types: descriptive, narrative and expository (explanatory/argumentative). Their research shows that the descriptive task proved the easiest, followed by the narrative task. This suggests a certain type of progression in writing tasks.

Macaro (2003b: 229) concludes from his examination of relevant research that

> there appears to be little evidence that the traditional and prevailing approach to FL writing which involves learning to produce 'sentence level, error-free text within a progression of tasks and under conditions of careful guidance' (Heilenman 1991) is successful in achieving holistic competence (i.e. focus both on content and form) with L2 writers. Learners may well find greater satisfaction, freedom of expression and ultimately motivation if they are allowed to experiment with drafting and redrafting of their own language, not necessarily at the end of a topic of work.

He suggests that the focus should be on the process, not the product of writing, on planning, formulating, monitoring and checking (p. 249). The finished product, he argues, gives a false impression of linearity and does not allow for an adequate analysis of the complexity of text production. He concludes that feedback from the teacher needs to focus on the difficulties and successes learners experience as they write and should be problem-orientated. As with other skills, strategy training and metacognition, i.e. awareness of learners about themselves as language learners, would appear essential (see separate section on learning strategies above). Correct models in and of themselves appear to be insufficient. Macaro also comes out in support of the use of bilingual dictionaries for writing, provided they are used effectively.

In their article focusing on an in-depth exploration of the factors differentiating FL writing from ESL writing, Reichelt *et al.* (2012) argue that L1 writing proficiency has a positive impact on FL writing proficiency and that transfer takes place. They also point out the merits of certain types of form-focused instruction, such as the explicit teaching of sentence combining and reformulations. In addition, they promote genre-based approaches. Typologically, they distinguish writing-to-learn and learning-to-write paradigms. The former views writing as a means to an end with writing being viewed as a vehicle for language practice. The latter emphasises content over linguistic accuracy, engages learners in collaborative interaction and focuses on the entire writing process rather than mainly the outcome. The act of writing would often be the culmination of a staged approach involving discussion, vocabulary-building, video viewing, brainstorming, group discussion, summarising, paraphrasing, sentence combining and synthesising.

With reference to the authors' own practice as well as the literature they examined, Reichelt *et al.* (2012: 35–36) identify the following uses for writing, especially in contexts where learners' real-life needs for writing in a FL are not immediately obvious:

1   Using writing to reinforce the orthography, grammar and vocabulary of the TL.
2   Using fun writing assignments to engage and motivate students.
3   Using writing to teach/test content, e.g. content related to the TL culture or literature.
4   Preparing students to survive in the TL environment.
5   Preparing students for studying in the TL environment, where they may need to write in academic TL genres.
6   Preparing students to write in business and other work-related genres, preparation for possible employment in a TL environment.
7   Using writing as a means of connecting with others around the world who speak the TL.

Hanauer (2012) focuses on meaningful literacy instruction and foregrounds personal experience, history and social contextualization in his core principles of FL writing: autobiographical writing, emotional writing, personal insight and authentic public access. In his poetry writing class, he uses the following syllabus outline (p. 113):

1   Introduction to poetry writing – reading others' poetry.
2   Thinking, imagining, reliving and talking about a significant life moment.
3   Investigating and exploring the genre of poetry.
4   Exploring personal experience – listing memories, discussion of unique, personally meaningful experiences; valuing one's personal history.
5   Poetry writing experimentation – checking your poetry in relation to its ability to 'show not tell' and to recreate your experience in another reader.
6   Classroom reading of poetry, peer and instructor interaction and the sharing of poetry with individuals the poet writer considers to be of significance beyond the classroom;
7   Production and sharing of a complete poetry book.

LEARNING AND TEACHING GRAMMAR

One of the ongoing debates in foreign and second language research is around the relative importance of implicit and explicit approaches to the teaching of grammar. Increasingly, it is believed that drawing attention to vocabulary and syntax explicitly – rather than spending long periods of time on message-orientated exchanges at the expense of meaning-based interaction – can enhance implicit classroom-based learning (Macaro, 2003b: 253–254). Focus on form as part of a meaning-based discourse, Macaro suggests (2003b: 254), 'provides the optimum amount of spot-lighting of new target-language models such that development of interlanguage can take place'. Macaro (2003b: 254) also reports a feeling among researchers and commentators that a focus on language awareness in the early stages of FL learning can be beneficial.

Nassaji and Fotos (2004: 126) agree: they argue that recent research has demonstrated that there is a need for formal instruction in order for learners to attain high levels of accuracy and they enumerate four reasons for the renewed interest in grammar (pp. 128–129):

1   According to their reading of relevant research, 'it is necessary for learners to notice target forms in input; otherwise they process input for meaning only and do not attend to specific forms, and consequently fail to process and acquire them'.
2   They point out that learners move through developmental sequences, some of which are fixed, i.e. they cannot be changed by grammar teaching, whereas others can be influenced.
3   There is a significant amount of research that suggests that mainly meaning-focused approaches are inadequate.
4   There is evidence in support of explicit grammar instruction, i.e. presenting structures, describing and exemplifying them, and offering rules for their use, compared with implicit grammar instruction, i.e. communicative exposure to target forms.

Nevertheless, Nassaji and Fotos (2004: 129) are keen to point out that there exists a complex relationship between grammar teaching and learning of target forms, which tends not to be direct. Noticing, they argue (p. 134), may be a necessary condition for acquisition, but it is not the only one.

They also report (p. 129) that some researchers question traditional approaches to grammar teaching where language is viewed as an object of learning and presented in a decontextualised way in support of which there tends not to be research evidence. With reference to Larsen-Freeman (2003), they posit that learners must have 'opportunities to encounter, process, and use instructed forms in their various form-meaning relationships so that the forms can become part of their interlanguage behaviour' (Nassaji and Fotos, 2004: 130).

With regard to possible approaches to grammar teaching, Nassaji and Fotos (2004: 131) argue for a 'focus on FORM', in which the teacher draws learners' attention to grammatical forms in communicative contexts, rather than a 'focus on FORMS', the selection and teaching of discrete structures in isolation. Focus on form, they argue, can be achieved through process or through design, reactively or pre-emptively.

Batstone and Ellis (2009) identify a set of principles that they argue should guide the selection of specific instructional procedures; they are:

1   Given-to-new principle: making new form/function connections involves the exploitation of what the learner already knows about the world as part of their schematic knowledge.

2   Awareness principle: making learners aware of how a particular meaning is encoded by a particular grammatical form. With reference to Schmidt (2001) they distinguish three levels of awareness: a) paying conscious attention to specific grammatical forms that arise in the input; b) understanding, i.e. recognising that the forms they have attended to encode particular grammatical meanings; and c) level of control: the controlled use of grammatical forms through monitoring.

3   Real-operating conditions principle: this views grammar as a communicative tool, whereas the other two tend to view grammar as an object. Learners need opportunities to practise language in the same conditions that apply in real-life situations, i.e. where the primary focus is on message conveyance rather than linguistic accuracy, including negotiation of meaning through corrective feedback in situations of communication breakdown. According to Batstone and Ellis, this can be problematic if it is done through recasts as they may not be perceived by learners as corrective; or by making target features explicit to learners in the course of them performing a communicative task which will require what they call 'time outs'.

Liamkina and Ryshina-Pankova (2012) also set out some key principles on language and grammar from a functional perspective, by which they mean a view of grammar as a rich resource for contextualised, culture- and language-specific meaning making; they are (pp. 272–276):

1   Grammar is a rich resource for meaning-making.
2   Grammar is a system of interrelated choices in relation to experiential, interpersonal and textual meaning.
3   Grammatical forms are in themselves meaningful: they help construe reality in particular ways for the purposes of linguistically based communication.
4   Each language – while usually having several alternative means to express particular meanings – has a preferred set of options that native speakers employ under 'ordinary' circumstances.
5   Grammar is mainly a supraclausal phenomenon.
6   Languages (first and subsequent) are acquired with the help of general cognitive mechanisms that are fully developed in adult learners. This potentially puts adults at a considerable advantage over children learning their L1 in terms of time required for acquiring the bulk of lexicogrammar and linguistic concepts that lexicogrammar realises. Utilising adults' L1 knowledge and literacy skills can help transform the classroom into an unparalleled rich context for adult second language acquisition.
7   Functionally based grammar instruction turns the language teacher into a language researcher and empowers the L2 learner.

Finally, in this section on grammar, we want to reference some of the work that has been carried out in recent decades under the banner of 'language awareness'. Svalberg (2007), in her state-of-the-art article, delineates the scope of language awareness with reference to work by James and Garrett (1991) as covering five domains: affective, social, power, cognitive and performance. They also refer to a definition offered on the Association for Language Awareness website suggesting that language awareness is the 'explicit knowledge about language, and conscious perception and sensitivity in language learning, language teaching and language use' (p. 288). Svalberg (2007: 290–291) also reports research, which suggests that both the quality and the quality of awareness appear to matter, and with reference to Borg (1994) reports five features of language awareness methodology:

1   It involves an ongoing investigation of language as a dynamic phenomenon rather than awareness of a fixed body of established facts.
2   It involves learners in talking analytically about language, often to each other.
3   It considers essential the involvement of learners in exploration and discovery.
4   It aims to develop not only the learners' knowledge about and understanding of language but also their learning skills, thus promoting learner independence.
5   The aim is to involve learners on both a cognitive and an affective level.

These she later reformulates as 'description (not prescription), exploration, "languaging", engagement and reflection' (p. 292).

LEARNING AND TEACHING CULTURE

Paige *et al.* (2000: 4), in their comprehensive review of the literature on culture learning, note that culture can sometimes be viewed as relatively static, comprising classifiable and observable, and thereby 'teachable and learnable facts', focusing on behaviour, rather than underlying value orientations. In such a view of culture, the variability within given target culture communities, the role of the individual in the process of culture creation, and/or the interaction of language and culture in meaning making are not always recognised (Paige *et al.*, 2000: 4). Other, more recent models view culture as more dynamic and changing, comprising variable behaviours and the construction of meaning through interaction and communication. Paige *et al.* (2000: 4) propose the following definition of culture learning:

> Culture learning is the process of acquiring the culture-specific and culture-general knowledge, skills, and attitudes required for effective communication and interaction with individuals from other cultures. It is a dynamic, developmental, and ongoing process which engages the learner cognitively, behaviorally, and affectively.

Implicit in this definition is a pedagogical approach that foregrounds notions such as 'interactional competence' inter alia comprising

1   learning about the self as a cultural being;
2   learning about culture and its impact on human communication, behaviour and identity;
3   culture-general learning, i.e. learning about universal, cross-cultural phenomena such as cultural adjustment;

4   culture-specific learning, i.e. learning about a particular culture, including its language;

5   learning how to learn, i.e. becoming an effective language and culture learner,

at the expense of the memorisation of cultural facts and sociolinguistic conventions (pp. 4–5). Characteristic of such an approach is also the foregrounding of culture-general domains of learning as opposed to culture-specific ones. Paige *et al.* (2000: 5–6) list the following in this context:

> the concept of culture, the nature of cultural adjustment and learning, the impact of culture on communication and interaction between individuals or groups, the stress associated with intense culture and language immersions (culture and language fatigue), coping strategies for dealing with stress, the role of emotions in cross-cultural, cross-linguistic interactions, and so forth. Culture-general skills include the capacity to display respect for and interest in the culture, the ability to be a self-sustaining culture learner and to draw on a variety of resources for that learning, tolerance and patience in cross-cultural situations, control of emotions and emotional resilience, and the like.

The authors also stress the importance of the affective, behavioural and cognitive domains of learning, which they (p. 8) see supported by the following three learning processes:

1   the learners' exploration of their own culture;

2   the discovery of the relationship between language and culture;

3   the learning of the heuristics for analysing and comparing cultures.

Meta-level awareness and cross-cultural comparison, according to the authors of the review, can be seen to lie at the heart of such a culture pedagogy.

The emphasis on the importance of meta-level awareness also chimes with a more recent review of literature on culture and language learning by Byram and Feng (2004), who note the problems of perceiving culture learning potentially as identity-threatening or as potentially leading to identity loss (p. 152). The authors also stress the importance of experience as a basis for learning and teaching (p. 152) and, with reference to Lantolf (1999: 29), problematise the feasibility of 'constructing and seeing the world through culturally different eyes' and the impact of decentring, i.e. reassessing that which is normally taken for granted (p. 161). They also identify a move towards an ethnographic and critical perspective in culture teaching (pp. 154–155), the former of which – the ethnographic perspective – to them manifests itself in the processes of 'observing, participating, describing, analysing and interpreting' and where the emphasis on negotiating relationships, rather than culturally appropriate and linguistically correct communication (p. 156). The latter, i.e. the critical perspective, in their view, has resulted in a reappraisal of some key notions such as the role of native speakers, standard varieties and cultural identity and diversity (pp. 158–159). In addition, they point to the importance of context, be it 'intertextual', i.e. referring to a diachronic dimension, or external and internal, i.e. pertaining to the social or individual factors respectively (p. 154). With reference to Doyé (1999), they refer to a pedagogical procedure which addresses the key domains of knowledge (cognitive), skills (pragmatic) and attitudes (attitudinal) by engaging learners in

> exploring pre-knowledge, creating cognitive dissonance, replacing stereo-typical images, exploiting related sources of information and non-verbal communication, comparing others with own and moving beyond the culture of the TLs.
>
> (Byram and Feng, 2004: 161)

In view of the difficulty in defining that which is to be studied, i.e. the cultural content, participation in a cultural community becomes a more appealing concept than acquisition of a cultural system with the overarching metaphor being that of socialisation, i.e. the 'participation in the community and internalisation of its beliefs, values and behaviours' (p. 163) with the role of the teacher being that of a mediator.

FL COMMUNICATION IN MULTILINGUAL CONTEXTS

In a think-piece, Kramsch (2006) moves the debate about communicative competence as a key aim of FL teaching and learning, and Communicative Language Teaching (CLT) as the dominant pedagogical model helpfully on by pointing out that we should be mindful of how the notion of communicative competence 'is being put to the service of instrumental goals' (p. 250) by being interpreted in and by the educational world as 'the ability to exchange information speedily and effectively and to solve problems, complete assigned tasks, and produce measurable results' (p. 250). She points out that in the move from predominantly monolingual to multilingual contexts, communication has become much more complex and breakdown in communication often is not due to 'a lack of linguistic comprehension, but because of a lack of understanding and trust of interlocutors' intentions' (p. 250).

> The exacerbation of global social and economic inequalities and of ethnic identity issues, as well as the rise in importance of religion and ideology around the world have created historical and cultural gaps that a communi-cative approach to language teaching cannot bridge in itself.
>
> (pp. 250–251)

Kramsch stresses the need not only for knowledge about language and an ability to communicate meaning, but also for an understanding of meaning-making itself in order to bridge these widening gaps. This, she cogently argues, has implications for language teaching and requires more sophisticated competences in what she calls 'the manipulation of symbolic systems' (p. 251). By that she means discourse competence in a range of modalities (speech, writing, images) with an emphasis on the representation and interpretation of meaning. Pedagogically speaking, she argues for the need for complexity and a focus on alternatives in the production of meaning, the tolerance of ambiguity as well as an appreciation of form as meaning (p. 251).

As could be seen in Paige *et al.*'s (2000) definition, the notion of culture is increasingly reconceptualised as a reflection of the multicultural and global nature of the world in which we live. The key concepts are intercultural understanding and intercultural communicative competence, depending on the relative importance of the linguistic component. In their review article, Perry and Southwell (2011) note that intercultural understanding encompasses cognitive as well as affective dimensions. At a cognitive level this includes knowledge about and similarities and differences between cultures. At the affective level it includes positive attitudes including empathy, curiosity and respect, also referred to as 'intercultural sensitivity' related to experiences of cultural difference. According to Perry and Southwell, there is no agreed definition of 'intercultural competence' but there is a general acknowledgement that it comprises the ability 'to interact effectively and appropriately with people from other cultures' (p. 455). With reference to Lustig and Koester, (2006), 'intercultural communication' comes into play according to Perry and Southwell around cultural differences making similar interpretations and expectations about how to communicate competently difficult. An important feature for them is the fact that this 'is not an individual attribute but rather a characteristic of the association between individuals'. In terms of pedagogical implications, they refer to work by Bennett (2008), which cautions that neither language learning nor the facilitation of cultural contact need necessarily lead to the desired outcomes, i.e. culture learning, competence development and/or stereotype reduction.

THE USE OF AUTHENTIC MATERIAL AND TEXTS

Groot (2000: 63) discusses the potential of exposure to authentic foreign language material with a view to bringing about the sort of incidental vocabulary learning seemingly important in mother tongue acquisition but quickly comes to the conclusion that this is not very realistic on account of the following reasons:

- authentic 'texts' do not tend to have the purpose of illustrating aspects of language usage but instead to communicate meaning;
- new words tend not to be particularly salient in authentic texts;
- clues for the meaning of new words tend to feature in the wider, rather than the immediate context of authentic texts which might not form part of the specific extract chosen by the teacher; and, most importantly for Groot,
- authentic texts tend to contain too many unknown words.

Macaro also discusses the issue of what research has to say on the issue of the use of authentic texts. He recommends (2003b: 147) that the use of authentic texts with beginners should be kept to a minimum. One study referred to (Maxim, 2002), carried out among beginner university language students, suggests that the reading of authentic fictional texts with recurring situations, accessible characters, culturally familiar genre and stereotypical behaviours can be implemented with positive outcomes early on in an in-class group reading situation where pupils can share their prior knowledge and their reading strategies. The question remains how transferable these findings are for pre-university age pupils. Another study quoted by Macaro (Anderson, 1999) suggests that the reading rate can be increased by

- textual recognition (spotting similar words later in the text);
- chunking bits of text;

■ line-by-line training (where the learner is encouraged to avoid following the line with the finger but instead to maintain concentration by placing a pencil at the end of each line of text and moving it vertically down the text as she reads).

Reporting these, and other studies, Macaro (2003b: 148) draws the conclusion that while teachers should explore the possibilities afforded by authentic texts and continue to aim for their use with advanced learners, the definition of 'authenticity' need/should not be too narrowly described, such as 'written by and for native speakers'. Also, with the right kind of support it might be possible to use authentic texts early on in the FL learning process in a measured way. Overall, Macaro comes to the conclusion (p. 151) that it is mainly by making the reading process more 'visible', i.e. by discussing it at a process level with pupils, that progress can be made.

More recently, in a state-of-the-art review, Gilmore (2007) identifies a number of inadequacies of current language coursebooks, be it in terms of linguistic competence, i.e. the representation of linguistic knowledge, pragmalinguistic competence, i.e. the availability of appropriate pragmatic models and discourse competence, i.e. the support provided in terms of realistic models for managing conversations effectively in the TL. At the same time, he also diagnoses a rather conservative approach by publishers concerning authenticity. Gilmore notes that authenticity can be located in a text, in participants and/or in contexts and the purpose of the communicative act. A number of explanations for these shortcomings are rehearsed, for example the context-sensitivity of discourse, problems around defining native speakerness, difficulties in codifying the lingua/cultura franca concept, the diversity of the potential cultural contexts and the risks of disenfranchising learners by introducing target culture(s), a lack of empirical foundations supporting claims about the motivational potential of authenticity or the comparative difficulty of authentic texts. Concerning the latter, Gilmore (2007: 109) reminds his readers of work by Brown and Yule (1983), identifying a range of factors affecting text difficulty:

1   different spoken genres can be represented on a cline of increasing inherent difficulty (description < description/instruction < storytelling < opinion expressing), depending on whether they represent static, dynamic or abstract concepts;

2   the number of elements in a text and how easily they can be distinguished from one other, so that a short narrative with a single character and a few main events will be easier to comprehend than a long one involving more characters and events;

3   the delivery speed and accents used in spoken texts;

4   the content (grammar, vocabulary, discourse structure and presumed background knowledge in a text);

5   the visual support offered in conjunction with listening texts (video images, realia or transcripts).

Other factors include the organisation of information, topic familiarity and degree of explicitness (Anderson and Lynch, 1988), complexity of sentence structure (Bygate, 1987), lexical density (Stubbs, 1986) and text length (Nunan, 1989).

TASK-BASED LANGUAGE TEACHING (TBLT)

Chapter 5 provides a summary of the main features of the TBLT approach and its application in the classroom. The purpose of this section is to provide an outline of the main areas of findings of TBLT research and their implications for the FLs classroom in schools. It should be noted that while TBLT is a familiar concept in the discourse of language teachers in many countries, in the UK it is still a relatively unfamiliar term and approach. For instance, Summer (2012: 10) reports that 'In Germany, TBLT is also a widely discussed methodological concept... Tasks are seen as additional pedagogical options that can be employed for reaching different curricular objectives – such as intercultural, literary, and communicative competence'. This is not to say, of course, that teachers of languages in the UK do not incorporate the use of tasks in their lessons but that until recently they have largely been unaware of TBLT as a theorised pedagogical approach.

As a reflection of this, TBLT research in the UK has been overwhelmingly located in the context of adult EFL teaching. Consequently, questions about the generalisability of the findings of such studies to the context of the school languages classroom need to be addressed. Nevertheless, it is worth considering some of the main features of this research in order to see how similar questions might be relevant to the foreign languages classroom.

As Ellis (2012: 197) has pointed out, the term 'Task-based Language Teaching' does not represent a single approach but has been used to refer to a wide range of pedagogical conditions with the common feature being an 'emphasis on creating contexts for natural language use and focus on form'. In this way, TBLT combines the CLT focus on authentic meaning with a focus on acquisition of the form of the language. Empirical research on TBLT has been prolific and varied in the last two decades or so. However, two broad strands of research can be identified. Cognitive approaches have tended to focus on 'how attentional resources are used during task completion; the influence of task characteristics on performance; and the impact of different conditions under which tasks are completed' (Skehan, 2003: 5). A good example is Skehan and Foster's 1997 study of the effects of planning and post-task activity on the fluency, accuracy and complexity of language performance on three tasks: personal information exchange (participants had to describe to their partner pleasant and unpleasant surprises about life in Britain); narrative (they were given two cartoon strips without dialogue and took it in turn to describe the story on their strip); decision-making (they were given three magazine agony aunt letters and had to agree on best advice to give to the letter writers). The subjects (aged 18–25) were forty part-time students of EFL at a college in London. The researchers found that pre-task planning resulted in less frequent pauses in oral production and greater accuracy for the personal information and narrative tasks but not the decision-making task. Planning also led to the production of more complex speech in the personal information and decision-making task but not in the narrative task.

In a similar study, but set in the context of a high school in Japan, Mochizuki and Ortega (2008) examined the effect of 'pre-task planning that embeds grammatical guidance' in relation to a specified TL structure on the frequency, quality, complexity and fluency in the students' oral production of the structure (the relative clause in English). The task in question was a picture-retelling task with audio-narrative stimulus and the participants were fifty-six 15–16-year-old learners of English. The three conditions were 'no planning', '5 minutes of unguided pre-task planning' and '5 minutes of guided pre-task planning'. The findings indicated that the no planning group were more fluent in their retelling (measured by words per minute) but that the guided planners were more accurate in their production of relative clauses. There was no difference between the groups in terms of complexity of the structures produced.

One can conclude from these and similar studies that the effects of tasks completion on TL performance and acquisition vary depending on the following variables:

- the differences in type of task;
- the level of complexity of the task;
- the focus of language performance (i.e. fluency, accuracy, complexity of language produced);
- the level of the students' ability.

The second main strand of research on TBLT has adopted a discourse-focused perspective that has entailed either analysis of 'negotiation for meaning' interactions between teacher and students in terms of the use of strategies such as recasts, repetitions, etc. when there is conversational breakdown or through sociocultural analysis of the way in which teachers and learners 'co-construct meaning while engaging in interaction' (Skehan, 2003: 5). The interest here, therefore, is in the quality of the classroom talk (mostly in the TL) around the completion of a task and in how it contributes to the students' learning of the language items targeted in the task. As Ellis (2000: 210) has pointed out, unlike cognitive approaches to research on TBLT which have dwelt on the link between intrinsic task features and successful performance outcomes, sociocultural approaches have examined 'how tasks are accomplished by learners and teachers, and how the process of accomplishing them might contribute to language acquisition'. In other words, the interest is in the process of scaffolding. Students, in this view, need to be motivated to engage with a task and that motivation is driven by their interpretation of the task, which in turn is scaffolded by the teacher.

Van den Branden (2009: 268) has shown (with reference to studies conducted in schools in Flanders) how in the school classroom context (as opposed to the out-of-classroom clinical research context or the adult learning context) the teacher often provides whole-class scaffolding of group task activities by modifying the implementation of the task designed by the researcher in one or more of the following ways:

- changing the educational format of the task, e.g. turning a group work into a lockstep discussion of the text;
- changing the main focus of the task (e.g. turning a reading comprehension task into a listening exercise);
- simplifying the input or modifying output demands, or adding additional challenges;
- differentiating between individual students in terms of support, focus on form, feedback, negotiation of meaning;
- skipping certain phases of task implementation;

■ introducing additional phases (e.g. stimulating the students to listen to a real radio news bulleting when the task only invited the students to create a fictitious news bulletin).

Van den Branden concludes (2009: 285):

> Though not dominating interaction in the classroom so much as more transmission-based approaches, the teacher remains a crucial interactional partner in task-based language classrooms, by taking the role of motivator (i.e. launching the students into action by constructing joint projects), organizer (making sure the students know what they are expected to do, and organizing temporal and spatial aspects of task performance), and last but not least, conversational partner and supporter, as the more proficient, knowledgeable interlocutor who can feed the language-learning needs of different students in a wide variety of ways.

CONTENT AND LANGUAGE INTEGRATED LEARNING (CLIL)

CLIL programmes have become increasingly popular, especially in contexts where the classroom is likely to be the only access point to the FL (Lasagabaster and Sierra, 2010). CLIL is a form of content-based teaching where a FL being learned is used as the medium for the teaching of other substantive content (e.g. science or history might be taught through French or Spanish). Such courses vary considerably in the proportion of time devoted to language and content (Lyster and Ballinger, 2011). Coyle *et al.* (2010) suggest a number of benefits that CLIL might bring; for example, content can be made relevant to learners' needs and interests, communication is developed as the meanings generated are more likely to matter, there is a higher level of cognitive challenge, and intercultural understanding can be advanced.

CLIL has been widely promoted in the European Union (EU) as one way of delivering policies such as 'mother tongue plus two', the aim of which is that all citizens should speak two community languages in addition to their L1. Indeed, the European Commission's action plan singles out CLIL as the approach that 'has a major contribution to make to the Union's language learning goals' (European Commission, 2003: 8).

There is a growing body of research into the outcomes of CLIL programmes, though to date the main focus has been on language attainment outcomes. In a detailed review of this research, Dalton-Puffer (2011) highlights the following main benefits for language learning that seem to result from participation in CLIL classes:

■ better spontaneous oral production;
■ greater receptive and productive vocabulary;
■ better listening skills;
■ greater pragmatic awareness;
■ better strategic competence.

Pronunciation, syntax and written development beyond sentence level are shown to be less affected by participation in a CLIL programme (Dalton-Puffer,

2011). She concludes that research has shown that students in CLIL classes can reach higher levels of competence than those following regular programmes, and that effects might be greater for students who are 'average', since high ability students might do as well in traditional classes (Dalton-Puffer, 2011).

In addition, some work on attitudes towards language learning as a result of participation in CLIL classes has found some positive effects on attitudes to language learning when compared to non-CLIL classes in the same institution (Lasagabaster and Sierra, 2009), but this initial surge in enthusiasm may not be sustained (Bruton, 2011).

There are mixed findings as to whether CLIL classrooms encourage more learner-centred practice, however. Coonan (2007), for example, found that teachers in an Italian setting reported a move to more pupil-centred teaching as a result of CLIL, whereas research carried out in Austrian schools by Dalton-Puffer and colleagues found evidence of 'increased teacher orientation in CLIL teaching because CLIL teachers' limited L2 competence may prompt them to adhere very closely to their preparation' (Dalton-Puffer, 2011: 189–190).

The research is growing but, at present, the extremely diverse nature of CLIL programmes means we need to be tentative in drawing conclusions with regard to their effectiveness in comparison with more traditional courses. In addition to the variables we mention earlier that need to be borne in mind when researching SLA, such as learners' age/proficiency level/the teacher, and so on, we need to bear in mind when evaluating CLIL programmes the fact that some students carry on with language classes at the same time as the CLIL classes; some learners have already been taught the content before in the L1; the L1 is sometimes used to explain difficult concepts and sometimes not; it is usually the more able or more motivated students that are selected out for CLIL classes; foreign language assistants or additional teachers might be working with CLIL groups; sometimes content specialist and sometimes language specialist teachers have responsibility for the classes (see Dalton-Puffer, 2011; Bruton, 2011).

The final question of who teaches the CLIL classes remains to be investigated more fully. Ting (2011) offers the interesting example of her observation in L1 science classrooms, where the language level has been so incomprehensible to the learners as to be like a FL, and points out that language educators are better placed than most to keep a close focus on the quality of language and its comprehensibility (Ting, 2011). Whether taught by language or subject specialists, the training implications arising from the research to date are the need for further teacher professional development, as well as institutional commitment to giving teachers time to plan and co-plan with colleagues (Lyster and Ballinger, 2011), and for further published materials that will support learning in CLIL contexts (Ioannou Georgiou, 2012).

LITERATURE AND LANGUAGE LEARNING AND TEACHING

In view of the renaissance of literature in the 2013 UK National Curriculum proposals, we also include a brief overview of some of the recent literature in the field. We begin with an overview by Pachler and Allford (2000) who set out to answer the question why to study literature in the FLs classroom. They outline the rationale for the inclusion of literature in the curriculum and pedagogical approaches to it diachronically, and conclude that literature can meaningfully contribute to the development of language and literacy skills, an understanding of culture and society, as well as to foster personal involvement in the learning process (see also Carter and Long, 1991). They refer to work by Kast (1985), which argues that literary texts require decoding at three levels: the linguistic-semantic, the linguistic-aesthetic and the cultural-semantic. They also refer to Stern (1985) who identified four inherent difficulties: syntactic, lexical, discoursal, semantic and contextual (cultural, pragmatic, sociolinguistic). In addition, Stern identifies the issue of the predisposition of the reader, such as limited or lacking preconceptions, or presuppositions, such as personal literary experience. Choice of text, Pachler and Allford suggest, will depend *inter alia* on criteria such as length of text, thematic appropriacy, story structure and available support material.

Barrette *et al.* (2010) argue the case for an integrated approach, of which they see the use of literary text to develop language proficiency, content knowledge and analytical skills as a key component. They consider literature to perform a key role by providing a rich sample of input. Within their interactive and process-orientated approach they do not view proficiency level as dictating whether learners can comprehend or analyse literature, instead, when they move from familiar to unfamiliar subject matter, they view task design, schemata and text selection as playing a more important role in textual meaning construction. Furthermore, they suggest the following task (p. 227).

At introductory level:

■ introduce elements of the text gradually;
■ enable students to identify the organization of the text;
■ encourage students to draw on and expand their world knowledge;
■ progressively build students' language proficiency and reading skills.

At intermediate level:

■ elicit appropriate background knowledge from students;
■ supply new information needed to contextualise or interpret the text;
■ guide students to link that information to the literary text's features or meaning;
■ identify new information in the text indicating that students should re-evaluate their prior knowledge;
■ encourage students to manipulate or apply that new information in interpreting or creating another text.

At advanced level:

■ identify and apply relevant background information for themselves;
■ evaluate how new ideas fit with existing background knowledge;
■ assess the contribution of language to the effect or meaning of a story;
■ justify or argue against an interpretation of a text from cultural, linguistic, and literary perspectives.

Finally, we want to report on work by Redman (2005) who, drawing conceptually on the work of Kern (2003), discusses what she calls 'Stationenlernen' and tends to be known as 'carousel work' in UK FLs classrooms:

Texts – written, oral, visual, audiovisual – offer learners new aesthetic experiences as well as content to interpret and critique. The point is not simply to give them something to talk about (content for the sake of practising language), but to engage them in the thoughtful and creative act of making connections between grammar, discourse, meaning, between language and content, between language and culture, between another culture and their own – in short, making them aware of the webs, rather than the strands, of meaning in human communication.

(Kern, 2003: 43)

Redman discusses an example of Stationenlernen where learners move through a series of tasks on a single subject in close succession individually or in groups at various stations around the classroom. This, she argues, casts learners in the roles of makers and receivers of the meanings of the text they work on, represents a journey through the multiple layers of and interpretative perspective on a text, and fulfils Kern's (2002: 22) four literacy needs of:

1   to be immersed meaningfully in written language;
2   to receive direct assistance in the complexities of reading and writing foreign language texts;
3   to learn to analyse and evaluate what they read;
4   to learn how to transform meaning into new representations.

TRANSLATION

Translation as part of the FLs curriculum has a rather checkered recent history, particularly in the context of communicative approaches to FL teaching and learning, leading some commentators to consider it 'counterproductive' despite the prevalence of translation as a natural and integral part of FLs use (see Allford, 1999: 230). As could be seen in Chapter 1, the 2013 curriculum proposals for England promote the role of translation.

Allford makes the distinction between translation as a teaching approach and as a means of assessment; he clearly favours the former and sees the advantage of translation in its ability to show 'how the TL conveys or encodes meaning differently from the mother tongue' (Allford, 1999: 231).

Translation activities, which require close scrutiny of vocabulary, structures and discourse (i.e. meaningful language as it occurs in coherent units larger than sentences) can sensitise learners to differences between the two languages that may be much less apparent if all work is conducted in the TL. Employing the mother tongue in this way is entirely compatible with extensive use of the TL, which is being complemented, rather than undermined, by cross-lingual comparisons.

(Allford, 1999: 231)

In his recent reassessment of translation in language teaching, Cook argues (2010: p. xi) that where there is potential for misunderstanding in cross-lingual communication, translation has a key role to play in avoiding misunderstanding.

One of the challenges about translation, according to Cook (2010: 55–56), is the fact that it involves transfer of meaning from one language to another, which inevitably involves a degree of loss of different kinds as a result of different languages not representing meaning the same. Another factor contributing to loss are different culturally defined sets of background knowledge of readers/listeners across language domains. The loss, Cook goes on to explain (pp. 56–74) can take place at different levels of equivalence and how they interact. He discusses in particular the following levels: meaning, pragmatics, function and discourse, culture, free versus literal translation.

One frequent reservation about translation in language teaching in the SLA literature, according to Cook (2010: m88), is that

> it obstructs development of an ability to use the language automatically. The process of translation is seen as a slow and laborious one, focused more upon accuracy than fluency, making it somehow impossible ever to escape this impediment. The person who has learnt through translation will forever be locked into this laborious process, always condemned to start production and finish comprehension in their own language, and unable – to use a popular formulation – 'to think in the language' they have learnt. Related to this is the popular idea that translation promotes 'interference' and 'transfer' from a student's own language.

This, Cook argues (pp. 95–96), need not be the case and points out that the notion of transfer can be positive – providing stimulation, variety and creativity – as well as negative.

Cook (p. 109) goes on to discuss a number of educational arguments in favour of translation which he calls, with reference to Allen (1983): technological, social reformist, humanistic and academic. Under the rubric 'technological', Cook questions the assumption that translation is only needed by translators and interpreters, and posits that in today's world characterised by cross-lingual and cross-cultural communication, there is an everyday need for translation, be it in the realms of politics, work, social interaction or personal use. This, he argues,

> is true whether we take translation in the established sense of producing texts and utterances which replace 'textual material in one language by equivalent textual material in another language' . . . , or in the looser sense of what is done by 'a bilingual mediating agent between monolingual communication participants in two different language communities'.

Under the heading of 'social reform', Cook (2010: 112) argues that translation can be justified not only from a utilitarian but also from an ethical perspective and under the 'humanist' rubric, he argues (pp. 120–121) that translation, as part of a bilingual approach to instruction, can contribute to personal fulfilment and student satisfaction. Finally, in relation to the academic rationale, Cook (p. 121) points out the association of translation with a deductive approach to grammar teaching and an emphasis on accuracy rather than fluency and that the use of translation tends to involve an academic dimension given the necessary involvement of declarative knowledge about language and the use of metalanguage.

In relation to translation as a pedagogical activity Cook (2010: 126) notes the difficulties caused by teachers not speaking their students' language or by multilingual classes, which are not uncommon in the English as a Foreign Language (EFL) context. Another, he notes (p. 129), are questions around the appropriacy of translation for beginners. Here again, Cook takes the view that bilingual explanations, i.e. the use of the mother tongue as part of FL teaching, often involves elements of translation, which he approves of. Finally, Cook (pp. 136–153) lists the following nine types of activities:

1   corrected close translation;
2   word-for-word translation;
3   teaching vocabulary;
4   discussion of translation problems;
5   'traditional' focuses in a 'communicative' frame;
6   communicative translation;
7   'sandwiching' as an aid to fluency;
8   translation in mixed-languages classes;
9   translation for teachers who do not speak their students' language(s).

For practical teaching ideas about translation, see e.g. Duff, 1989 and Gonzàlez Davies, 2004. For machine translation in foreign language learning, see Niño, 2009.

SUMMARY

In terms of a 'moral of the story', or an overall conclusion of this overview of pertinent SLA and FLL research findings, two things can be said. First, we once again want to refer to Macaro (2003b: 253) who notes the importance of principled eclecticism as opposed to what he calls 'highly delineated methods of teaching', i.e. on the basis of available research evidence he is of the view, as are we, that it is counterproductive to impose or rely on restricted practices in the classroom and that variety is the spice of life.

Second, this review and summary of available research raises important questions around the extent to which UK government statutory requirements and non-statutory guidance and policy making are, indeed, informed by research.

FURTHER READING

Ellis, R. (2012) *Language Teaching Research and Language Pedagogy*. Malden, MA: Wiley/Blackwell.
This book focuses on how research on language teaching can inform pedagogy. It is aimed at teachers interested in 'theorising' about language teaching and seeks to point out possible causes of pedagogical action it might be interesting to explore.

Lightbown, P. and Spada, N. (2013) *How Languages are Learnt* (4th edn) Oxford: Oxford University Press.
This book aims to introduce the reader to some relevant language acquisition research with a view to helping them evaluate and adapt coursebooks in line with their own understanding of how languages are learnt.

Macaro, E. (2003) *Teaching and Learning a Second Language: A Guide to Recent Research and its Applications.* London: Continuum.

This book surveys second language acquisition research and links it to language pedagogy. The book takes into account the views of foreign language teachers about perceived gaps to be filled and personal knowledge to be extended.

CHAPTER 4

TRANSITION FROM PRIMARY TO SECONDARY

INTRODUCTION

A combination of the effects of FLs education policies in England over the last few decades and those of the growing global context of education and of cross-border demographic mobility has meant that it has become increasingly the case that the start of the Secondary school experience does not represent the start of a pupil's experience of learning a FL. The proportion of pupils in their first year of Secondary schooling in England, who learn a foreign language *ab initio* is diminishing as it has been for a longer period of time in countries such as Scotland, France, Germany and the Netherlands where the statutory teaching of a FL at Primary school has had a longer history. Indeed, statistics by Eurostat (www.epp.eurostat.ec.europa.eu/cache/ITY_OFFPUB/KS-SF-10-049/EN/KS-SF-10-049-EN.PDF) suggest that since the European Council set the target of 'mastery of basic skills, in particular by teaching at least two FLs from a very early age' in 2002 (www.consilium.europa.eu/uedocs/cms_data/docs/pressdata/en/ec/71025.pdf), the number of Primary pupils studying a FL increased significantly between 2000 and 2008. What are the implications of this classroom reality for student teachers of FLs at Secondary level?

First, unlike proponents of the 'clean slate' approach to FL teaching in the Secondary sector, which is premised on the mistaken belief that it is best to assume no prior knowledge of the TL in order to have more control over the pace and content of progression of learning, we believe that the Secondary FLs teacher needs to have some knowledge of the prior FL learning experiences (both formal and informal) that the Year 7 pupils, aged 11, have had before arrival at the school. There are several types of benefit that one can gain from this knowledge. First, the Year 7 FLs classroom is often referred to as a 'mixed experience' classroom on the basis of different degrees of prior knowledge of the TL. FLs teachers need to develop skills to accommodate this reality as much as they need to develop skills in mixed ability teaching. Second, it is widely accepted that knowledge is acquired through a process of building on existing understandings and competences that a pupil has already acquired; therefore, encouraging awareness (for both teacher and the pupil) of what has already been learned can provide a useful platform for new learning. Third, awareness of the form of FL teaching that the pupil has been receiving will be useful to the Year 7 teacher as it will help her plan the right amount of familiarity and novelty of approaches in their lessons. It is important to avoid both stultifying repetition and bewildering novelty in the content of lessons and in the teaching approaches adopted if progress of learning and teaching between Year 6 (last year of Primary) and Year 7 (first year of Secondary) is to be maintained. This chapter provides an outline of key features of the areas that, in our view, inform effective transition of FL learning and teaching across the two sectors.

OBJECTIVES

By the end of this chapter you should:

- have an overview of FLs provision in Primary schools in England;
- have an idea of the different models of Primary FLs provision;
- have an understanding of key curricular and pedagogical issues relating to Primary FLs;
- be aware of Key Stage 2–3 transition issues and effective strategies;
- have some knowledge about research findings on the effects of an early start on FL acquisition.

MODELS OF PRIMARY FLs PROVISION

The teaching of FLs at Primary school level is in some ways a much larger logistical enterprise than at Secondary school level. For instance, in 2009–10 there were 16,971 maintained Primary schools in England compared with 3,127 maintained Secondary schools (DfE, 2010). In countries where FLs are a compulsory subject at some point in the Primary schooling years, planning the teaching of the subject is a major undertaking and involves large numbers of staff. Introducing the subject on to the curriculum more or less from scratch, as has been the case in England recently,

---

▪ **Table 4.1** Main models of FL teaching in maintained Primary schools in England (percentage of schools in 2008)

Class teacher working alone	37
Class teacher working with teaching assistant	15
Class teacher working with FLs assistant	4
Internal peripatetic specialist FLs teacher	8
External peripatetic specialist FLs teacher	11
Higher level teaching assistant working alone	3
Mixed	18
Other	2

Source: Wade et al., 2009: 35.

therefore, involves a significant reorientation of the workforce. According to a national survey (Wade *et al.*, 2009) conducted in 2008, 92 per cent of maintained Primary schools were providing FL teaching in class time. French was taught in nine out of ten of the schools offering FLs, Spanish in 25 per cent of the schools, and German in 10 per cent of the schools. According to the survey, there is a wide range of models of FL teaching provision, which possibly reflects the fact that with the absence of the subject from the Primary curriculum and the consequent lack of sufficient numbers of suitably qualified FLs teachers, schools have needed to deploy a range of strategies to teach the subject.

EMPIRICAL RESEARCH ON THE AGE FACTOR IN FLs ACQUISITION: DOES AN EARLY START GIVE LEARNERS AN ADVANTAGE?

The Critical Period Hypothesis (CPH) has generated much debate in the literature on second and foreign language acquisition. With regard to FL learning, the CPH has claimed that there is an 'offset point', identified by some as being at the age of puberty, beyond which FL learning becomes more difficult. Lenneberg (1967: 176) claimed that after puberty FLs needed to be learned consciously and in a 'laboured' way and that learners beyond this age have difficulty in developing native speaker competence with pronunciation.

However, there has been plenty of evidence to indicate that there is little or no advantage, per se, to starting FL learning at an early age. In her summary of the findings of studies comparing the L2 learning rates of adult and older children over those of younger children, Ortega (2009: 28) concludes that adult and older children have an initial advantage of one or more years, after five years the early starters 'catch up and are better than late starters in second language contexts'. However, and crucially for us, she adds that this is not the case with FL learning: 'In foreign language contexts, by contrast, the lagged advantage for an earlier start has not been observed, even after five years'. Researchers are increasingly distinguishing between the effects of age on second language acquisition in naturalistic settings and their effects on FL acquisition in instructional settings. While there is clear evidence of positive effects in the former context, this is not the case in the latter.

In their comparative study of children aged 5, 7 and 11 learning French in schools in two state schools in Newcastle, Myles *et al.* (2012) found that there was little difference between the groups with regard to acquisition of receptive vocabulary, and that older children had an advantage in terms of grammar acquisition.

Muñoz's comparative study (2006 and 2010), the *Barcelona Age Factor* (BAF) project, examined differences between school learners of English with starting ages of 8, 11, 14 and 18+, and similarly found that older starters had an advantage in terms of rate of acquisition.

If there is no comparative benefit or advantage to starting early, we need to formulate the question differently and focus on the beneficial effects of an early start per se. In what ways, then, can an early start enhance a learner's acquisition of a FL? First, there is empirical evidence that length of exposure to the FL, rather than starting age, leads to improved acquisition of the FL. For that reason alone, especially in the context of schools in England where currently very many children drop the subject at the age of 14, this provides justification for starting the process of that exposure at KS2 or earlier. There is an argument, therefore, to be made that learners should start early and end their study of a FL late if they are to develop an appropriate level of communicative competence in the FL purely on the basis of formal instruction. Second, there is evidence that early learners benefit from tuning in at a relatively early age to the sounds of the FL and to the cultural context of the FL and its speakers, building early positive motivation and attitudes towards learning the FL. Third, by starting at an earlier age and establishing a basis of elementary competence in the FL at KS2, FLs learners at Secondary school can engage in more cognitively appropriate tasks using the FL.

In their summary of research findings on the advantage of an early start, Singleton and Muñoz (2011: 418) conclude:

> Accordingly, any advantage of an early start in the instructional context needs to be seen in terms of educational and attitudinal benefits that may accrue – benefits that do not automatically flow from an early learners' biological circumstances but require, in addition to larger amounts of language input, high quality teaching, including high-grade input.

THE CONTENT FOCUS OF PRIMARY FLs

The first place to look for indications of curricular content of FLs provision in Primary schools is that of the national frameworks and policy guidelines that were designed with the aim of ensuring continuity and progression of FL teaching and learning. While it is true that in many cases the picture will be fairly eclectic and individual schools will be planning their FLs provision on the basis of their own needs and availability of staffing and resources, national documentations at least give us a sense of the expectations and objectives of the enterprise as a whole. It would be wrong also to assume that there is a universal Primary (or indeed Secondary) FLs curriculum that is fundamentally the same in different national contexts. Let us look briefly at two contrasting national approaches.

England

In England, the development of a curricular framework for FL teaching has a fairly recent history. In 2011, a report by the Expert Panel for the National Curriculum review recommended the statutory provision of one FL across Key Stages 2–4 (pupils aged 5–16) inclusively:

> It is worth noting at this point that the optimum age at which to introduce **modern foreign language** teaching remains a contested matter that requires careful consideration of evidence; this is not yet fully resolved and we therefore present modern foreign languages in lower Key Stage 2 as a query [. . .] However, we do believe because of its importance that it should be included in the National Curriculum at upper Key Stage 2, which represents a change to the existing arrangements.

> (DfE, 2011b: 27)

The Key Stage 2 Framework for Languages (DfES, 2005a), which until recently provided guidelines for the teaching and learning of FLs in Primary schools, targeted provision for learners in Years 3–6 (ages 7–11). Although this document is no longer functional as an official framework, it nevertheless remains as the most detailed attempt at an outline of objectives for FL teaching in Primary schools in England and therefore continues to merit some attention.

The document consists of five strands, three of which are described as 'core strands' (Oracy, Literacy and Intercultural Understanding) and two as 'cross-cutting strands' (Knowledge about Language, Language Learning Strategies). The following is a summary of the objectives of the five strands for Year 6.

The implicit rationale behind the Oracy strand was the widely held view that the most tangible effect of learning a FL at pre-Secondary school age is gain in terms of the learners' phonological competence in the FL. At an early age, children appear to be more receptive to the sound of a language and, therefore, can develop appropriate pronunciation and intonation in their own oral output more easily than older, post-adolescent learners. As the list indicates, the focus of the Oracy objectives was also largely communicatively orientated and encourages public performance in the TL. In this way, the building blocks are set up for the development of communicative contexts for FL learning in later stages of schooling. The development of presentation skills can be seen as a communicative spin-off from the usually high-motivation context of interactive classroom oral activities, helping children to

---

■ **Table 4.2** Oracy in the KS2 Framework for Languages

O 6.1 Understand the main points and simple opinions in a spoken story, song or passage

■ listen attentively, retell and discuss the main ideas
■ agree or disagree with statements made about a spoken passage.

O 6.2 Perform to an audience

■ recite a short piece of narrative either from memory or by reading aloud from the text
■ develop a sketch, role-play or presentation and perform to the class or an assembly.

O 6.3 Understand longer and more complex phrases or sentences

■ retell using familiar language a sequence of events from a spoken passage, containing complex sentences
■ understand and express reasons
■ understand the gist of spoken passages containing complex sentences, e.g. descriptions, information, instructions.

O 6.4 Use spoken language confidently to initiate and sustain conversations and to tell stories

■ participate in simple conversations on familiar topics
■ describe incidents or tell stories from their own experience, in an audible voice.

Source: DfES, 2005a: 56.

appreciate 'the power of language' (DCSF, 2009: 6). Oracy is also seen as contributing to the development of the children's literacy in the wider sense: 'Talk is the underlying key factor in the development of literacy' (DCSF, 2009: 6), enhancing learners' awareness of differences in sound and register and allowing them to experiment with speech as they progress from single words to longer utterances in the TL.

Table 4.3 Literacy in the KS2 Framework for Languages

L 6.1 Read and understand the main points and some detail from a short written passage

- read and respond to, e.g. an extract from a story, an email message or song
- give true or false responses to statements about a written passage
- read descriptions of people in the school or class and identify who they are.

L 6.2 Identify different text types and read short, authentic texts for enjoyment or information

- read for enjoyment an email message, short story or simple text from the internet
- read and understand the gist of a familiar news story or simple magazine article.

L 6.3 Match sound to sentences and paragraphs

- use punctuation to make a sentence make sense
- listen carefully to a model, e.g. a video recording, recorded story or song, and reconstitute a sentence or paragraph using text cards.

L 6.4 write sentences on a range of topics using a model

- apply most words correctly
- construct a short text, e.g. create a *PowerPoint* presentation to tell a story or give a description.

Source: DfES, 2005a: 56.

Table 4.4 Intercultural understanding in the KS2 Framework for Languages

---

IU 6.1 Compare attitudes towards aspects of everyday life

- recognise similarities and differences in attitudes among children in different cultures
- learn about role models for children in different cultures.

IU 6.2 Recognise and understand some of the differences between people

- discuss similarities and differences between the cultures they have learned about
- recognise and challenge stereotypes.

IU 6.3 Present information about an aspect of culture

- perform songs, plays, dances
- use ICT to present information.

Source: DfES, 2005a: 56.

The interdependence of the sound and written forms of the TL was also a feature of the Literacy strand (L 6.3). The strand portrayed a balance between a meaning-focused orientation to literacy development (L 6.1 and L 6.2) and a more form-focused approach (L 6.3 and L 6.4). This latter dimension is further supported by the Knowledge about Language strand referred to below.

The Intercultural understanding strand was perhaps the least developed of the objectives and teachers needed to draw on external resources such as authentic materials relating to the target culture(s) or direct contact with the countries and its peoples through visits or other means, virtual or face-to-face. The intercultural focus had an overall aim of encouraging tolerance in terms of attitudes towards cultural difference. The strand is structured according to the contexts of understandings relating to everyday life (IU 6.1), people (IU 6.2) and culture (IU 6.3). What was arguably missing is a linkage with the plurilingual identity of learners themselves.

The final two, 'cross-cutting' strands consisted largely of lists of activities that develop knowledge about language or language and learning strategies.

■ **Table 4.5** Knowledge about language in the KS2 Framework for Languages

- Recognise patterns in the foreign language.
- Notice and match agreements.
- Use knowledge of words, text and structure to build simple spoken and written passages.
- Use knowledge of word order and sentence construction to support the understanding of the written text.
- Use knowledge of word and text conventions to build sentences and short texts.
- Devise questions for authentic use.

Source: DfEs, 2005a: 56.

■ **Table 4.6** Language and learning strategies in the KS2 Framework for Languages

- Discuss language learning and reflect and share ideas and experiences.
- Plan and prepare – analyse what needs to be done in order to carry out a task.
- Use language known in one context or topic in another context or topic.
- Ask for repetition and clarification.
- Use context and previous knowledge to help understanding and reading skills.
- Practise new language with a friend and outside the classroom.
- Listen for clues to meaning, e.g. tone of voice, key words.
- Make predictions based on existing knowledge.
- Apply a range of linguistic knowledge to create simple, written production.
- Evaluate work.
- Compare and reflect on techniques for memorising language.
- Use a dictionary.

Source: DfES, 2005a: 56.

How far were these broad objectives targeted at actual classroom practice? In the conclusion of their longitudinal case study of sixteen Primary schools in England, Cable *et al.* (2010: 146–147) pointed to the following patterns of acquisition and pedagogy in relation to the teaching of the three core strands of the *KS2 Framework for Languages*:

10.7 Oracy

In common with practice reported elsewhere oracy was considered the main aim of languages learning by teachers in the case study schools. The focus on oracy began in Year 3 and largely involved the word level naming of objects and short question and answer routines. These were frequently revisited as children expanded and added further information to their utterances. Pedagogy centring on the topic-related teaching of vocabulary and sentence forms to express personal information or describe events persisted throughout Key Stage 2. An emphasis on memorisation rather than experimentation was evident as was the ability of the majority of children to produce memorised language items and formulaic phrases rather than their own independent sentences. Some of the older children, who have experienced continuous teaching, were able to engage in sustained dialogues and draw on previous learning to enhance question and answer routines.

10.8 Literacy

Children engaged in more literacy activities as they moved through Key Stage 2. Older children were involved in more work at sentence level and, in some instances, at text level. Older children also received greater visual support for oracy work in the form of written words and sentences. Although literacy activities did not form a substantial part of most lessons, as noted in other studies (Ofsted, 2005), there was evidence of an increase in the type and length of literacy activities over the three years of the study. Teachers suggested that the length of lessons constrained the amount of time they spent on literacy activities. It may also be the case that teachers who were still developing their linguistic knowledge felt less confident teaching literacy and that less attention was paid to this aspect in the training attended.

10.9 Intercultural understanding

Teachers were beginning to include objectives relating to the teaching of intercultural understanding in their languages lessons. In line with findings elsewhere (LACE, 2007), children were learning factual knowledge and expressing attitudes, e.g. about similarities and differences between practices or institutions in different European countries. There was little evidence of children developing the other *savoirs* referred to by Byram (1997). . ., and no evidence of assessment of objectives relating to intercultural understanding. For resources relating to intercultural understanding, teachers were drawing increasingly on commercially produced material. A number were integrating contributions from native speakers, including foreign language assistants or visiting students, or staff who have visited the country.

There was evidence of an increase in the number of whole school events focusing on developing children's knowledge and understanding of other cultures and languages, and of the development of international links and partnership projects which supported the development of intercultural understanding, although these were not usually related directly to the objectives in the Framework. A need for further professional development in this area was evident (see also Evans and Fisher, 2009). Staff need to be well informed and confident in order to encourage discussion and reflection and to ensure children are provided with a range of perspectives with clear implications for both initial teacher education and ongoing professional development. Developing their own knowledge and understanding, through training, encounters and experience is of fundamental importance for all Primary teachers whatever their role in languages.

France

Comparison with the FLs programme in France is interesting as it provides us with an example of an educational system in which English is taught and conceived as a FL and not as a first or second language. From an English perspective it is also interesting since it is the main FL taught in schools, links with schools in France are numerous, and a significant proportion of teachers of French in England are French nationals. Comparing the two systems can therefore provide useful insights.

The French pre-Secondary school system is divided into the following stages: *Ecole maternelle* (nursery school for children aged 3–5 years) and *Ecole Élémentaire* (Primary school for children aged 6–10 years). The latter is divided into two 'cycles': Cycle 2 – the first two years of Primary; and Cycle 3 – the next three years of Primary.

FL learning is a compulsory component from the first year of Primary school (*Cours préparatoire* – CP) and aims at attainment of level A1 of the *Common European Framework of Reference for Languages* (Council of Europe, 2001). The focus here is mainly on sensitisation to the TL through exposure to oral input: '*Dans un premier temps, c'est en exposant l' élève à la langue orale et en privilégiant la communication orale, qu'on établira les bases d'un apprentissage*' [In the first instance, it is through exposing the pupil to the spoken language and through focusing on oral communication that one can establish the foundations of FL learning]. This approach draws on what is seen as the foundational focus on oral competence and sensitisation promoted in nursery schools:

> *C'est à l'école maternelle que les élèves forgent leurs premières compétences langagières. À trois, quatre et cinq ans, l'oreille est sensible aux différences de prononciation, de prosodie. C'est aussi à cet âge que se fixe la façon de prononcer et d'articuler, et que les enfants ont le plus de facilité à reproduire des sons nouveaux. Au cours de cette période, les références culturelles, lexicales et phonologiques, qui serviront d'appui à l'apprentissage de la langue, se déterminent naturellement. En leur faisant entendre une autre langue (l'anglais le plus souvent), mais aussi par le chant et les comptines, en leur proposant de petites interactions verbales, l'enseignant prépare l'enfant aux séances d'apprentissage qu'il connaîtra en CE1.*
>
> (Ministère d'Education, 2011: 13)

[It is at nursery school that pupils develop their first language competences. At three, four and five years, the ear is sensitive to differences of pronunciation and of prosody. It is also at this age that methods of pronunciation and articulation are established and that children are able to reproduce new sounds. During this period, cultural, lexical and phonological references, which will support the learning of the language, are established naturally. By letting them hear another language (English in most cases), but also through songs and rhymes, by engaging them in brief verbal interactions, the teacher prepares the children for the learning sessions they will encounter in CE1.]

In the second year of Primary school (*Cours élémentaire niveau 1* – C1), the statutory requirement is one and a half hours of FLs lessons per week. In 2004 the French Ministry of Education produced a framework ('*socle commun*') of knowledge and skills to be targeted in the different phases of schooling. FL teaching relates to one of the following languages: Arabic, Chinese, English, German, Italian, Portuguese or Russian. Each of these languages has a separate programme that highlights the broad areas of learning within communicative skills, the four language skills, grammar and vocabulary, and cultural awareness. Interestingly, there is some attempt to exemplify progression of learning. For instance, the following progression is suggested with regard to teaching and learning basic forms of greeting and politeness expressions in English.

Cycle 2	Cycle 3
– How are you today, Tasmin?	– Hi Kate! Are you all right?
– Fine, Liz. And you?	– Oh hi, Karen! Yes I am, thanks, but I'm a bit tired.
– Very well, Tasmin, thank you!	

In this case, progression is marked in terms of fullness of length of utterance. This includes the use of adverbs ('a bit'/'very') and connectives ('but'), and a switch of register from formal ('How are you?') to informal ('Hi'). In this way linguistic progression from one year to the next is highlighted in linguistic terms rather than in broad language skill terms, which tends to be the case in the English *KS2 Framework for Languages*.

We want to conclude this section on the curricular focus of Primary FLs by posing a string of interrelated questions:

■ What is the nature of progression in FL learning?
■ How does progression in FL teaching and curricular planning relate to progression in FL learning and acquisition?
■ Is progression best characterised as linear, bell-shaped, recursive, like a spiral or some other spatial metaphor?
■ And, in the context of the theme of this chapter, how can progression in FL teaching and learning be best supported and developed during transition from Primary to Secondary schooling?

Task 4.1 **SOME QUESTIONS ABOUT PRIMARY FLs**

Based on what you have read so far, as well as any prior experience, what are your answers to the questions posed above? Then compare your answers to those of some peers.

TRANSITION AND CONTINUITY

International comparisons

A project funded by the European Commission on transition between Primary and Secondary language teaching that drew on the experiences of Austria, France, Germany, Hungary, Spain, Sweden and Switzerland (Sygmund and Smith, n.d.) identified similar issues in the different national contexts, with the exception of Sweden where transition issues are less problematic due to the nine-year compulsory schooling span of the Primary school (from age 7 to 16) whereby pupils can attend the same school throughout this period (and in which English and a 'FL' are compulsory subjects). The report made the following recommendations.

TEACHER EDUCATION

A difference of approach was noted in the training of Primary and Secondary FLs teachers. This was not always due to differences in the level of the student teachers' subject specialist knowledge. It was noted, for instance, that in Spain, Primary FLs teachers were language specialists who received training in pedagogy and yet problems of transition persisted because of a lack of communication between FLs teachers in the two sectors. The report, therefore, recommended the introduction of modules on transition in the two programmes as well as in-service training sessions to raise teachers' awareness of transition issues for FL teaching.

CONTACT BETWEEN PRIMARY AND SECONDARY SCHOOL TEACHERS

The report recommended the encouragement of liaison meetings between FLs teachers in the two sectors in order to support continuity of learning and to avoid 'the start again effects' that currently prevail. The use of the European Language Portfolio (www.coe.int/t/dg4/education/elp) is promoted as a useful tool for this purpose. The authors also comment that in the few cases where meetings between Primary and Secondary FLs pupils have been arranged, this has enhanced the Primary learners' experience of transition in their FLs learning.

LEARNING MATERIALS

The conclusion here is that textbooks alone will not bring about a smooth transition of FL learning between Primary and Secondary schools, simply by incorporating a diversity of different pedagogical approaches and a wide range of supplementary materials. There is a need to develop materials that address transition issues in the context of FL learning and to raise teachers' awareness of age-related differences in FL learning.

TRANSITION STRATEGIES

In his *Independent Review of the Primary Curriculum*, Rose (2009) pointed to the importance of transition strategies as a means of supporting the process of Primary to Secondary transfer. While research evidence of the relative effectiveness of different approaches is lacking, the review referred to a report from the London Challenge programme (DfES, 2005b), which identified five broad educational 'transition bridges' that constitute 'good practice': administrative; social and personal (improving Primary pupils' and their parents' familiarity with the environment of the Secondary school and the pastoral support available); curricular (continuity of learning from Year 6 to Year 7); pedagogical (continuity in classroom practice between Year 6 and Year 7); autonomy and management of learning (pupils as active participants in the transition and learning process). While these bridges may seem self-evident and at times imprecise, they are useful in highlighting the multilayered nature of the transition experience from a broad contextual point of view. Subject learning is not a purely mental or cognitive experience but is embedded in the particular physical and institutional contexts in which it takes place, and the pupils' experience of change will be filtered through that context. However, while it would seem incontrovertible that teachers and schools should strengthen their cross-sector practice and thinking for the benefit of their pupils, one should resist the temptation to over-value the idea of continuity at the expense of change and novelty from the pupils' perspective.

As Jones and Coffey (2006: 157–159) point out, children at Primary school go through a series of 'mini-transitions' in relation to their learning. These relate to organisational skills (e.g. from carpet to sitting at a table; from group work to individual seating), social skills (e.g. from responsibility for self to responsibility for others; from being relatively uninhibited to adolescence), and learning skills (e.g. from being a 'lone player' to a group collaborator; from doing best for the teacher to responsibility for their own learning; from being a non-reader to a reader). Transition, therefore, is arguably a key feature of the natural process of learning and development.

In addition, 'transition' is a temporal notion since it implies a momentary period of change from one condition to the next. It is a temporary link in the chain of the teaching and learning experience. How far should a FLs teacher dwell on and exploit this link and how far should pupils have their attention drawn to this aspect of their FL learning experience? Let us deal with the latter question first.

Pupils' views

It would appear that children tend to think of their FL learning experience in terms of chronological progress, as in the following quotations from Year 8 pupils in schools in England (Evans and Fisher, 2009). When interviewed on the subject of the value of learning languages at Primary school, pupils identified the benefits in terms of having a head start in languages, and learning the basics at Primary school and, therefore, being able to progress faster at Key Stage 3:

They would achieve higher marks when they got into Secondary school and did GCSE because they would already know the basics of the language, so when they come up to Secondary school, you can move straight on to the more difficult and complex stuff.

I think it would be good if you started at Primary and got all the simple stuff done and when you came here you would do more complicated stuff. You could get higher levels because you wouldn't have to go over the basics.

When you start early you've got more years to learn, haven't you? So you know more and if you carry on at high school, it would be a benefit because you already know some of the stuff.

Some also believed that language learning was easier at an early age:

When you are younger you remember things a lot better than when you're older, so when you're my age you tend to forget a lot of things.

I think actually it would be easier to learn it from a younger age because you've been doing it longer and it's something to do with your mind taking in more things.

A third common reason given by the pupils in support of the learning of FLs at Primary school was that it provided them with greater confidence when starting: 'It helped me because I felt a bit more confident starting off'.

Bridging activities

It is increasingly recognised that reflection on, and planning of 'boundary practices' (Wenger, 1998) can play an important role in facilitating the between-school transition experience of children. These practices take the form of strategies and activities that focus on some aspect of the transition experience itself or that explicitly aim to build on the subject learning that bestrides the period of transition.

Pre-transfer visits from pupils in feeder schools constitute one form of boundary practice that is commonly used by Secondary schools. In the FL teaching context these visits normally take the form of participation in taster FLs lessons or attendance of Year 7 FLs classes. The latter serve the dual purpose of introduction to Year 7 FLs pedagogy and overcoming peer-related anxieties by mixing the two groups in the classroom setting.

However, more creative conditions can also be designed that combine the development of Primary pupils' reflection about the future Secondary school environment they are due to enter with FLs-related activities. This would be one way of preparing the grounds both for the FL learning and the institutional contexts of school transfer. For instance, Evans and Fisher (2012: 170) report on an example of 'bridge-building' activity in which Year 5 pupils from feeder Primary schools collaborate with Year 7 pupils at the Secondary school in a joint project that involved thinking about the architecture of the school and making suggestions for improving aspects of the environment:

I led a project with our feeder Primary schools and our Y7 and it was a transitional MFL project [. . .] Our objective was to transform an area of external premises using sculpture, sound, video, art and modern languages. [. . .] They went round photographing the school and then we'd take words and language and they made sculptures of how they wanted to change the school [. . .] It was about transition as well. That's why they had to go round the school and photograph the ugliest bits and say what they wanted to do with it. And they were like mini-architects, sculptors.

This kind of 'transitional FLs project' has many potential advantages which operate on different levels. First, as a collaborative activity between Year 7 and Year 6 pupils, it helps the latter to overcome peer-focused anxieties in relation to the forthcoming move to the new school. Second, the activity gives the future newcomers a psychological boost by encouraging them to comment on and to improve the environment they will be joining, thus strengthening their sense of ownership of the place of their future learning. And third, by integrating FL learning with other subject activities (in this case, Art and Design) the status of FL learning can be raised in the pupils' minds. Such projects are, of course, exceptional and logistically difficult to organise for large numbers of Year 6 pupils. However, they can form part of a larger 'transition plan' to support this period of change for the pupils.

Jones and McLachlan (2009: 127) list the following 'transitional learning activities running through the end of Year 6 into the early part of Year 7':

YEAR 6

- Sampling a lesson from a Yr 7 textbook.
- Enjoying a simple story, reciting and acting as the words are looked at to establish phone-grapheme correspondence.
- Simple spelling and basic grammar challenges (linking these to literacy).
- Learning to write a few sentences.
- Writing notices in the foreign language for around the classroom and school.
- Short emails to pen pals.
- Reading aloud or memorisation competitions.

YEAR 7

- Devising challenge activities based on the year 7 textbook that clearly identify primary coverage such as interview scenario, a poem, a song.
- Formative integrated assessments in the form of quizzes in the early weeks to build up a picture of what the pupils know/do not know/do not know well, as part of the auditing procedure.
- Topic work that enables pupils to use what they know, e.g. create a brochure on their town or about a French town.
- Creating mini-plays in groups that require pupils to use previous as well as new learning.
- Skills lessons, e.g. vocabulary builders and pattern/grammar mind maps.

INTERVIEW WITH KATHERINE KELLY, TEACHER OF FRENCH AT FOUR PRIMARY SCHOOLS IN THE EAST OF ENGLAND

Kate Kelly, who trained as a Key Stages 2/3 FLs teacher, is peripatetic teacher of French and FLs co-ordinator at four Primary schools in the Eastern region of England. We present an extract of an interview she gave for this book in March 2013 so that you can gain insights into the issue of cross-sector transition from the perspective of an experienced Primary school FLs teacher. The interview is not intended as representing the views of all Primary teachers nor indeed of a Primary FL teaching paradigm. Instead, it should be read as a stimulus for further reflection about the issues involved in managing the FL learning experience of pupils from Primary to Secondary:

Interviewer: Do you think that somebody who is trained entirely at Key Stage 3 and above would need to adapt in any particular ways if they were going to be involved in teaching at Key Stage 2?

KK: I think they would need to be prepared to adapt. Yes. I think one has to not expect too much from the children. In the course of a year, one can perhaps expect the children to actually have learnt and be able to reproduce a limited amount, to be honest. Usually there is a lot of repetition, finding different imaginative ways of doing much the same thing over and over again. I think teaching in real bite-sized chunks of new teaching is important. I think it is important that you don't make assumptions about what the children know. You have to assume that you have to teach them everything. I used to fall into the trap of assuming that children would infer things, which is actually obviously a much more mature skill. In fact, the younger children, except for the really perhaps gifted ones, very often don't have those thinking skills so you have to spell things out: 'What does this word mean?' I've just said it instead of just assuming that they will understand it as a whole but what does it actually mean? And get them to say it rather than just assume that they've understood.

I think I was quite taken aback by having to, with the younger children, be a bit more pastoral. The children will come in from playtime and they will expect me to deal with friendship issues that they have happened at playtime – knocks that they have had – which for a French specialist you might find that a bit difficult. I think it's important with younger children that they are moving about more, that they're not just sitting at their desks for half an hour an hour at a time. Lots of activities that keep their interest. That sort of thing.

Interviewer: What are some of the more effective strategies you have used in classroom teaching at this level? Please give examples.

KK: I try to think of activities that the children would probably be doing anyway for fun, for interest. And then do them in French. So we do a lot of singing. Watch videos of French children, which I think is very important because I'm not always sure that the children have had a lot of experience of travelling to other countries or even of listening to other languages and so it's just make sure they understand that what we're doing is for real, this is for real, that people use this language for communicating in normal ways. Play a lot of games, playground games, very repetitive games, sometimes where the same language is used over and over again but because of the game element the children are still engaged and enjoy it.

Interviewer: What sort of games would these be?

KK: Well, for example, this is very, very simple but the most effective way I have found of learning to count up to 12, say, or 20 or whatever number you want is simply to put them in a circle and then get them to count out loud while you point round the circle and number 12 sits down. And it's as simple as that. And it sounds terribly tedious but the children find it absolutely really exciting because they want to be the last person standing and whenever somebody sits down they think that's hilarious and actually what you are doing is exposing them to counting up to 12 thirty times without getting bored and that sort of any simple game anything that you can put a game element into so that you can get away with making it very repetitive.

They love role plays of any sort and if you can get concrete objects in for them to use as part of their role play so much the better. Physically moving them around. Combining role play with repetitive activities. One of the role plays they love is in Year 3 if you're just teaching a basic question like '*Comment tu t'appelles*?/ *Je m'appelle. . .*' something as basic as that. Tell them that something terrible has happened and that there's a French child who has gone missing in the village and the police would like some help. Somebody who can ask some questions in French to find where this child is and then send a child out while you choose somebody in the room to be the French child. The person comes in to help the police with their enquiries and it's just '*Comment tu t'appelles*?' and she just asks everybody and again it is really repetitive and boring but for them it's just a game and they just enjoy hearing the same question over and over again.

What else? Anything to do with using all the senses. So, putting things in bags and getting the children to feel them and talk about them so that could be whether it's using adjectives to describe what they feel like or whether it's just using nouns, what the object is. If they learn something like fruits, just a vocabulary set, fruits, not just to look at them but possibly smell them, taste them, put them in little boxes and get them to smell them and identify them that way. So anything to do with all the senses.

Puppets! Puppets for role play. So again, in order to be able to repeat things without getting bored if the children are using finger puppets, they can assume different identities. They can be using essentially the same language but instead of always '*Je m'appelle*' there can be an element of surprise. So when they talk to somebody else in the class it can be: 'Actually, I know what your name is, so what's the point of asking you?' There's the element of finding out what all the puppets are called and that sort of thing.

Interviewer: What about writing? What sort of approach do you think is most effective with that age range?

KK: I do a lot of writing on whiteboards so that the children have an opportunity to easily edit their own work. I think there are some children who are a bit nervous about writing something on a piece of paper that's going to be handed in and marked. They're worried it's not going to be accurate. So I do quite a lot of writing on whiteboards so they know it's temporary. When they're first beginning to write, really just beginning, we do things like writing in the air, writing on people's backs. Not actually writing anything that you can actually see but just getting used to . . . We do quite a lot of phonics work in Year 3 and Year 4, particularly so they get used to the idea that when they spell a word they can't necessarily follow the same rules that they would for English. And then I like to give their writing a purpose if I can, so if I can't get them linked with maybe a school in France where they can actually write to a French child, I like to link them up with another class in England so that at least they are communicating with people they don't know but through the medium of French.

Interviewer: How useful has the KS2 Framework been in the planning of your lessons, if at all?

KK: I think the KS2 Framework for FLs is really good. I think it's more useful for people who haven't got a background in FLs and who haven't done any training to teach a FL because it is definitely all good stuff and I do refer to it quite a lot but it's not something I think . . . I could manage without it but I think for a lot of non-specialist teachers it must be really useful because it must be difficult to know what progression in a language looks like if you have no background. I think there might be a temptation to think 'We'll tie in the French with the topics that we are doing anyway in other subjects', which is a great idea but I think there would be the temptation to just teach loads of nouns, loads of vocabulary. For instance, 'We're teaching space in Year 5, let's teach the planets', without taking it beyond that.

Again, when I'm starting out with my planning I don't use it that much. I use commercial schemes quite a lot and they've already got the Framework objectives written into them but then I stray from those quite a lot and when I'm straying from those and thinking of other ideas I quite often refer to the Framework and say 'Well, does this fit in with the Framework?' And if it does, all well and good, but if it doesn't then I'll quite often do it anyway if I think it's valuable. I think in the introduction to the Framework it says that it is a climbing frame not a cage and I think so as long as you use it in that way I think it's really helpful for guidance rather than feeling constrained by it.

Interviewer: Do you have, for instance, assessment materials, marks or profiles of the Year 6s that you pass on to the Year 7 teachers?

KK: What I do do in the second half of the summer term of Year 6, partly because I think it may be useful for the Secondary schools to get it, but also for my own personal ease of life because the children after SATs have got their sights on Secondary school and so they are not that interested in what goes on in Primary school any more, so what I do with them is what we call a 'Year 6 project'. It's a written project all in French where they write everything they can about themselves, their families, their interests, anything they can write. I don't give them any help with that at all and I say to them 'This is to introduce yourself to a new French teacher. They'll get to know a bit about you as people as they'll get to know what you like and don't like and also they'll get to know a bit about what you can do in French.' So I do it that way and I get them to write the project and I actually think it's quite a good way of doing it because it really does show the difference in what they've achieved and what they can do by the time they go into Year 7. I mean, there are some children who are working at level 4, they're using dictionaries, they've got a good understanding of grammar, they are constructing sentences on their own. And then there are other children who can barely write a sentence. That's really realistic by the end of Year 6 that's really a realistic range of ability. And it needs to be taken account of I think so I get them to do these projects and they put photos in them and stuff and I send them up to the Secondary school. They do get information via that means about what the children can do (but it's all written).

Interviewer: Finally, if you were a Secondary school teacher teaching Year 7 French, how would you cater for your pupils' prior experience of FL learning at Key Stage 2?

KK: It's very difficult and I acknowledge it's very difficult as there is a wide range of children and they won't have had the same experience and they're not all going to achieve the same amount with the same experience. So it's difficult, I appreciate that. But I think if they know at least what's been taught that's one thing and if they've got some idea of which pupils have picked it up quite well and which haven't, then I think they can be at least sensitive at Year 7. I mean, for example, if you're going to teach them certain skills, certain structures then at least put them in different contexts to the ones they've had at Primary school if you can. Because that way, even if you're going over some of the ground, then at least it won't look that way to some of the children because I think I rather suspect that what quite often happens is that over the summer holidays the children forget a lot anyway and during the four years they are at Primary they cover a lot of stuff that they forget because they're not reinforcing it enough and I suspect that over the Year 7 it seems to the Year 7 teachers that they don't know very much because they have forgotten a lot of it or it's just not at the top of their heads, plus they are quite shy because they come to new classes with people they've never met before, new teachers. It probably seems they never knew too much. If at least they know what they've done before, even if they got to go over the same ground as before, it won't seem so bad because it will seem fresher for the children because I do hear quite a lot children saying 'We just do the same things'.

So I think that's important. I think just very often the children won't need very in-depth revision if they've done something in Primary. Quite often in Year 4 I've done something just for a couple of years, we've only got to spend a few minutes on it and they can remember it. I had a trainee from the Secondary school come to observe Primary languages at BG. His comment was that you do all this at Primary school and then when they come to Year 7 we start from scratch and we go through everything a bit too fast and some children can't keep up. So I think if they are aware in the first couple of years they can brush over a few things, and go into depth more quickly, they wouldn't need to rush through Year 8 and Year 9. The balance is wrong. Doing it all again in Year 7 is not necessary.

Task 4.2 **OBSERVATION OF FLs PROVISION AT A PRIMARY SCHOOL**

Arrange for a visit to a Primary school either before or during your period of teacher education.

Find out about the FL teaching that takes place at the school, e.g. factual information such as which FLs are taught and by whom, which pupils are involved, whether this is in curriculum time, and so on.

Observe some FLs lessons, where possible, and note the techniques the teacher uses with this age range. Ask the teachers (those teaching FLs and others, if possible) about their views on the value of FL teaching at their school.

SUMMARY

For the student teacher of FLs the issue of Primary to Secondary school transition may seem daunting with respect to its impact on classroom experience. As we have seen in this chapter, different national education systems have confronted the issue in different ways through the conception of their FLs curricula and through the structure of their schooling system. With the expansion of FLs provision in Primary schools in England, the default option of the 'clean slate' approach to FL teaching, which in the past has been applied by languages teachers in Secondary schools, is no longer acceptable, least of all to the pupils themselves who come with a pre-existing knowledge base. In this context the individual teacher needs to acknowledge the reality of the extent of the Year 7 learners' prior knowledge of the TL and prior experience of formal instruction in the subject and to develop strategies in terms of interaction and formative feedback with individual pupils which take account of that experience. We have also seen that cross-sector transition needs also to be supported at institutional and professional development level to facilitate the individual teacher's management of the learners' experience of progression of FL learning in the first year of Secondary school and beyond.

FURTHER READING

Evans, M. and Fisher, L. (2012) Emergent communities of practice: secondary schools' interaction with primary school foreign language teaching and learning. In *The Language Learning Journal*, 40(2): 157–173.

This paper explores defining features of the process of cross-phase interaction and the role that collaborative practice plays in generating change in perceptions and pedagogical practice of languages teachers in schools in England.

Jones, J. (2010) The role of Assessment for Learning in the management of primary to secondary transition: implications for language teachers. In *The Language Learning Journal*, 38(2): 175–191.

This article reports on a study of KS2–3 transition, drawing on evidence from a group of twelve pupils from two mixed Primary schools in Jersey who were tracked from Y6 through to Y8 at their Secondary school. The paper discusses pupil interview data collected at three stages during this period.

PEDAGOGY
RELATED

5 PEDAGOGICAL APPROACHES

INTRODUCTION

Having considered in Chapter 3 some historical developments in language teaching and key research findings in FLL and SLA, in this chapter we present some of the main pedagogical approaches adopted by FLs teachers. The pedagogical approaches discussed in this chapter come under the banner of Communicative Language Teaching (CLT) or 'non-synthetic' approaches to FL teaching. By non-synthetic we mean approaches that present language in a more *holistic* way, using it to perform communicative tasks, in contrast to synthetic approaches that focus on specific aspects of the language system (e.g. on grammatical structures, functions). The approaches under consideration are Presentation–Practice– Production (PPP), Task-based Learning and Teaching (TBLT), and Content and Language Integrated Learning (CLIL).

First we must ask the fundamental question: 'What is a pedagogical approach?' In our view it is a (more or less) coherent blueprint for teaching and learning that classroom teachers have drawn up explicitly (see Leach and Moon, 2008). This blueprint is not based necessarily on the teacher's own learning experiences, historicity, familiarity, and so on, but rather is derived from principles that might arise out of an understanding of empirical research in the field, out of a teacher's reflection on his or her own work, and reflection on the work of educators in other contexts and other cultures (Leach and Moon, 2008).

We begin by examining features of Communicative Language Teaching, which has, in fact, become rather a cover term for a somewhat eclectic assortment of traditional and novel approaches to FL teaching. The way in which CLT has been interpreted and understood has been the focus of a great deal of recent discussion (see e.g. Pachler, 2000; Spada, 2007; Broady, 2014). As Spada (2007) notes, what it is and how it is interpreted differs from individual to individual. Generally, though, it prioritises the development in pupils of an ability to communicate in the TL, and all agree that CLT is a primarily meaning-based approach. The differences lie in how much attention teachers believe should be paid to language *form* – i.e. to grammar and issues of accuracy.

We consider first a framework for teaching that draws loosely on PPP. This is a common, but not universally accepted, framework for FL teaching (see Pachler,

2000) that presupposes the need to provide pupils with essential language input, followed by work on exercises, activities and tasks to enable them to develop effective language habits. The process can be said to be complete when the pupils are able to use and manipulate the language to satisfy perceived needs, i.e. to generate language themselves.

From this we move on to consider two other pedagogical approaches that sit under the same umbrella of CLT: Task-based Learning and Teaching, and Content and Language Integrated Learning. In task-based learning, lessons are structured around core tasks. There may be some pre-task preparation and post-task evaluation, but the main activity in the classroom is the completion of these tasks, which often aim for 'real-life' applications of language beyond the classroom. TBLT therefore constitutes a form of CLT, where the teacher acts as facilitator and learners are using the language to learn it, rather than learning it to use it.

The term CLIL was coined officially in the EU in 1994 (Coyle *et al.*, 2010) and is a form of content-based language learning. In this approach the teaching of another subject area (e.g. History, Science, Geography) is carried out through the use of a second language, with an equal emphasis on both substantive content of the subject and the FL itself. Some advantages of CLIL might be the higher level of cognitive challenge for learners involved in the study of other disciplines through a FL and the space created in the curriculum for the study of other FLs.

OBJECTIVES

By the end of this chapter you should:

■ have developed some understanding of the methodological underpinning of current FLs practice;
■ have gained awareness of the main tenets of CLT;
■ have familiarised yourself with a framework for developing the main tenet of CLT, communicative competence;
■ have developed an understanding of task-based learning and its possible applications;
■ become familiar with the concept of CLIL and ways in which it might be incorporated into FL classrooms.

COMMUNICATIVE LANGUAGE TEACHING

Traditional approaches to FL teaching focused on 'synthetic' forms of learning and emphasised language structure rather than language use, as we saw in Chapters 1 and 3. In the 1970s with the theory of 'communicative competence' (Hymes, 1971) came the idea that knowing a language involves not just grammatical knowledge. CLT arose out of the great deal of work on developing models that were more wide-ranging and included a focus not just on linguistic competence but also on areas such as sociolinguistic competence (e.g. formal and informal registers) and strategic competence (e.g. using a range of strategies to get meaning across). CLT built on the understanding that the purpose of language is to communicate, and that communication (see Halliday, 1976, as summarised in Richards and Rodgers, 2001: 70–71) is:

- instrumental (to get things);
- regulatory (to control others);
- interactional (to engage with others);
- personal (to express personal meaning);
- heuristic (to learn and discover);
- imaginative (to create a world of imagination);
- representational (to communicate information).

The move towards a more communicative approach to FL learning was reflected in FLs syllabi in the UK, as we discussed in Chapter 1. FL teaching methodology in the UK has been characterised by an emphasis on communicative competence with intercultural communicative competence coming increasingly to the fore. This represented a redefinition and broadening of what was deemed to constitute proficiency in FL learning away from the ability to translate, read and write texts towards an ability to respond, often by way of the spoken word, to aural and oral stimuli. One key feature of CLT is its principal aim of providing pupils with the necessary language and communication skills to use the TL effectively and in a purposeful way. This involves communicating to satisfy personal needs as well as the structuring and sequencing of the learning experience.

With CLT, 'authenticity' of texts and tasks became increasingly important, as did using the TL in 'real' contexts for communicative purposes. The focus was on the ability to use the TL to communicate personal meaning rather than on knowledge about the TL, together with an emphasis on active participation of learners and language use outside the classroom (see Mitchell, 1994; Pachler, 2000). Classroom activities were to maximise opportunities for learners to use the TL for meaningful purposes, with their attention on the messages they are creating and the task they are completing, rather than on correctness of language form and language structure.

In a bid to improve the ability of pupils to communicate in the TL, emphasis has increasingly been placed on the use of the TL for instruction and interaction. As contact with FLs for Secondary school pupils often comes through language learning (the structured and limited exposure to the TL in a classroom environment), rather than acquisition (subconscious development of language skills devoid of formal explanation), the emphasis on TL use and the focus on 'authentic' material can be seen as an attempt to counterbalance the 'context-reduced' (Roberts, 1992: 21) nature of the FL learning process.

A CLT approach implies that FLs teachers need, among other things, to do the following:

- structure the language that pupils are exposed to;
- select relevant, varied, appropriate and, where possible, authentic material for them;
- provide them with ample opportunities to practise and develop, among others, the skills of listening, speaking, reading and writing;

- devise suitable communicative outcomes from their work;
- prioritise the development of a TL-rich environment where the TL is the language of communication;
- facilitate the development of their independence as language learners and confidence in their own ability; and
- develop their cultural and structural understanding.

While CLT has been, and continues to be very influential in FL teaching and learning in the UK, 'it is not the panacea of FL teaching' (for a detailed critical examination of CLT, see Pachler, 2000). CLT was criticised in the UK context mainly for its over-interpretation in the late eighties and nineties, where it was frequently characterised by a marginalisation of grammar in the learning process and a diminishing focus on accuracy. Howatt (1984: 279) usefully notes that CLT has been interpreted in 'strong' and 'weak' versions. The strong version sees language as *acquired* through communication, where a teacher would avoid explicit grammar instruction expecting that the learners will acquire it in an input-rich environment. Strong versions of CLT might mean in practice the virtual absence of any rules or application of grammar, and the supremacy of an (almost) exclusively TL environment where L1 has little or no function. However, the distinction between language acquisition and language learning is important in an FLs context in the Secondary school as pupils are, in the main and for a host of reasons, unable to immerse themselves in the TL and the target culture(s). Hawkins (1987: 99) memorably described the FLs experience of British pupils through the metaphor of 'gardening in a gale' of English. The limited time available in the school curriculum and the limited exposure to the TL make it difficult for pupils to retain what they have learnt in the classroom when re-entering the world of English outside, as what happens there does not usually reinforce the learning that has taken place in the classroom. In this context, strong interpretations of CLT in the FLs classroom, where there is little space for focus on forms for metalinguistic analysis, or for a focus on FLs learning strategies which are increasingly accepted to contribute to better FL learning outcomes, are therefore less likely to yield productive FL learning.

Bearing in mind the criticisms of 'over-interpretation', in the discussion of PPP below we outline a 'weaker' form of CLT that an observer of UK FLs class-rooms today might recognise. At its core is a recognition that the impoverished opportunities for meaningful engagement with the FL outside the classroom means that the classroom itself must be the context for as much meaningful input as possible, including high levels of interaction in the TL.

A FRAMEWORK FOR SEQUENCING: PPP

On the basis of the discussion of aspects of CLT, one way of developing pupil independence through a structured approach to FL learning might be to use a framework for sequencing, summarised in Figure 5.1. The framework we present here builds on the traditional Presentation–Practice–Production paradigm. According to Nunan and Lamb (1996), the PPP model is based on a view of learning as a linear process of understanding, internalising and activating knowledge. At the different stages of the model, the teacher and learners have different roles (e.g. model, facilitator, monitor; listener, performer, interactor) and they feature different activity

Presentation	1 Introducing the topic	Continuous formative assessment
	2 Presenting new language/imitation	
Practice	3 Practising language/focus on form	
Production	4 Exploiting the language: using it 'for real'	
	5 Assessment and evaluation	

■ **Figure 5.1** A framework for sequencing

types (e.g. exposition, information gap, role play) and interaction modes (e.g. whole class, pair, small group). Nunan and Lamb (1996: 46–47) conclude that the PPP model, while simple, is effective and useful for meeting *discrete* language objectives. For more contextualised and integrated objectives, however, more sophisticated models are required.

Drawing on the framework for sequencing, the following sections explain the steps in more depth.

PRESENTATION

Introducing the topic

The introduction of a new topic is important for generating pupil interest and for helping them to understand what they will be learning in the short to medium term – i.e. in this or over a series of lessons. The introduction of a topic can involve the negotiation of appropriate objectives in order to meet individual pupils' needs but should involve making explicit the learning objectives, where possible in the TL. This gives pupils a sense of where they are going and why these activities might be useful. Pupils should be aware of the value of a topic and, on occasion, they can be asked to identify for themselves key language that might be needed. This process of negotiation and discussion enables the teacher to establish her role as a facilitator of the learning process and helps the pupil in adopting an active, participatory role.

One possible strategy that can be adopted when introducing a new topic is what Grell and Grell (1985: 105–106, 117–133) call 'to send positive reciprocal emotions'. In order to foster an atmosphere conducive to learning and to motivate pupils to learn, Grell and Grell suggest the teacher might, for instance, show personal enthusiasm for a given topic and relate it to personal experiences. She might tell the pupils something funny or express positive expectations about what they are about to learn. Visual stimuli relating to the topic might be used to prompt pupil comments and responses. Careful consideration needs to be given to whether and how this can be done using the TL.

One strategy that enables pupils to draw on their existing knowledge of the TL and culture and which can be applied to a number of different contexts is brainstorming (Figure 5.2). Although we do not suggest using brainstorming every time a new topic is introduced, we feel it is a good example of a strategy, which allows future learning to build on existing knowledge – i.e. learning is scaffolded. Again, careful consideration needs to be given to whether and how this is done using the TL.

1   You ask pupils to brainstorm words they associate with the topic in small groups. A nominated scribe notes down all words that group members can come up with. Asking pupils to work within a given time limit can add pace and a sense of urgency.

2   The pupils group their list of lexical items into categories, for instance, buildings, subjects, qualifications, people. Pupils should be encouraged to use the TL and explain contributions to one another.

3   Next you ask the pupils to produce an illustrated guide in the TL on what they feel they ought to know about the topic 'school' for display.

4   Public display of the various guides allows critical analysis of the pupils' work by the teacher through comparison of outcomes of different groups. The emerging gaps in knowledge can be formulated into learning objectives. The teacher's role is to place the content of displays and the learning objectives into a communicative context. This way, through a consolidation of existing knowledge and skills, pupils should be able to experience some sense of ownership of and interest in the topic.

■ **Figure 5.2** Brainstorming on the topic of 'school'

Presenting a new language focus

Having identified objectives and particular linguistic and learning needs, the teacher needs to expose pupils to the language content required. The teacher is the principal (linguistic) resource in the classroom and needs to select and organise the content into manageable chunks to include the teaching and learning of vocabulary, phrases and structures (see Field, 2014, for some more practical examples) and encouraging the development of the skills of listening, speaking, reading and writing within a communicative context. In Chapter 7 we outline in more detail how individual and sequences of lessons might be planned.

The aim at this stage is to begin the process of mastering the linguistic forms so that, at a later stage, pupils can draw on these in real communicative situations for themselves. The presentation stage should be set within a communicative context. Visual aids, such as PowerPoint presentation, Interactive Whiteboard (IWB) activities, video and audio clips, realia, flashcards or mime and gesture can be employed to help learners to assimilate new language. There are numerous reasons for presenting new language in a communicative context, such as the development of pupils' inductive language learning skills (can they work out meaning from context?), the opportunity for working with authentic materials and for developing pupils' cultural learning. Independence in FL learning requires pupils to use dictionaries, reference material and (contextual) clues to interpret meaning. As a consequence, the teacher needs to ensure that pupils have the skills to carry out related tasks.

Pupils need lots of chances to repeat new language. Being able to repeat a word does not necessarily mean they have acquired it. In the light of this you might do the following:

■   Especially at the beginning, make sure you plan for this by explicitly writing the presentation question sequence and repetition strategies into your lesson plan. Think carefully about how you will use definite or indefinite articles, negatives, etc.

■ When presenting language, think about the variety of ways you can repeat and get pupils to imitate new language (e.g. speed, tone/volume of voice, different groupings, different number of times, repeat only if it is correct, etc.).

■ You also need to consider the variety of resources through which you can present language.

■ Consider the variety of questioning strategies you can use from yes/no questions and alternative prompts (e.g. is it a cake or a sandwich?) to more open questions requiring higher-order thinking skills (e.g. why do you think it's like this?)

Task 5.1 **PRESENTING NEW LANGUAGE FORMS**

During lesson observations, note the different resources and methods used by different FLs teachers to introduce new language.

Discuss with pupils to what extent gestures, colours, size, position, voice modulation or movement can help them memorise new language and test out these ideas in your own teaching.

PRACTICE

Practising the language

There is no clear dividing line between the presentation and practice of language forms but, instead, there is a gradual change of emphasis. Practice is one stage in the continuous process of internalising selected language and is, some would argue, the most important phase. Without sufficient practice, pupils will be unable to produce or manipulate new language. It is important to break the language into chunks that are easily accessible, considering what the pupils need to know before they can move on. For example, we cannot assume they can use the third person because they can use the first, or the negative because they can use the affirmative.

Class management problems are often very closely bound up with planning (e.g. lack of clarity or suitability) or practice issues (i.e. pupils do not feel confident about the new language and are, therefore, daunted by the production activity). Repetition exercises can be effective and it is possible for them to be directed by pupils, provided they realise the value of the exercises and can see the ultimate goal (there is great value in emphasising to pupils why a certain activity is valuable in the language learning process; even better if the pupils themselves can identify why a task or activity is of benefit). Class surveys, for example, can allow the repetition of simple questions avoiding the possible boredom arising from having to say the same thing to the same person repeatedly. There are many ways in which such surveys might be carried out. Dependent on the class, it may be most appropriate from a management perspective to limit the survey to a small group of pupils sitting together, whereas in a different class, pupils could select (e.g. ten) pupils to question. The survey can be differentiated by encouraging the inclusion of an additional question of the pupils' own choosing should they wish. For more on classroom management and grouping, see Chapter 14.

Although the skills of listening, speaking, reading and writing can be developed independently of each other, this is not advisable as pupils must understand the need to integrate skills in order to be able to communicate effectively. Not to work towards the integration of skills poses the risk of producing 'walking phrase books' incapable of using language spontaneously and of generating their own language in response to stimuli. Coursebooks often provide effective exercises to allow pupils to practise and to experiment with language. Written exercises must relate to the pupils' need to write and listening exercises must contain the type of language which is comprehensible to them. 'Authentic' texts, or texts made to look 'authentic', provide a link between the classroom and the outside world, FLs learning and its use.

At this stage the teacher might focus on any grammatical forms that are intended as part of the learning goals framed within a communicative context. Having introduced the forms in context, at this stage the teacher might draw pupils' attention to form, asking them to identify features of the form and then to use it.

Task 5.2 **PRACTISING LANGUAGE**

Observe a number of FLs lessons and note the types of activities teachers use to allow pupils to practise language. How valuable did you find these to be? How did the practice activities that the teacher chose to do link to her lesson objectives? What evidence of learning was there? How valuable did pupils find the different activities? Try to ascertain from pupils exactly what they understood to be the purpose of a particular activity.

PRODUCTION

Exploiting the language: using it 'for real'

At the production stage pupils get to use the language they have practised to communicate something 'for real'. Drawing on work carried out in this and in previous lessons, pupils now get to generate their own meanings. For example, a beginners' class has been working on the topic of food and drink. In the production phase they get the chance to communicate genuine opinions on the topic, for example, to discuss their likes and dislikes with a partner, to agree and disagree with one another, to say what they usually eat, and so on.

The production stage differs from the practice stage as at that point pupils were using language that *may* have, but did not necessarily 'belong' to them; they were practising set structures. Now they *use* what they have learned to generate real meanings. This is the stage where learning becomes activated and helps learners see how the language they have been learning is relevant, can be used in numerous situations and can be pertinent to them.

ASSESSMENT

Assessment, which needs to cover the skills of listening, speaking, reading and writing equally, should not only be seen as coming at the end of the learning process but as an integral part; it should, therefore, be both continuous and summative, both assessment of learning and assessment for learning – that is, assessment which incorporates feedback indicating how a learner can improve. Pupils do not progress at the same rate in all four skills and they need to be aware of the progress they make. Diagnostic feedback, i.e. the teacher telling pupils (and the pupils finding out for themselves) what they need to do to improve, is an important part of the learning process. Assessment should serve to motivate and inform pupils, but also inform the teaching process and feed into planning and the evaluation of learning opportunities. Assessment and feedback are central aspects of FL teaching and learning and are discussed in detail in Chapter 15, illustrating how effective assessment can move pupils forward in their learning (see also Barnes and Hunt, 2003; Black and Jones, 2006).

TASK-BASED LEARNING AND TEACHING (TBLT)

With its roots in the 'CLT family' (Spada, 2007), TBLT is another pedagogical approach that has enjoyed a good deal of interest worldwide, although less so in the UK. In TBLT the task is the organising unit of classroom work and these tasks are constructed to allow the learners to solve problems or negotiate meaning to achieve a particular goal. In this way 'tasks provide an organizing focus for the individual components of language (structures, vocabulary, and so on) that students have to learn in order to communicate' (Littlewood, 2004: 324).

What, though, constitutes a task in a TBLT context and how does it differ from other classroom activities or exercises? This is an area of some confusion for teachers and indeed has been an area of some contention for researchers within the field of SLA. One way that researchers have attempted to define a task is by differentiating it from an exercise. Ellis (2003), for example, draws the distinction between the two as being determined by their goals; an exercise is 'synthetic' – i.e. it is primarily form-focused in its goal whereas a task is more holistic and meaning-focused. However, Widdowson (1998) suggests that *meaning* distinguishes the two: whereas exercises are concerned with semantics (the meaning of words and phrases), tasks are concerned with pragmatic meaning (the use of language in context).

Drawing on a number of other authors, Ellis summarises the critical features of a task (2003: 9–10) as follows:

- A task is a *work plan.*
- A task involves a *primary focus on meaning* and will incorporate some form of 'gap' in information that has to be filled.
- A task will reflect real world processes of language use. Task therefore suggests the need for some form of *authenticity.*
- A task may involve any of the *four language skills*. This can be both in writing and speaking, and reading and listening, although often the literature on tasks is concerned purely with productive skills and spoken outcomes in particular.

■   A task engages *cognitive processes*. Ellis argues that there is also a cognitive skills dimension to carrying out tasks, e.g. selecting, reasoning, classifying information.

■   A task has a clearly defined *communicative outcome*.

In short, task-based approaches emphasise the functional sense of language, the goals that people usually have in using language. They might allow for more holistic approaches where the learner can see by trial and error what works, receive feedback as the task is being carried out, work out explanations as to why it succeeds or does not. Because TBLT places emphasis on the practical tasks that a learner is likely to need to be able to achieve using the FL, language use beyond the confines of classroom is stressed. Pupils might, therefore, be better able to see the practical applications of investing time and energy in learning, and this might in turn have some effect on their motivation for engaging with FL learning.

Norris (2011: 580) argues that TBLT draws on the theoretical and empirical basis for good pedagogy and presents a number of advantages of using tasks, such as that TBLT:

■   involves 'real' communication;

■   respects learners' interests and is learner-centred;

■   attends to learners' interlanguage development;

■   is motivating with relevance to applications outside the classroom;

■   offers real outcomes (with tangible success criteria – you get what you ask for outside the classroom);

■   allows for trial and error in the classroom.

While earlier models of task-based learning adopted primarily a strong form of CLT, more recent interpretations of TBLT have made a focus on forms a more integral part of the learning process as we shall see below.

Designing a task-based approach

Setting up a task-based approach in the classroom may be rather demanding on the teacher, requiring careful thought as to how learning goals will be achieved through choice of tasks that must offer all learners the capacity to progress their language learning at a rate suitable for them. Authors have noted a number of elements that most task-based programmes will need to incorporate (see Long and Crookes, 1993 and Long and Norris, 2000). These include:

■   A preliminary needs analysis: what do the language learners in this classroom context need to know? This will include close planning with regard to syllabus requirements.

■   Tasks selection and sequencing: how are tasks to be chosen and ordered?

■   Materials and instruction design: what sort of materials are needed to support the task completion?

■   Teaching: how will the task be introduced? How will different learner needs be catered for?

■   Assessment: how will the learning be assessed?

■   Programme evaluation: how will the success of the task-based learning be evaluated?

Once the teacher has a medium-term plan in place, the lessons themselves need to be designed. Ellis (2003) notes that all designs put forward for structuring lessons around tasks have in common three principal phases. These are the *pre-task phase,* the *during task phase* and the *post-task phase*, although he notes that only the during task phase is obligatory. Drawing on Ellis's summary we consider the main components of each phase below.

Pre-task phase

This will involve setting up the task, explaining its purpose and importance, and generally getting pupils motivated to carry out the task. As in the PPP model we discussed earlier, the teacher may want to start by trying to reduce the cognitive or linguistic demands on the learner by brainstorming and revising language the learners may already know or by predicting language they may need to use. In terms of planning for carrying out the task, the teacher will need to consider, based on his/her knowledge of the learners, whether the students can work out what to do independently or whether the task should be more tightly structured for them. In this pre-task phase the teacher might provide some input, modelling what the task outcome might look like (e.g. modelling a role play). The learner can at this stage start to notice gaps in what they can and cannot currently do.

During task phase

As in any teaching situation, the teacher will have a number of *pedagogical decisions* to take as the task completion progresses. Are the pupils making progress? Do they need more support or can I withdraw some of the support materials once they can be more independent? How much time do I give them at this point? Should there be time limits? Ellis (2003) notes that there is some evidence that allowing more time for learners to complete the task increases complexity and accuracy of the outcome, although fluency might be enhanced with stricter time limits.

Post-task phase

There are a number of activities that teachers might want to do to 'debrief' the task. Ellis (2003) offers three main categories: repeat performance; reflecting on the task; and focusing on forms.

Repeat performance: this might be useful as there is some evidence that performance, particularly fluency and complexity, is improved the second time around.

Reflecting on the task: as a key component of Assessment for Learning teachers might encourage learners to reflect on and evaluate their own and others' performance. They could consider the decisions they took in completing the task and evaluate these in terms of effectiveness and work out what they would do differently next time in order to improve.

Focus on forms: it is in the post-task phase of TBLT that most commentators advise focusing on grammar and structures so that the task phase itself remains primarily concerned with developing fluency and communication strategies.

In summary, TBLT requires commitment and careful planning by the teacher. As Norris notes (2011: 585):

> It should be clear that much more goes on in the task-based classroom than simply turning learners loose on tasks (or vice versa). Teachers play an essential role throughout the task lesson cycle, motivating, schematising, scaffolding, monitoring, intervening, and so on.

TBLT AND PPP

How, then, does TBLT differ from the PPP model presented in the previous section? Ellis (2003) notes that tasks in PPP are used to *support* the learning in the 'production' stage, whereas in TBLT, the tasks are the basis of the entire curriculum. TBLT might be said to be PPP in reverse (see Skehan, 1996 and Klapper, 2003), where the final stage, pupils' use of the language 'for real', is the starting point for TBLT. Some questions remain over how practical TBLT really is. Researchers have questioned whether TBLT is actually suitable for the beginner and early stages of language learning as would be seen in a Secondary school classroom, being more suited to more advanced and adult settings (see Bruton, 2005). In addition, the emphasis usually being on one skill (often speaking) does not work for teachers who have to offer integrated course on all four skills, and is difficult to manage constructively in terms of language development.

Despite these reservations about its application at beginner level, teachers are experimenting variously with task-based learning to try to achieve particular goals. Newly qualified teacher Habi O'Grady was keen to discover whether she could improve the motivation of her Year 8 French group using a TBLT approach to their work.

Habi explains how she used a task-based approach:

> Right from the beginning of term I altered the prior departmental SoW, so that instead of the familiar scaffold based on the PPP (Presentation–Practice–Production) sequence that pupils were used to, I introduced a new way of delivering the language with less teacher control. The TBLT programme focused on developing motivating and enthusing goal-orientated tasks, with good levels of peer-interaction and collaborative working. Tasks were planned and structured in order to give maximum chances of successful completion of the task and also give scope for initiative, inventiveness and metalinguistic thinking.

An example of one task:

Le chef de rayon (carousel activity)

Situation: *Vous êtes chefs de rayon d'un grand supermarché. Vous voulez créer un rayon continental européen. Avant de commander des produits français, vous goutez les produits et vous décidez en groupe si vous acceptez les produits ou si vous refusez les produits.*

Resources:

a)   *liste des 7 produits acceptés ou refusés +*
b)   *prix Feuille de vocabulaire positif + négatif*
c)   *Feuille de vocabulaire pourquoi? parce que . . .+ raisons*
d)   *Bon de commande individuel*
e)   *Cahier, stylo, Calculatrice*
f)   *Dictionnaire*

Actions:

1   *En groupe: Vous mangez un croissant, un mini pain au chocolat, une tranche de brioche, une madeleine, de la baguette et du brie (excepté le foie gras).*
2   *En groupe: Vous acceptez ou vous refusez le produit. Vous expliquez pourquoi.*
3   *Finalement, vous remplissez le bon de commande. Vous calculez les quantités de produits que vous voulez pour le magasin et le prix total.*

All tasks had to be completed in the TL. Tasks that were completed were considered as successful regardless of the language accuracy so long as the task goal was reached. Information was obtained orally and always recorded in writing in their exercise books or on a worksheet to allow for task appraisal. The language or results produced were marked (with a focus on both form and meaning) and I provided feedback to help learners improve.

Pupils worked in groups of three and, at first, saw group work as an opportunity to chat. It was important for me to 'train' pupils using the reward or sanction approach as a way of avoiding the frustration of having them idling their time during the task, which was longer than anything they were used to previously. Encouraging the pupils to work collaboratively, though, helped to make them aware of their knowledge gaps and to address these gaps together. It was equally important to put pupils in situations where they had to activate their existing linguistic knowledge to cope with the tasks requirements together.

All this meant that lessons switched from a teacher-controlled structure to a pupil–pupil interactive approach. The language scaffolding was gradually removed to allow pupils to work together and scaffold the language learning process themselves. The risk in asking learners to complete a task without prior teacher scaffolding is that it could have destabilised their confidence, inhibited their intrinsic engagement and the quality of the peer interaction process needed in completing the task. However, this didn't seem to happen as I monitored what they were doing closely, encouraged them to ask for help when needed and praised their efforts generously. In fact, they became more self-reliant and sorted out issues and problems for themselves, though did seem more willing to ask language-related questions than in the usual teaching environment.

The authenticity of the task seemed to stimulate the pupils' interest and engagement as the situation resembled a real-life situation and pupils were becoming aware that they need to be able to cope with and solve problems that are pertinent to real-life contexts and situations.

The pupils' response when they were asked how they felt about it afterwards was enthusiastic: 'it seems more meaningful because sometimes in lessons you think that this is never going to help you in life but when you're in a real life situation you think that could happen'; 'you use your brain to work it out'; 'you feel like proud'.

As Habi's example demonstrates, TBLT, even at beginners' level, may have mileage as a pedagogy that develops learner independence, engages interest and develops a range of skills such as problem-solving. It needs, however, a good deal of planning and preparation on the teacher's part and a willingness to adopt a more pupil-centred methodology.

CONTENT AND LANGUAGE INTEGRATED LEARNING (CLIL)

A good deal of interest both in the UK and internationally has been generated by the final pedagogical approach, CLIL, which also sits under the umbrella of CLT. The term CLIL, which has come to be used widely in Europe since the 1990s, is in many ways not completely new, being closely related to bilingual education and immersion programmes. The novel aspect of CLIL is its equal focus both on the substantive content that is being delivered through the medium of the foreign language, and on the learning of the language itself. Coyle *et al.* (2010: 1) define CLIL as:

> a dual-focused educational approach in which an additional language is used for the learning and teaching of both content and language. That is, in the teaching and learning process, there is a focus not only on content, and not only on language. Each is interwoven, even if the emphasis is greater on one or the other at a given time.

As Coyle *et al.* (2010) point out, education in a language that is not the first language of the learner goes back centuries with, for example, the Romans educating their children in Greek. However, in its dual focus on both language and content, CLIL differs from content-based forms of education that concentrate on the subject instruction only. For example, a foreign language teacher might co-plan a unit of work with a geography teacher on the topic of rivers. The substantive content knowledge might be to learn about erosion, while the language learning objectives might be the production a piece of extended writing in the TL on the advantages and disadvantages of living near rivers, with a focus on a particular linguistic feature such as negative forms/use of modal verbs. There is, however, great diversity in the ways teachers and departments might adopt CLIL, which we explore later in this section. If we refer back to some of the aims of CLT outlined earlier in this chapter, it is clear why CLIL might be attractive to languages teachers. CLIL seems, in theory, to have the potential to take forward some of CLT's aims, especially where authenticity is concerned, as it involves learners using language for meaningful purposes, in this case *using* the target language to learn about another subject.

Why is CLIL attractive to FLs teachers?

Language teachers recognise that there is often a fairly big discrepancy between the learners' cognitive levels and the level of their target language. Because they are unable to operate linguistically at a level of high cognitive demand (e.g. in analysing and evaluating information), as FLs teachers we often ask students to perform tasks that require very little in the way of intellectual demand (e.g. recognising, copying, writing descriptively). By engaging with CLIL approaches, learners can be stretched appropriately both in terms of their language learning and engagement with content. In an attempt to conceptualise a framework for the advantages that might arise from introducing CLIL into the curriculum, Coyle *et al.* (2009: 13) assert the following benefits:

CONTENT

- CLIL provides contexts relevant to learners' needs and interests.
- CLIL allows for integration of language into a broader curriculum.
- CLIL can be explicitly linked to literacy joining first and second language and EAL.

COGNITION

- CLIL promotes learner progression in both language skills and knowledge construction.
- CLIL helps to redefine the curriculum sharpening the focus on the interconnections between cognition and communication.
- CLIL accelerates creativity in taking independent control of language using – this process leads to refining thinking and applying skills.

COMMUNICATION

- CLIL involves using language in the here and now to construct new knowledge and skills.
- CLIL offers direct opportunities to learn through language and to make meanings that matter.
- CLIL offers genuine opportunities to interact face-to-face and through the use of new technologies – e.g. the Internet, video-conferencing, international projects.

CULTURE

- CLIL is particularly relevant in classrooms where learners bring diverse language and cultural experiences.
- CLIL is an appropriate vehicle for exploring the links between language and cultural identity, examining behaviours, attitudes and values.
- CLIL involves contexts and content which enrich the learners' understanding of their own culture and those of others.
- CLIL strengthens intercultural understanding and promotes global citizenship.

The authors note that while these 4Cs can be outlined individually, each element does not exist separately and planning requires making connections between them (Coyle *et al.*, 2009).

At present there is not a great deal of empirical evidence as to CLIL's outcome on learning (though there is a lot of reported benefit from schools that have adopted CLIL approaches; see Coyle *et al.*, 2009 for more detail). Dalton-Puffer (2011) points out that the ability to get messages across despite limited language resources, or strategic competence, is strong in CLIL students. There were still, she notes, some students in traditional FLs classes who did very well. Where CLIL classes seem to show benefits is in generating

> a significantly broader band of students just below the top level. In other words, people with special language-learning aptitude may reach high proficiency levels via traditional foreign language classes, but CLIL significantly enhances the language skills of a broad group of students whose foreign language talents or interests are average.
>
> (Dalton-Puffer, 2011: 187–188)

Planning for effective CLIL learning

According to Coyle *et al.* (2010: 21–22), there are a number of models for introducing CLIL, such as:

- dual-school education, where some classes are taught at schools abroad and technology is used to communicate;
- bilingual education where learners study a significant part of the curriculum through the medium of a second language;
- interdisciplinary modules where learners engage in a cross-curricular module are taught in the second language and involving teachers from different disciplines;
- language-based projects which differ from the interdisciplinary module as the language teacher takes primary responsibility for the delivery. Learners view it as part of language teaching but see it as an authentic way of using language to learn non-language content.

The most commonly introduced models from this list tend to be the interdisciplinary model and language-based projects. The former requires subject area specialists (e.g. history, geography or science teachers) to work closely with FLs teachers to determine what is to be taught.

Given the dual focus on offering learners appropriate challenge in both content and language, CLIL requires very careful planning. Planning to incorporate the 4Cs in two different areas requires a very sophisticated syllabus and skilled teacher. Coyle *et al.* (2010) suggest constructing a mind map consisting of all the elements that need to be included before attempting to translate this into activities with accompanying materials.

Coyle *et al.* (2010: 19–20) also note some concerns that may be raised about CLIL. Teachers may have concerns that the curriculum is 'dumbed down'. The amount of planning necessary might not happen. Non-specialists may end up teaching a subject that they have no training in. If, for example, the FLs teacher teaches history, do they have the necessary training in this discipline to teach it effectively? If the history specialist is teaching, do they have enough language to allow for a focus on this? In practice it would seem that in the secondary area it is mainly the FLs teacher that would take responsibility for the delivery of the CLIL lessons. Assessment also needs careful consideration: what is to be assessed and how? There are also issues about operating in the L2 exclusively when there are reasons why it might be beneficial to draw on learners' L1 at some points and so this would have to be considered carefully.

Some UK teachers are developing their own modules of work that have a CLIL focus. One such teacher was Ronak Punjabi, a student teacher at Cambridge in 2010–2011, who was nicknamed 'evangeli-clil' by his school-based mentor due to his enthusiasm for all things CLIL. Ronak decided to devise a medium-term scheme of work for his Year 10 Spanish group on the topic of healthy eating in collaboration with his placement school's technology department. Here he describes how he decided to work with the technology department and his planning for teaching a sequence of lessons:

> I focused on how language lessons in the Scheme of Work could be adapted so that the grammar and target lexis was maintained but taught within a context that was more cognitively challenging for the students. The next main topic on the SoW was 'Food and drink as aspects of culture and health'. The obvious subject on the National Curriculum to draw content from was Food Technology. I set up a meeting with the head of Food Technology at my placement school to discuss what sort of content I could teach to my Spanish class and to ensure adequate subject knowledge on my part. There was a significant overlap between 'The advantages and disadvantages of different diets' from the Spanish Scheme of Work and the module on nutrition in GCSE Food Technology. The technology teacher was able to provide her teaching resources and we discussed her typical lesson plans for delivering such materials. My task was then to translate these authentic materials into Spanish and consider how to use them so as to develop students' understanding of nutrition.
>
> I devised a module of work focused on: the foods that various groups of people (e.g. the elderly, teenagers, religious groups) should eat; the role of vitamins and minerals in preventing conditions such as anaemia; producing healthy food (we made guacamole in class from an authentic recipe). This was devised in conjunction with the key grammar, here modal verbs, e.g. the construction 'deben + infinitive' ('deben comer') and the vocabulary of foodstuffs.
>
> In evaluating the project I noted that students said that the CLIL intervention allowed them to build on their general knowledge: student M enjoyed learning 'about the different religions as well and why the Muslims only ate . . . that Halal meat, . . . 'cause it's just improving your general knowledge as well'. There were motivational aspects too where students felt that studying the subject in a foreign language 'makes you feel smart'.

SUMMARY

CLT encompasses a number of different approaches to FL teaching, aiming ultimately to develop independent communication by the pupil. CLT is a methodological framework and a teacher needs to determine his/her own teaching style within it, according to personal and contextual factors. Outcomes differ according to the interests of pupils, their backgrounds, their motivation, their perception of themselves and, of course, their abilities.

The pedagogical approach adopted by most teachers in the UK seems to be one of a 'weak' version of CLT, where lessons generally follow a Presentation–Practice–Production structure, with some focus on forms and some metalinguistic or strategy-based classroom work on issues such as how to learn vocabulary. A number of questions still remain, such as what the role is of grammar in such a framework, which we consider in Chapter 11, and whether the L1 constitutes a resource that might be drawn upon in the communicative classroom, which we consider in Chapter 8.

PPP is generally accepted to be a more teacher-centred pedagogy, as is CLIL, where teaching of the substantive subject area such as history or science is carried out through the TL with an equal focus on the learning of both. TBLT, where teachers devise tasks that require pupils to work towards goals, solving problems, usually in a co-ordinated effort with classmates, is by comparison more pupil-centred. Of course, teachers do not necessarily need to stick to one pedagogical approach only. As Broady (2014) rightly reminds us, teachers encounter in their classrooms a range of *individuals*, with varying interests, preferences, motivations and needs. There simply is no one approach that will suit everyone. Increasing interest across Europe and the rest of the world in CLIL and TBLT approaches and in developing skills such as critical thinking and team work has led to consideration of alternative pedagogical approaches that might complement a teacher's practice with certain groups at certain times to fulfil certain goals, for instance in offering challenge for more able students or in improving motivation.

FURTHER READING

Pachler, N. (2000) Re-examining Communicative Language Teaching. In Field, K. (ed.) *Issues in Modern Foreign Language Teaching*. London: RoutledgeFalmer, pp. 26–41.
This chapter explores the issues surrounding the key features of communicative language teaching and their interpretation and implementation.

Coyle, D., Hood, P. and Marsh, D. (2010) *CLIL: Content and Language Integrated Learning*. Cambridge: Cambridge University Press.
This book provides an excellent overview of CLIL as an approach, with practical advice on incorporating CLIL in languages classroom teaching.

Ellis, R. (2003) *Task-based Language Learning and Teaching.* Oxford: Oxford University Press.
A thorough handbook on task-based learning which offers a comprehensive overview of the theory and practice of TBLLT.

CHAPTER

6

THE ROLE OF DIGITAL TECHNOLOGIES

INTRODUCTION

For many years now, the use of technology has had a meaningful role to play in FLs classrooms. Where it tended to be mainly traditional writing and reading tools such as coursebooks, tape recorders, overhead projectors (OHPs), and TV and video recorders, there is now a plethora of digital technologies including (portable) computers and mobile devices (including tablets), which have become an integral part of the resource ecology of the FLs classroom. The distinction between 'traditional' and 'digital' technologies is, of course, in many ways artificial and flawed. For example, TV and video are increasingly available digitally and the OHP has been replaced by visualisers in FLs classrooms for many years. And an even older technology, the board, is increasingly being replaced by large displays linked via a data-projector to a computer, the so-called interactive whiteboards. Also, computer-assisted language learning applications (CALL) have largely been replaced by apps on mobile devices. Therefore, the field is characterised as much by 'evolution' as it is by 'revolution'. In this chapter we will use the terms 'digital technologies' and 'educational technologies' and we will do so relatively interchangeably as the latter term for us not only comprises technologies specifically developed for educational purposes, but also the use of any technology for such purposes.

The world of communication, a central concern for FLs teachers, is experiencing something akin to a 'revolution': as Kress (2010b: 6), for example, draws attention to in his writing about multimodality, texts are changing radically in terms of form and function both in relation to productive and receptive domains. He sees writing/text production affected by the following four factors:

1   Texts are becoming intensely multimodal, that is, image is ever-increasingly appearing with writing, and, in many domains of communication, displacing writing where it had previously been dominant.
2   Screens (of the digital media) are replacing the page and the book as the dominant media.
3   Social structures and social relations are undergoing fundamental changes, as far as writing is concerned, predominantly in changes of structures of authority.

137

4   Constellations of mode and medium are being transformed. The medium of the book and the mode of writing had formed a centuries-long symbiotic constellation; this is being displaced by a new constellation of medium of the screen and mode of image. The consequences of this shift are profound.

At the level of the text, we argue (see e.g. Pachler *et al.*, 2010), that they are increasingly open, rather than fixed, subject to constant modifications and comprise different modalities to be contextualised and recontextualised according to specific situational requirements.

As FLs teachers we have to consider the implications of these factors on our understanding of, and approaches to, texts and the associated skills of reading and writing or text reception and production. What impact do digital technologies have on language itself and on language in use and how do we respond to them in our FL teaching?

Task 6.1 A 'REVOLUTION' IN COMMUNICATION

Consider the notion of a 'revolution in communication' (Kress, 2010a: 6). Do you agree?

Reflect on your personal acts of text reception and production. What role do digital technologies play in them?

In a second step, engage your pupils in a discussion about their literacy practices: what use do they make of digital technologies in their everyday lifeworlds?

Finally, consider the implications of your findings for your teaching.

The term 'multimedia' refers to the use of teaching resources involving different presentational formats that engage the learner in a range of cognitive processing activities: listening, viewing, reading, speaking and writing. Digital technologies have made possible greater interaction between the different sensory systems and between the different systems of representation during the process of learning. The educational psychologist Mayer (2001: 46) has argued that 'humans possess separate processing channels for visually represented material and auditory represented material'. The term 'multimodality', therefore, refers to the learner's use of different senses during the learning process. Mayer's empirical studies have led to him to formulate three key 'assumptions' of a cognitive view of the way learners best assimilate multimedia information.

ACTIVE PROCESSING ASSUMPTION

Learners actively process input in three stages:

- selecting relevant material;
- organising the material;
- integrating the material with prior knowledge.

Spatial contiguity principle: 'Students learn better when corresponding words and pictures are presented near rather than far from each other on the page or screen' (Mayer, 2001: 81).

Temporal contiguity principle: 'Students learn better when corresponding words and pictures are presented simultaneously rather than successively' (Mayer, 2001: 96).

DUAL CHANNEL ASSUMPTION

Humans process visually represented and auditory represented information separately.

Learners learn better from words and pictures than from words alone.

LIMITED CAPACITY ASSUMPTION

Multimedia input should exclude redundant information (i.e. interesting but irrelevant information).

In the context of FL education, this theoretical framework has been most frequently researched with reference to the potential benefits of subtitles (onscreen text in the L1) and captions (onscreen text in the TL) on vocabulary acquisition and comprehension accompanying video material. For instance, Guichon and McLornan (2008) report on a pilot study of the impact of multimodality on the comprehension performance of French undergraduate students of English. Participants were divided into four groups in relation to their processing of a three-minute BBC news report: 1) sound alone; 2) image and sound; 3) image, sound and captions in English; 4) image, sound and subtitles in French. The researchers found that the third group reproduced the largest percentage of correct information when asked to produce a detailed written summary after viewing the report. Similarly, Lwo and Chia-Tzu Lin (2012) applied Mayer's framework in their study of the effects of captions on the multimedia processing of junior high school Chinese learners of English as a FL. Four groups of pupils viewed an animation with English narration under different conditions: no captions; Chinese subtitles; English captions; and Chinese subtitles + English captions. The viewing was followed by tests of vocabulary and comprehension. In contrast with Guichon and McLornan, and others, Lwo and Chia-Tzu Lin did not find a significant difference in results on the basis of the different modalities. They did, however, find a difference in performance based on the pupils' level of proficiency in English and in the nature of the test activity. For instance, they conclude that the higher attainers performed better in the no captions condition and that the lower attainers seemed to find 'English or Chinese + English captions was helpful for comprehending simple sentence structures; with complex structures only Chinese + English captions had a positive effect on the correct repetition of the sentences' (2012: 204).

In recent years there has been a significant growth in online learning, which is outside the scope of this chapter. Here we focus mainly on educational technologies that support face-to-face FL teaching and learning. If you are interested in all aspects of technology-enhanced FL learning, see e.g. *Language Learning & Technology* (www.llt.msu.edu). If you are keen on keeping up with new developments in digital technologies more widely, you are encouraged to visit the webpages of the EDUCAUSE Learning Initiative (www.educause.edu/eli), in particular the '7 Things You Should Know About' series of briefing sheets (www. bit.ly/7-things-you-should-know). In addition, you should read the annual K-12 Edition of the Horizon Report published by the New Media Consortium jointly with EDUCAUSE available at www.nmc.org/publications/2013-horizon-report-k12. For a discussion of digital technologies in FL teaching and learning, see also Strasser and Pachler, 2014.

OBJECTIVES

By the end of this chapter you should:

■ understand the rationale behind the use of educational technologies in FL teaching and learning and how they can contribute to achieving FL learning objectives;

■ understand the potential and some of the characteristics of digital technologies and how to exploit them;

■ be able to make decisions about when, when not and how to use them in your FL teaching;

■ be able to evaluate some key applications and their contribution to FL teaching and learning.

DIGITAL TECHNOLOGIES IN FLs: AN OVERVIEW

Figure 6.1, created in the mind-mapping package Inspiration®8, attempts to provide a rough conceptual overview of digital technologies and FLs in classroom contexts. Please note that it does not seek to be comprehensive.

Roughly speaking, technology can be seen to support teaching as well as learning by virtue of its characteristics and potential, what the literature calls afford-ances, as well as the applications and tools designed and programmed to exploit them. Rather than adopt a skills-based approach, this chapter focuses on the dimension of applications and tools, and examines some in terms of their relative merits for teaching and learning in general, and for FL teaching and learning in particular.

Technologies are being used to enrich pupils' FL learning experience and have allowed learners to practise language skills independently according to need. A wide range of tools and resources exists, too numerous to list or discuss in any detail here.

Early applications tended to be computer-based rather than web-based and to follow a behaviourist, drill-practice paradigm. Simple text manipulation pro-grams and exercise generators remain popular; examples include Hot Potatoes (www.hotpot.uvic.ca) and web-based applications such as Quia (www.quia.com).

Text manipulation software allows pupils to make changes to previously written text. Hewer (1997: 2), for example, distinguishes the following types of activities:

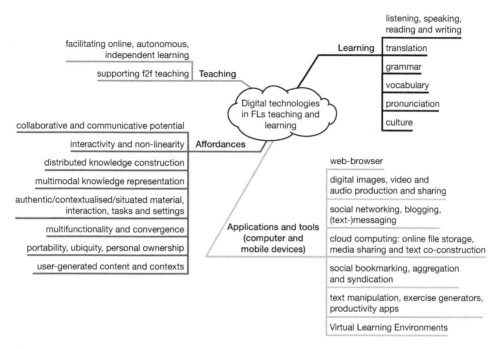

■ **Figure 6.1** Digital technologies in FLs teaching and learning

---

Task 6.2 **EXPLORING TOOLS AND RESOURCES**

Familiarise yourself with the range of tools and resources tagged on a popular social bookmarking service called Diigo by one of the authors. These lists are regularly updated:

www.bit.ly/tools-tag
www.bit.ly/resources-tag

- ■ sequencing words, sentences and/or paragraphs;
- ■ replacing existing words;
- ■ inserting additional words;
- ■ gap filling, including cloze tests;
- ■ unscrambling words or chunks of text;
- ■ reconstructing a text in part or in its entirety.

She (p. 12) deems text manipulation to have the potential to produce tasks that:

- ■ improve (pupils') knowledge of structure;
- ■ improve their knowledge of form;

- apply and improve their knowledge of collocation;
- consolidate and improve their vocabulary;
- consolidate and improve their spelling and punctuation.

The same applies to developments in digital audio and video. Programs such as Audacity (www.audacity.sourceforge.net) or Pocket Voice Recorder (www.xemico.com/pvr) as well as various digital video (DV) editing packages such as Movie Maker or iMovie allow for the straightforward production of DV artefacts by teachers and/or learners (see Burn and Durran, 2013) and online photo- and video-sharing services such as Flickr (www.flickr.com) and Picasa (www.picasa.google.com) or YouTube (www.youtube.com) and Vimeo (www.vimeo.com) allow users to post and access a huge range of visual material that can be exploited for language and culture learning in creative ways. There are also many mobile apps offering audio and/or video recording and editing functionality. Importantly, care needs to be taken that copyright issues are taken into account and only images that are copyright free, often published under a Creative Commons licence (see www.creativecommons.org), are used.

Technologies can give learners access to a range of resources in the TL and enable them to find out about how people of TL communities speak and live. Proponents of the social-interactionist view of FL learning (that is, through social interaction in the TL with others) stress the importance of technology as a tool for communication. In an interesting review of research on networked language learning, Kern *et al*. (2004) discuss what is currently known in the field with particular reference to linguistic interaction and development, intercultural awareness and learning, and the development of multiliteracies and identity. They point out that online communication does not necessarily lead to more complex FL production, that cross-cultural and intercultural understanding does not automatically result from online communication and that connectivity does not necessarily translate into learning. Among other things, the role of pedagogical mediation or 'orchestration', as it is frequently called in the literature – that is, managing the complex interrelationship of variables impacting on, and influencing learning, is important. They also report research by Kramsch and Thorne (2002) who argue that it is not linguistic misunderstanding but a clash in cultural frames and communicative genres that impede learners, and that demands on communicative competence and negotiation may be different on the Internet. Furthermore, they refer to Thorne (2003) who points out that communicative practices are 'tightly bound to the materiality of the medium' through so-called 'cultures of use', i.e. differences in the norms, attributes and use of applications, programs and tools across generations, social groups, interest groups, national groups, professional groups, etc. With reference to various pieces of work by Warschauer and Lam, Kern *et al*. (2004: 254) draw several conclusions for language pedagogy and research from their literature review:

> First, because language learners do not just speak a language (a standard singularity) but speak from particular social positions (a plurality), teachers and researchers should be less concerned with learners' conformity to standard language norms in their online language use and more concerned with how well learners can use all their available linguistic, cognitive, and social resources to negotiate the linguistic, interactional, and cultural demands of

online discourse. Second, what is important about language and literacy development on the Internet is not just the ability to read and write in comprehensible language, but also the ability to negotiate new roles and identities.

Socialization and identity construction can have either a facilitating or restrictive effect on language and literacy development, depending in part on whether instructors encourage learners to participate as creative producers of new media and as agents of purposeful communication and action.

In short, they posit that technology-enhanced FL learning and teaching is less about teaching 'old things in new ways' but instead about '(helping) students enter into a new realm of collaborative inquiry and construction of knowledge, viewing their expanding repertoire of identities and communication strategies as resources in the process'.

(Kern *et al.*, 2004: 254)

Technology-enhanced or -mediated FL learning, therefore, needs to be seen as a highly complex endeavor.

PERSONAL DIGITAL LITERACY AND EFFECTIVE PEDAGOGICAL PRACTICE

It is important to stress that the effectiveness of technology in supporting FL teaching is linked to your own personal digital literacy as well as that of your learners. Given the rapid developments in the field of educational technology as well as the proliferation of available resources, it is important to keep abreast of recent developments.

Task 6.3 USING THE WEB AS A PROFESSIONAL DEVELOPMENT TOOL

One effective way of developing personal digital literacy is by following blogs in the field of educational technology and language education. We recommend you do so by setting up an RSS feed reader and by subscribing to some interesting blogs. For information about RSS feeds, see e.g. www.elearningstuff.net/2009/06/10/a-guide-to-rss or www.freetech4teachers.com/2011/03/rss-or-how-do-you-keep-up-with-all-of.html.

To get you started, we suggest you have a look at the following blogs:

www.freetech4teachers.com
www.daily-english-activities.blogspot.co.uk

Another useful resource is the newsletter produced by Jürgen Wagner at the Landesinstitut für Pädagogik und Medien available at: www.wagner-juergen.de.

Task 6.4 **THE DIGITAL LITERACIES OF PUPILS**

Talk to relevant colleagues at your school. Find out what digital literacy pupils are expected to develop between the ages of 11 and 16.

Then consider how their digital literacy relates to the scheme of work of the FLs department at your school across different year groups and how their FL learning can contribute.

In a study commissioned by BECTA, the former quango responsible for supporting the education sector in making effective use of educational technologies, Cox and Webb (2004: 6–7), who use the term ICT to refer to educational technologies, identify the following as being central to effective technology-related pedagogical practice:

- Teachers need to understand the relationship between a range of ICT resources and the concepts, processes and skills in their subjects.
- Teachers need to use their subject expertise to obtain and select appropriate ICT resources that will help them meet the learning objectives of a particular lesson.
- Teachers need knowledge of the potential of ICT resources, not only in terms of their contribution to pupils' presentation skills but in terms of their facilities for challenging pupils' thinking and extending pupils' learning in a subject.
- Teachers need confidence in using a range of ICT resources, which can only be achieved through frequent practice.
- Teachers need to understand that some uses of ICT will change the nature and representations of knowledge and the way the subject is presented to and engages the pupils.
- Teachers need expertise in organising pupils when using ICT resources within the class – understanding when pupils should work on their own, how working in pairs and groups should be organised, and when to use ICT for whole-class teaching.
- Teachers need to know how to prepare and plan lessons where ICT is used so that lessons challenge pupils' understanding and promote reflection and thinking.
- Teachers need to know which kinds of class organisation will be most effective for the learning tasks, e.g. individual/pair/group work or a whole-class presentation.

In a large number of schools Virtual Learning Environments (VLEs) are available for use by teachers and pupils. The extent and quality of VLE use across the board varies. VLEs, whether commercial or open source (e.g. Moodle (www.moodle.org) or Edmodo (www.edmodo.com) tend to have similar features, but they can differ significantly in relation to their orientation to openness of content: are users being locked into the content provided within the system or is the system open? This can be significant for you once you have started a process of online 'curation' (see

---

Task 6.5 **EFFECTIVE TECHNOLOGY-RELATED PEDAGOGICAL PRACTICE**

Carry out a self-assessment in relation to the issues identified by Cox and Webb (2004): on a scale of 1–5, with 1 being 'very good' and 5 being 'not at all', rate your personal state of readiness. Where do you need to improve?

Task 6.6 **KEEPING A PERSONAL ELECTRONIC PORTFOLIO**

Keep a personal electronic portfolio relating in particular to the technology-enhanced aspects of your pedagogical practice throughout your period of study on your teaching programme. Here are some questions against which you may wish to collect evidence in your portfolio:

■ What technology-related skills did I have at the start of the course?
■ What have I learnt about educational technology and what technical and pedagogical skills have I developed?
■ How have I used educational technology during the course?
■ How have my pupils benefited?
■ How have I used educational technology for my personal professional and linguistic development?
■ What have I learnt about when educational technology is (not) appropriate?

Your evidence might comprise the following documents:

■ resources tagged on a social bookmarking site with annotations how they can be and/or were used for teaching;
■ lesson plans featuring educational technology use and their evaluation;
■ evaluations of resources, tools, apps and other web-based material;
■ personal technology skills audit;
■ logs of personal technology use, e.g. a personal blog;
■ reflection tasks;
■ handouts, Web-based worksheets, printouts, annotated background readings;
■ resources you have developed throughout the year;
■ pupils' work.

---

e.g. Wong and Looi, 2010): will the resources you create be portable to another system or service should the need arise or will you have to start from scratch?

A VLE provides an integrated environment giving access to the following: communication facilities such as chat rooms, blogs, bulletin boards; pedagogical facilities such as course modules, online assessment and marking; learning facilities such as independent access to online resources and links to useful language learning sites. As a school facility, a VLE can also support homework learning for pupils, support follow-up activities to supplement work done in the languages classroom and develop pupils' independent language learning skills.

One popular tool for FLs writing are so-called Wikis, websites allowing shared multimodal content and knowledge creation; they lend themselves very well to collaborative project work and asynchronous communication, provided users are comfortable with the notion of shared authoring and editing. Google Drive (www.drive.google.com) is a widely used collaborative knowledge creation and document-sharing tool. For detailed advice on its use for educational purposes, see the guide by Richard Byrne at www.scribd.com/mobile/doc/92629651. One important issue to explore with learners in relation to the use of such cloud computing services is data protection: what happens to the ownership of the data? Where is the data stored? How is it processed? Who has access to it? What uses can the service provider make of it? Wikipedia (www.en.wikipedia.org), the multilingual, free content encyclopedia project, has added considerably to the popularity of Wikis, particularly in the context of developing writing skills and of collaborative knowledge construction.

AFFORDANCES OF EDUCATIONAL TECHNOLOGIES

A realistic understanding of the characteristics of, and an ability to assess, the potential and benefits of educational technologies is essential at all times. The overriding rationale for their use has to be determined by their effectiveness in helping teachers and learners to meet FLs-related aims and learning objectives. They should not be viewed as an end in themselves but as a means to an end. They should be used to support genuinely meaningful FL learning activities and not just because they are available.

Educational technologies – tools, applications, services and resources – have specific characteristics, of which users need to be aware and which allow teachers and learners to do new things in new ways. As Figure 6.1 showed, they include:

- collaborative and communicative potential;
- interactivity and non-linearity, particularly relevant in terms of active learner engagement and the provision of feedback;
- the potential for distributed knowledge construction, allowing learners who are not co-located to work together in real or delayed time on the production of digital artefacts;
- multimodal knowledge representation, i.e. the combination of the written and the spoken word with still and moving images;
- access to authentic/contextualised/situated materials, interaction, tasks and settings
- multifunctionality and convergence, i.e. the availability of multiple tools in one device linked to online services, networks and repositories;
- portability, ubiquity, personal ownership;
- the potential for user-generated content and contexts.

For a more detailed discussion, see e.g. Chapters 7 and 8 in Allford and Pachler, 2007.

PLANNING AND CLASSROOM ORGANISATION

Invariably, as in all FL teaching, planning and classroom organisation are important considerations in ensuring the effective use of educational technology. Most, if not all, points raised in relation to planning and classroom organisation in other chapters apply and we will not reiterate them here. Similarly, many tried and tested approaches to FLs pedagogy can be adapted for ICT use. Nevertheless, the introduction of an additional, and inherently complex variable in the ecosystem that is the FLs classroom increases the degree of unpredictability. While it might well lead to serendipitous learning, it might also become a potential barrier to learning unless you minimise the chances of something going wrong by careful planning. This should normally include a 'Plan B' in case something goes wrong, e.g. the equipment malfunctions. Applications and programs not only have different technological features but also different temporal, spatial and organisational as well as pedagogical requirements which you need to be aware of. For example, is a tool/application/ program to be used with the whole class, a group of pupils or are some pupils going to work independently? How do you gain access to the necessary equipment? How can you ensure it is fully operational?

As we have noted earlier, as a general rule, it is the curricular objectives that should determine the use of technology, i.e. technology should only be used if it can be seen to have a meaningful contribution to make to achieving the learning objectives identified on lesson plans and schemes of work.

Effective use can be seen to be characterised by cognitive engagement of learners and when the technology is used as a mediational tool that enables the learner to actively engage in meaning-making, knowledge-building and communication.

In our view, one particular value of digital technologies lies in the potential for the agency for learning to be transferred to the learners and for them to become actively involved in the production of content and contexts in the process of FL learning (see e.g. Pachler *et al.*, 2010). This change in agency from the teacher to the learner has considerable implications for traditional notions of classroom organisation, the role of the teacher and the learner, as well as of individual, pair and group work.

Task 6.7 **CLASSROOM ORGANISATION AND THE USE OF EDUCATIONAL TECHNOLOGY**

Carry out a number of FLs lesson observations focusing on the implications of educational technology use on classroom organisation. Note any issues.

Strategies for classroom organisation in the context of educational technology use both in the classroom and the computer room can be different from the regular techniques you use as a FLs teacher. Invariably, the methods employed to manage pupil learning and behaviour depend upon the nature of the technological aids used and whether the lesson takes place in the classroom or the computer room. Just as in lessons that do not feature educational technology use, good pace, challenging activities and high teacher expectations are important.

Task 6.8 **EDUCATIONAL TECHNOLOGY AND TL USE**

Observe a number of lessons in which different types of educational technologies are used. Note any issues affecting effective TL use by the teacher and pupils (positive and negative).

EVALUATING TECHNOLOGICAL RESOURCES AND TOOLS

The choice of which technological resources to use or which products to buy requires careful consideration, not least because of the considerable cost of many resources:

> The very nature of multimedia, vast, non-linear and readable only through the computer screen, means that it is difficult to assess the scope and quality of a title or source without spending considerable time on it. There is no equivalent to picking up and flicking through a book which will give an experienced teacher a clear view of its coverage and relevance.
>
> (McFarlane, 1996: 4)

Research suggests that the choice of which resource to buy or use is often informed by the quality of support materials available to help you with use in the classroom such as teacher notes and activity booklets.

The creators of technological resources make certain assumptions about the learning process, pedagogy and the knowledge, skills and understanding of the intended user group. You need to explore these assumptions before using the resource. Also, constraints in technical possibilities exist. Therefore, the ability to evaluate technological resources and tools is an important skill for you to have.

We focus here on general criteria for assessing the value of technological resources and tools for FL teaching. For specific criteria relating to mobile apps, see e.g. Seipold *et al.* (2014):

■ What assumptions are made about how pupils learn?
■ What assumptions are made about pupils' cognitive abilities, i.e. what are the prerequisites for the use of this resource?
■ Are the conceptual and linguistic/lexical assumptions clear and appropriate?
■ Are the scope and the aims of the resource explicit?
■ Can links with existing learning objectives/schemes of work be easily established?
■ Is there an appropriate indication as to the possible contexts of use?
■ What skills/knowledge/understanding are being developed by using this resource?
■ How do I use this resource?
■ In what socio-cultural context is learning situated?
■ What types of pupil–teacher, pupil–pupil and teacher–pupil interactions are facilitated?

- ■ How flexible is it, i.e. does it stimulate individual work, pair work and/or group work?
- ■ Is the resource user-friendly and appropriate for the age of the learners?
- ■ Is the resource interactive and, if so, how?
- ■ Is differentiation built in?
- ■ Has appropriate use been made of multimedia?
- ■ Does the concept work and is functionality given, i.e. do all the 'buttons' work and is there a clear navigational structure?
- ■ Is the user able to pursue her own path through the material?
- ■ Is there an 'About' page or a user guide?
- ■ Is the authorship transparent and subject expertise given?
- ■ Is the content accurate, reliable and up-to-date?
- ■ Is the resource comparable with similar resources, e.g. what does it do that a more traditional resource, such as a book, doesn't/can't do?
- ■ Is online help available and are error messages clear?
- ■ Are there technical/compatibility problems?

Task 6.9 EVALUATING TECHNOLOGICAL RESOURCES AND TOOLS

Put the criteria above in order of your personal preference. What do you consider to be most important in technological tools and resources for FLs?

Then use this checklist for the evaluation of one or more tool(s) and resources(s).

Finally, ask your pupils what they think. Compare your views with those of your pupils.

KEY TOOLS AND RESOURCES

Digital video

Through the video recorder, and more recently the so-called personal video recorder (PVR) or digital video recorder (DVR), which allow users to record programs straight on to hard disc, two different types of material can be accessed: off-air recordings (in the TL) produced for non-educational purposes and language programmes produced specifically for educational purposes either stand-alone or accompanying /accompanied by printed or online material. Both types are readily available from national, satellite and foreign television stations as well as often on-demand on the Internet.

An example of material not explicitly produced for educational purposes are the many clips to be found on video sharing and social networking sites such as YouTube or Vimeo. These online repositories, to which users can easily add, feature a wide range of mostly amateur video clips providing interesting insights into culturally diverse episodes and practices from everyday life. Users can also post comments in a threaded discussion and view the profiles of those who have posted or commented on clips. Such DV repositories tend to allow users to fairly easily embed videos in webpages. Useful extensions exist for web-browsers, such as a Cleaner Internet (www.clea.nr), which 'declutter' the video viewing experience and strip out often unwanted elements for use in the classroom, such as advertising, etc.

The clips often feature real language use by real people, which does, of course, pose certain challenges for you in terms not only of reliability and representativeness but also appropriacy. According to Godwin-Jones (2007: 16), one problem results from the lack of prescribed or even recommended tags, which makes effective searching for appropriate material difficult. He also notes that there can be a problem in relation to the availability of particular clips due to the use of copyrighted audio and video material which can lead to certain clips being removed from the site.

One of the reasons for using video material in your FL teaching is that it is often intrinsically motivating to pupils. It offers a degree of familiarity and with it security.

There is also an increasing range of software that enables the qualitative analysis and annotation of DV and audio such as Transana (www.transana.org). This software package allows users to transcribe video and audio material, identify relevant episodes, organise them into meaningful categories and apply keywords.

In terms of the exploitation of DV for FL learning, there is little, if any, difference to the analogue format and most, if not all, established pedagogical routines and approaches remain valid. As Hill pointed out (1989: 3), recordings in the TL can provide useful examples of real life, which are potentially up-to-date and offer an intercultural perspective on life. Off-air recordings can bring the culture(s) of the target countries into the classroom.

As a teaching and learning resource, the DV offers useful listening material. The visual support allows pupils to make use of paralinguistic information and also to contextualise language use. The use of DV provides you with many options. Depending on the learning objectives and the language skills to be developed, sound can either be on or off, the picture can be on or off, frames can be frozen and passages fast-forwarded or rewound. Each of these uses can support a range of different learning processes. DV offers the user more control and flexibility. For example, video and audio tracks tend to be separate, which offers the possibility to pupils to record their own audio track. Depending on the compression rate of the video, the audio and video quality can be better and it is easier to manipulate episodes and create extracts.

Simply playing an excerpt with strong visual clues can lead to passive understanding. Hill (1989: 8) argues that this passive understanding is a necessary precursor to oral work and that '[there] is also considerable evidence to suggest that learners will begin to speak when they are ready' (p. 19).

Williams (1982: 69) recommends what he calls the 'witness activity' to stimulate a higher level of engagement. Learners are required to listen and observe, and are quizzed on their non-verbal observations. This is intended to focus the pupils' interest on the context.

Swaffar and Vlatten (1997: 175) argue that 'identifying values implied by ... pictorial messages ... helps students recognize how pictorial messages are underscored and elaborated in a video's spoken language'. They also report research on children and adult foreign language learners that suggests that, 'when compared with students who have only print or auditory texts, learners supplied with video materials understand and remember more'.

Needless to say, certain DV resources lend themselves better to FL teaching and learning than others. Television-based resources with relevance to FL learning are:

News items which have a short life-span but a high level of topicality. Watching news bulletins allows structured note-taking and can serve as an excellent stimulus for discussions. Keywords can, for instance, be matched with newspaper headlines and comparisons between the presentation of a story in different media are possible.

Advertisements, on the other hand, have a longer 'shelf-life'. They often represent, yet also distance, 'real life' through symbolism. Often little language is used and consequently the stimulus is essentially visual. The 'freeze-frame' is particularly useful, as is guessing the product by playing the sound-track only.

Drama, notably soap opera, offers a wealth of transactional language. Short sequences can be used as stimuli for role plays by pausing at key moments of narration, by fast-forwarding or by switching off the sound. Prediction of events to come and the recapping of past events allow pupils to manipulate tenses. Soap operas lend themselves to speculation about future events, which can lead to short dramatic performances by pupils. For drama work at a more basic level, scenes watched on screen can be copied.

Web-based DV resources, such as amateur video, can also be divided into different genres such as ethnographic pieces, comedy, entertainment, film, animation, how to, music, people, news, sport, travel, animals, etc., all of which can be relevant in some way to FL teaching and learning.

Task 6.10 **THE RELEVANCE OF WEB-BASED DV RESOURCES**

Following the example of television resources above, consider the relative merits of web-based DV genres such as 'how to' clips or ethnographic pieces.

In addition to presenting brief segments of thirty seconds to three minutes of longer video 'text' or choosing shorter 'texts' such as commercials or newscast excerpts, Swaffar and Vlatten (1997: 177) argue the case for real-life video 'texts' of longer duration (between ten minutes and one hour) on the grounds that they require pupils to produce their own language to generalise about what they have seen where shorter extracts focus pupils' attention on the precise language used in the video text. Shorter extracts, they argue, deprive pupils of redundant and contextual information such as story line.

Task 6.11 **USING DV RECORDINGS**

With a particular unit of work and its learning objectives in mind, record/select snippets of different programmes or select some online material and devise a range of activities for each programme type.

In what way can any of the recordings/snippets be used to enhance this unit of work? What preparatory work needs to be undertaken in order to use the recordings successfully?

What viewing tasks could pupils undertake and how would you follow them up?

Podcasts

Increasingly, newscasts and other source material, including transcripts and sometimes even activities for exploitation, are available as podcasts or videocasts or vodcasts. Put simply, they are audio or video files that are uploaded together with a Really Simple Syndication (RSS) file which notifies users through their podcatching software, such as iTunes, and alerts them to available downloads. In the FL learning context, a quick websearch will throw up various pod- and vodcasts with a pedagogical orientation. However, in our experience it is pod- and vodcasts that have not been produced for a native speaker audience which yield more promise for FL learning purposes, particularly at intermediate and advanced level. Television and radio stations make a wide variety of programmes available for download, which lend themselves very well for listening for pleasure.

Another important dimension of DV is the use, by pupils, of a range of recording devices from camcorders to mobile phones to produce DV material. Recordings can be made by the teacher or by pupils.

In considering the production of a podcast as part of a FL learning activity, the genres identified by the ufi/learndirect and kineo guide to podcasting (ufi/learndirect and kineo, 2007: 8–10) are useful: the monologue, the interview, the magazine show, the documentary, the audio tutorial and the marketing/promotional podcast. Which format is most suitable for a particular topic? The guide points out (p. 10) that in addition to genre, frequency and length are important issues in podcasting and it considers the production of an interview-based podcast in more detail (p. 12), noting that effective design makes a difference. It advises potential podcasters to think through carefully what they want to achieve in an interview and lists the following key steps in achieving it:

- Always write questions in advance – don't wing it, even if you know your subject well. Respect their time and know what you want to get from the session.
- Research your subject – are you aware of their views already?
- Do you want to cover points they've already expressed in other formats, or explore new ground?
- Think about the listener – what will be engaging?
- Are there points of controversy to explore?
- What are the absolute core messages that you must cover?

Keep your question list to 5–7 questions, allowing opportunity to ask follow-up questions to pursue a topic further if a particular question merits deeper examination. Always submit your questions in advance and get confirmation that the subject is willing and able to address them.

Clearly, the need to ask the questions in the TL and to ensure the podcast is comprehensible as well as engaging for a non-native speaker audience adds complexity to the task. The ufi/learndirect and kineo guide (2007: 12) suggests the following interview questions. Open questions are your best opportunity to engage a subject – here are five standard journalist questions you can nearly always ask to elicit answers that are useful to your listeners:

- What's the biggest lesson you've learned in X . . .?
- What's your key piece of advice on X . . .?
- How would you explain topic X to a newcomer?
- What keeps you interested in X . . .?
- What drives you mad about X . . .?

And the catch-all bonus question:

- Is there anything we haven't covered that you want to get across about X . . .?

If you are using podcasts as an outcome of a FL learning activity, you might well want to bear this advice in mind.

Pupils use a wide range of skills to produce their own information-based, documentary-type video clip such as a tour of their school in the TL. This requires a script and research. The case study ('German School Project') described on p. 154 is an example of such a project.

At a more advanced level, you can use DV and multimodal texts effectively in the context of more advanced cultural enquiry. In a very interesting paper, Beers (2001: 1) argues that FLs teachers should be using ICT to address curricular objectives around intercultural sensitivity and tolerance rather than factual knowledge, and she argues the case for ethnographic methods to interpret complex, multimodal texts from the target culture(s). She identifies four skills (2001: 10–12) needed to carry out such research:

1   thick observation: shedding yourself of prior static, product-based notions of culture for more process-based ones that recognise the fluidity of your identity in relation to the social context in which you interact;
2   thick interpretation: determining the relations between each of the elements observed within the power structures of the larger cultural context;
3   thick comparison: examine aspects of your identity in relation to the home and target cultures;
4   thick description: compile selected observations and link them to a representative, though partial, account of the cultural event.

The paper presents a project based on the creation of a short DV around cultural interpretations of an everyday object.

Digital storytelling operates in a similar vein; it combines narrative with digital media to create a short movie. We believe that the construction of narrative and its telling to an audience involves a range of important skills and can lead to effective FL learning. Normally, the process starts with the production of a script for which the storyteller assembles a range of media, including DV, photos, animations, music, audio files, etc. to communicate the intended meaning. Learners will also benefit from an introduction to universal story elements such as (see www.wiki.answers. com/Q/What_are_the_elements_of_a_story):

■ characters (description, actions, dialogue, stream of consciousness);
■ plot (events that govern relationships between characters);
■ conflicts (problems characters encounter; external, internal);
■ setting (time and place);
■ theme (meaning behind events);
■ narrative (point of view);
■ style of writing.

For useful tools and resources, see www.bit.ly/digital_storytelling.

The 'German School Project' (case study by Roswitha Guest) arose out of a need to 'kick start' a highly motivated and enthusiastic small group of Year 10 pupils at a school in west London, who had chosen German as their second FL examination option, having had one lesson per week for two years.

The overall objective of this project was to capitalise on pupils' enthusiasm and motivation and to stretch them intellectually as well as linguistically despite the deficit in their language skills over a conventional first FL German group.

The aims of the project were:

■ to practise, consolidate and extend beginner level language;
■ to provide pupils with an opportunity to take charge of their learning and to 'own' their project, assuming responsibility for planning, execution, outcome and evaluation;
■ progression from beginner to intermediate language situations bearing in mind pupils' linguistic limitations;
■ to utilise the individual interests and special talents within the group, e.g. technical skills.

An article in German about the German School in Richmond in the *Education Guardian* (see Kasten, 1995) intrigued the pupils who, despite its proximity, had not been aware of the school's existence. This article provided the stimulus for the project.

The German School has approximately 600 German native-speaking pupils from the age of 5–19 and a mixture of English and German staff. It is very much a German environment and the working language at the school is German.

Once the go-ahead for the project had been given by both schools, the pupils' first task was to agree on a realistic programme for their visit to the German School. After lengthy discussions they settled for the production and presentation of a video for peers at their own school of:

- the school environment at the German School (buildings and grounds);
- two or three lessons in the lower school there;
- interviews with three of four pairs of Year 3 pupils;
- breaktime in the dining hall;
- lunch in the dining hall.

The preparations involved:

- organising all technical equipment, etc.;
- writing a commentary for filmed items;
- writing cue-cards and link sequences between items;
- interview question cards to be prepared using phrase books, dictionaries, coursebooks, etc.

The preparation of the interview cards involved the pupils in the recycling of all language items they already knew, starting with the topic of 'personal identification' and moving on to many more as they became more adventurous with their questions. Because the interviews were designed for young pupils (aged 8–9 years) at the German School, the visiting pupils' limited linguistic competence was appropriate for the audience.

The cue cards and link sequences required a more descriptive type of language. Pupils gathered the information for these from brochures and articles about the German School.

On the day of the visit the pupils were excited but quite nervous about their project. They were particularly worried about having to speak German all day and about how the German pupils would react to their linguistic efforts. But the day went very well.

The filming of a German lesson (pupils composing a poem about the topic 'spring'), a handicraft lesson (German Easter decorations) and a PE lesson (a German ballgame) turned out remarkably well on film – and visiting pupils enjoyed and understood the lessons.

The most valuable part of the project turned out to be the interviews with the German pupils. Each pair of pupils visiting the German School interviewed a German boy and girl. It was most impressive how visiting pupils adapted their questions to suit the individual pupils displaying an impressive linguistic agility. At the end of the interviews the visiting pupils 'pooled' their questions and interviewed an additional pair of German pupils using the questions that had worked best previously. This last interview consequently formed the basis of the follow-up work to the project.

Visiting pupils found it challenging to produce items in the TL that were clearly spoken and easily understood. They also realised that there was a real difference between authentic language production and role plays and found that the most useful items turned out to be those that had been thoroughly discussed, carefully prepared and fully scripted.

Back at their own school, pupils spent a considerable amount of their own time editing a final version of the video, having decided a running order and what to cut. The transcribing of the individual interviews was followed by the preparation of a worksheet for their peers at beginners level.

The next stage of the project was the presentation of the film and the worksheet to beginners' level German as a FL pupils.

The pupils were surprised how much work was involved to turn their 'raw product' into something usable, but they rose to the challenge. After the project they were also much more appreciative of any FLs videos they watched.

In addition, they wrote many thank-you messages to various teachers and pupils at the German School and to their German Foreign Language Assistant whose help was invaluable.

As an evaluation of their experience and the project, pupils wrote an account of the day in the past tense. They all wanted to repeat the activity and do everything much better.

The list of achievements – apart from the pupils' enjoyment of, and pride in, their work – is long; it covers in particular language skills, language learning skills and cultural awareness.

Photographs were taken and other items of information material gathered at the German School were displayed in the languages corridor at the school and generated considerable interest from pupils, staff and parents.

SOCIAL NETWORKING

One of the main advantages in terms of FL learning of the Web has been, and continues to be, access to authentic, up-to-date material. Of late, one of the significant shifts in the use of educational technologies has been that towards user-generated content, particularly in terms of the many social networking tools, including blogging and photo sharing, becoming available. *Social bookmarking* software, such as Diigo can be used as a tool for locating, organising and sharing of web-based resources. Social bookmarking tools are designed to allow users to store and share bookmarks on the Web, rather than on their computer, which means they can access them from anywhere. It also enables them to access bookmarks of other users. These features can be particularly useful in the context of project work, for example.

Digital technology-mediated communication

A particular benefit of digital technologies for FLs teachers and learners is the ability they afford to communicate with TL speakers. They allow both real-time (synchronous) and delayed-time (asynchronous) communication. In real time, teachers and pupils can communicate with TL speakers through *instant messaging* programs such as Google Talk/Hangout (www.google.co.uk/talk) as well as Skype (www.skype.com), many of which also have voice-Internet-based telephony, and video-sharing facilities.

Chats are based on written text while videoconferencing combines text and picture. In research terms, the jury is still out on the extent to which the video channel actually makes a noticeable difference in terms of learning.

The potential of *e-mail* for project and group work with partner schools in the TL is great and a number of web-based partner-finding services are available, for example: the British Council's Schools Online (www.schoolsonline.british council.org/partner-with-a-school), which offers a partnership database with schools from all over the world; ePals (www.epals.com), a commercial learning community

Task 6.12 **EXPLORING SOCIAL BOOKMARKING TOOLS**

Explore a range of social bookmarking tools such as Diigo (www.diigo.com). How can you use its functionality to collect web-based resources, sorting them, sharing them with others, annotating them, etc.?

Similarly useful for information retrieval and sharing can be *social networking sites* such as Facebook (www.facebook.com); they allow users to join networks based on location or other groupings, such as professional or political interests, and create and share online identities and resources, and interact with members of these networks. However, caution is advised and particular attention needs to be paid to privacy issues and how much control a tool or service offers, for example, around who can and cannot view their information. Social networking sites such as Facebook are based on a relationship model of 'friends' and network membership. One of the drawbacks of using social networking sites is the fact that activities can lack substance; however, integration in an educational project can overcome this potential problem. Another increasingly noticeable drawback is the strong push towards commercialisation and monetisation of such services. Use of social networking tools needs to go hand in hand with an explicit problematisation of e-safety issues. For useful resources on e-safety, see e.g. www.bit.ly/infonet-e-safety or www.freetech4teachers.com/2013/01/17-cartoon-videos-explaining-internet.html.

Other relevant social networking tools are online photo-sharing sites such as Flickr (www.flickr.com), which offer a rich repository of visual resources for FL learning and teaching. Images lend themselves very well as stimulus for activities such as vocabulary learning, description, analysis, narrative, exemplification of cultural practices, etc. As already noted, it is important to pay attention to copyright issues.

of teachers and students offering ideas for classroom projects and related resource such as collaboration tools; and eTwinning (www.etwinning.net), an online community for schools in Europe. (See also e.g. Pachler, 2007.)

Webquests, online inquiry-based activities, are similarly an appropriate use of the Internet in FLs teaching and learning. As Mittergeber (2004) points out, webquests offer three basic pedagogical options: problem resolution; product-orientation and/or process-orientation:

- a problem resolution – or a quiz-based format, in which learners have to search for answers to pre-determined questions;
- a product-oriented approach, in which pupils work towards a tangible outcome mostly in the form of an artefact, e.g. a webpage, a portfolio, a presentation;
- a process-orientated approach, which involves learners in formulating their own questions and/or in developing points of view and positions in relation to complex subject matter.

A useful starting point for the exploration of webquests is www.webquest.org; the website offers online tools for webquest creation as well as a searchable database of webquests created by others. Ostensibly, as teacher you have to devise a series of activities using the template available that focus on the systematic and creative engagement with a range of carefully selected online resources. (See also e.g. Pachler, 2007.)

Blogs are tools that allow users to publish personal commentaries and diaries on the Web. They are particularly interesting in the FL learning context as cultural artefacts in that they offer personal perspectives which are grounded in different social, generational, political and cultural traditions, etc. and often lead to 'discussions', i.e. cross-referencing, and community building between bloggers and their readers. Blogs lend themselves very well to the writing of reflective and learning diaries and to sharing them with peers and colleagues. Blogs are online journals and allow for multimedia content. RSS allows for readers to be alerted about new postings and delivers them to users. Many blogs allow readers to post feedback and comments on the blog page. They are increasingly used in the academic world as a tool for knowledge sharing and building across different communities of interest but also function as personalised discussion forums. They are very useful for capturing and disseminating user-generated content and lend themselves well to the development of reading and writing skills in the context of sharing personal ideas and opinions and interacting and communicating with others. For some related resources, see e.g. www.bit.ly/blogging-tag.

The TESL-EJ (Campbell, 2005) offers a useful comparative review of different weblog applications for FL teaching and learning, and distinguishes nine features that you might take into account when choosing which tool to use including a user-friendly intuitive interface, a WYSIWIG text editor, ability to moderate comments and set access levels, customisability to the interface, built-in social networking features and aggregator, spell-check function and multimedia content functionality.

Blogger (www.blogger.com) is one of the popular tools. Services geared to use in educational contexts include Edublogs (www.edublogs.org) and Wordpress (www.wordpress.com). Hipcast (www.hipcast.com) allows the posting of audio, video and podcasts to blogs.

Godwin-Jones (2006: 10–11) rightly notes that through blogs writing has moved to the public domain, the so-called blogsphere, and blogs offer pupils ample opportunity to write in a public sphere, but courseblogs are also very popular. In their discussion of a blog pedagogy, Fernheimer and Nelson (2005) argue against what they polemically call a 'cacophony' of individual pupil blogs and instead, in favour of a class blog as 'a locus of civil discourse bound by social rues, but constituted by individual expression'. The ideal community, in their view, is 'agonistic, deliberate, and collaborative', one that functions as 'a public space in which people do not simply speak to each other but one in which they [also] listen' and one which prompts students not only to express their positions, but also to acknowledge and then engage the positions and opinions others express. Ideally, students would then revise their positions, both argumentative and subjective, based on these 'real' and virtual classroom interactions, thus evolving the depth of their understanding, opinions and constructions to account for the differences they encounter. For us, this classroom would encourage students to express their points of view freely and civilly, but civility would not be emphasised to the extent that it precluded 'true' argument, which we imagine as allowing and encouraging genuine dissent. In other words, a space that is conducive to high-level language use.

In recent years, microblogging has become very popular. The term can refer to two phenomena, either the publishing of blog entries directly from a mobile device or, and this is the definition we will use here, the use of services such as Twitter (www.twitter.com), which allows users to send and read text-based messages of up to 140 characters. These are known as 'tweets' and are 'tagged' using the # sign followed by a keyword to enable users to exchange ideas and URLs. One important feature to consider in relation to its use in educational contexts is the fact that tweets are by default public; however, message delivery can be restricted to what is known as 'followers', i.e. users who have subscribed to receiving tweets from other users. As we have already noted, mobile devices are increasingly allowed into the (FLs) classroom, for example to support independent language learning by pupils, e.g. to search for information such as online dictionaries etc., or for the use of language apps. For a detailed discussion of mobile learning, see e.g. Seipold *et al.*, 2014.

Interactive whiteboards (IWBs)

The introduction of IWBs, large, touch-sensitive screens on to which a computer screen can be displayed via a projector and through which a computer can be controlled, into British schools has been extensive and fast and was supported by the government. The government has produced a range of guidance material, e.g. DfES (2004). Critics wonder whether IWBs are really value for money and whether they have the potential to transform teaching and learning. Two main types of IWBs can be distinguished: boards with a hard magnetic surface and soft boards, and are supported by specific software tools that need to be installed on the computer. IWBs can be used as presentation tools, e.g. to present pupils' work to the rest of the class or to use web-based resources in whole-class teaching, but also for pedagogical practices such as analysing language, visualising concepts, illustrating explanations with video or audio files, manipulating information, etc. The ability to move items on the screen supports a range of activities such as matching, labelling, categorising, sorting, gap filling, sequencing, etc. – all frequently used in FLs classrooms. Material can, of course, be stored digitally and reused as is or in a modified form in future lessons which also supports recaps and revision activities. IWBs enable users – teachers and pupils – to embed a wide range of multimodal digital resources in their teaching and/or learning. For you as a FLs student teacher, IWBs offer great potential for making language and concepts less abstract and specific teaching points visually more salient through the use of colour, annotations, glosses, movement, etc. One inherent danger in the nature of the IWB is a tendency to transmission-based, whole-class teaching.

A report published by Becta (2003: 1) presented findings from research in support of IWBs; it listed the following key benefits:

■ encourages more varied, creative and seamless use of teaching materials;

■ engages pupils to a greater extent than conventional whole-class teaching, increasing enjoyment and motivation;

■ facilitates pupil participation through the ability to interact with materials on the board.

The government commissioned an evaluation of the educational and operational effectiveness of the project and to assess the impact of IWB use (see Moss *et al.*, 2007). The research found that IWBs are mainly used as data projectors, as a surface to generate dynamic display and to enhance presentation from the front of the class. The majority of texts used are the teachers' own but teachers appear to be struggling to incorporate design principles which establish clear reading paths for pupils; this difficulty also gets in the way of teachers designing resources that can be shared independently of their author. The research also shows that the introduction of IWBs does not in and of itself transform existing pedagogies and it concludes that the main emphasis should be on the appropriacy of pedagogical approaches not the use of the technology per se.

To a large extent the kinds of changes the technology fosters depend on what teachers think it is for. There are three key themes that dominate thinking about the role of IWBs in changing pedagogy. These are: increased pace of delivery; increased use of multimodal resources, incorporating image, sound and movement in new ways; and a more interactive style of whole-class teaching. The research suggests two important caveats to these anticipated benefits.

First, it is possible to approach pace, multimodality and interactivity with either a surface or deep understanding of what they contribute to pedagogy. A surface approach rests at the level of the technical or physical attributes of the technology. From this perspective, making pedagogy interactive means using particular features of the IWB such as drop and drag, or moving between multiple screens during lesson time. A deep approach embeds the use of the technology more specifically in a broader pedagogic aim. This means assessing more precisely how particular features of the IWB can achieve a wider pedagogic purpose, which is itself centred on increasing pupil understanding of key aspects of relevant subject knowledge.

Second, the value of particular attributes of the technology and their capacity to achieve meaningful change depend on how these features fit with existing pedagogic approaches and priorities embedded in the particular subject domain and its existing practice. So fast pace in teaching is perceived as much more of a virtue in Maths than in other subject domains. This is also where the technology is most likely to be used to this effect. From this point of view, the introduction of IWBs to Secondary schools may reinforce, or even distort, rather than reconfigure the dominant approach to pedagogy in particular subject areas (Moss *et al.* 2007: 6).

Moss *et al.* (2007: 7) also note that IWBs offer an opportunity to think about the strengths and weaknesses of whole-class teaching. Discussion between colleagues about how IWBs can be used to support and transform existing practice, they argue, is important to ensure effective use of IWBs. A focus on interactivity as a technical process, for example, is not inherently beneficial and can lead to some relatively mundane activities being over-valued:

> Observations for this project suggest that developing good materials for use with the IWB is not just a matter of solving a range of technical or logistical problems but also means considering more fundamentally which kinds of texts can most usefully be shared in this way.

(p. 8)

Moss *et al.* (2007: 8) identify two potential drawbacks to the ways in which IWBs are currently being used. The technology can:

- ■ Reinforce a transmission style of whole-class teaching in which the contents of the board multiply and go faster, while pupils are increasingly reduced to a largely spectator role.
- ■ Reduce interactivity to what happens at the board not what happens in the classroom.

This, we argue, you must guard against when using the IWB.

SUMMARY

In this chapter we discussed the role of education technologies in FLs teaching and learning. They should not be seen as a possible replacement or challenge to your importance as an FLs teacher. Indeed, their use makes your role more important but it requires new pedagogical skills, such as the ability to evaluate multimodal resources.

Educational technologies offer a range of affordances which enable them to play a key role in the development of listening, speaking, reading and writing skills, as well as transferable skills such as independent learning and the use of reference material and prepare pupils for their (working) lives in modern society. They can also support other important aspects of FL teaching and learning such as vocabulary acquisition, grammar practice and translation.

Educational technologies should be used on the basis of its appropriateness in achieving FL-related learning objectives, as a means to an end and not as an end in themselves.

They can be used effectively inside and outside the FLs classroom and has great motivational potential for learners. They can meaningfully enhance and enrich pupils' FL learning experience.

Last, but by no means least, educational technologies have considerable potential for continuous professional development and networking.

FURTHER READING

Allford, D. and Pachler, N. (2007) *Language, Autonomy and the New Learning Environments*. Frankfurt am Main: Peter Lang.
This book explores, with reference to relevant research findings, how digital technologies create new possibilities for foreign language teaching and learning, such as knowledge construction through computer-mediated interaction and learner autonomy in online networks.

Evans, M. (ed.) (2011) *Foreign Language Learning with Digital Technology*. London: Continuum.
Chapters of this book include a review of the evidence of the impact of ICT policy on learning and discussions of different pedagogical applications of ICT in the foreign language learning context, including the use of CMC between pupils in different countries, classroom use of ICT, and online foreign language learning materials.

Leask, M. and Pachler, N. (2013) (eds) (3rd edn) *Teaching and Learning in the Secondary School using ICT*. London: Routledge.
This book addresses the question of how digital technologies can be used for teaching and learning. It provides a starting point for exploring the possibilities that digital technologies offer to schools, teachers and pupils.

PEDAGOGY RELATED ■ ■ ■ ■

Language Learning & Technology. Available online at: www.llt.msu.edu

Language Learning & Technology is a refereed, online journal which disseminates research related to technology and language education to foreign and second language educators.

CHAPTER 7

PLANNING AND REFLECTING ON CLASSROOM PRACTICE

INTRODUCTION

Planning lessons and reflecting on practice are central to the profession of teaching. In this chapter we consider first the role of observation in developing understanding of the practice of others and in informing your own planning for learning. Lesson observation and collaboration with experienced teachers provide unique opportunities to gain insights into the learning and teaching process, and are essential parts of the learning process for a beginning teacher.

The second section concerns the planning of lessons, both developing 'one-off' lessons as well as thinking about medium-term planning. Planning and evaluation are integral parts of effective teaching and form the foundation for successful pupil learning. Wringe (1989: 25–26) points out that only through planning 'is it possible to see present work in its due perspective and appropriately adjust the emphasis of one's work in the light of what has gone before and what is to follow'. The role of colleagues in joint planning is also considered.

There are many different pro formas for observation and planning in use, of which many include similar features. The exemplar pro formas we use in this chapter are not meant to be prescriptive, nor do they purport to be the only appropriate or possible way of recording observation, planning and evaluation. They are intended as a starting point for you and need to be tailored to local needs and preferences. The pro formas attempt to bring together the most important features of what we perceive to be good practice.

Teacher education programmes often lay a great deal of weight on evaluation and reflection. This is because the development of a disposition to continually seek to improve the learning that goes on in the classroom is at the heart of becoming a teacher. Furthermore, it is through establishing a rigorous process for reflecting on the quality of the learning that our planning and teaching has resulted in, that we continue to improve throughout our professional lives.

The professional decisions we make in planning and teaching need to be subjected to rigorous evaluation, first in relation to individual lessons, then of sequences of lessons, and potentially followed by the investigation of a particular aspect of practice through the conduct of small-scale practice-based enquiry projects.

The third and final part of the chapter concerns the why and how of conducting evaluation of our teaching, and opening up the learning and teaching in our classrooms to close scrutiny.

OBJECTIVES

By the end of this chapter you should:

■ recognise the importance of observation and collaborative teaching in learning to teach FLs and be able to carry out lesson observations effectively and professionally;

■ be able to understand the issues attendant to the planning of FLs lessons as well as the construction of outline medium-term plans, i.e. unit of work plans;

■ understand the planning/teaching/assessment cycle;

■ understand the importance of self-evaluation for effective FL teaching and maximising pupil learning;

■ be aware of the ways in which a FLs teacher can research his/her own practice.

OBSERVING AND WORKING COLLABORATIVELY WITH FLs TEACHERS

Familiarisation with departmental policies and documentation

A first step in understanding an unfamiliar FL teaching context might come from any available documentation, such as the departmental handbook. Departmental handbooks might contain policies on relevant aspects of the work of a FLs teacher in a given school, such as the use of the TL, assessment and marking, homework, discipline procedures, staffing and resourcing of the department, organisation of the FLs curriculum, accommodation, teaching methods used, the departmental development plan, extra-curricular activities available to pupils through the department, job descriptions of individual team members and any other information useful to outsiders or colleagues arriving new to the department, such as newly qualified teachers, inspectors and/or student teachers.

Familiarisation with these policies and practices allows you to understand better the 'ethos' of this particular department and allows for the classroom practice observed to be set in context. Understanding why a FLs teacher uses certain strategies when giving instructions in the TL, for instance, might become easier when set against the background of the departmental TL policy. Departmental policies should also inform the planning carried out by student teachers. It is, for instance, important to know that certain procedures for the setting and returning of homework are in place when planning lessons.

Task 7.1 **DEPARTMENTAL DOCUMENTATION**

Ask your mentor for a copy of any relevant departmental documentation such as policies and handbooks. Read the information carefully. What has the department set out to achieve? What important general processes and procedures for the conduct of FLs lessons are stated? What policies are in place? What priorities emerge for you as a student teacher from the information you have read?

LESSON OBSERVATION

In her book on observation tasks for the language classroom, Wajnryb (1992: 19) makes a very important point about how lesson observation needs sensitivity on the part of the observer:

> Observers need to maintain a sensitive awareness of the potential for vulnerability that inevitably accompanies any observation of teaching. When a teacher opens the classroom door and extends a welcome to a visitor, a basic trust in motive and professional ethic accompanies that welcome. This must be respected.

This needs to be borne in mind when observing lessons, the point of which is not to evaluate critically the practice of experienced FLs teachers against performance indicators; this is the responsibility of their senior colleagues internally or externally. The aim is to learn as much as possible about the complexity of the teaching and learning process, and possible approaches/strategies to maximise pupil learning. Information obtained from any lesson observations should, therefore, be treated confidentially. Figure 7.1 outlines an observation etiquette.

- ■ Ensure the person you are observing knows who you are and why you are there.
- ■ Be aware of the 'background' to this lesson about which you know almost nothing: the relationship built up with the class, the whole range of reasons why the teacher has chosen a particular approach today, etc.
- ■ Few lessons are ever perfect. Please bear this in mind when observing teachers and commenting to them afterwards.
- ■ If you make critical comments on any observation pro forma, make sure these remain confidential and constructive.
- ■ When observing, you should always be able to learn something from the experience.
- ■ Take opportunities, where appropriate, to become involved (e.g. when pupils are working in pairs or groups). Don't feel that all observation must be done at the back as if you were invisible but make sure the teacher is happy with this.
- ■ Make sure you thank the teacher for the chance to observe the lesson.

■ **Figure 7.1** 'Observation etiquette'

In this chapter we describe a systematic approach to lesson observation, which focuses on the gathering of mainly qualitative data – that is, verbal descriptions of certain occurrences during the lesson linked to a small number of observation foci per lesson. The foci for observation will change regularly. Parkinson (1992: 20) notes: 'It is a common beginner's mistake to try to capture everything, but you will soon find it impossible to look for more than one or two things in any one observation.'

It is important, though, that observation foci relate to your development needs, whether these have been generated by you yourself or are linked to targets set by your mentor or tutor.

The approach we propose is systematic in that it is based on the completion of a generic pro forma per lesson observed (see Figure 7.2). Before the lesson, the observer decides on one or two foci (rubric: 'observation foci') and notes why she has done so (column: 'comments'). During the lesson, the observer completes the columns 'time' and 'description of action'.

This approach does not make use of fixed observation categories but, instead, allows the observer the freedom and flexibility to concentrate on changing foci. To some extent the lesson observation foci depend on particular lesson objectives. For instance, a Spanish lesson in the computer room, where pupils compose e-mail messages to their e-pals, invariably offers different opportunities for observation than a classroom-based lesson taught in collaboration with the foreign language assistant (FLA) focusing on the oral practice of transactional language relating, for example, to the topic 'clothes'. It is, therefore, important to find out from the teacher prior to the lesson what the objectives and the content of the lesson are.

Observation can be a very effective learning experience, but where the observation is vague and unstructured, then potentially valuable insights into the teaching and learning process are lost.

Figure 7.3 lists a number of possible observation foci. Given their importance, particularly at the initial stages of a teacher education programme, classroom organisation/management issues are listed not under teacher behaviour here but as a separate category. It might be possible to use the *discussion* of observation notes as evidence of meeting certain aspects of teacher standards. Structured observation notes may not only be useful in facilitating the reflection process but can also be used as evidence of having addressed certain standards.

Lesson observation sheet			
Class: 9L	Time: 2.10– 3.20	Date: 08.10	Teacher: M. Beauchamp

Observation foci	Comments
Target language use: teacher–pupil.	I wanted to see how a unit of work can be introduced and to collect ideas on how to give instructions and explanations, how to organise the classroom and how to conclude a lesson in the target language.

▪ **Figure 7.2** Sample lesson observation

Time	Description of action	Reflection
2.10	Pupils enter the room individually returning the teacher's greetings: T: 'Bonjour . . .' 'P: 'Bonjour, Monsieur. Comment ça va?' T: 'Ça va bien, merci. Et toi?' P: 'Ça va +/~/-'	Pupils used to routine and responded automatically.
2.15	Oral introduction of topic 'school life'. 'Aujourd'hui nous étudions le système d'enseignement, l'éducation en France. Qu'est-ce que c'est 'l'enseignement' en Anglais? . . . Oui c'est ça.'	Used able pupil to translate to ensure comprehension.
2.18	Activity introduced by using able pupil to demonstrate how to brainstorm vocabulary relevant to school life. 'Peter. Donne-moi du vocabulaire associé avec l'éducation. Tu parles et moi, j' écris.' Gestures and teacher writes answers on board.	Pupil followed instructions without hesitation.
2.24	Pupils put into groups of four: 'Vous allez travailler en groupes de 4'. Teacher uses gestures and counts 1–4 to clarify. Teacher repeats the demonstration. 'Peter, encore une fois. Tu parles et j'écris. Du vocabulaire associé avec l'éducation, s'il te plaît.' Number 'ones' in group asked to identify themselves. They are then told that they are scribes. 'Numéro un . . . lève la main . . . numéro un, tu écris. Joanne, tu es numéro un, oui, alors tu écris. Voilà le stylo, tu écris. Marie . . . tu écris . . . OK? Numéro un . . . lève la main . . . Tout le monde comprend? . . . Vous écrivez.	Why were pupils put into groups after the demonstration? Giving pupils a number helped; by asking pupils to identify themselves there was no confusion.

■ **Figure 7.2** continued

Time	Description of action	Reflection
2.28	Ground rules of the brainstorm explained in English. IWB clock used to ask time and to set a ten-minute time limit for group work. Teacher issues instructions and time scale using IWB clock. *'OK. Il est deux heures et demie. Regardez! Il est quelle heure? Oui, deux heures et demie. Vous avez dix minutes. Dix minutes. Combien de minutes Sharon? . . . Oui, dix minutes. Fatima, vous finissez à quelle heure? Tout le monde répète: "Nous finissons à deux heures quarante."'*	Why was the TL not used here? Process of setting a time limit seems a useful device. Pupils all on task. I guess they are used to brainstorming.
2.40	Brainstorm of known vocabulary brought to a close. *'OK. Il est deux heures quarante. Posez le stylo. C'est fini. Regardez moi. . . . Regardez moi. Lucy . . . c'est fini . . . regarde moi.'* Teacher asks each group: *'Vous avez combien de mots?'*	Would the element of competition have added motivation?
2.45	Teacher revises key words – *les matières, le personnel, les bâtiments* – with the use of flashcards and graded questioning.	According to plan these words would serve as headings to allow pupils to put words into categories. Purpose of this activity not entirely clear.
2.47	Distracted pupil shuffles and talks to partner. *'Tais-toi, Lucy'* and gestures used.	Some pupils seemed unsettled. The fact that the teacher knew the pupil's name was very useful.
2.55	Teacher writes category headings on board. Asks for some words from the whole class. *'Voilà des catégories . . . les bâtiments, le personnel et les matières. Donne moi un exemple d'un bâtiment . . . l'école . . . trés bien, le bureau, oui. Et le personnel? . . . le professeur, merci, le directeur, très bien. Et une matière? . . . l'anglais. OK. Voilà vous comprenez.'*	Did there need to be more examples? The teacher assured that all pupils understood what he was doing. Questions targeted: more able first then less able pupils.

■ **Figure 7.2** *continued*

Time	Description of action	Reflection
2.55 cont.	As they shout out teacher asks which category to put the word in, repeats the words and writes them on the board. 'L'université, c'est une matière. Tout le monde, oui ou non? Non . . . et alors . . . Martin? Oui, c'est un bâtiment. Et le directeur . . . un bâtiment aussi, non? Excellent c'est une personne.'	
3.00	Pupils asked to work in groups to categorise words. 'Allez-y, continuez en groupes.' Teacher walked around targeting groups that needed help. 'Vous comprenez? Les maths, c'est une matière? Oui, très bien. Donnez-moi d'autres matières. Regardez la liste. La géo? . . . oui la géographie. OK. Ecrivez la géographie ici. Bien. Une personne? Le surveillant, bien . . . ici. Très bien vous comprenez. Continuez. . . .'	No one had to translate the instructions. Most pupils used English when deciding which categories words from brainstorm should go in. Could some sort of forfeit have been used to make pupils aware that use of English is not desirable?
3.10	Teacher interrupts pupils still in full flow, although some off-task. Teacher targets individuals with questions. 'Donnez-moi trois exemples des matières, du personnel, etc.'	Teacher asked pupils who seemed to have been off-task.
3.15	Homework set: pupils have to copy the instructions into their homework diary. 'Les devoirs. Ecrivez trois phrases au sujet des matières à l'école . . . ça commence avec "J'étudie . . .". Ecrivez trois phrases pour les bâtiments: par exemple "Le collège se trouve à une distance de . . .". "Il y a trois salles de français . . .". Et écrivez trois phrases au sujet du personnel: "Mon professeur de français s'appelle M. Beauchamp . . ."' Able pupil translates.	Might it have been easier for all in the class and quicker to use English to set the homework?
3.20	Bell rings. Pupils dismissed in twos saying: 'Au revoir' to the teacher on exit.	Lesson running over. Do pupils think about what they are saying when they go through the routine?

■ **Figure 7.2** continued

PUPIL LEARNING AND RESPONSE

▨ contexts and type of TL use by pupils;
▨ amount of productive language use by pupils per lesson;
▨ amount of receptive language use by pupils per lesson;
▨ nature of pupil participation in teacher-led activities nature of pupil involvement in pair and group work;
▨ independent pupil learning, e.g. use of dictionaries and glossaries pupil time spent on-task;
▨ types of off-task behaviour, e.g. talking, inattentiveness, possible reasons for off-task behaviour;
▨ pupil achievement of lesson objectives.

TEACHER STRATEGIES AND BEHAVIOUR

▨ engagement of pupils: use of starter;
▨ use of the TL for instructions and interaction use of body language, gesture, mime;
▨ development and revision of previous learning outcomes choice of activities in relation to objectives;
▨ ways of communicating objectives to pupils;
▨ ways of presenting new language;
▨ amount and characteristics of teacher talk and pupil talk;
▨ use of questioning techniques: question-and-answer exchanges;
▨ use of open-ended versus closed questions;
▨ use of differentiation;
▨ (variation of) pace;
▨ use of strategies to motivate pupils;
▨ use of teacher-led activity, group work, pair work, individual work;
▨ role of the teacher in group work, pair work and individual work;
▨ teacher movement around the classroom;
▨ strategies for teaching linguistic structures;
▨ balance of teacher-centred and pupil-centred approaches strategies for continuous assessment and feedback to pupils;
▨ administration of homework;
▨ strategies for error correction;
▨ use of plenaries (during and/or at the end of the lesson).

CLASSROOM MANAGEMENT/ORGANISATION

▨ settling pupils down;
▨ arrangement of seating and classroom layout issuing books and equipment;
▨ establishing a code of conduct;
▨ strategies for reminding pupils of rules grouping arrangements for specific tasks;
▨ use of the TL for classroom management/organisation use of praise and sanctions;
▨ use of the TL for dealing with discipline matters; strategies for dealing with disruptive behaviour.

▨ **Figure 7.3** Foci for lesson observation

Lesson observation of the student teacher is, of course, also carried out by mentors. The foci identified in Figure 7.3 can equally be used by teachers observing (parts of) lessons taught by you. Dedicated lesson observation pro formas are usually provided by the HEI for use when observing you.

Task 7.2 CARRYING OUT LESSON OBSERVATIONS

Using the lesson observation in Figure 7.2 as an example, carry out a number of lesson observations of your own. Choose one or two observation foci per lesson from those identified in Figure 7.3.

After the lessons, complete the 'reflection' column. NB: Remember to keep your evaluative comments to yourself. You might want to ask yourself reflective questions such as:

- What were the lesson's short-term objectives?
- What about the longer-term aims?
- How were the differing needs of pupils approached?
- How did the teacher deal with any issues that arose (behaviour, misunderstandings, etc.)?
- What learning took place exactly and how do you (and the teacher) know?
- What have you learnt? (ideas, activities, strategies – both positive and negative; changes to how you think you might plan your lessons).

The approach to lesson observation suggested above is suitable for a wide range of observation foci and does not require any specific preparation on the part of the observer such as the design of specific observation instruments.

On the basis of targets set, you might, however, want to design specific observation pro formas or recording sheets for colleagues observing your lessons, such as, for example, a tally sheet to record how often you support TL instructions with gestures or how often you elicit answers from specific pupils.

Task 7.3 LINKING LEARNING OBJECTIVES TO TEACHING ACTIVITIES

Carry out some lesson observations of your own, linking lesson objectives and learning activities. Ask the respective teacher before the lesson what the learning objectives are and note them in different columns. When observing the lesson, categorise the learning and teaching activities according to these columns. Do all the activities relate to one of the lesson objectives?

COLLABORATIVE PLANNING AND TEACHING

The typical progression route for FLs student teachers is one from lesson observation via small-group and collaborative teaching to 'solo' whole-class teaching. Student teachers may also teach a section of a full lesson, e.g. a starter activity with one group while teaching a full lesson independently with another. At the forefront are the training needs at that time: in which situations will you be able to develop your skills most effectively at this particular point? (see also Fleming and Walls, 1998 and Crozier *et al.*, 2003). During collaborative planning and teaching, student teachers gradually assume responsibility for planning and teaching (parts of) lessons with support from the class teacher (assessment should also play a part in these short teaching and learning episodes). By our definition, collaborative teaching is different from team-teaching, which involves the cooperation of two experienced teachers.

The student teacher working collaboratively with the class teacher is in a unique position. She occupies the place of the learner, but gradually assumes responsibility for what goes on in the classroom, allowing for a developing understanding of the skills required for 'solo' teaching. Moving from observation to collaborative planning and teaching involves discussions about, for example, how learning objectives are to be achieved, the teaching strategies and activities to be used and how these relate to the learning objectives identified.

In collaborative teaching the class teacher retains overall control and authority and allows the student teacher to participate in aspects of teaching which she is ready to develop. The level of student teacher involvement gradually increases. Invariably, careful planning features prominently in this process. Both the student and class teacher need to be clear at every stage of the lesson who is responsible for what. For a useful analysis of collaborative teaching with examples of effective practice, see Arthur *et al.*, 1998: 123–125.

The gradual shift in responsibility from the class teacher to the student teacher might follow the stages we list below:

1   student teacher observes and assists while class teacher plans and teaches;
2   student teacher takes small group while class teacher plans and teaches;
3   student teacher takes class for parts of lesson with class teacher planning and teaching most;
4   collaborative teaching: student teacher increasingly involved in joint planning;
5   student teacher plans and teaches, class teacher advises on lesson plan, offers support and advice and observes; and
6   student teacher plans and teachers 'solo' and class teacher observes and offers diagnostic feedback.

PLANNING INDIVIDUAL AND SEQUENCES OF LESSONS

Lesson planning and the student teacher

Up to now in this chapter we have been referring to planning collaboratively. Planning lessons is one hurdle many FLs student teachers find challenging at the start of their course, and many find that it is tempting to spend hours trying to produce the 'perfect' lesson plan. First, there is no such thing as a 'perfect' lesson plan; second, too much time spent on planning takes away from the energy you need to teach; and, third, planning is a skill in which you will develop confidence and effectiveness with practice and feedback. In order not to be misunderstood, this is *not* to suggest that planning is unimportant; far from it, effective planning is essential and should start from a focus on the objectives:

■   What do the pupils need to learn in this lesson/series of lessons?

This is closely followed by the supplementary question:

■   How can this learning come about?

As background to both these questions is the third one:

■   Where are the pupils now with their learning?

LESSON PLANNING

Individual lesson plans need to be seen in the context of medium-term planning, the so-called units of work. These units of work relate to the scheme of work, which outlines what is to be covered over a period of time such as an academic year or a period of study defined by examination specifications.

Lesson plans outline how a particular aspect of a unit of work is to be taught. Initially, you will be concerned with planning at micro-level – that is, with (parts of) individual lessons, rather than at macro-level, the unit of work level. Nevertheless, these (parts of) lesson plans need to be firmly rooted in unit of work planning:

> In planning our lessons the all important question becomes not 'How can I occupy them in tomorrow's lesson?' but 'What is now the most pressing thing for them to learn in order to be able to perform the final activity satisfactorily?' 'What is the most effective and economical way of doing it?' and above all 'If they are to do that successfully, is there anything I must do first?' It is no longer a matter of generating activities that are sufficiently novel, stimulating or innocuous to be included but the more finite and easily manageable problem solving one of finding the most efficient means to ends.
>
> (Wringe, 1994: 13)

When planning a FLs lesson you need to consider a number of important issues, which are discussed below. The most important thing to remember is the planning/teaching/assessment loop. Assessment is not something that gets tacked on at the end but an integral part of your planning and teaching, and can be used to evaluate the quality of the learning that your planning and teaching have led to so as to provide more information to be used in planning the next lesson. This is exemplified in Figure 7.4, a sample lesson plan and discussed below.

Lesson plan			
Class: *8E*	Time: *1.30–2.40*	Date: *25.11*	Language: *French*

Learning objectives		
At the end of the lesson pupils should be able to:	**Language needed:**	**Assessment: how will I know if learning objectives have been met? Evidence?**
Core:	*Core:*	*In pair work can all ask question and use card to locate place on grid?*
Ask directions to places in the town from memory (S)	Pour aller au, à la, à l' + places in town (S,L)	
Understand when someone gives directions (L)	Prenez la première/deuxième rue à gauche/droite, etc. (L)	*In listening can pupils show they understand directions by placing cards correctly?*
Extension:	*Extension:*	*Devising rule: how many seem to grasp it?*
Give direction to places in town (S)	Prenez, etc. (L & S) Correct form of au, à la, à l'	*How many can give directions from memory?*

Previous learning outcomes
Vocabulary for key places already introduced. Pupils have labelled a map. Pupils have learnt the song 'La première rue à droite'.

Resources
IWB presentation of places, pair cards of places, MP3 listening files containing dialogue asking the way and giving directions, gapped text of transcript, grid/town plan

Time	Activities	AfL opportunities
1.30	Starter: IWB game to remind pupils of key places: teacher-led repetition, graded questioning: **'C'est . . . ? C'est . . . ou c'est . . . Qu'est-ce que c'est?'** *Introduce Objectives*	*How well do they remember the places? Do I need to revise more before moving on?*
1.35	Use same presentation to introduce 'Pour aller. . .?'; teacher-led: Pupil comes to front blindfold pupil; elicit 'Pour aller . . .?' from others; blindfolded pupil points to screen from memory **'Peter, où tu veux aller?'** . . . *le cinema* . . . **'OK. Pour aller . . . oui . . . au cinéma? Alors, Peter. Répète: Pour aller au cinéma?'**	*Can all remember the phrase from memory? Do I need to do a little more whole-class repetition at this point?*

▪ **Figure 7.4** Sample lesson plan

Time	Activities	AfL opportunities
1.50	Pair work: pair cards, colour coded by gender, face down; one pupil asks 'Pour aller . . .' other points out flashcard from memory; gender serves as a clue **'OK. Travaillez avec un partenaire. Vous êtes "A" et "B". "A", tu poses la question: "Pour aller à la ou". "B", tu reponds la-bas et tu indiques la carte. Vous avez beaucoup de cartes. Vous devez vous souvenir de la bonne carte.'**	As I circulate I'll try to spot anyone who is struggling. Again here I can do more whole class repetition if I think quite a few would benefit.
2.00	In pairs: pupils devise a rule for au, à la, à l'. . . Debrief as a whole class and write rule in books	Which pairs do I need to support in this activity?
2.10	Teacher-led listening activity: asking the way to places and giving answers; pupils use the cards to locate the places mentioned on a grid/town plan follow the directions to arrive at the place they are directed to.	Can they follow? Is anyone finding the Prenez . . . construction difficult? In debrief remember to differentiate questions.
2.20	Individual work: gapped transcript to reproduce the listening text using the pair cards as guide; able pupils asked to reproduce text without the gapped transcript **'Voici un texte à trous. Le texte sans mots importants. Ecrivez le texte, mais il faut remplir des trous. Utilisez les cartes pour vous aider.'**	How much are they able to reproduce? Are the more able working without the cards for support?
2.30	Extension activity for those who finish: can you direct your partner to places on the grid from memory	Move those who can on to this activity as soon as possible and monitor.
2.36	**Plenary: What have we learnt today? What are you able to do that you couldn't do before?**	What do their responses tell me about their confidence with the new material?
2.38	**'Les devoirs. Sortez le journal de devoirs. Copiez les instructions.'**	Write up homework in homework diary in English.
2.40	Dismiss class **'Levez-vous. Derrière les chaises. Ramassez les papiers. Silence. Au revoir tout le monde.'**	
Homework		
Using the gapped transcript as a guide, write a set of directions for the French exchange students to get them from the train station in town to your school		

■ **Figure 7.4** continued

Evaluation
Quality of pupil learning
From circulating during the pair work speaking activity I could see that most of the class were using the key phrase 'pour aller à . . .', though Simon, Daisy and Asif were not working from memory. An estimated two-thirds were getting the au/à la/à l' form. In the first pair work all seemed comfortable asking for directions. They were able to recognise the directions, (Simon seemed unsure) as I could see from the listening. Karima, Scott, Danny and Florence worked without the support grid and could give directions. Otherwise no-one got to this point.
Quality of my teaching
The material was fine and they seemed to get a lot out of the pair work especially. I should have been more insistent in the final activity that the support grid was just for that purpose i.e. to support them if they were struggling. Too many pupils referred to it instead of trying to work from memory and so the level of challenge might have been higher in the lesson. My timings were off so I didn't get to do as much as I wanted in the final plenary.
Forward planning
I need to offer more challenge and monitor better how differentiated activities are working, e.g. today too few pupils stretched themselves and worked with the support grid. In future lessons I need to establish the principle of personal challenge more strongly in advance of their starting the task and monitor more closely as they are working. I need to build in more opportunities for pupils to self-assess. This is connected to the issue of challenge above and I need to think of ways to make the two work in tandem.   *I need to offer more opportunities for pupils to use the language 'for real', e.g. to say how to get to their house. This may also help me 'sell' the lesson to them – they can see a real outcome and it will seem more authentic to them.*

▨ **Figure 7.4** *continued*

It is very important to have *clear learning objectives* for individual lessons which are spelled out at the beginning of a lesson. They help pupils realise where they are going, what is asked of them and what potential (future) application it may have. To articulate learning objectives in terms of 'By the end of the lesson, you will be able to . . .' statements can assist pupils in recognising the value of the work in hand and can also assist in making the necessary links between lesson objectives and activities. Pupils understand why they are working on certain activities, what they will be able to do when they have finished the activities, what knowledge, skills and/or understanding they will have gained and how the work in class helps them towards achieving the overall objectives. There might, however, be some lessons, where an element of surprise or discovery might be preferable.

The choice of objectives has to be firmly rooted in the context of the overall unit of work. At the beginning, it is difficult for a student teacher to see beyond the 'one-off', but it is important that even with the first plan, which may be only for one activity within a lesson otherwise taught by the class teacher, that you keep in mind as far as possible what the pupils have done previously and where they are heading, i.e. why *this* activity will help them make progress.

Importantly, lesson objectives should be multidimensional, embracing, among others, the following skills:

- ■ lexical;
- ■ structural/grammatical;
- ■ functional (e.g. expressing likes and dislikes);
- ■ 'communicative' (e.g. objectives concerning discourse and strategic competence);
- ■ (socio-)cultural;
- ■ transferable (e.g. use of reference material).

As we stated earlier, lesson objectives will be defined on the basis of previous learning outcomes and the teacher will be aware of these having closely evaluated previous lessons. New learning objectives need to build on what has come before by either consolidating it, extending it or applying it to different contexts. When planning a lesson you need to ask yourself questions such as: what can pupils realistically be expected to know already? Do certain words/phrases/concepts need to be revised or do they need to be introduced first? Are there any issues arising from previous lessons such as unfinished activities or homework to be collected in and marked? The sample lesson plan in Figure 7.4 includes a rubric on previous learning outcomes where you can note relevant points.

Objectives of a lesson should also be differentiated. The majority of pupils should achieve core objectives but some will be able to carry out extension work. Some pupils might, for instance, only be expected to remember five new items of vocabulary in a lesson whereas others can realistically be expected to remember eight as well as use them in conjunction with what they learnt in previous lessons such as expressing likes and dislikes. For a detailed discussion of differentiation, see Chapter 13. It is important to be specific about what you want learners to achieve so as to be able to evaluate the success of your lesson later on. For example, do you want them to be able to give directions (speaking) as well as understand when they hear them (listening)? Make this explicit on the lesson plan. This makes it easier when a teacher at some point in the lesson summarises with the pupils what was learnt, checks on what was learnt or asks pupils to reflect on how well they think they have met the objectives. While this sort of 'bookending' of lessons, where objectives are stated at the beginning and the extent to which they have been met reviewed at the end, may not suitable for every class, we deem this to constitute good practice generally.

Once learning outcomes have been identified, suitable activities can be selected in order to achieve the objectives. As can be seen on the sample lesson plan in Figure 7.4, assessment criteria need to be thought about in advance and in relation to the activities chosen. It is important that activities are closely linked to objectives, i.e. that lessons are objective-led and not activity-led. Only in this way at the end of the lesson is a teacher likely to have a) met the objectives and b) have some evidence that there has been learning. These can then be used to feed directly into the evaluation of the quality of the learning.

When choosing lesson objectives, contextual factors, such as the day of the week and the time of day, also need to be borne in mind. When did pupils have their last FLs lesson? Do pupils come straight from Physical Education? Is it the first or last lesson in the day? These and other questions need to be asked as pupils' concentration spans, and physical and mental readiness for certain types of activity depend on such factors. Is it a 35-minutes single or 75-minutes double period? This has implications, for instance, for the choice and sequencing of activities, the variety of tasks or the amount of work to be covered. This is the sort of valuable information that can also be gleaned from effective lesson observation carried out by you as student teacher, as well as activities such as pupil tracking, likely to be organised by your school experience school.

As part of the planning process you need to give some thought to what strategies you will use to set up and explain the various activities. For example, what TL instructions are appropriate or what type of interaction mode is best: teacher-led, group, pair and/or independent work? How will pupils best see the value in activities?

You also need to try to anticipate potential problems/disruptions that may arise. For instance, do seating arrangements have to be changed between a teacher-led activity and the following group work activity? Such changes are best kept to a minimum. Where they are required, they need to be well managed: prediction and prevention of class management issues are key.

The sequencing of activities is very important. The paradigm of 'introduction–presentation–practice–exploitation–assessment' applies to individual lessons as well as unit of work planning. Content should be broken down into manageable steps and, usually, input should come towards the beginning of the lesson when the receptiveness of pupils is highest (see Harris, 1994: 34). Often, revision of work carried out in the previous lesson is necessary prior to new input.

It is important to remember that pupils will be able to *recognise* new language before they are able to *produce* it. This has implications for sequencing of activities and questioning. For example, if introducing new vocabulary of animals, activities and questions which require recognition only – e.g. listening and reading activities and closed questioning (*C'est le chat ou la souris? Le chat, c'est quel numéro?*) should generally precede activities and questions that require production of the new language, speaking and writing tasks and open questions (*C'est quel animal?*). This is so as to give pupils more exposure to the new language before they are required to produce it themselves. For more discussion, see Chapters 9 and 10 on teaching the receptive and productive skills.

The timing of activities is another essential consideration. Anticipating the length of a particular activity helps to make sure that a realistic amount of work has been prepared. Estimating how long activities will take can be initially very difficult for student teachers. Realistic use of lesson observation to time activities can help. Pupil responses to classroom tasks vary, yet all types provide some feedback for you about pupils' readiness to move on. Pupils' facial expressions, the number of hands going up, the tone of voice and body language can all be signs of enthusiasm and confidence or boredom and inattentiveness. Pupils' willingness to engage in pupil–pupil and pupil–teacher TL activities gives you an opportunity to monitor the progress of individual pupils. Atkinson (Atkinson and Claxton, 2000: 81) suggests that there are other signs that tell you something about learners – e.g. learning difficulties might be expressed by trying to copy from neighbours, furrowed brows, etc.

Timing activities precisely also helps to pace a lesson appropriately – that is, to ensure that the change from one activity to the next happens at the right time. 'Pace' is often cited as a necessary improvement to a lesson, but what exactly is 'pace'? It certainly includes:

■ a clear focus and purpose;
■ making good use of the time available;
■ keeping on track without being unduly distracted;
■ ensuring administrative and organisational tasks are carried out efficiently;
■ not creating an imbalance between 'teacher talk' and 'pupil learning/doing';
■ reacting to pupils' responses (or lack of) to the learning activities in an appropriate manner.

As exact timing is not always possible it is advisable to have a number of end-of-lesson 'fillers' ready in case there are a few minutes left at the end of a lesson to reinforce what has been taught. These 'fillers' might be in the form of a quick game, which should be linked to the learning objectives of the lesson/unit of work providing opportunities for pupils to practise known vocabulary and/or linguistic structures, for instance, noughts and crosses, blockbusters, hangman or lotto, number drills or songs. For useful ideas, see Rumley and Sharpe (1993) and Griffith (2007). It is a very good idea to collect some generic-style games to use with any class. As your repertoire grows, you will become more confident in your adaptability in this area.

The availability of equipment, facilities and resources clearly also needs to be considered when planning and checked before teaching a lesson. Have I got the correct listening material? Is there an IWB? How can I get the equipment into the classroom in time for the beginning of the lesson? Is everything on my memory stick too and do I have back up?

Lesson plans provide an opportunity to demonstrate how the programme of work meets the statutory framework in the country you are working in. This needs be done in terms of which aspects of the curriculum are being addressed. This can be done at a unit of work level (see below).

The sample lesson plan in Figure 7.4 also features a rubric for homework. Homework needs to be planned in advance in relation to the learning objectives identified for a particular lesson. Is a learning homework most suitable, followed by a short test at the beginning of the next lesson? Should a worksheet be administered asking pupils to match up the newly encountered words and phrases with pictures or symbols? Should pupils be asked to write a short dialogue using the new language?

PLANNING A SEQUENCE OF LESSONS/UNIT OF WORK

Planning a unit of work is more than simply ensuring the coverage of the content specified in the curriculum, examination specifications or a chapter of a coursebook. Medium-term plans ensure that learning is planned over a period of time and occurs step-by-step. Unit of work planning enables you to think carefully about the exact nature of learning intended to take place over time and can help ensure progression, which needs to be built in by teachers in a multifaceted manner, from

pre-communicative	→	communicative activities
simple	→	complex language
short	→	longer spoken and written texts
implicit	→	explicit knowledge of grammar
scripted/didactically prepared (more salient)	→	authentic (less salient) language
known/familiar (e.g. classroom, self)	→	unknown/unfamiliar (world knowledge, target country) words and topics
teacher-led/aided (e.g. graded questions, examples)	→	independent (e.g. use of glossary, dictionary and other reference sources; pair-work, groupwork) interaction and working modes
concrete	→	abstract ideas
factual	→	non-factual/fictional spoken and written texts
predictable	→	unpredictable situations
less controversial	→	more controversial issues

(Pachler and Redondo, 2012)

The process of planning a series of lessons raises a whole host of issues related to providing appropriate learning opportunities. Teachers need to ensure medium-term plans feature variety, breadth and balance. From an initial overview of the forthcoming year's work it may become apparent that some units are more interesting and have more potential than others. Some may be more difficult and may contain more material and so need extra time, or are best not begun near the end of term. Equally, it may become apparent that some units of work seem thin and may need supplementing with additional material, and may offer plenty of opportunity for incorporating language covered in earlier units.

Importantly, learning opportunities must articulate with the statutory framework. If certain learning opportunities are not contained within one unit of work but required by the curriculum framework, they need to be included in one of the following units and progression in each of the four skills of listening, speaking, reading and writing considered. For example, in developing reading proficiency we need to be wary of going back to word/sentence level reading each time a new topic is introduced.

The coursebook can also offer a useful basis for planning and can contain many appropriate tasks and much useful material, particularly for listening. However, it is clearly not appropriate to set pupils certain tasks just because they are in the coursebook. Planning for series of lessons, just as it does for each individual lesson, starts from the learning objectives. The coursebook may have suitable activities that will help the teacher meet these objectives. Or it may have material that can be adapted. Frequently the teacher will need to find material from elsewhere.

While many coursebook writers suggest the level of performance demanded by particular tasks, the teacher needs to relate these notional levels of task difficulty to the pupils' levels of attainment and adapt the material accordingly.

In our view, there is no such a thing as the ideal coursebook as certain skills and topics tend to be handled differently and more to the liking of the teacher by different coursebooks. However, having a coursebook can be a useful resource for learners as it visibly structures the teaching and learning material they encounter and provides another source for reading and revision (see also Chapter 14).

Many departments pursue what could be described as a 'pick-and-mix' approach, sharing a number of PowerPoint or IWB presentations, writing their own worksheets, having sets of certain coursebooks, which they use for different topics. Such an approach can work very well but tends to be more demanding in terms of planning time.

It is important to note that FLs student teachers should not plan units of work in isolation from colleagues. Schemes of work and departmental handbooks need to be seen as collaborative efforts. As Hurren (1992: 11) points out, the scheme of work acts as:

■ a tool for developing coherent ideas on policy, methodology, priorities, subject matter, etc.;

■ a basis for pooling expertise, sharing workloads and apportioning responsibility;

■ a means of ensuring a cohesion of approach, objectives, teaching methods and standards among colleagues;

■ a device for monitoring the effectiveness of current practice;

■ a means of expressing the department's work to other departments, to newly appointed colleagues, to headteachers and curriculum managers, parents, governors, advisers and inspectors;

■ a device for interpreting into practice the guidelines of local policies, national criteria, National Curriculum, desirable methodology, etc.

Many FLs student teachers fear that they will fall behind more experienced colleagues by taking too long over particular aspects of units of work. Identification in advance of the number and length of lessons available for teaching a unit of work can help pace pupils' progress. This gives you, and of course pupils, a time frame to work to.

A medium-term plan should indicate what pupils should achieve by the end of the unit. As in lesson plans, they should be multidimensional and differentiated into core and extension outcomes. Main language items/structures refer to the vocabulary, phrases and structures to be covered. Although much is accounted for by examination specifications, important decisions for the teacher do remain even there. These include the identification of a core, which applies to all pupils in the group, and an extension for those who can carry out additional work. Some individuals may need additional support to achieve the core objectives and this should be included in planning. In addition, the teacher may need to consider which phrases need to be explained with reference to metalanguage and which can/should be taught as lexical items.

Once the objectives are clear, activities can be identified. These activities should cover the language skills of listening, speaking, reading and writing, and include intercultural learning and development of skills for independent learning.

Many teachers value mulitmodality as a way of ensuring that all learners have their needs met in the classroom. By varying the types of learning activities, the teacher can make a judgement as to whether pupils of all learning styles and abilities have been catered for equally well; pupils' enjoyment of and engagement in lessons has to be taken into consideration. Periodical audits might be useful to monitor the extent to which teaching and learning are varied, and that more pupils can feel involved and enthused by the work they are doing (see Task 7.4).

Task 7.4 **HOW OFTEN DO YOU EMPLOY THE FOLLOWING TEACHING AND LEARNING ACTIVITIES IN YOUR TEACHING?**

Feel free to add to the list. 5 indicates 'very often' and 1 means 'never'.

investigation	5	4	3	2	1	Example
problem solving	5	4	3	2	1	Example
hypothesising	5	4	3	2	1	Example
trialling	5	4	3	2	1	Example
testing	5	4	3	2	1	Example
explaining	5	4	3	2	1	Example
exploring	5	4	3	2	1	Example
communicating	5	4	3	2	1	Example
memorising	5	4	3	2	1	Example
repetition	5	4	3	2	1	Example
drilling	5	4	3	2	1	Example
improvising	5	4	3	2	1	Example
inventing	5	4	3	2	1	Example
designing	5	4	3	2	1	Example
brainstorming	5	4	3	2	1	Example
role playing	5	4	3	2	1	Example
evaluating	5	4	3	2	1	Example

Does this information help you identify how FL teaching may contribute to the fulfilment of the aims and objectives of a unit of work for all pupils in the class?

Source: Field *et al.* (2000)

Importantly, unit of work plans also need to give an overview of the opportunities provided to assess and monitor pupils' progress. As we have emphasised previously, activities need to be tightly linked to objectives and may need, particularly on a medium-term plan, to be cross-referenced to the statutory framework. Activities carried out in class should serve to provide meaningful information to help monitor and assess pupils' progress in relation to the objectives. Summative assessment tasks, such as end-of-unit tests and end-of-unit goals, might be devised in line with the practices at the placement school (for more information on assessment, see Chapter 15).

Homework to be carried out to reinforce and extend work covered in class, prepare pupils for future learning or involve them in creative activities should be considered as part of the medium-term plan. It is important that homework is carefully planned and contributes to the fulfilment of the stated objectives.

Unit plans require considerable thought and can be time-consuming to prepare. However, they facilitate the process of individual lesson planning and help to ensure progression and continuity, and the inclusion of variety and differentiation. Finally, unit planning should also take into account the need to provide pupils with the opportunity to become more independent in their approach to FL learning. Evaluation should include a review of whether such learning opportunities have, or have not, been provided. This information should, of course, be used to inform future planning.

Task 7.5 **UNIT OF WORK PLANNING**

Observe a sequence of lessons with the same class taught by an experienced colleague.

Identify what you think the key objectives are and identify the activities planned to prepare the pupils to achieve these.

How is the learning monitored and what action is taken by the teacher to compensate when successful learning has not taken place?

LESSON EVALUATION AND DEVELOPING PRACTICE THROUGH ONGOING FOCUSED REFLECTION

In their requirements as to what teachers should know and do, governments in many parts of the world are explicit on the need for continuing professional development through reflection on practice. In the UK, for example, both England and Scotland make reference to this in their standards for qualification as a teacher:

> A teacher must . . . reflect systematically on the effectiveness of lessons and approaches to teaching.
>
> (DfE, 2012: 8).

> Student teachers . . . know how to access and apply relevant findings from educational research; [and] know how to engage appropriately in the systematic investigation of practice.
>
> (GTCS, 2012: 11).

Indeed, in Northern Ireland (NI) the concept of the reflective profession underpins all of the professional standards and teachers are told that 'reflective practice needs to be internalised as part of a teacher's professional identity; it cannot simply be bolted on as an additional skill, rather it becomes part of the professional mindset and it is integrated within all the competences in a holistic way' (GTCNI, 2011: 12).

Equally, in the US, the ability to reflect on one's own practice forms part of the performance guidelines and student teachers should 'frame their own reflection and research questions and show evidence of engaging in a reflective process to improve teaching and learning' (ACTFL, 1998).

We agree that becoming a professional teacher is inextricably connected to ongoing reflection on the quality of what we are doing in our lessons. Most student teachers will begin by reflecting on individual lessons they have planned in terms of the learning outcomes, moving on as their classroom teaching increases to consider evaluation of sequences of lessons or units of work. Finally, the teacher becomes a *researcher* of his/her own practice, where evaluation of lessons continues, but the teacher focuses more in-depth attention on an aspect of teaching or a professional problem that they would like to investigate further.

Lesson evaluation: individual lessons

How should this reflection on lessons be carried out? While you are teaching only part lessons or planning collaboratively you may want to evaluate more 'holistically', asking simply 'how did it go?' Once the responsibility for planning and teaching a whole lesson has passed to you, it is important that each lesson is evaluated more rigorously.

We suggest focusing evaluation on three areas:

■ quality of learning;
■ quality of teaching;
■ forward planning.

It is useful to try to separate out learning and teaching when evaluating lessons because, naturally, early on student teachers tend to focus any evaluation on themselves and are concerned with 'performance' in the classroom. Requiring a focus on the *learning* in a lesson shifts the focus from teacher to learner, so keeping at the forefront of your mind the fact that this is all about the pupils. It also takes the emphasis off often trivial lapses in behaviour (e.g. a pupil off-task for some of the time in a pair work activity); incidents like this start to be seen in better perspective if framed in terms of the overall learning in the lesson.

The main question that needs to be answered in the review of the lesson is:

■ Did the pupils learn what I set out to teach them in the lesson and how do I know?

Below we suggest questions you might ask after a lesson and offer examples of responses that are *focused* and, wherever possible, *evidence-based*. The evaluation is imagined as a response to the teaching of the lesson outlined in Figure 7.4.

The quality of pupils' learning

Here the teacher reviews the evidence that pupils learned something and how that relates to the lesson objectives that were set. There should be reference to *evidence* as to how well pupils (both individuals and groups) met the learning objectives (examples in italics).

■   What evidence do I have that the pupils learned?

In the listening all seemed comfortable and were able to recognise the directions as I could see from asking them to raise their hands if they got six correct. I could see from circulating during the pair work speaking activity that most of the class were using the key phrase 'pour aller à . . .', though Simon, Daisy and Asif were not working from memory. I could see in addition, an estimated two-thirds were getting the au/à la/ à l' form correct. Karima, Scott, Danny and Florence worked without the support grid.

■   How clear were the pupils on how much they had learned?

I agree with Carol's [class teacher] comments that pupils did not see the point of the first listening activity. I didn't have time for a proper plenary where I might have used hands down questioning and a possible summarising listening activity to see if any of them could recognise sentences on mini whiteboards. I did not have time for a traffic light activity either, which would have helped them to think about what they felt they'd learned today.

The quality of the teaching

Here you comment on the effectiveness of your planning and on your own teaching performance in the classroom. The questions below will guide you on this as well.

■   How was the quality of the planning? Was the teaching material suitable for the age, abilities and aptitudes of the pupils? Was it well-ordered, relevant, sufficiently challenging or too difficult?

The material was fine and they seemed to get a lot out of the pair work especially. I should have been more insistent in the final activity that the support grid was just for that purpose, i.e. to support them if they were struggling. Too many pupils referred to it instead of trying to work from memory and so the level of challenge might have been higher in the lesson. My timings were off so I didn't get to the final plenary.

■   Did I build in activities that allowed me to gauge whether the learning objectives had been met? Did I diagnose and assess pupils' difficulties? Did I respond to them? Did the homework set seem appropriate to the age and abilities of the pupils? Was homework handed in on time or did I have to 'chase it up'?

I need to develop a closer link on the plans between objectives and activities that will provide me with evidence that the pupils can do what I set out to do with them. Here I could have offered more opportunity to use the language 'for real', for example, by moving some on by asking them to describe how to get to their house from the school. This would have allowed me to gauge better whether they could work from memory.

■   How successful were my questioning techniques? Did I give all or most of the pupils a chance to answer something?

Yes, I spread the questions pretty well using the pupils' names and making sure I differentiated the questioning. (Did I ask any higher-order questions though?) David did particularly well and may need stretching.

■ How were levels of pupil interest and activity? How would I change my activities if I were to teach the same lesson again?

I could have 'sold' the lesson objectives (and so the activities) much better to the pupils at the beginning. I need to think of ways to make the learning more relevant to them. They were a little subdued and bored looking. Were there cultural opportunities that I missed? I need to give this more thought. Maybe something about the features of French towns?

■ How much opportunity did I and the pupils get to speak in the foreign language? Did they all hear and understand what was being said?

Partly. They all took part in the pair-work and I didn't notice too much off-task behaviour. I did not always check comprehension and I should use more examples and modelling rather than launching pupils into the activities too quickly.

Forward planning

■ What do you need to do in the subsequent lesson(s) with the group in the light of your evaluation to build on the progress made in this lesson? Note here specific things to bear in mind (e.g. planning, teaching points, as well as catering for individual pupils' needs).

I need to offer more challenge and monitor better how differentiated activities are working – e.g. today too few pupils stretched themselves and worked with the support grid or from memory in producing the directions. In future lessons I need to establish the principle of personal challenge more strongly in advance of their starting the task and monitor more closely as they are working.

I need to build in more opportunities for pupils to self-assess. This is connected to the issue of challenge above and I need to think of ways to make the two work in tandem.

I need to offer more opportunities for pupils to use the language 'for real' – e.g. to say how to get to their house. This may also help me 'sell' the lesson to them – they can see a real outcome and it will seem more authentic to them.

It is important to note that there will be many positives as well as many areas for development in any lesson. It is impossible to focus on every developmental point in every lesson. In the 'forward planning' section of any evaluation it might be wise to focus on only one or two key areas for development and put these into action in the coming lesson rather than try to do everything at once.

Lesson evaluation: sequences of lessons

Once a sequence of lessons is underway, it may make more sense to start to jointly evaluate a number of lessons in the sequence, using the same headings as above (quality of learning, quality of teaching, forward planning). Because at this point the student teacher is aware of the medium-term as well as short-term goals that

---

Task 7.6 **LESSON PLANNING AND EVALUATION**

In consultation with (the) respective class teacher(s), prepare a number of lesson plans using the format suggested in Figure 7.4 for a specific class, which you have observed on a number of occasions already.

Discuss the lesson plans with the respective class teacher, teach the lessons and evaluate them against the quality of pupil learning and the quality of personal teaching, forward planning.

---

need to be achieved across a unit of work, it makes sense to evaluate how well the overarching objectives have been achieved. For example, a short unit of work entitled 'When I was younger. . .', where the goals are for pupils to speak and write about things they used to do when they were young children but do not do any more, would incorporate use of the imperfect tense as well as a number of key lexical items. Rather than (or perhaps as well as) evaluating how one lesson has gone, it would seem sensible to reflect after maybe three or four lessons on the short unit of work, focusing on the extent to which the medium-term objectives have been met: what is the evidence that pupils *can* communicate meanings about their earlier childhood? How accurate is their ability to use the imperfect or to understand when others use it? What do I need to do in the next lesson or in future units of work to reinforce and revisit this learning? How has the teaching contributed to these outcomes and how might future teaching be improved? And so the cycle of planning/teaching/assessing and reflection begins again for the next unit of work.

As we develop our understanding of the context we are working in and start to see patterns in our practice, we may need to re-evaluate what we are doing more fundamentally. We asserted earlier our view that professionalism develops as a result of the constant review of our work in the light of all knowledge at our disposal. This knowledge might be generated by the reading we have done in the substantive area of SLA research and research on FL teaching as well as in tangential areas, such as social psychology (see Chapter 3). It will likely be generated from listening to the judgements and feedback on our work other professionals give. It will be generated from the observations you yourself and others have carried out in different contexts. Finally, and most importantly, it is through the process of reflecting on the professional decisions you have made, both in your planning (pre-action) and in the teaching (in-action) that you will refine and develop your practice so as to achieve the best learning for the pupils.

Professionalism consists of taking all of this knowledge and making sense of it so as to apply it as wisely and effectively as possible to arrive at the methodological choices that are most likely to achieve the best learning outcomes in the future. The application of this professional knowledge will have to take into consideration the nature of the varied school and classroom contexts and the varying needs of the learners within these contexts. As Zeichner and Liston (1996: 1) remind us, reflection needs to be set within a wider picture of a teacher's situation and his/her beliefs:

If a teacher never questions the goals and the values that guide his or her work, the context in which he or she teaches, or never examines his or her assumptions, then it is our belief that this individual is not engaged in reflective teaching.

The teacher as researcher: evidence-based inquiry into teaching and learning

We started this section by considering why a teacher, in the interests of developing professionally, might need to evaluate her practice carefully. Now we consider how focused, evidence-based evaluation of lessons might provide a basis for researching some aspects of practice more thoroughly. Developing the skills to research practice systematically is an invaluable tool that teachers can draw on again and again through their careers. In addition, as Taber (2007: 7) reminds us: 'The message is that all teachers are now required to be able to demonstrate research-informed and evidence-based practice'.

To this end, most teacher education programmes now require student teachers to carry out a practice-based inquiry project or some other form of in-depth investigation of their work in the classroom at some point during their programme of study. This substantial project must show familiarity with an area of academic research, an aspect of which is then explored through a study in the classroom based on primary data collection.

There are a number of steps that help establish a focus for such a piece of practitioner research (see Macaro, 2003a for some useful suggestions). The first is to ask some fundamental questions: 'What do I want to find out more about? Is there an aspect of my practice I feel needs some more attention? Is there a professional "problem" that I'd like to solve?'

Having established an area of interest in, say, the use of the TL in the classroom, you might then explore what you already know about the topic, reflecting on your teaching experiences to date (both as teacher and learner) and your current beliefs about the issue of TL use. You might then look for relevant reading and draw on advice from mentors, tutors, and so on and ask: 'What writing exists on this topic?' This might be either reviews of literature or empirical studies carried out in similar topic areas, writing in professional journals, and so on. Exploring what is known already about a topic can help focus the enquiry and allow for the next stage which is producing the research questions for this inquiry. The research questions that will frame the design need to be clear and most importantly answerable. To do this it is useful to work out *how* they might be answered as they are being written, rather than later on. This is more likely to keep the questions realistic and manageable.

Once the questions are established, the data-gathering tools need to be devised. There are a number of books that will help a teacher construct a project to investigate their practice. We recommend Taber (2007), Denscombe (2007) and Wilson (2012) in particular. The tools frequently used are interviews (both individual and focus groups), questionnaires, classroom observation schedules, records of pupil progress (test and homework results) and documents (policy documents, both national and departmental). Once the tools are designed and a time-frame established, the research can begin.

Often the project will involve the gathering of some baseline data. For example, if your research question is: 'To what extent does the introduction of a range of strategies to encourage pupil TL use affect the amount of TL spoken in class?' you could begin by asking how things are at present, e.g. 'What is the current level of pupil use of TL?' Data gathering for this stage might involve asking the usual class teacher to observe some of your lessons against an observation schedule designed to note when, how often and who uses the TL in the classroom. Another relevant question might be: 'How does introducing the range of strategies to promote use of the TL affect pupils' attitudes towards TL use?' for which baseline data might be gathered using a pupil questionnaire and/or through interviews with some pupils.

At this point you might carry out an intervention, changing an aspect of your TL practice (e.g. introducing strategies that encourage more TL use – using deskmats with key phrases for support; building in rewards for effort with TL; using flags to indicate blocks of time when all will use the TL only) and then evaluate what has happened as a result. This might involve further observation, a second round of questionnaires, interviews, analysis of lesson evaluations, and so on.

Careful thought needs to be given to analysis by considering: 'How will I make sense of the data?' Most important is to be rigorous in considering the learning that arose from the focus on this aspect of professional practice, and then to reflect on how it might influence future practice. To what extent has carrying out this project led me to change my understandings and so my practice, and how?

Having completed the investigation, it might be helpful to share the outcomes with others, perhaps at a professional conference, in a departmental meeting at the placement school, during sessions with other student teachers, online via a teacher forum, or even more informally via Facebook groups or over coffee in the staffroom.

Essentially, this form of researching of practice is just a stage on from rigorous evaluation of lessons. It is important to remember that the *process* of carrying out such research is often as important as the outcome. Once the skills of thinking about and investigating practice in this way are in place, it can be done again and again throughout a teacher's professional life.

SUMMARY

Lesson observation is an effective way to learn about FL learning and teaching, and can represent an invaluable tool in the development and formation of an individual approach to FL teaching. It is impossible to focus on everything you will see in a classroom, so it helps to have defined areas to focus on in a particular lesson. The aim is not to be critical but to learn as much as possible from each lesson observed. The model of moving from observation → collaborative teaching → student taking responsibility for teaching one-off whole lessons → teaching sequences of lessons is commonly followed by student teachers since it constitutes a helpful model of progression. To this end effective short- and medium-term planning is vital, where evidence of understanding of the planning, teaching, assessment loop can be seen in lesson plans and evaluations. The process of rigorously reflecting on professional choices, taking into consideration evidence of pupil learning in previous lessons, your wider understanding of how FLs are learned, and the particular school and classroom context, is an integral part of becoming a teacher.

PEDAGOGY RELATED ▨ ▨ ▧ ■

FURTHER READING

Crozier, M., Gidley, R., Lertoria, T., Murphy, D., Slater, S. and Wardle, M. (2003) Starters and plenaries – a practical resource. In *Deutsch: Lehren und Lernen*, 28: 11–14.

A very clear introduction to the issues involved in planning for learning in FL. Practical ideas to incorporate in plans for foreign language teaching and learning.

Macaro, E. (2003) Second language teachers as second language researchers. In *Language Learning Journal,* 27: 43–51.

This paper discusses classroom-based research as an integral part of teaching and learning, and provides some advice not only on how to approach the reading of empirical work but also suggests some techniques for carrying out research in the foreign language classroom.

Wajnryb, R. (1992) *Classroom Observation Tasks: A Resource Book for Language Teachers and Trainers*. Cambridge: Cambridge University Press.

This text remains a very good guide to aspects to be considered when observing in foreign language classrooms.

CHAPTER 8

TEACHING IN THE TARGET LANGUAGE

INTRODUCTION

The use of the TL involves some key methodological decisions for FLs teachers. These include:

- how to ensure the TL is used most effectively for instruction, interaction and communication and how to structure target language discourse in the classroom;
- how to elicit effective TL use by pupils;
- when and how the use of English may be appropriate in the FLs classroom.

OBJECTIVES

By the end of this chapter you should be able to:

- view the practice of teaching in the TL from the perspective of a basic understanding of theoretical issues and recent policy developments;
- assess the desirability and aims of teaching in the TL;
- assess the practicability of teaching in the TL in everyday FLs lessons;
- reflect on different patterns of classroom TL interaction;
- reflect on different functions of TL use in the classroom;
- understand strategies for effective TL use.

Rather than discussing TL use as a recurring theme in various places in the book, we cover them in one single chapter in order to provide a coherent overview of relevant issues. Therefore, the examples given need to be seen in the context of the respective chapters they are linked to; for instance, examples of how to teach grammar in the TL need to be related to the overall approach to teaching and learning grammar outlined in detail in Chapter 11. In this chapter we briefly examine the theoretical arguments and discuss practical suggestions for effective TL use. In addition, issues of TL teaching with particular relevance for you as a student teacher are included.

THE TL IN THE FLs CLASSROOM: A SUMMARY OF OFFICIAL POLICY VIEWS ON THE RELATIVE VALUE OF THE USE OF THE TL AT KEY STAGES 3 AND 4 (FOR PUPILS AGED 11–16) IN ENGLAND

A brief historical perspective on the use of the TL in the National Curriculum in England

The successive versions of the National Curriculum Orders in the 1990s established the expectation of TL use as the 'normal means of communication' (DES/Welsh Office 1990: 6) in the classroom. This was largely premised on the belief that for successful FL acquisition to take place, pupils should be exposed as much as possible to the TL.

More recently, the debate surrounding TL use in England has incorporated the question of whether or not to include the use of English in the FLs classroom. Is there a legitimate case for using English as L1 in certain circumstances? Can it further pupils' learning in FLs? The debate has thus shifted from the focus on clarity and progression of TL instructions to that of the development of a more inclusive rationale for the role of the L1 in improving pupils' FLs skills. The shift, therefore, has to some extent moved from a quantitative view of the effect of TL use (the maximalist position) to a qualitative perspective (the optimalist position) which seeks to define the best form of TL use in the FLs classroom.

Developments with the National Curriculum reflected to some extent this change in focus. While the National Curriculum Orders implemented in the early and mid-1990s promoted the maximalist position on TL use, which assumes that 'there is probably no pedagogical value in learner use of L1 and almost certainly none in teacher use of L1' (Macaro, 2000: 184), the publication of a revised National Curriculum at the end of the 1990s saw a shift towards the so-called optimal use position, which sees 'some value in teacher use of L1 and some value in learner use of L1' (Macaro, 2000: 184). Although the 1999 National Curriculum document contained no explicit references to the medium in which teachers should teach, expectations concerning pupil use of the TL were clear:

> The target language is the modern foreign language that pupils are learning. Pupils are expected to use and respond to the target language, and to use English only when necessary (for example, when discussing a grammar point or when comparing English and the target language).
>
> (DfEE/QCA, 1999: 16)

In addition, the 1999 National Curriculum stated:

Pupils should be taught to:

Use their knowledge of English or another language when learning the
target language.

The 2007 National Curriculum, however, made a number of references to
English (or another language) as being potentially helpful to learners when
comparing languages, memorising or considering language patterns:

> use their knowledge of English or another language when learning the target
> language . . .
>
> . . . make links with English at word, sentence and text level . . .

The recently published framework document for consultation on revisions to
the National Curriculum (DfE, 2013) makes reference to specific uses of English
to support FL learning at both Key Stage 2 and Key Stage 3. At Key Stage 2, teachers
are encouraged to draw their pupils' attention to grammatical similarities and
differences between the TL and English to help them

> understand basic grammar appropriate to the language being studied, such
> as (where relevant): feminine, masculine and neuter forms and the conjugation
> of high-frequency verbs; key features and patterns of the language; how to
> apply these, for instance, to build sentences; and how these differ from or
> are similar to English.
>
> (DfE, 2013: 174)

In the proposals for Key Stage 3, this process is developed further through
the reintroduction of the practice of translation. This would take the form of
developing a competence in translating 'short, suitable material' into English and
translating 'short written text into the foreign language' (DfE, 2013: 176).

THE USE OF TRANSLATION AS A PEDAGOGICAL TOOL IN THE FLs CLASSROOM

The official revival of the role of translation in the 2013 version of the National
Curriculum in England has provoked renewed interest in the idea that translation
can contribute to FL teaching and learning in schools. To some extent this is a formal
recognition of what has, in fact, been occurring in the majority of schools, even at
the height of the popularity of the communicative paradigm: for instance, through
regular vocabulary testing, the use of the pupil as interpreter, or the use of
dictionaries. However, given that it is important to align classroom practice with a
justifiable framework for a pedagogical approach, it is worth reflecting explicitly
on the implications of this pedagogical strategy.

It is important to bear three points in mind when formulating your position
about the role of translation in FL teaching. First, most specialists in the field of
translation studies point to the inherent deception in the concept of 'translation',
which is captured in the Italian adage *traduttore, traditorre* (translator, traitor).
The act of translation does not usually involve the transference of linguistic meaning

from one language to another, but the search for equivalent formulations. However, exact equivalences do not always exist between two languages and different cultural connotations are often attached to the translations. What, furthermore, is the distinction between translation and interpreting? Second, while translation is most often advocated by FLs teachers of advanced or university-level students, the arguments in favour of its use at Secondary school level need to be situated in this context. For instance, for some pupils the translation process presents obstacles to performance not only in relation to the TL but to the L1 as well. In contemporary multilingual Britain translating into English can be problematic for pupils whose L1 is not English, as well as for those for whom it is but whose literacy competence is weak. While translation exercises may arguably be useful for such pupils to support their FL learning, using the results as an assessment of their knowledge of the TL would not be appropriate. Finally, the revival of the use of translation as part of the repertoire of the FLs teacher's strategies should not be seen as a return to the 'grammar-translation' approach to FL teaching which dominated in the nineteenth and early twentieth centuries and which consisted mainly of the development of a 'mental discipline' (Richards and Rogers, 2001: 5), focusing almost exclusively on reading and writing, on literary texts, on sentences as the basic unit of teaching and learning, and on accuracy in learner output. Instead, you need to develop ways of integrating the strategy within the broader teaching and learning objectives of the curriculum. For instance, key sentences or short paragraphs for translation can be extrapolated from prior textual material used for comprehension or dialogue activities in order to consolidate or monitor prior learning.

GENERAL CERTIFICATE OF SECONDARY EDUCATION (GCSE)

The 2000 GCSE subject criteria for FLs (QCA, 2000: 3) explicitly highlighted the requirement for maximal use of the TL in candidates' responses:

> A specification must require candidates to express themselves in the modern foreign language when speaking and writing. In listening and reading, where a response is spoken or written, it must be in the modern foreign language, except where response in another language is a necessary part of the task (for example, in an interpreting exercise) or where a non-linguistic response is a natural and appropriate alternative to a response in the modern foreign language. A maximum of 10% of the total marks for the subject may be awarded for answers in English, Welsh or Irish. No more than half of this maximum allocation may be assigned to any particular assessment objective.

From this, clear inferences can be made about expected teacher use of the TL. However, subsequent versions, including the 2011 Ofqual subject criteria, available at www.rewardinglearning.org.uk/docs/regulation/gcse_criteria/nov11/gcse-subject-criteria-modern-foreign-languages.pdf, make no mention of the use of English and are generally less explicit about the use of the TL.

The 2000 GCSE criteria also stipulated that 'instructions to candidates (other than general instructions) should normally be in the language in which the candidate

---

You are shopping in (target-language country) and want to buy a gift. Below are some suggestions for points to include but you will also have to answer unexpected questions about this topic.

The following points are suggestions of the information you can include:

1   Say what you want to buy and who/what it is for.
2   Say what you like or dislike about any gift suggested or offered.
3   Ask a question about the gift (e.g. is it popular/traditional/fragile/is there a guarantee?).
4   Explain why you do or do not want to buy it.
5   Ask a question about another item in the shop.
6   Say what you have liked about the area and what you would like to do (e.g. a particular place you want to see or visit or an activity you would like to do).
7   Explain what you have done/seen during your visit and what it was like.

■ **Figure 8.1** OCR specimen French GCSE speaking test exemplar task 3 – role play

is expected to respond, except where the nature of the task would make the instructions too difficult to understand' (QCA, 2000: 3). A policy of testing in the TL requires pupils to learn rubrics and instructions in the TL. This alone does not lead to increased spontaneous use of the TL by pupils as these rubrics are part of standard classroom vocabulary and pupils are expected to learn them like other transactional phrases. (For a detailed discussion of assessment issues, see Chapter 15.) In the 2007 and 2011 GCSE criteria, the only stipulation is that boards list the TL rubrics to be used.

The use of rubrics in exam tasks is an interesting and potentially awkward issue as it raises key questions about the role of the L1 in the process of FL learning. As a scaffold to the assessment task, the L1 can help clarify the candidates' understanding of what is required in the assessment task and, therefore, their performance can be measured more confidently. In their FAQs pages of guidance to the introduction of the new GCSE FLs examinations, one of the Awarding Bodies – education bodies appointed by the government to offer approved qualifications, OCR – justify the use of English in the rubrics for examination tasks on the basis of feedback from teachers and FLs teacher associations, which stressed that 'the focus should be the testing of understanding of target language through the material, not through the questions' (p. 3). However, beyond clarifying the focus and requirements of the task, the English instructions may trigger, however implicitly, different cognitive reactions than if they were absent from the rubrics. Take the oral test prompts in Figure 8.1 as an example.

What might this task tell us about the type of knowledge that the candidate would display here and what role does the prompt in English play in completion of the task? How far does the rubric encourage the candidate to think in English first before producing the TL utterance?

OFSTED INSPECTION EXPECTATIONS

Ofsted, the UK body responsible for inspecting and regulating services that care for children and young people, have consistently used teacher and student TL use as a yardstick for measuring effective teaching and learning. In *The Changing Landscape of Languages* (2008: 5) Ofsted reported that 'barriers to further improvement at KS3 were teachers' lack of use of the TL to support their students' routine use of the language in lessons'. A subsequent report (Ofsted, 2011) pointed to an absence in many lessons observed of the teaching of strategies for responding to 'everyday requests and thus routine work in the TL' (p. 6). Conversely, the same report identified outstanding practice through reference to teacher use of the TL: 'Teachers presented very good role models for speaking as they used the target languages consistently, using English only when appropriate to do so' (p. 28).

THE VALUE OF TL USE AS MEDIUM OF INSTRUCTION AND CLASSROOM INTERACTION

Teacher TL use as source of input

There is a general consensus among linguists, SLA theorists and FLs educators that TL input plays a key role in a learner's acquisition of that language. This may seem self-evident, but language learners are not going to develop competence in a FL out of fresh air. The process requires input as the basis of language development. That input can be either explicit or implicit. The former normally consists of explanations and information about the TL, which can be given either in the TL or in another language (most often in the L1, of course). Implicit input is almost always provided in the TL and takes the form of 'natural spoken language' (Whong, 2011: 96) or authentic written texts. While substantial exposure to TL input is necessary for learners to develop competence in the language, it is not a sufficient condition. It is, of course, not necessary to be exposed to all items of a language to be able to produce them. Humans have the capacity to process and develop their language competence independently once they have acquired a basis of knowledge acquired through explicit and implicit input.

This input needs, of course, to be pitched at an appropriate level for the class or individual learner. Krashen (1982: 21), for instance, argued that the input needs to be 'a little beyond the [learner's] current level of competence $(i + 1)$'.

The teacher is not, of course, the only source of TL input. This is also available through exposure to TL speakers through audio, video and digital means. In some cases, these other sources provide valuable enhanced naturalistic exposure of the TL which is superior to what the non-native speaker languages teacher can offer linguistically. So what are the distinctive benefits to be gained from teacher TL use? Figure 8.2 is a list of different ways in which teacher TL use is an invaluable tool for scaffolding the language learning in the FLs classroom.

Pupil reactions to their teacher's use of the TL in lessons

One commonly hears comments from pupils and others that there are problems with TL comprehension in the classroom when perhaps the approach has not been

- ■ Teacher TL use helps to model the language in the learners' mind as a tool for communication rather than simply as an object of study.
- ■ The teacher knows their class and can, therefore, adapt the TL to optimal effect to make it comprehensible to the class through the use of appropriate strategies.
- ■ The teacher can use paralinguistic strategies (e.g. gestures, facial expressions, intonation, exaggeration) to support the expression of meaning through the TL.
- ■ The teacher can model the formal features of the language through whole-class TL interaction (repetition, games and drills).
- ■ The teacher can exemplify different functions of the language through TL use (e.g. questioning, requesting, admonishing).
- ■ The teacher can manage the discourse to allow for unpredictable and spontaneous use of the TL.
- ■ Teacher TL use can reinforce correct pronunciation of the TL.
- ■ Teacher use of the TL can develop the learner's listening competence in the TL.
- ■ Teacher TL use can incorporate a range of language items that can be picked up incidentally by the learners through intermittent exposure over time.
- ■ Teacher TL use can also be valuable in enabling feedback through recasts, repetition and other strategies which allow the learner to self-correct their own TL output.

■ **Figure 8.2** Teacher TL use for scaffolding language learning in the FLs classroom

effectively thought through. But what about when teachers do use the TL consistently and effectively? How do the pupils respond to that? Consider the following extract of an interview with a group of Year 8 pupils at a Cambridgeshire 11–16 school learning French where the FLs department has followed a strong policy of communicative use of the TL in lessons:

Researcher: What do you think about the use of the language in the lesson because we've noticed your teachers use the language quite a lot? How do you find that? Do you think that helps you to learn?

Several: Yeah.

Ad: Key words trigger what you think is going to happen and I think it just kind of widens your senses almost, so you're trying to understand things by just certain words.

Al: And then, yeah, it's good to kind of . . . again it's with the tapes, when you're listening to tapes, it doesn't matter if you don't understand every word they're saying. You're just picking up the words you know and you can kind of make out what they're trying to get at out of that. And so when they will be talking a lot in the language, the teacher will always say, 'Well, does anybody know what I'm talking about?' in English. And then the person that does will explain, so then the rest of the class will understand if they didn't.

Researcher: So the teacher checks usually. So she or he uses the language but they always have a way of checking?

Ad: There was one teacher in Year 7 that would, when we were in forms until we were split up into groups, would just talk to us in French like we're French, and then she would stop and say and, like, stop for a certain short period of time for English time, so that she would talk in English, but that would only be a short period and then she would just speak in French for a long time. And I sort of found that slightly difficult but after a while I think I caught on because you'd certainly hear words after a while and you'd certainly catch on to what they'd mean.

Ce: I certainly understand the reason why the teachers did that just so we could get used to the language when we started in French. One of the teachers, in our forms, she would always like speak French and then there would be a period of time to ask her questions in English or whatever. And she would like us to speak in French as well so that we got used to it more.

Task 8.1 **PUPIL RESPONSES TO TL USE BY THE TEACHER**

What can you learn from the comments in the interview, both in terms of the pupils' perceptions of the TL experience and also in terms of effective TL practice?

LIMITATIONS IN THE USE OF THE TL: THE ROLE OF THE L1

Factors affecting the amount of TL use in the classroom

TL use is an important issue for all FLs teachers, whether they are non-native or native speakers of the TL. FLs teachers who are native speakers of English face challenges such as developing the requisite subject knowledge and confidence in TL use for sustained periods of time. Native speakers of the TL need to take care to ensure their use of the TL is pitched correctly according to the linguistic proficiency of their pupils.

It is widely acknowledged that the artificiality of the classroom frequently militates against maximum TL use by pupils and teachers. Maximum TL use requires a certain suspension of disbelief both on the part of pupils and teachers, i.e. the willingness to pretend that neither party speaks English and that the transactions and interactions of the classroom are 'authentic', which can be difficult to sustain. The effort required both by pupils and by teachers to maintain maximum TL use can lead to reduced levels of 'performance' on the part of teachers and alienation from the learning process on the part of pupils, and the ultimate objective of ensuring progression in the pupils' learning may suffer in the long run. The development of good social relationships between teachers and learners, it can be argued, requires non-curriculum specific TL discourse, which learners do not have at their disposal. There can be, in short, practical difficulties associated with maximum use of the TL. Nevertheless, these are not arguments for not aspiring to optimum TL use.

The nature of TL used by teachers can depend on many factors such as:

- ability and size of the group;
- motivation;
- group dynamics;
- receptiveness of the pupils;
- environmental factors;
- incidents during previous lesson or break;
- topic area;
- tasks to be attempted;
- discipline problems;
- interruptions from outside, etc.

These factors can have a bearing on the amount of TL used by the pupils to respond to, or initiate exchanges with the teacher and/or peers. Established classroom routines, adequate preparation and a feeling of confidence and security are vitally important in this respect.

Despite the fact that mother tongue use deprives learners of exposure to TL models, teaching in the TL needs to be systematic and planned in order to be effective. There are occasions when TL use can become a barrier to understanding; there are certain circumstances when it is not appropriate and there are some when it is simply impossible. What is important is the systematicity of TL use and that use of the mother tongue is principled and carefully thought through. Teacher talk is different from native speaker talk (see Pachler, 1999a or Macaro, 2000) and, therefore, classroom-based exposure to TL is different from that in the real world: the language is, of necessity, segmented, partial and carefully built up. In his review of research literature, Macaro (2000: 179) stresses that the mother tongue is the language of thought for all but the most advanced learners and that, therefore, it warrants careful consideration as a learning tool. Code-switching (i.e. switching between the TL and the L1) is described by him as a natural and legitimate operation despite the possibility of interference from the mother tongue. Macaro questions whether interference from the mother tongue is sufficient 'to counterbalance any beneficial cognitive processes that making links between L1 and L2 might bring about' (2000: 179). He points out that beginners use the mother tongue to help them decode texts and that beginners and more advanced learners use it to help them write texts. Also, Macaro suggests that progression from formulaic expression to more 'creative'/independent use of the TL may well require some recourse to the mother tongue as the language of thought. In addition, learners need to feel clear about what they are doing and why.

Teaching in the TL can be tiring for teacher and pupils. A lot of thought has to be given not only to the lesson plan but also to the wording of instructions and the level of the 'incidental' language ensuring that pupils do not get left behind. It takes great concentration and perseverance not to do the 'natural thing' – that is, to answer the questions in the language in which they are asked. There is often the temptation to answer a pupil's question 'What page are we on?' with 'Top of page 48'. One possible strategy is to appoint language guardians, who call the teacher to order in such circumstances, e.g. with '*Auf Deutsch bitte, Frau/Herr . . . !*' ('In German, please Ms/Mr . . . !').

Pupils' limited attention span can also be a challenge. A lesson of 50 minutes or more is a long time for pupils to concentrate and for some pupils this can be a struggle. Indeed, in his study Macaro (2000: 187) found that lessons that were more than 50 minutes long elicited less pupil use of the TL in teacher-centred activities than lessons which lasted approximately 35 minutes.

Factors limiting the effectiveness of TL use

For those pupils who think that FLs are beyond them, unstructured teaching in the TL can confirm their feeling of inadequacy, potentially leading to demotivation and frustration and all the associated discipline problems. As FLs teachers, we need to try to build up positive dispositions in pupils and try to avoid any (sense of) failure to understand.

This problem can be overcome by careful lesson planning: if the pace of the lesson is brisk, if the activities are varied, if a range of skills are being practised and if there is a balance of 'stirrers' and 'settlers' (see Halliwell, 1991: 26), then unacceptably long spells of continuous TL should not normally occur. Using the TL language should be a stimulating challenge for you and your pupils.

TYPOLOGY OF TL USE

There are three dimensions to the phenomenon of TL use in the FLs classroom, each of which represents a set of different options available to the teacher: different types of participant relations in the interaction; different patterns of discourse interaction; and different functions of the use of the TL in lessons.

Different participants in the interaction

The National Curriculum Council non-statutory guidance, still valid despite its early publication date, offered the diagrammatical representation of TL use in Figure 8.3: the teacher and pupils interacting with each other inside the classroom as a preparation for TL use beyond the classroom. The diagram identifies three sets of interactional relations:

- teacher–pupil;
- pupil–teacher;
- pupil–pupil.

Often FLs departments identify key lexical items and phrases for each of these categories as *aide-mémoires* for members of the team in order to encourage appropriateness of TL use in relation to the level of proficiency of pupils as well as to foster standardisation across the department. For pupils, these lists become part of the passive and/or active vocabulary they are expected to know (see Macdonald, 1993).

Evidence suggests that, while a structured and well-planned approach can facilitate the coherent use of the TL by the teacher when interacting with pupils and – to a lesser extent – pupils responding to or even initiating interaction in the TL with the teacher, TL use between pupils is most difficult to achieve.

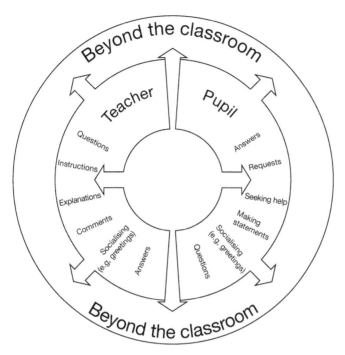

■ **Figure 8.3** Using the TL

Source: NCC, 1992.

Task 8.2 **DEPARTMENTAL POLICY ON TEACHING IN THE TL**

Obtain a copy of the departmental policy on the use of the TL by pupils and teachers. What approach do you feel it encourages: maximal or optimal, or is the message less clear? Compare practice at your placement school with the experience of fellow student teachers in other schools.

Transactional language, i.e. the language that refers to classroom objects and events, classroom interaction and classroom communication, needs to be taught just like other topic-related language. Possible strategies in this context are, for instance:

■ the use of visuals (IWB, PowerPoint, OHP or flashcards) depicting key words and phrases;

■ classroom displays, which are regularly referred to in the course of teaching;

■ building up a list of useful phrases and expressions in the back of pupils' exercise books;

■ the encouragement of TL utterances by pupils when entering and leaving the classroom or when the register is called;

- the use of pupils as 'translators' to verify meaning in English;
- variation in voice and intonation as an incentive to pupils to repeat words or phrases many times, e.g. *'leise'*, *'ganz leise'*, *'schnell'*, *'ganz schnell'*;
- the so-called 'sandwich' method of 'wrapping' mother tongue instructions into two 'layers' of TL, e.g. *'Stellt euch leise hintereinander auf'* – 'Line up quietly' – *'Stellt euch leise hintereinander auf'*.

Task 8.3 **TEACHING TRANSACTIONAL TL**

Design some visuals in a format of your choice or other material for the teaching and practice of some specific transactional TL phrases for pupils in their first year of study of the FL. Test these out with your classes and revise them on the basis of pupil feedback and your reflection.

Patterns of interaction

The second dimension of classroom TL use in schools is that of choices between different patterns of discourse interaction. While it is true that FL lessons often consist of a variety of different discourse patterns, it is useful to be conscious of what the different templates are and how they impact on teaching and learning in different ways. In that way you will be better able to balance your lessons with the right mix of appropriate discourse strategies. The following are two broad patterns that one can find in operation in FLs classrooms at this level.

IRE/IRF

Arguably the most conventional patterns of classroom discourse are what are called IRE (Initiation–Response–Evaluation) and IRF (Initiation–Response–Feedback). Often, and especially in the context of FL teaching, these two patterns are combined, as in the following example.

EXAMPLE 1: IRE/F INTERACTION IN A BEGINNERS' FRENCH CLASS

Teacher (shows a PPT slide of items of food on the whiteboard): *Mémorisez. Quelque chose va manquer. Attention. Un, deux, trois.* (Clicks to a new slide with one item missing.)
Qu'est-ce qui manque? [Memorise it. Something is going to go missing. Pay attention. One, two, three. What's missing?]
Paul: *De la poulet.* [chicken – *wrong gender*]
Teacher: *C'est correcte, Tina?* [Is that correct, Tina?]
Tina: *Du poulet.* [chicken – *correct gender*]
Teacher: *Oui, c'est ça. Du poulet. Très bien!* [Yes, that's right. Chicken. Well done!]

Example 1 illustrates some of the following common features of the IRE/F pattern of interaction as conducted in a beginners' FLs classroom:

■ The exchange consists of clearly defined units of interaction. Although the interactional pattern is triadic (I–R–E/F), this can be extended (as in the example above, where the teacher turns to a different pupil for the correct answer) to involve more individuals within the unit of exchange.

■ The teacher speaks in the Initiation and Evaluation/Feedback turns and the pupil in the Response turn. The teacher is the expert directing the interaction and evaluating the accuracy of the response. The evaluation in this example is represented by the comment 'Du poulet. Très bien!' and the corrective feedback focuses on the gender of '*poulet*'.

■ The unit of interaction is opened (often in the form of a question) and closed by the teacher who is thereby in control of the exchange.

■ The focus of the exchange tends to be on learning and practice rather than on open communication.

■ The IRE/F pattern is generally suitable for carrying out whole-class oral drills and supports consolidation of language use through repetition and correction.

INSTRUCTIONAL CONVERSATION

An alternative mode to the IRE/F pattern is an interactional pattern that gives more space for learner influence on the direction of the interaction and which focuses more on real dialogue, elaborating on unpredicted responses. There are different variants of this more constructivist approach to classroom interaction (such as the 'dialogic approach' described by Mercer (2004) and others that relies on a sociocultural view of learning). For an in-depth analysis of 'spontaneous teacher–learner interaction' in the context of third-year German classes taught by different teachers in the same school, see Hawkes, 2012. The notion of 'instructional conversation', originally developed in bilingual educational settings, is defined by Toddhunter (2007: 604) as 'collaborative, extended verbal exchanges in which students develop a coherent topic, supported by the teacher's contingent questions and feedback'. Toddhunter applied the strategy in a case study analysis of the teaching of Spanish as a FL to third-year high school pupils in south-western Pennsylvania, US.

Example 2 below is an extract from one of the lessons and follows on from the teacher asking the class how they had spent their weekend.

EXAMPLE 2: CHRISTMAS LIGHTS (SOURCE: TODHUNTER, 2007: 603–604)

Eduardo: *uh Yo uh . . . ¿Yo uh . . . uh poni?* [uh I uh . . . I uh . . . uh put?]
Teacher: *¿Puse?* [put – correct past form]
Eduardo: *Yo puse* I knew it XXX *¿Yo puse uh la luces de Navidad?* [I put – I knew it XXX I put uh Christmas lights?]
Teacher: Sí. [Yes]
Eduardo: *y . . . Mi uh yard* [And . . . my uh yard]
Teacher: *Sí, ¿En tu patio?* [Yes, in your yard?]
Eduardo: *En mi patio uh ¿es un lightbulb grande?* [In my yard uh is a big lightbulb]
Teacher: *Es un grande ¿ Una bombilla así?* (Draws on board.) [It's a big lightbulb like this?]
Eduardo: Sí. [Yes.]

Teacher: *¿Sí?* [Yes?]
Eduardo: Sí. *Muchos luces.* [Yes. A lot of lights.]
Teacher: *Much– Muchísimas luces de Navidad, ¿sí?* [Very many Christmas lights, yes?]
Eduardo: *Sí.* [Yes.]
Teacher: *¿De colores o todas en blanco?* [Coloured or all white?]
Eduardo: *. . . Todas en blanco.* [. . . All white.]
Teacher: *Todas en blanco. Aah.* [All white. Aah.]
Teacher: *¡Qué elegante! ¿Verdad?* [How elegant, right?]
Teacher: *¿Quién más tiene luces en sus–* (*many hands raised*) [Who else has lights in their –]

In this interaction we can see the following:

▓ It is the pupil who has introduced the topic of 'Christmas lights' which is the focus of the conversation and which the teacher later extends to interaction with other classmates.

▓ The pupil uses code-switching to support his speech and the teacher is tolerant of this.

▓ The pupil provides the information in the conversation and the teacher expresses an interest ('¿Sí?')

▓ There are no right or wrong answers with respect to the content of the discussion.

▓ Correction is made through subtle recast (adjectival ending: '*muchos luces*'/'*muchísimas luces*').

Further ideas about strategies to support conversational interaction are provided below.

Task 8.4 OBSERVING INTERACTIONAL PATTERNS

When you observe other teachers on placement, make a note of the different whole classroom interactional patterns using the TL. How do the pupils respond to more conversational forms of interaction?

THE FUNCTIONS OF TL USE IN THE FLs CLASSROOM

Transmitting information versus real communication

According to one point of view, the focus on active work with the TL by pupils rather than passive learning elevates TL use to authentic communication. A closer examination of the communicative tasks of the classroom would suggest that very often pupils engage in little more than transactions devoid of an important criterion for communication – namely, the desire to pass on personally meaningful and valued information: buying railway tickets, making dental appointments or giving directions to a cathedral in some foreign city do not normally fulfil this criterion. The fact that these tasks are conducted in the TL often makes very little difference to the pupils' perception of a 'real' conversation topic and rarely makes the topics more appealing. The issues pupils generally consider worth communicating about can be difficult to incorporate in lessons because they are personal and often do not related to the task or topic in hand. Many of the situations pupils are expected to communicate in seem contrived as they are not commonly conducted by pupils in English, let alone in the TL.

In terms of classroom transactions and interactions there are, however, a number of opportunities for real communication such as '*Ich habe mein Heft vergessen*' ('I forgot my exercise book'), '*Darf ich einen Kuli haben?*' ('Can I borrow a pen?'), '*Darf ich aufs Klo gehen?*' ('Can I go to the toilet?'). In subsequent years this list needs to be expanded and built upon to ensure progression; whereas in the first year of learning German '*Entschuldigung, ich habe mein Heft vergessen*' ('Sorry, I have forgotten my exercise book') is acceptable, in Year 10 one might expect an explanation as well '*Entschuldigung, ich habe mein Heft vergessen, weil . . .*' Not to encourage pupils to use the TL in these contexts can be considered to be wasting valuable opportunities for TL use.

A great number of pupils can convey and transmit information, which is, indeed, a success criterion in examinations. What most of them cannot do, however, is to communicate their own ideas, deeply felt emotions, strongly held opinions and all those abstract thoughts many pupils find challenging to communicate in their own language.

TL use for the management of pupil behaviour

One particular and common topic of interaction in the FLs classroom is behaviour and, if handled appropriately and consistently, the use of the TL for pupil management can be very effective. For instance, when pupils break a classroom or whole-school rule, they are usually well aware of their misdemeanour. They are also familiar with the sanctions commonly used in their school and the expectations of their FLs teacher. The teacher can safely admonish the pupils in the TL. Even if the pupils do not understand the words, the situation has made the meaning quite clear.

Supported with gestures and near cognates such as '*Du sollst nicht auf deinem Stuhl schwingen!*' the message usually gets across, occasionally with the help of another pupil: 'She says you must not swing on your chair.' The tone of voice in which the reprimand is delivered, as well as the context, make comprehension possible. This approach does, however, assume that pupils know the rules of the FLs classroom. These should be made very clear in the first few weeks in English and subsequently reinforced and added to.

The teaching of grammar and TL use

Grammar is often perceived to be a difficult – if not the most difficult – part of the subject to be taught in the TL (see Dickson, 1996; Macaro, 1997; Neil, 1997). However, quite a number of grammar points can be taught in the TL, particularly if there is an element of physical demonstration and visualisation. A playful approach as well as the continuous use of certain 'stock' types of activities, which can be used for a range of different topics, can help to minimise the need for complex instructions and explanations in English and make it easier to teach grammar in the TL. Demonstrations, illustrations and examples are worth many complicated explanations. The examples given in this chapter are to provide ideas and to be adapted appropriately to the relevant TL. You will need to plan the specific linguistic focus carefully.

Many pupils have difficulties with the German word order when a sentence starts with an adverbial of time. The following activity works well in the second year. Having taught the activities, e.g. '*Ich gehe ins Kino*' ('I go to the cinema'), days of the week, e.g. '*am Montag*' ('on Monday') and the question word '*wann*' ('when') the teacher writes the words *[ich] [gehe] [ins Kino]* and *[am Montag]* on individual A4 cards. A bigger sign is made for *[wann?]*. The class is divided into groups of five. The first three pupils go to the front and hold their words up in the correct sequence to form and speak the sentence. Pupil 4 holds up the *[wann?]* sign and asks the question. Pupil 5 – *[am Montag]* – joins them and four pupils re-form physically to make the correct sentence: *[Am Montag] [gehe] [ich] [ins Kino]*. Pupils then make their own sentences (on cards) and perform them.

Word order, in particular in the past tense, can be practised with cut-up sentences (auxiliary verb and past participle in different colours) mixed up in small envelopes. This task is almost always performed in the TL using familiar phrases such as '*Ist das richtig?*' ('Is that correct?'), '*Nein, das ist falsch!*' ('No, that is wrong'). It works particularly well if the same colours are used when introducing the past tense (on PowerPoint, for example).

Pupils' speaking skills are often restricted by the number of verbs they know, which limits their communication. Verb endings are a frequent source of error. Pupils can revise and practise verbs and verb endings in the form of the following game (Figure 8.4).

Two hexagons are drawn on the board (side by side). Each corner of the hexagon represents a personal pronoun. Elicit two verbs (regular verbs to begin with, then irregular and modal verbs much later) from the pupils and write them inside the hexagons (Figure 8.5). The class is divided into two teams, the members of each team are numbered, the numbers written on pieces of paper and put in a box. A pupil picks a number and the two corresponding pupils from each team go up to the board. At the command '*Auf die Plätze, fertig, los!*' ('On your marks, get set, go!'). Pupils write the relevant verb forms at each corner of their hexagon (Figure 8.6). Conferring with their team is permitted. The first pupil to finish gets 10 points. One point is deducted for each mistake. The second pupil gets one point per correct verb form. This ensures that the fast and careless pupils do not always win.

Question forms are also difficult to learn for pupils. They can be learned playing the battleship game. From a grid (Figures 8.7 and 8.8) each pupil has to select one square per row and per column without showing it to their partner. By asking relevant questions, e.g. '*Kommst du mit dem Auto zur Schule?*' (Figure 8.7) or '*Saugst du manchmal Staub?*' (Figure 8.8), they then try to find out what choices their partner has made. If they guess correctly, they can ask again; if not, their partner asks a question. The winner is the pupil who has found out all of her partner's answers first.

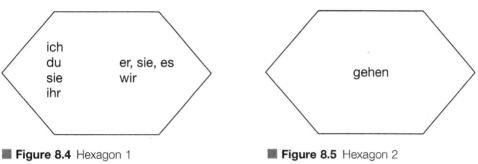

■ **Figure 8.4** Hexagon 1   ■ **Figure 8.5** Hexagon 2

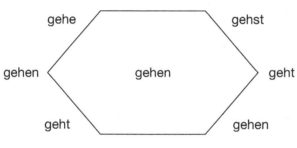

■ **Figure 8.6** Hexagon 3

	ins Schwim- mbad	in die Stadt	nach Amerika	nach London	zur Schule	zum Bahnhof	zum Golfplatz
mit dem Zug							
mit dem Bus							
mit dem Rad							
zu Fuß							
mit dem Flugzeug							
mit der U-Bahn							
mit dem Auto							

■ **Figure 8.7** *Wie kommst du . . .?*

	Spülst du ab?	Mähst du den Rasen?	Wäschst du das Auto?	Führst du den Hund aus?	Räumst du dein Zimmer auf?	Kochst du?	Saugst du Staub?
oft							
manch-mal							
nie							
ab-und-zu							
einmal in der Woche							
zweimal am							
nur für Geld							

■ **Figure 8.8** *Hilfst du im Haushalt?*

This works particularly well in the TL if the questions are quite cumbersome to translate into English. Provided the questions have been well practised before the game starts, most pupils tend to use the TL rather than switch back to English. Pupils would be familiar with the game from Year 7 where the language items used are much less complex.

Successful language games are usually said:

■ to be based on known games;
■ not to be too long;
■ not to need lengthy explanations;
■ to have clear objectives;
■ to produce a winner.

Information gap exercises, such as finding out about somebody's timetable, work well if pupils are properly prepared: '*Was hast du montags in der ersten Stunde?*' is no more complicated than 'What subject do you have on Monday in the first period?'.

Kofferpacken (packing a suitcase) is another excellent activity for practising word order in the past tense as well as vocabulary; it also increases fluency.

In the *Kaufhaus* (department store) variation each pupil writes on a piece of paper an item to be bought in a department store. The class is then divided into groups (between six and ten pupils). The first group lines up at the front of the class (getting them to pick a number from 1 to 6 out of a hat will prevent the scramble to avoid being the last in the line). The first pupil starts the sentence: '*Ich war im Kaufhaus und habe* . . . (mentions his or her item or items) *gekauft*' ('I went to the department store and bought . . .') and puts the piece of paper into a (an authentic) shopping bag. The second pupil starts again: '*Ich war im Kaufhaus und habe ein . . .* (previous pupil's item) *und einen . . .* (own item) *gekauft*' – and so on to the last person in the line, who has, of course, the most difficult task of remembering all the items. Strangely enough, pupils tend to forget the '*gekauft*' (past participle), but remember all the shopping items. The *Kofferpacken* version (packing your suitcase) works very well with a real suitcase and real items.

Building conversational skills in the TL

One of the aims, if not the ultimate aim of FL teaching is to enable pupils to conduct conversations in the TL. They need to be well prepared for this and given the skills and confidence to use the TL in a carefully nurtured atmosphere.

Conversations in FL learning usually grow from learned phrases and role plays. For a discussion of how to develop speaking skills in pupils, including the use of role plays, see Chapter 10. Role plays do have their limitations, though, as this example of a keen and very able pupil's frustration at the lack of conversational skills during an exchange visit demonstrates: 'I can ask for the butter at the breakfast table and what time we have to leave for school because we've done that. But I can't have a proper conversation and it makes me mad!' A purely transactional approach, therefore, seems too narrow. In order to go beyond the scripted, pupils need to be taught conversation strategies such as opening gambits, hesitating, agreeing, disagreeing, asking for help and support, expressing surprise and disbelief and many more. Much of this can be achieved by adding an element (albeit small) of drama, creativity or challenge.

Adding an element of unpredictability such as a lost granny, boiled eggs or their memory can make a routine role play such as *Im Fundbüro* (at the lost property office) much more interesting and entertaining for pupils. Introducing realia into role plays can liven things up considerably. Most pupils like bringing in unusual clothes, food (real or plastic) or toys – or pictures of these items, either cut out of magazines, drawn or computer-generated.

For papers on the use of drama, see also the special issue of *German as a foreign language* 2004(1) available at www.gfl-journal.de/Issue_1_2004.php.

Apart from conversation strategies, there are other ways of organising role plays so as to encourage spontaneity. Instead of asking pupils to prepare a role play together with their partner, e.g. the shopkeeper together with the shopper, they can be grouped with peers in the same role, e.g. shopkeepers and shoppers in different groups. This way, when shopkeepers and shoppers come together, communication is more realistic and spontaneous because, while shopkeepers and shoppers do prepare possible answers in advance, they have to listen very carefully to each other in order to be able to respond meaningfully.

Another way you can help pupils make the transition from learned response to genuine manipulation of the TL is to record the general conversations of groups and discuss with pupils how they can be improved to sound less like an oral examination and more like a real conversation. Pupils who remain reluctant to 'spontaneously adopt the FL as their own language of self-expression in the FL classroom, even where the teachers have done so to a considerable extent' (Mitchell, 1988: 164) continue to be a real challenge for FLs teachers.

DEVELOPING YOUR COMPETENCE IN TL USE

As can be seen in this chapter, you can use the TL meaningfully and effectively for a number of types of interaction in the FLs classroom.

Competence in TL use, as so many aspects of good practice, is difficult to achieve and requires a lot of practice. You can benefit from considering all aspects of TL use and should develop strategies to address them. Here are some targets a student teacher at the Institute of Education set herself for her induction year:

1   *Be supportive*: when a pupil wants to use the TL, I need to offer help and support. The nature of the support given may vary according to the age and the ability of the pupil.

---

1   Contextualisation increases comprehension. Always ensure pupils know what is going on. Pictures, demonstrations and examples must be carefully selected to avoid ambiguity.
2   Use of cognates or near cognates, particularly in German, not only increases the chances of comprehension, it makes pupils feel more confident and less apprehensive. (Over-reliance on cognates, however, should be avoided.)
3   Simplification of language, not only for teacher input but also for pupil production – a single well-chosen word can go a long way. A pupil's *'Entschuldigung, Amir'* ('Sorry, Amir') – he had interrupted Amir – can make the point quite adequately.
4   Pupil access to language – this can take the form of 'clouds' with the most useful phrases and key words prominently displayed and lists in pupils' exercise books or on word mats on desks.
5   Teaching of key phrases – such as *'Wie heißt das auf Deutsch?'* ('What is the German word/phrase for . . .?') *'Wie sagt man . . . auf Deutsch?'* ('How do you say . . . in German?'), *'Darf ich bitte English sprechen?'* ('May I please speak in English?'), *'Ich habe ein Problem, Herr/Frau. . .'* ('Sir/Miss, I have a problem'), *'Können Sie mir bitte helfen?'* ('Can you help me, please?'), *'Ich bin fertig.'* ('I have finished').
6   Rewarding pupils' spontaneous use of the TL – words and phrases remembered from previous lessons, an ambitious attempt (successful or not) at a new construction or a combination of words, etc. deserve to be praised by the teacher and their efforts recorded (in a separate column) in the mark book. Pupils can also keep a tally of when they use the language spontaneously in their books and get a reward after a certain number of contributions.
7   Screening out unwanted English contributions – this usually just means ignoring them.
8   TL-only sessions: during a designated (previously announced and cleared with parents) period of 15 minutes of a lesson only the TL may be spoken. Everyone who speaks English (including the teacher) suffers a forfeit. Initially these sessions tend to produce silent minutes. As pupils get used to them they get braver and more adventurous in their use of the TL.
9   Request box: pupils write phrases they need on a card and put them into the box. The TL phrases are compiled and presented and taught to the whole class.
10 Incorporation of 'real life' TL into speaking and writing: expressions of disbelief, how to pretend you're interested, how to compliment someone, etc.

■ **Figure 8.9** Strategies to support TL use

Everyday routines, classroom management and maintaining discipline	Instructions and explanations by the teacher	Pupil interactions with the teacher	Pupil interactions with other pupils
Taking the register	Presenting new language	Asking for clarification	Asking for material/equipment
Getting ready for the lesson	Setting up activities	Expressing problems and apologies	Carrying out pair and group work activities
Tidying up at the end of the lesson	Making oral comments	Requesting explanations	Initiating information exchange
Dismissing the class	Checking comprehension	Giving excuses	Playing games
Offering praise and rewards	Asking questions	Asking for material/equipment	Expressing agreement and disagreement
Reprimanding and sanctioning pupils	Making written comments in exercise books	Making evaluative comments	Assessing the work of peers
Friendly asides, humorous remarks		Asking for confirmation	Using fillers
		Requesting permission, answering questions, giving information, humorous remarks, linguistic experiments.	

■ **Figure 8.10** Using the TL for classroom instruction and interactions

2 *Be consistent*: I need to try hard to use the TL as often as possible to be a good role model. Sometimes it might mean claiming not to understand what they are saying just because they speak English.

3 *Be realistic*: I need to remember that the use of the TL is meant to enhance classroom teaching, and not to become an intolerable burden. It is sometimes a good idea to have a set period in the lesson when pupils know that they can speak to me in English and when problems can be dealt with.

4 *Be non-critical*: I must greet any attempt at using the TL positively or the pupil might not try again. The most important thing is communication, and any understanding of the message should be rewarded.

5 *Be challenging*: while asking for the impossible is demotivating, equally demotivating is asking for that which is banal and far below a pupil's capabilities. I need to build progression into both my use of the TL and theirs, using, teaching and expecting more complex phrases with older and more able pupils.

6 *Be flexible*: if I want to encourage the use of the TL, I must be sufficiently flexible to respond to what happens in the classroom and to what pupils have to say.

7   *Make it worthwhile*: I must reward and acknowledge any efforts, be aware of what pupils are doing in the classroom and listen to two or three pupils each lesson so I can keep a record of their individual achievement as regards TL use.

8   *Involve the pupils*: pupils are much more likely to be motivated if they are involved. I can ask them to note and tick useful phrases or expressions in their exercise books each time they use them in the lesson.

9   *Promote a positive attitude*: the most important thing is that pupils do not feel threatened and it is up to me that they don't. I must present the TL as something I am going to do with them and in which all have a part to play and not as something that I am imposing upon them.

Task 8.5 **THOUGHTS ON TL USE**

How relevant are the above targets for your own practice? Draw up a list appropriate for the different groups of learners you work with.

SUMMARY

There is no doubt that 'optimal' use of the TL as a medium for instruction and communication in the FLs classroom is a powerful tool that enhances pupils' progress in learning the language. Such optimal use also means an awareness of when it is appropriate to use the L1 in lessons, to accept its presence in the pupils thinking and output, and to vary the degree to which it is used with different classes and individuals.

Furthermore, teacher TL use should not be considered separately from the pedagogical approaches and aims and objectives of FL teaching. A teacher's decisions about how they use the TL at a particular moment of a lesson should be linked to the teaching and learning objectives of that moment. As this chapter has demonstrated, teacher TL use is not only valuable in terms of giving the pupils exposure to the language but also in terms of scaffolding their learning of the language.

Note

Many thanks to Roswitha Guest for her contribution to earlier versions of this chapter.

FURTHER READING

Butzkamm, W. (2003) We only learn language once: the role of the mother tongue in foreign language classrooms: death of a dogma. In *Language Learning Journal*, 28: 29–39.
    This paper discusses the issues surrounding the use of target language and mother tongue for foreign language learners and clearly sets out the arguments in the debate.

Macaro, E. (1996) *Target Language, Collaborative Learning and Autonomy*. Clevedon: Multilingual Matters.

A close examination of the use of target language and its effectiveness in foreign language learning.

Thoms, J. (2012) Classroom discourse in foreign language classrooms: a review of the literature. In *Foreign Language Annals*, 45(1): 8–27.

A review of empirical studies on target language classroom discourse in foreign language contexts, examining the relationship between classroom talk and foreign language learning.

CHAPTER 9

TEACHING
RECEPTIVE SKILLS
Listening and reading

INTRODUCTION

An important aim of FL teaching in the Secondary school is the development of pupils' ability to learn and use the FL independently, which of course necessitates the development of the skills of listening, speaking, reading and writing. While we have chosen to consider the skills under the headings of 'receptive FL skills' (listening and reading) in this chapter, and the 'productive FL skills' (speaking and writing) in the following chapter, we recognise that a multi-skill approach in which no one skill is taught discretely, usually does and should prevail in the classroom. Successful FLs lessons integrate a number of activities and exercises developing different (FL) skills, which are carefully chosen to build on previous knowledge and understanding. Both listening and reading can be responded to, and writing and speaking need input and modelling from reading and listening to inform their development.

We also include in this chapter a section on vocabulary learning, a fundamental building block in pupils' language repertoire. Without an adequate vocabulary, learners find it particularly difficult to access meaning and, of course, cannot generate their own meanings. We include discussion of the role of vocabulary for language learning progression as well as strategies to help pupils learn it.

The stages of vocabulary learning discussed here (discrimination, under-standing meaning, remembering, and consolidation and extension of meaning), are similar to the developmental sequence that we suggest in the subsequent sections on listening and reading. Here the stages move from pre-listening/reading activities → listening/reading for gist and detail → focusing on linguistic structures and forms → rebuilding selected language forms to express personal views. These stages are not proposed as a simple formula, which can be repeated lesson after lesson, unit of work after unit of work. The nature of the task or given learning objective(s) might not make it possible and/or desirable to cover all stages at any particular time.

Simply doing more reading or more listening does not necessarily mean that a pupil will improve. We therefore prioritise learning strategies in our discussion of the four skills, and begin this chapter with a definition of learning strategies and a presentation of its key characteristics. Learning strategies are specific actions or techniques that learners can adopt to improve their performance in language learning. Helping pupils to become better aware of how they learn and how this might be improved is key to continued progression.

OBJECTIVES

By the end of this chapter you should:

■ understand the importance of vocabulary teaching and learning and have a range of teaching ideas for doing it;
■ appreciate how listening and reading can be taught;
■ be aware of a range of learning to learn skills that pupils can employ to help with vocabulary learning, listening and reading;
■ understand how cultural awareness may be developed through reading and listening.

LEARNING STRATEGY

One aspect of FL teaching which has received increased attention in recent years is learner training, i.e. teaching pupils how to learn. If pupils are to become independent and autonomous learners, we need to teach them the skills to be able to do this.

Learning strategies have been found to be a powerful learning tool, as recognised by some of the pioneering researchers in this field (Rubin, 1975; O'Malley *et al.*, 1985; Macaro, 2006; Oxford, 2011). Strategies are essentially: *a set of actions taken by the learner that will help make language learning more effective – i.e. will help a learner learn, store, retrieve and use information.*

Communication strategies and learning strategies are commonly distinguished in the research literature. Communication strategies allow the learner to overcome a limited linguistic repertoire to ensure communication of meaning takes place. They appear to be more difficult to teach as they occur as a result of a breakdown in communication. Canale and Swain (1980: 31) state that 'such "coping strategies" are most likely to be acquired through experience in real life communication situations but not through classroom practice that involves no meaningful communication'. Learning strategies have been categorised into 'metacognitive' strategies (concerned with managing learning), 'affective' strategies (preparing oneself emotionally and attitudinally for the learning process) and 'social' strategies (pertaining to the interaction with other pupils or language users) (see Oxford, 1987: 16–21; Ellis and Sinclair, 1989: 151–154 and Harris, 1997: 5–6).

Some researchers (see Griffiths, 2008) have identified the following six essential features of strategies:

■ they are *active* – they are what pupils do (both mental and physical behaviour);

- they are *conscious* (although they can become automatic, at some level learners are partially conscious of them even if not attending to them fully);
- they are *chosen* by the learner (there needs to be active involvement, hence the strategic element);
- they are *purposeful* (towards the goal of learning the language);
- they are used by the learner to *control* or regulate their own learning;
- they are about *learning* the language (not employing what's been learned).

Work with strategies is essentially about:

- making *explicit* the processes pupils are already using to help them learn;
- *exposing* them to a greater range of strategies so as to widen their repertoire of useful strategies that might make their FL learning even more effective.

There is a consensus view that strategy instruction should be explicit rather than implicit, that is, pupils should be aware of the strategies they are using as this makes it easier for them to increase the range of strategies they use. There is more debate about whether such strategy instruction should be taught in an integrated way – i.e. when doing authentic language learning tasks, or whether strategy training should be done as a discrete unit. We tend to the view that strategy instruction should be as integrated as possible and, therefore, in presenting the following sections we build strategy work into our discussion on how to approach vocabulary learning, listening and reading in class. Whichever way a teacher chooses to approach strategy training, most important is that pupils need *reminding* to use strategies. Suggesting some strategies as a one-off in class and not returning to them again later is likely to mean that pupils either forget to apply them, or remember only one or two strategies and apply these constantly. Teachers need to remind pupils regularly of the range of strategies available to them and ask for feedback on which they are using.

For a detailed discussion of learner strategies, see also the 2007 two-part Special Issue of the *Language Learning Journal,* 35(1) and 35(2).

MEMORISING, AND LEARNING HOW TO MEMORISE, VOCABULARY

While most teachers and researchers agree that learning vocabulary is very important for making progress in language learning (Schmitt, 2008), there is less confidence as to the best way that this might be done. Clearly, teaching vocabulary is not straightforward, otherwise we would simply provide our pupils with long lists to take home to assimilate and come back into class ready to use. A growing number of empirical research studies (for a review see Laufer, 2009) have found that the best results for vocabulary learning are likely to result from input followed by activities that *engage* at a word level – i.e. activities that draw learners' attention to new words and make learners do something with them. Schmitt (2008) argues that vocabulary learning *can* happen incidentally – i.e. during independent reading or listening, but is likely to be much more effective if engaged with explicitly.

Revisiting vocabulary at various points in the future and in different contexts is also important for longer term retention.

How much vocabulary do learners need, and are we offering enough opportunities for them to increase their vocabulary? Some studies suggest that UK pupils learn vocabulary on average at the rate of between 170 and 200 words a year (see Milton and Meara, 1998 and Milton, 2006) and that the average pupil entering for the GCSE, the UK school-leaving examination at 16, knows around 850 words on a recognition test (Milton, 2006). However, this is arguably too little to allow access to anything but very basic texts. Milton argues that even knowing the most frequent 2,000 words of French gives only 80 per cent coverage, making it just about possible to get the gist of a normal text. See also our discussion of this issue in Chapter 3. This suggests the need to devote energy to helping pupils build their knowledge of vocabulary, and particularly of the highest frequency words.

The main point noted in most research is the importance of vocabulary learning for progression in FL learning, and the need for active and explicit engagement with vocabulary learning. As we suggest below, a staged approach to teaching vocabulary, set within a communicative framework for language learning, as presented in Chapter 5 of this book, is likely to lead to successful outcomes.

We draw here on Grauberg's (1997: 5–33) process for vocabulary acquisition, which is similar to our framework. He distinguishes four stages – discrimination, understanding meaning, remembering, and consolidation and extension of meaning – all of which require active intervention on the part of the teacher, yet which serve to guide the learner towards a greater degree of independent language use.

Discrimination: the role of phonics

Discrimination is the ability to distinguish sounds or letters from each other and also to be clear about meaning. Grauberg (1997) maintains that this is usually straightforward, though some FLs teachers might disagree. In listening, for example, distinguishing sounds clearly – i.e. trying to disentangle one word from the next, is something many learners struggle with as discussed below. As teachers we need to remember how difficult some learners may find it and that it is usually a cause of error. This makes the teaching of ways of discriminating all the more important.

Students can use either 'top-down' or 'bottom-up' processes when trying to make sense of new input. Top-down processes are more 'global', for example, using world knowledge to try to make sense of various clues in text or predicting what someone might be talking or writing about. Bottom-up processes require engagement at word level to make sense of it: how do I break this sentence or word up? How do I sound it out? It would seem sensible to suggest that pupils need a mix of both top-down and bottom-up approaches to dealing with input. Never engaging with bottom-up strategies for dealing with new language makes it much more difficult for pupils to discriminate – i.e. to distinguish letters and sounds from each other.

In order to use bottom-up processes pupils need to understand the grapheme/phoneme correspondence (GPC) of the language they are learning. Research evidence suggests that this decoding ability is not picked up implicitly (see Woore, 2009). The implication is clear: teachers need not only teach important top-down strategies, but also to engage with systematic phonics to teach explicitly how the sounds of the new language relate to written forms.

As Woore (2009: 5) notes, if we are to give pupils the tools to build their vocabulary and with it their independent use of the language to express their own meanings, then we have to be explicit about GPC:

> Being able to generate phonological forms for unfamiliar written words therefore provides a key to acquiring new vocabulary; vocabulary knowledge, in turn, underpins all other aspects of L2 proficiency.

A number of schools are now incorporating systematic teaching of phonics into their schemes of work, either as discrete units of work near the beginning of pupils' FL learning experience or in more integrated ways. This involves drawing pupils' attention explicitly to sound combinations and their written equivalents. Consistent revisiting of the sound/written word correspondence is required, as is discussed in subsequent sections.

Understanding meaning

Usually, new vocabulary is situated in a functional/communicative context; just as we do not use words in isolation of each other, so it makes little sense to present them in isolation to learners, and situating new vocabulary in a context allows for more challenging discrimination than presenting words in isolation. Teachers might use a range of teaching material and visual aids (spoken and written text, PowerPoint, the IWB, flashcards, posters, video, photographs, etc.) to set this new vocabulary in a broader cultural and communicative context. Presentation by the teacher should not be purely a passive activity for pupils. Exposure to new lexical items and phrases can include the practice of pronunciation, the association with gestures and movement, the association with previously taught language and the answering of a range of questions.

Teachers are often guided in their presentation of key lexical items by the department's schemes of work, which may in turn be based on an established coursebook. Exam specifications also often provide defined lists in relation to given topics. For pupils to understand meaning in a multidimensional way – e.g. functional, grammatical, etc. – there is a need for explanation by the teacher and this is usually followed by pupils' recording of vocabulary for future learning. For beginner learners there seems to be some evidence to suggest that noting L1–L2 links can be helpful (see Schmitt, 2008), though we would also encourage pupils to note down a meaningful example of use in context as well as the TL and mother tongue meanings of the new lexical item or phrase. The categorisation of vocabulary can be undertaken in several ways – grammatically, by topic, in the form of mind maps or in the context of stories, songs, rhymes and poems. A varied approach seems advisable. Field (2014) offers a range of practical ideas on introducing new vocabulary and structures.

Remembering

Having encountered the new vocabulary what happens to it? We might test it in class but a criticism of repeated classroom vocabulary testing is that pupils learn new lexical items for a specific, short-term and decontextualised purpose. This can, though, be seen as a necessary prerequisite to consigning the vocabulary to the long-term memory, which we discuss in the next section. We need to be clear what is meant by *learning* vocabulary – for example:

■ to recognise the word when written;
■ to recognise when heard;
■ to use the words in speaking;
■ to use the words with accurate spelling in written form;
■ does this include gender and accents?

Students usually can perform better in the *receptive* skills of listening and reading than when asked to *produce* the spoken or written form. Are both receptive and productive aspects being assessed? We feel that it is important to present pupils with a range of vocabulary learning strategies in order that they can adopt strategies to suit their own learning styles.

Field (1999: 55) suggests a range of ways of learning vocabulary:

■ alphabetical listing;
■ listing according to grammatical concepts (verbs, nouns, adjectives, etc.);
■ semantic field mind-mapping;
■ repeated use in context;
■ recital;
■ colour coding or preference ranking.

To these can be added:

■ Using the 'Look–Cover–Say–Write–Check' method.
  – *Look* at the word.
  – *Cover* up the written form.
  – *Say* it aloud to yourself.
  – *Write* it from memory.
  – *Check* against the correct form.
  – *Repeat* for those you get wrong.

■ getting a friend or family member to test;
■ teaching someone else;
■ devising mnemonics or rhymes;
■ matching synonyms;
■ matching opposites;
■ matching words to symbols;
■ gapped texts and dictionary activities;
■ making up a song with the words included;
■ devising tests and games for classmates.

Pupils should be encouraged to experiment with all these methods from early on in their learning process. Certainly, teachers could draw on a range of strategies that mirror the different 'intelligences' identified by Gardner (1983) in his well-known work *Frames of Mind* – i.e. some learners may benefit from 'tactile' activities, where they have to move cards and match them up to learn vocabulary, while others may feel recording the words and meanings on a cassette or as a podcast may be more beneficial for them. It is worth stressing at this point that the enthusiasm

---

Task 9.1 **HOW DO YOU LEARN VOCABULARY?**

1   Set a vocabulary learning homework.
2   In the next lessons ask the students how they learned the vocabulary.
3   Make a class list of the methods used which is copied to everyone.
4   Ask learners to choose a strategy new to them the next time they have to learn vocabulary and to report back on its effectiveness.
5   Add to the list when someone has something new (suggest some of the above where they are not mentioned).
6   They might complete a table as in Figure 9.1.

Vocabulary learning strategy	Used: 14/2/12	Used: 2/3/12	Used 25/3/12
Use Look–Cover–Say–Write–Check	✓	✓	
Other (allow space for student to add their own language learning strategy)			

■ **Figure 9.1** Vocabulary learning table

for the notion of multiple intelligences and their potential for pedagogy is not universally shared. For a critique of Gardner, see White (2005). Graham (1997) notes that pupils feel that vocabulary learning is more successful and enjoyable if it forms part of a game. Puzzles, word searches, quizzes and challenges can all be usefully deployed.

Consolidation and extension

By consolidation and extension we mean the stage at which learners transfer vocabulary from the short-term to the long-term memory. Some activities suggested above, as well as active use of new language for personal communicative reasons, will help consolidation. In any case, if we do nothing with new vocabulary beyond immediate testing then we can be pretty certain that it will be forgotten. This learning needs to be revisited regularly in what Bruner (1996) refers to as spiralling back, where the teacher links new learning constantly to things gone before. Repeat testing at a later date, where pupils are required to revise again for testing may also have some positive effects. Revisiting the new language in a different context to that in which it was first met helps to embed language and needs to be considered as an integral part of planning.

Task 9.2 **MATCHING VOCABULARY STRATEGIES TO MULTIPLE INTELLIGENCES**

Some of Howard Gardner's different types of intelligence:

- ■ logical intelligence;
- ■ linguistic intelligence;
- ■ bodily kinaesthetic intelligence;
- ■ spatial intelligence;
- ■ musical intelligence;
- ■ interpersonal intelligence;
- ■ intra-personal intelligence.

1 Can you categorise the vocabulary learning strategies below by the type of intelligence they may appeal to? (NB: any activity can fall into more than one category.)
2 Place the activities under each category into a sequence following the stages discussed above.
3 Where are there gaps? Consider additional activities, which can be placed into the model.

Some vocabulary learning strategies:

Repetition, recital, categorising by grammar, categorising by topic, colour coding, testing oneself, being tested, placing in communicative context, matching to symbols, developing puzzles, completing puzzles, formal teacher-led tests, word searches, finding synonyms, finding opposites, dictionary work, rote learning, mnemonics, identifying key words in extended texts, etc.

TEACHING RECEPTIVE FLs SKILLS (LISTENING AND READING)

The process for making sense of any new input means that pupils have to first identify key vocabulary, phrases and structures in the spoken and written input and to apply meaning to new language forms. The pupil needs to proceed from the recognition of new forms via practice to using them in an individualised and personal way, rebuilding language within 'authentic' and realistic contexts. The model of progression is one then of moving from recognition to incorporation into one's own repertoire of language in use.

LISTENING

Listening to a(n extended) passage without preparation can be challenging for FLs learners. While for reading the text is visible, which makes it easier to see where one word stops and another begins, segmenting listening material where sounds seem run together can be daunting, particularly for lower-proficiency learners. There are two ways that pupils approach listening. One is as discussed in the vocabulary learning section above, using bottom up-strategies to try to establish where one sound starts and another begins, and the other is using more global top-down strategies for processing the new input. Teaching bottom-up processes for listening is not so straightforward, though, and in fact some researchers recommend top-down strategies only (see Vandergrift, 2007 for a fuller summary).

We begin with top-down strategies but consider bottom-up strategies as appropriate in the later stages. We suggest a scaffold that moves through the following stages:

- pre-listening activities;
- listening for gist and detail;
- focusing on linguistic structures and forms;
- rebuilding selected language forms to express personal views.

Pre-listening activities

To understand the location and context of a text facilitates comprehension and so asking pupils to complete some pre-listening activities can be useful. Pupils can be set a number of lead-in tasks such as input and practice of key linguistic items through word associations or work with sentence cards taken from the text.

Prior to the first listening, particularly when the task consists of fairly straightforward questions and answers, learners could predict what they might hear/what the answers might be, and then the listening itself serves as a 'real' activity to check their predictions. (For a wide range of pre-listening and listening activities and discussion of some of the issues involved in listening, see Graham, 2003; Fernández-Toro, 2005; Vandergrift, 2007; Field, 2008).

In terms of metacognitive thinking before the task, pupils might be encouraged to ask themselves:

- do I understand the task I have to do?
- are there any clues (titles/pictures)?
- which vocabulary do I know about this topic?
- what's likely to come up in this topic? – i.e. what common sense can I apply here?

Listening for gist or detail with a focus on content

To record details verbally and/or non-verbally while listening to a 'text' and to recall details after listening can be demanding. For this reason listening activities are often best broken down into manageable chunks to suit the particular learning objectives of the lesson and/or the unit of work. It is helpful too if different foci are provided for each time the recording is listened to or video watched. So, for example, the first listening might be for gist only, to find out what the listening is about, how many speakers are participating, the location of a dialogue and guess the mood of speakers.

During the second listening, pupils can be set activities to which they are asked to respond verbally and/or non-verbally. Possible verbal responses are listed

Response type	Ranking
completing diagrams	
drawing	
gap filling	
labelling	
mixing-and-matching	
multiple choice	
physical movement	
ticking boxes	
true/false	

■ **Figure 9.2** Non-verbal response types

Response type	Ranking
agreeing/disagreeing	
answering in full sentences	
correcting	
gap filling	
interpreting	
mixing-and-matching half sentences	
one-word answers	
paraphrasing	
rebuilding text	
sequencing	
summarising	
translating	
unjumbling text/scripts	

■ **Figure 9.3** Verbal response types

in Figure 9.2 and non-verbal responses in Figure 9.3. These responses can be used at a later stage as stimuli for follow-up work. Examples of non-verbal responses include the ticking of boxes within a grid, identifying statements as true or false, answering simple multiple-choice questions, and matching simplified text to pictures and symbols while verbal responses include sequencing, correcting or summarising.

Pupils can also be asked to focus on specific details by having to answer 'closed questions' to which there is a specific answer and which can be found in the stimulus material such as prices, times, directions, ages, descriptions.

A third playing of the recording might allow some of the pupils, who have not managed to do so already, to complete some of the activities above. It might allow others to listen out for additional details or complete additional tasks – e.g. requiring them to make inferences.

How does a teacher choose appropriate listening material? It can be very motivating to listen to real people speaking the language we are learning and the

Web is awash with authentic material – i.e. material that has not been adapted for a pedagogical purpose. Finding *appropriate* authentic listening – i.e. listening pitched at the correct level for the pupils and including some of the key language being taught, is the holy grail of the FLs teacher. Listening material from textbooks tends to be well pitched at learners' level but can also date quickly. It is rarely authentic, having usually been recorded in order to be pitched at the right level for the course it is supporting.

While it is, of course, important to try to keep material as authentic as possible, teachers need to consider carefully the listening they ask pupils to do; believing that you have not understood a word of what has been said can be very demotivating. Listening to authentic material such as news bulletins, interviews and stories *can* spark interest and build confidence if the teacher chooses material carefully, structures and differentiates tasks and helps learners to apply listening strategies. It is also helpful to keep expectations realistic by reminding pupils that even fairly fluent speakers of a language find it difficult to understand all that is said when native speakers are talking to each other. In this way as pupils' proficiency and confidence increase, they can be led gradually towards more challenging authentic material.

Below we list some further top-down strategies that may be suitable for supporting listening:

■ work out the type of text (conversation/news, etc.);
■ work out the level of formality;
■ work out the topic under discussion (gist);
■ pay attention to any background clues (background noises, back scene if video);
■ think about tone of voice;
■ make use facial and body language (if video);
■ seek out familiar words and phrases;
■ seek out cognates (where languages share common roots).

To discriminate sounds and try to establish meaning, as a learner I might:

■ raise my hand when I hear a certain word or phrase;
■ hold an unfamiliar section in my head and replay it over and over;
■ try to get the break between words;
■ try to write down bits I can't understand and relate this to language I know;
■ listen for clues from tense word order.

For useful examples, see Harris (1997) and Rampillon (1994). Macaro's work (e.g. 2000) provides some very interesting insights into the use of strategies in FL learning and work by Graham (2003 and 2006) illuminates some issues with listening. For further practical ideas for listening, also see Chambers (2014). Task 9.3 below has some suggestions of ways to try out strategy work on listening with learners to make them more aware of the sorts of strategies they might be using and how to increase their repertoire.

Task 9.3 **DEVELOPING LISTENING STRATEGIES**

1   Which strategies are we using?

Set a listening task.

After its completion, brainstorm with the class all the different listening strategies they used when completing the task.

Compare the list they come up with some of those suggested above. Ask pupils which of the strategies they had not thought about before strikes them as quite useful.

Do another listening task and ask the class to incorporate one or more new strategy. Evaluate with them how successful they thought this was.

2   Teacher modelling

Using a 'think aloud' technique, model what you would do to tackle a piece of listening.

'What might I do first? Well, I would look for clues as to what this listening text is about . . .'

'I would listen through once to get the gist, listen out for names or key words . . . Let's do that now . . .'

Then you might give out the transcript to identify with learners the problem areas and suggest together ways forward for next time.

Remind them to use the strategies each time before listening.

Pupils will also benefit from input on strategies concerned more with how to manage and monitor their learning – for instance, setting themselves short-term, achievable targets, keeping listening diaries and revision notes, focusing their learning on areas of perceived weakness, how to go about finding and identifying relevant resources or evaluating the success of their learning. Regular opportunities for reflection on these issues should help pupils become more successful and effective FLs learners and teachers can make pupils aware of the following ideas:

After listening I could . . .

- ■ reflect on what went well and note it in my listening diary;
- ■ reflect on strategies I used and what I might do next time;
- ■ carry out some more listening at home and apply the strategies learned in class.

Focusing on linguistic structures and forms

To stretch pupils further, activities focusing on the linguistic structures and forms contained in the stimulus material can be devised. Pupils could, for instance, be asked to verbalise the non-verbal responses made initially. One of the ultimate goals of listening activities is the ability of pupils to communicate and express themselves by transferring the language contained in the stimulus material from their passive to their active vocabulary.

Devising a gap-filling activity or providing a transcript out of order requiring pupils to find the correct sequence, and asking them to match beginnings and ends of sentences, can all be used to make them more familiar with the language forms, as can replacing key vocabulary with synonyms or correcting inaccurate sentences.

Consideration needs to be given to the extent of preparatory work on key vocabulary and essential linguistic structures. Figure 9.4 provides some practical hints.

- Be aware of the level of the group – is it set or mixed ability? Only then select the listening material. The length of texts will depend on the ability level of the group. Bear in mind that more able pupils tend to have a longer concentration span.
- Listen to the recording yourself first: a transcript does not indicate the speed at which language is spoken, nor the clarity of speech.
- With mixed ability or lower ability groups it is advisable to do a series of short aural activities during the course of a lesson with other activities in between. This could be a long dialogue played in sections or several shorter exchanges broken down into clusters of two or three rather than all being played at once. This strategy also gives pupils the opportunity to improve on their last score within the same lesson, thus boosting their confidence in their listening ability.
- Play the recording at least twice but don't forget to explain exactly how you are going to do this. For instance, will you play the whole passage through with pauses for answers and then repeat it? Or will you play it in sections and repeat each section? Pupils find listening particularly difficult, as it demands considerable concentration. Careful explanation at the outset can prevent unnecessary anxiety or constant interruptions during the exercise. If the quality of the recording is not so good, do not be afraid to repeat certain phrases or words yourself or to play it again. Those who could understand will have already completed the task by then, while those struggling will receive extra help discreetly and not feel that they have failed.
- Do pupils need to be familiar with all the language in the text in advance? In most cases this is essential in order to build up their confidence in what can for many be a difficult and demanding exercise. However, in short extracts where many words are recognisable, e.g. hobbies, pupils will enjoy the fact that they can easily identify the new vocabulary with little effort.
- The use of answer forms: a quick table on the board or on a worksheet can be an effective way to elicit answers and useful for oral or written work afterwards. Gauge carefully the amount of information pupils have to give according to their ability. Also, stopping the recording and asking pupils to write down the last word they have heard can be fun and pupils will succeed provided that the speech is not too fast or indistinct.

▉ **Figure 9.4** Some practical hints and considerations by Jo Bond

Rebuilding

Once pupils have a very clear understanding of the content of the stimulus material and also of how these details have been expressed, the focus can shift towards rebuilding the text. This can take the form of a literal rebuilding where the listening material is played and learners try to construct it in writing (a form of dictation), which may help with their awareness of segmentation. The transcript can later be provided and the listening material replayed with the teacher drawing attention to features of pronunciation and intonation that differ from English. This should gradually lead pupils away from trying to segment according to the rules of their L1 (see Graham, 2006).

Pupils can also construct their own précis of the text, either orally or in writing, using notes taken in previous activities. A framework of targeted questions provided by you might offer further support with this, moving from the expression of factual details to the expression of personal opinion. In this way listening can be used as a basis for developing other skill areas such as speaking and writing.

Independent listening

Pupils can be asked to develop their listening skills independently. For example, they might work in groups, using appropriate equipment and following a pre-planned, differentiated programme, with open-ended 'subtasks' given to them. They would handle the recorded texts, assign tasks to each other, address and complete all required elements in whatever order they feel is suitable and ensure that they have completed the activity fully according to expectations. A self-assessment aspect can be included so that pupils can present their complete work, evaluate what they have done and how, and consider how to improve their listening, communication and collaborative skills. This style of task can also be given for the development of reading and other language skills.

READING

Top-down and bottom-up processes

As a receptive skill, the process of reading is not dissimilar to that of listening. Through reading, pupils can be exposed to new language forms and structures, the main difference being that stimulus material is more varied and, crucially, visible to pupils. Source material is, therefore, more permanent and the idea of 'reading for pleasure' can be discussed with the pupils.

As considered in the sections above, for learners to be able to read well it is important that they are able to use both top-down or global strategies (e.g. inference from clues), as well as bottom-up processes that help them to distinguish the sounds they are reading – i.e. that they are taught grapheme-phoneme correspondences (GPC). Baddely, Gathercole and Papagno (1998) posit that the 'phonological loop' processes written language into sound during all reading whether we aware of it or not. This means that as we read we are in effect subvocalising the words in our working (or short-term) memory in order to try and make sense of what we are reading. So, if we do not teach our FLs learners the GPC for the TL, they will simply attempt to use their English sound system to do this as this is the only one they have (see Erler, 2004).

Is this really necessary for FL learning, though? As Woore (2009) points out, decoding may have positive effects on our comprehension in our L1 in particular, as we know many more words to hear than we do written down. Subvocalising may, therefore, bring potential benefits if we, say, recognise words we already have heard. The fact that we are more or less *simultaneously* hearing and learning to read a new FL makes it arguably less beneficial. Where the written language is closer to our L1 than spoken language (as is the case in French with, for example, cognates like 'nation'), it may be even more confusing. Nevertheless, as Woore (2009) argues, all learners will still have heard more than of the TL than they think, e.g. classroom language, and will be able to use this to help them make links between spoken and written forms.

In a similar vein to the scaffold suggested for listening, we suggest the following stages for reading, with a focus on synthetic phonics integrated as appropriate:

■ pre-reading activities;
■ reading for gist and detail;
■ focusing on linguistic structures and forms;
■ rebuilding selected language forms to express personal views.

Preparatory activities

As with listening, pupils can benefit from some preparation before being exposed to written texts. At this early stage the pupil can predict the content of the passage with the help of visual clues or headlines. Also, word associations can be used to reactivate key lexical items. It may be that a particular text contains few clues or, indeed, an abundance of them. Newspaper articles contain headlines, subtitles and pictures. Cartoon strips tell the story in pictures supported by text. Texts containing 'direct speech' indicate the number of speakers. Advertisements consist of slogans and visual clues. All of these can be extrapolated from the main body of the text and serve as material in their own right. (For examples of the use of clues, see Brandi and Strauss, 1985; Powell and Barnes, 1996.) The following ideas might be helpful for pupils:

In advance of reading, as a learner I could . . .

■ check I understand the task I have to do;
■ look at title/pictures/graphs or charts or any other clues;
■ think about the vocabulary I know in relation to this field;
■ apply world knowledge (what's likely in this scenario).

Reading for gist or detail with a focus on content

Once pupils have activated relevant linguistic items and structures and are familiar with the context of the text, they are ready to carry out a closer examination. Often it makes sense to encourage pupils to get a global understanding of what the text is about before mining it for key facts and figures. Both individual and pair work activities can encourage a closer examination of the text. Questions should be graded and structured, from closed to open, to maximise pupils' opportunities to answer correctly and gradually encourage longer verbal responses (for further ideas on reading, including on strategy instruction and types of task, see Hill, 2004; Wright and Brown, 2006). The teacher can provide tables, diagrams, true/false exercises, multiple-choice activities to elicit non-verbal responses or single word/phrase answers, which serve to summarise the content of the text.

Harris (1997: 7) lists the following further strategies for reading:

- ■ Recognising the type of text: poem, newspaper article, brochure?
- ■ Examining pictures, the title, etc. for clues.
- ■ Going for gist, skipping inessential words.
- ■ Using punctuation or clues; question marks, capital letters, etc.
- ■ Using knowledge of the world to make sensible guesses.
- ■ Substituting English words, e.g. 'she something on his head'.
- ■ Analysing unknown words, breaking a word/phrase down and associating parts of it with familiar words, e.g. '*hochgewachsen*'.
- ■ Saying the text out loud and identifying 'chunk boundaries'; how a sentence breaks down and which parts of it to work on at one time.
- ■ Identifying the grammatical categories of words.

As we did for vocabulary learning and for listening, in Task 9.4 we suggest some activities that help pupils to consider the strategies they are using and for teacher modelling.

Task 9.4 **DEVELOPING READING STRATEGIES**

1   Which strategies are we using?

Set a reading task.

After its completion, brainstorm with the class all the different reading strategies pupils used when completing the task.

Compare the list they come up with, with the one above. Ask which of the strategies they had not thought about before strikes them as quite useful.

Do another reading task and ask class to incorporate several new strategies. Evaluate with them how successful this was.

2   Teacher modelling

Using a 'think aloud' technique model what you would do to tackle a piece of reading. Try to use a mix of top-down and bottom-up strategies.

Use large text projected on to a screen. Begin by saying something along the lines of the following:

'What might I do first? Well, I would look for visual clues as to what this text is about. I can see a picture of a city centre here and lots of people. There are also a lot of figures, numbers and statistics in the text, so I'm starting to think this is a news piece maybe about city living or something . . . , etc.'

Use a highlighter pen to show clearly where the clues are, and then work through the other strategies – e.g. 'now I'm going to read the text 'aloud' in my head and try to get the gist of what it is about'.

Learners do follow-up task with texts. They might mark in different colours different sorts of 'clues' in the text.

3   Group reading task

Take a longer reading passage and divide it up into sections (paragraphs might work well).

Divide the class into small groups and give each group a section. They must work out the meaning of their section. It should not be translated – they go for the overall meaning. While they are working this out, they jot down the strategies they are using.

Pupils should be asked to speak aloud about the strategies they are using to break the text down – in this way they learn from each other. Someone in the group makes a list of the strategies used.

Encouraging pupil reflection on their reading might follow the same pattern as suggested for listening:

After reading I could . . .

■   Reflect on what went well in my diary.
■   Note down useful words and phrases and reuse as soon as possible in writing or speaking.
■   Reflect on strategies I used and whether I'll use the same and/or different ones next time.
■   Join in class discussion of what worked well.
■   Read more widely at home a range of materials that I'm interested in and/or suggested by the teacher as homework.
■   Maintain a reading diary.

Focusing on linguistic structures and forms

Teachers select texts based on the objectives of the particular lesson, for example texts that contain vocabulary relevant to the topic being taught or that feature a grammar point that the teacher wants to draw attention to. Once the text has been mined for meaning, the texts can be used to draw attention to whichever key language point the teacher wishes to emphasise. Teachers might ask pupils to find certain groups of words or identify how a particular structure works based on its use in the context of the reading (for more on this sort of inductive grammar teaching see Chapter 11). The teacher can devise activities requiring pupils to reproduce the specific structures introduced by a text – e.g. gap-filling exercises focusing on particular grammatical forms such as text with verb/adjective endings missing, requiring pupils to complete certain sections from memory. Texts can be rewritten by substituting certain lexical items. Also, for 'jigsaw readings', sections of the text can be reproduced in a jumbled form, again requiring pupils to reconstruct the passage in a meaningful way. This can be livened up by chopping the text into chunks and positioning it around the classroom for pupils to go around, memorise and recreate either verbatim or in summary back in their seats.

Rebuilding

By this stage pupils should be fairly familiar with the text and follow-up activities can serve to develop pupils' speaking and writing skills (see Bramall, 2002). Pupils can be asked to continue a story, provide an explanation of the events portrayed or produce an alternative account. They can be asked to talk or write about their favourite character from the reading text and what distinguishes her from others. A response to a text of this nature is individual and personal. Reference material needs to be made accessible to facilitate the expression of opinions and interpretations.

Reading for pleasure – examples from and reflections on classroom practice

Due to the limited time available in lessons it can be difficult to include reading for pleasure in the weekly diet of FL teaching, though some teachers try to build a short slot for reading for pleasure into their planning. If this proves difficult, learners can still be encouraged to read as much as they can in the FL outside of the classroom. A key to getting pupils to read seems to be finding material that they will find interesting – and what one pupil finds interesting another may not. Someone interested in food and cooking might like to read recipes or a food blog; someone else might prefer a motorcycling magazine and someone else some short stories.

Krashen (2013) points to the benefits of 'free voluntary reading' by FLs learners and to research evidence that the effects of extended reading in the TL on reading comprehension and vocabulary acquisition are more positive than control groups that only expose students to intensive reading in the TL. Therefore, what is required, it would seem, is to enable pupils to discover the pleasure of reading in a FL (see Swarbrick, 1998) despite all the obstacles that might be entailed. Here are some things to consider when planning the inclusion of extended reading with beginners and intermediate level learners:

■ Children seem to enjoy narrative particularly, so it would seem sensible to engage them with stories. Primary methodology often involves reading fairy stories or reworked stories that the learners are familiar with, so why not Secondary? However, we need to avoid selecting material that is either too simple in terms of content or too difficult in terms of language. Books aimed at teenagers are likely to deal with topics pertinent to young people that they would like to read about. Excerpts from translated books that the class may be familiar with such as J.K. Rowling's *Harry Potter*, or books by Roald Dahl or Neil Gaiman may well engage interest and while the level of language might be high, familiarity with content can offer some compensation.

■ Narratives can also be played out through role plays or acting out scenes from a film. Pupils can provide potted descriptions of key characters, predict what will happen in the next chapter or scene in a play, or provide an alternative ending to a story. In this way they can be encouraged to engage actively with the narrative and develop their critical and interpretive skills.

■ Another solution is to invest in specially edited readers that adapt fictional texts with interesting stories for young language learners. For instance, the 'Easy Readers' collection, available through the European School Bookshop publishes edited texts under four categories of difficulty (600, 1,200, 2,000 and 2,500 word vocabularies) with supplementary notes and visual support, word definitions and questions after each chapter. Online readers are also available and can be used either with laptops or iPads in class or as homework. For instance, the Instituto Cervantes provides a free site with annotated Spanish text readers with pre- and post-reading activities, and lexical support provided by clicking on highlighted words (www.cvc.cervantes.es/aula/lecturas/default. htm). The beginner level texts are suitable for pupils aged 14–16.

■ One drawback with translated books and stories is that the cultural value of reading authentic material is lost and this is one of the main bonuses of reading in a FL. Even if a pupil is reading only supermarket flyers or a cinema listing, if it is authentic, then she has not only engaged with a real cultural 'artefact' but has the satisfaction of having made sense of it. Teaching learners how to access the material that interests them on the Web may well be the best uses of classroom time for encouraging reading. When they know what is out there to be read in their TLs, be it the Paris Saint-Germain football club website, Italian fashion blogs, German rap groups' websites, or Neruda's poems, and how to find what interests them, then they are far more likely to get reading.

SUMMARY

In this chapter we have presented an outline for progression in listening and reading that moves through pre-tasks to understanding meaning to focus on form and structure to rebuilding the input. The importance of selecting appropriate material and devising structured activities that allow pupils to be successful at accessing what they hear and read are discussed. We suggest that the development of pupils' vocabulary furthers all progression in reading and listening, and suggest ideas for teaching and embedding vocabulary learning.

We have emphasised throughout the chapter the importance of learning how to learn – i.e. encouraging pupil reflection on questions such as: how I am tackling vocabulary learning or reading and listening tasks? How I can improve my repertoire of learning strategies? To this end we have offered possible strategy lists that are not meant to be exhaustive; you will be able with your pupils to add to the lists.

This learning how to learn should be integral to the development of pupils' receptive skills and we cannot assume that they can do it without being shown how to. We argue that including in our teaching a mix of bottom-up and top-down strategies is most likely to lead to success in reading and listening, and that this will allow pupils to become more independent, using what they have heard and read to create their own meanings. This is the focus of our next chapter.

FURTHER READING

Grauberg, W. (1997) *The Elements of Foreign Language Teaching*. Clevedon: Multilingual Matters.

This book explores a wide range of fundamental issues in the teaching and learning of foreign languages, and provides excellent insights into aspects such as phonology, vocabulary and the four language skills.

Pachler, N. and Redondo, A. (2014) *Teaching Foreign Languages in the Secondary School: A Practical Guide* (2nd edn). London: Routledge.

This book provides a good source of further thoughts concerning the issues introduced in this chapter as well as for most of the other chapters in this publication.

CHAPTER 10

TEACHING PRODUCTIVE SKILLS

Speaking and writing

INTRODUCTION

Until the mid 1980s, writing, for instance in the form of translations, dictations and essay writing, as well as reading, tended to predominate in FL teaching, certainly in UK Secondary school classrooms. Since then, multi-skill approaches, in which no one skill is taught discretely, have become the norm. The use of terminology such as 'respond', 'react', 'summarise' in the curriculum guidance and examination specifications encourages the integration of skills.

With the growing popularity of communicative approaches to FL teaching, and their maxim of 'communicative competence', speaking has become an increasingly important feature of FL classrooms. Teaching speaking is, however, challenging and not infrequently is realised in the form of repetition drills, the rendition of memorised dialogues and reading aloud.

Vocabulary is a key prerequisite for both speaking and writing, and has been discussed already in the previous chapter as well as, in some detail, in the review of research in Chapter 3.

Pronunciation – i.e. knowledge and skills relating to sounds and their combination (segmental) as well as intonation and rhythm (suprasegmental) – is an important precursor to speaking, which is an often neglected area of FL classrooms.

Orthography, including spelling and punctuation, is an important element of effective and accurate writing.

As could be seen in the previous chapter, listening and reading also have a number of productive features, in particular in relation to cognitive activity and meaning making. And, the ability to manage the 'sound code' of a language is an important part of the reading process.

Both speaking and writing can be transactional or interactional, and there exist clear differences between spoken and written language. Writing, in other words, is not 'written speech'. The spoken word tends to be much more ephemeral than the written word; due to the increased cognitive load of language production in real time as well as increased levels of anxiety, it tends to be characterised by more informal and colloquial language, hesitation, false starts, improvisation, repetition, redundancy, paraphrasing, etc. Writing, given the greater amount of time for composition and opportunity for reflection available, tends to show a higher degree of density in lexis and grammar and complexity. Spoken and written language also are context-dependent and determined by social factors and/or characterised by genre conventions. In addition, both speaking and writing are characterised by different modes: Bernstein (1971) famously distinguished 'restricted' and 'elaborated' codes of speaking, with the former not making meaning verbally explicit and expressing personal uniqueness; in writing normally narration, description, exposition, persuasion are differentiated. How meaning is expressed will depend not only on the mode but also on the genre. From a pedagogical perspective, this suggests the desirability of texts as models and to activate schemata. Interesting texts can, of course, also be used as stimuli. In the language classroom both speaking and writing often function as learning activities as well. Through speaking and writing, pupils' progress in the skills of listening and reading can be ascertained. Often a distinction is made between process and product approaches. While the latter focuses on the composition and the artefact resulting from writing, the former pays attention to idea generation, structuring, drafting, reviewing, redrafting, etc.

A recurring challenge in FLs lessons around productive skills in particular revolves around fluency and accuracy – i.e. the extent to which experimentation and creative expression are allowed and encouraged and lack of correctness is tolerated. Another key challenge relates to the creation of a clear communicative purpose.

In this chapter, we will focus on the teaching of speaking and writing at beginner to intermediate level. For approaches suitable for more advanced learners, see e.g. Pachler 1999a.

Another consideration in the area of productive skills, as Bachmair and Pachler (2013) have recently shown, is the fact that the semiotic resources for composition used in formal educational settings do not tend to take (full) account of the transformations of contemporary representational resources in everyday life in which multimodal resources dominate. This is an area FLs teacher will increasingly have to take into account: what is happening to language (use) in a world in which digital devices with their multiple affordances are increasingly used as communication tools? What are the implications for FLs pedagogy?

OBJECTIVES

By the end of this chapter you should:

■ appreciate how speaking and writing can be taught at beginner and intermediate level;
■ be aware of the need for a gradual integration of skills;
■ be aware of the importance of pronunciation and the role of reading aloud;
■ realise the importance of pupils taking control of input and use them creatively, generating their own, personalised language;

■   be aware of important criteria for selecting learning activities as well as the need for the sequencing of activities;

■   be able to devise suitable learning objectives and use appropriate teaching strategies that provide beginner and intermediate FLs learners opportunities for engaging in speaking and writing with an appropriate degree of accuracy and independence.

THE IMPORTANCE OF SEQUENCING AND THE INTEGRATION OF FLs SKILLS

As has been noted in previous chapters, the development of communicative competence in pupils is an important aim of instructed FLs learning. Real communication consists of more than drawing on a bank of statements and questions suited to a given topic area. It requires language to be tailored to fulfil specific objectives by drawing on situational language and lexical phrases.

For Littlewood (1981), successful 'social interaction' is an important outcome of language use, which requires a certain level of linguistic and communicative competence and is reached via a number of phases of development. It can be very difficult to develop social interaction skills, particularly in a classroom setting. Therefore, we see it as one of the aims of FL teaching to make pupils aware of the components that comprise successful communication.

One of the challenges for FL teachers is to devise a programme of learning which progresses from a reliance of pupils on the teacher towards their independence, developing in pupils the ability to generate language of their own within a communicative framework. Both the teacher and pupils must be aware of the importance of the role of the teacher as an agent of learning.

Another challenge is the appropriate sequencing of teaching and learning activities. Their development needs to be fitted within a coherent approach, which involves careful monitoring of learning and the selection of appropriate activities.

Although 'meaningfulness' of tasks and activities, e.g. 'authenticity' and the meeting of perceived needs, is important to further the development of language skills in pupils, the 'pre-communicative' phase is equally important in which 'context-reduced', i.e. less than communicative activities, occupy a valid place (see e.g. Barnes, 2007).

In this chapter we identify various stages of development for both speaking and writing as we did in the previous chapter for listening and reading. These stages should not be viewed as a simple formula, which can be repeated lesson after lesson, unit of work after unit of work. The nature of the task or given learning objective(s) might not make it possible and/or desirable to cover all stages per skill. In particular, progression does not only take place within an isolated FL skill but across a number of skill areas. Therefore, successful FLs lessons integrate a number of activities and exercises developing different FL skills, which are carefully chosen to build on previous knowledge and understanding. The examples given in this chapter by no means represent an exhaustive list.

from:	to:
repetition and copying	generation of own language

■ **Figure 10.1** Progression in productive FL skills

Imitation of 'foreign' sounds and the reproduction of accurate written forms comprise the earliest stages of developing productive language skills. Repetition and copying rely heavily on examples provided by the teacher. Eventually, the aim is the generation of personalised language by the pupil in order to satisfy a perceived communicative need.

PRONUNCIATION

As already discussed in Chapter 3, the teaching of pronunciation is an often neglected, yet very important prerequisite for success in spoken language production as well as in reading. Particularly in England, where pupils are extensively sensitised to its importance through the study of their mother tongue, i.e. in the form of a particular approach to phonics teaching, FLs teachers can expect not only a certain degree of awareness of its importance but also a certain ability to engage with it at a metalinguistic and reflective level.

The National Reading Panel, convened in the late 1990s at the request of Congress in the US, reviewed research on reading instruction which culminated in *The Report of the National Reading Panel: Teaching Children to Read* in 2000. In it, the Panel concludes that the learning of the alphabetic system, i.e. letter-sound correspondence and spelling patterns, as well as how to apply it as essential. It goes on to delineate a number of approaches to systematic phonics instruction including synthetic phonics, analytical phonics, embedded phonics, analogy phonics, onset-rime phonics and phonics through spelling, all designed to support children with their reading. It defines the various approaches as follows (2–89):

> Synthetic phonics programs teach children to convert letters into sounds or phonemes and then blend the sounds to form recognizable words. Analytic phonics avoids having children pronounce sounds in isolation to figure out words. Rather children are taught to analyze letter-sound relations once the word is identified. Phonics through-spelling programs teach children to

from
awareness raising
imitation
explanation
practice
to

■ **Figure 10.2** Pronunciation – an overview

transform sounds into letters to write words. Phonics in context approaches teach children to use sound-letter correspondences along with context cues to identify unfamiliar words they encounter in text. Analogy phonics programs teach children to use parts of written words they already know to identify new words.

The Panel also acknowledges the existence of whole-language programmes which have an emphasis on meaning-based reading and writing activities, and which integrate phonics instruction on the basis of the professional judgement of the teacher.

We outline these different approaches to the teaching of phonics here as in the UK one particular approach to the teaching of phonics has been promoted, synthetic phonics, which impacts on the L1 reading experiences that learners will bring with them to the L2 classroom.

One useful starting point to the teaching of pronunciation might be to sensitise learners to similarities and differences in pronunciation of their L1 and the L2 they are studying. This could relate to things like individual phonemes, specific phoneme combinations and pairs, vowel length and quality, consonant clusters, word stress, intonation patterns.

The stage of awareness-raising can then be followed up with imitation, explanation and practice – a procedure recommended, for example, by the BusyTeacher website (www.busyteacher.org), which also recommends the use of tongue twisters, entertaining listening activities such as rhyming games and reading aloud at the practice stage. For a useful discussion of pronunciation practice in English, see also Hewings (2004) and Schneider and Evers (2009). In the imitation phase, your learners will benefit from a focus on individual phenomena at a time. One guiding principle in making decisions about which phenomena to foreground might be perceived learner difficulty.

Task 10.1 SIMILARITIES AND DIFFERENCES IN PRONUNCIATION

Carry out some research and draw up a list of similarities and differences between English and the FL(s) you are teaching across different categories. List a number of examples mapped on to the lexical syllabus of different year groups.

Also, discuss the relative merits of the use of phonetic symbols with colleagues in your placement school.

READING ALOUD

In the specialist SLA and FLL literature, reading aloud has found occasional advocates, for example Gibson, 2008 who makes the case (p. 29) that reading aloud can help reading by reinforcing grapheme–phoneme correspondence. She also posits that it can aid the acquisition of prosodic, i.e. suprasegmental, features and help develop writing skills. She acknowledges that the practice of *unprepared* reading aloud in the class can be dull and boring as well as anxiety inducing, and it offers little, if any benefit for listeners. She (p. 30) also draws attention to criticism of reading aloud, which suggests that due to the cognitive demands on the working memory of decoding, recoding and articulation that often little is left for comprehension and that reading slowly interferes with semantic proposition formation, which hinders understanding. Not only is reading aloud a difficult thing to do, the efficacy in relation to a positive impact on pronunciation is also in doubt.

However, according to Gibson, there is a growing awareness that L1 reading strategies can be different from those in the L2 and that, consequently, there is a need to develop them actively, including in relation to the links between graphemes and phonemes, which reading aloud – Gibson argues – forces learners to do.

Gibson goes on to discuss possible ways of overcoming the potential problems with reading aloud she has identified and concludes (p. 33) that reading aloud can be beneficial but needs to be used sparingly, with listeners being given something to listen for, with an emphasis being placed on anxiety reduction, for example by audience or text length reduction and with reading aloud not being used for comprehension purposes.

Reading aloud is an activity that is seen less frequently in class. There are some obvious reasons for this: it can be hard to maintain other pupils' engagement when only one is reading; giving feedback is tricky where some pupils are struggling with pronunciation and/or may be uncomfortable reading in front of peers. As with all possible choices for classroom activities, reading aloud can be useful if there is a clear pedagogical objective for its inclusion. For example, if you were aware that certain sounds were being mispronounced often (e.g. the '–ent' ending in French), you might ask some pupils to read aloud and ask their peers to listen out carefully for when this sound was pronounced accurately and raise a hand when they heard it. If, having worked on the meaning of the text, you were trying to get the class to develop their intonation to help convey meaning, you could give them ten minutes to rehearse reading aloud some sections of the text with a partner and then hear some examples in a plenary.

In the literature, there is also a considerable amount of discussion about parents and teacher reading out texts aloud and the beneficial impact that can have on reading development. However, space prevents us from discussing this fully here.

SPEAKING

The speaking activities discussed in this section span the continuum from repetition to free expression. For further practical examples of speaking activities, see Graham, 2014.

from
repetition and controlled activities
structured pair work and guided activities
open-ended role play
creative expression and exploratory talk
to

■ **Figure 10.3** Speaking – an overview

REPETITION

Repetition exercises are a first step towards the development in pupils of speaking skills and often include choral and individual repetition.

Use of visual aids

The use of visual aids allows pupils to follow the process of labelling concepts, which can render the translation of words unnecessary. Many items of key vocabulary can be introduced and presented effectively in a visually recognisable form such as through digital technologies, flashcards, real objects, images or posters.

First of all, pupils should listen to the teacher. Once an item has been presented, pupils can be asked to repeat what they have heard. Often, young people prefer not to repeat in front of their peers because of feeling embarrassed or finding the task difficult. This can be overcome by the teacher encouraging the pupils to 'have a go' by using voice modulation, singing, imitation or speaking in pairs. Longer words and phrases often cause problems. Chanting and clapping to a rhythm can be useful strategies.

The teacher should not simply go through the list of lexical items, assuming that, once covered, learning has taken place. Images already shown need to be returned to and pupils asked to recall the relevant vocabulary. This can increase the pace of the lesson and keep the pupils attentive and interested.

Pantomime competitions

Also, the class can be divided into smaller groups to carry out 'pantomime competitions' where pupils act out – through mime and gesture – what is depicted on individual visual aids. When pupils recognise what peers act out they say the word or phrase in question. All pupils should be encouraged to participate and the last rendition of a word or phrase should be pronounced correctly so that the correct pronunciation is reinforced.

Building up phrases backwards

Building up phrases backwards can also be of help, e.g. '*Je regrette, je n'en ai pas*' becomes '*pas, . . . n'en ai pas, . . . je n'en ai pas, . . . je regrette je n'en ai pas*'.

Repeating a word or phrase if it is correct

In this activity the teacher presents a visual image to the whole group and makes either a correct or an incorrect utterance. Pupils are asked to repeat after the teacher only if what she has said is correct. If what she has said is incorrect, pupils should remain silent. The activity works best if most of what the teacher says is true (adapted from Buckby, 1980: 7). Nominating a pupil to lead the activity is one possible strategy or the class can be divided into smaller groups with some pupils acting as group leaders. Those learners with a real aptitude for the language or those who are more extrovert can be asked to lead the groups.

Pupils are required to think, to demonstrate what they know and also to participate as group members. The skills of identifying and memorising language are beginning to be developed in this way. Support by the teacher is evident through providing choices.

Guessing

If the teacher conceals the visual aids and asks pupils to guess the corresponding word or phrase in the TL, pupils are encouraged to use the TL even if they invariably make some mistakes. An element of challenge can be introduced, for instance, by counting attempts.

In activities of this kind pupils are required to use their memory and to listen to peers. Correct articulation is rewarded and pupils practise the initial stages of communication.

Distributing visual aids

A natural progression towards communication is to use the same visual aids within a communicative context. There, the teacher encourages pupils within a whole-class situation to ask for the items represented on the visual aid in the TL. The 'reward' for an accurate request is for the pupil to receive the visual aid. The pupil hides it from the rest of the class. Once all the items have been distributed, the class is asked to find out from individual pupils what their particular visual aid depicts. If the request is correct, the visual aid is revealed; if the guess is wrong or the utterance is incorrect, an appropriate response should be made, e.g. '*Lo siento, no tengo . . .*' ('Sorry, I haven't got it') or '*Lo siento, no es correcto*' ('Sorry, this is not correct'). The activity continues until all the items have been revealed. In this activity communication does take place, albeit within a supported environment.

STRUCTURED PAIR WORK AND GUIDED ACTIVITIES

The next step towards the development of speaking skills in this framework is structured pair work and model dialogues.

Card games

A natural sequel to the activities above is, for instance, to provide cue cards for pairs to perform similar communicative acts in pairs. Reduced-size copies of the visual aids can be produced. Pupils work in pairs and successful communication is rewarded by the pupil making a correct utterance retaining the card. The game is over when one pupil has gathered all the available cards. This game can be played a number of times in succession.

Information gap activities

Information gap activities are another way of getting pupils to use the newly encountered linguistic items and structures in a communicative context.

Scripting and acting out role plays

On the basis of such preparatory speaking activities, but also listening and reading tasks, pupils can use the new language to script and act out role plays. These structured pair work activities encourage repetition of set linguistic items and structures. Pupils neither respond nor communicate spontaneously, yet they do use functional language for a particular purpose.

OPEN-ENDED ROLE PLAYS AND CREATIVE EXPRESSION

From structured pair work pupils can move on to open-ended role plays. To make classroom communication of pupils more like 'real' communication, pupils need to be given opportunities to define and express their own needs. In open-ended role plays the language to be used for communication is not restricted to what has been introduced in a given unit of work but pupils have an opportunity to transfer linguistic items and structures from previous units and/or use new ones found in glossaries, dictionaries or other resource material.

In one possible activity pupils write their own 'shopping list' and purchase these articles from an imaginary store. This store can be 'staffed' by pupils, who have a defined list of articles available. As a consequence, pupils cannot predict what their peers will say. As dialogues progress, needs and requests will inevitably change, requiring original use of language. This might allow for a sense of ownership of the language used. Differentiation can include the use of images for items to be purchased. Care should be taken that pupils, in an attempt to help each other, don't just show their lists to their partner. Praise may encourage pupils to persevere with their speaking efforts.

The introduction of an element of fun or unpredictability can help to make certain topics more immediately interesting to pupils. Rather than script a standard role play in a restaurant, pupils can, for instance, be encouraged to invent a scene featuring a confused or reluctant waiter mixing up things and bringing the wrong orders.

Asking pupils to write their own mini-plays, and to rehearse and perform them is a useful activity not least because of its open-ended nature allowing for a range of outcomes and for the use of a number of language skills. Video-recording pupils' performances gives them a chance to review their language production later and consider possible improvements. The review process can be linked to assessment criteria, thereby engaging pupils in processes of self- and peer-assessment. Public performances of their plays to a wider school audience, for example in assembly, can provide pupils with a sense of achievement and impact positively on their motivation.

Pupils can also make recordings of their role plays under the supervision of the foreign language assistant (FLA). When all groups had their turn, some of the recordings are played in class. This way, pupils can practise their pronunciation, improve their accent and intonation and use their imagination.

Depending on the level of the learners, discussions and debates, often with pre-assigned roles for which pupils can prepare themselves, and simulations based around specific scenarios also lend themselves to creative expression.

EXPLORATORY TALK AND CREATIVE EXPRESSION

One important feature of many classrooms, including FLs classrooms, is teacher talk. As we have already shown in Chapter 3, IRF or IRE is the dominant interaction pattern with often rather restricted scope for language production by pupils.

Here we want to report on the work of Rojas-Drummond and Mercer (2003) who *inter alia* discuss the educational value of teacher-led discussion. They (p. 101) – rightly in our view – argue that teacher questions need to go beyond a control mechanism of classroom talk and a mechanism to evaluate pupils' performance against pre-defined criteria, e.g. by being designed to elicit one single, and often brief correct answer often not going beyond a reiteration of information supplied by the teacher. Instead, teacher's questions should:

a) encourage children to make explicit their thoughts, reasons and knowledge and share them with the class;

b) 'model' useful ways of using language that children can appropriate for use themselves, in peer group discussions and other settings (asking for relevant information possessed only by others, or asking 'why' questions to elicit reasons that are relevant to both functions (a) and (b));

c) provide opportunities for children to make longer contributions in which they express their current state of understanding, or to articulate difficulties.

They go on to argue the importance of learners' productive engagement in collaborative activities through exploratory talk:

> Exploratory Talk is that in which partners engage critically but constructively with each other's ideas. Relevant information is offered for joint consideration. Proposals may be challenged and counter-challenged, but if so reasons are given and alternatives are offered. Agreement is sought as a basis for joint progress. Knowledge is made publicly accountable and reasoning is visible in the talk.
>
> (Mercer, 2000: 98)

Exploratory talk can, therefore, be seen as an important next step up from more carefully scaffolded speaking activities.

WRITING

While writing should be introduced after new lexical items and phrases have been heard and seen, the written word should not be withheld, as there is the danger of pupils beginning to imagine their own spellings.

The simplest form of writing is copying. At the other end of the continuum is the free expression of ideas within the constraints of the vocabulary and active knowledge of the grammatical forms available.

COPYING

Copying is not as simple a task as it might at first seem. Pupils need to copy accurately as a first step towards developing writing skills in the TL, but also as a

from
copying
targeted practice
guided writing
free expression through writing
to

■ **Figure 10.4** Writing – an overview

means of recording language forms for future use. Pupils cannot simply be expected to be able to copy without instruction and practice.

Many pupils find it difficult to concentrate and copy accurately. This difficulty can be overcome by providing activities requiring more focused attention than 'simply' copying. 'Mixing and matching' activities require pupils to select a meaning for a particular word. Pupils might be asked to complete a sentence by filling gaps, choosing words from a jumbled list or unjumble letters to make a meaningful word or phrase out of them, e.g. locogie = '*colegio*'. Computer programs such as ordinary word processor packages or 'Fun with Texts' can be used effectively for this purpose, as can a wide range of websites allowing the teacher to input a list of vocabulary that is then used as the basis for a variety of web-based matching, copywriting, etc. activities.

You clearly have a key role in identifying and/or correcting misspellings.

TARGETED PRACTICE

From copying, pupils can progress to targeted practice such as the following.

Substitution

The replacement of words by alternatives and the use of appropriate reference material is a valuable skill and possible next step. Similarly, unjumbling sentences can also be used to encourage accuracy. You should insist on accuracy and demonstrate the value of correct spelling. Pupils might occasionally be given the opportunity to design crossword puzzles and wordsearches containing key vocabulary as this requires them not only to know the vocabulary/phrases in question but also to reproduce these accurately.

Repetition exercises

Writing is traditionally the form used to practise grammatical structures. Repetition exercises can reinforce correct forms of language. At the same time, work on grammatical exercises out of context can inhibit the aim of free expression. Grading activities in terms of difficulty can help to overcome this risk. You can provide alternative answers for, say, verb endings followed by pupils having to apply rules without such support. Such activities only tend to be perceived as meaningful by pupils if the teacher uses them in preparation for a communicative tasks such as, for instance, the writing of letters, e-mails, memos, faxes and messages requiring the use of information and linguistic structures in a meaningful way.

Responding through writing

Some activities outlined in the sections on listening and reading clearly require pupils to respond in writing in the TL. Support comes in the form of the text provided as a stimulus.

GUIDED WRITING

One increasingly popular approach to targeted practice, linked to the increasing emphasis on phonics in L1 teaching, is the use of writing frames. In the UK, writing frames have been promoted in particular by Wray and Lewis (see e.g. 1998 and 2000). They argue that writing frames are an effective strategy of developing non-fiction writing in particular with the following 'genres': recounts, reports, instructions, explanations, persuasion and discussion. In essence, writing frames are a skeleton outline operating as a scaffold and consist of key words and phrases such as starters, connectives and sentence modifiers enabling learners to 'concentrate on communicating what they want to say, rather than getting lost in the form' (Wray and Lewis, 1998: 1) and, in the process, enabling learners to become increasingly familiar with formal aspects of writing. In particular, they (pp. 1–2) outline the following benefits of writing frames:

- providing experience of a range of generic structures;
- offering a structure in which the given connectives maintain the cohesive ties of the text, thus helping pupils maintain the 'sense' of what they are writing;
- offering a varied vocabulary of connectives and sentence beginnings, thus extending children's experience beyond the familiar 'and then';
- encouraging pupils to give a personal interpretation of the information they have gathered by the careful use of personal pronouns. It is tempting to talk about this process in terms of giving children ownership of the information they are working with;
- asking the children to select and think about what they have learned by encouraging pupils to reorder information and demonstrate their understanding rather than just copying out text;
- enabling all pupils to achieve some success at writing, a vital ingredient in improving self-esteem and motivation;
- preventing pupils from being presented with a blank sheet of paper – a particularly daunting experience for some children, especially those for whom sustained writing is difficult;
- giving children an overview of the writing task.

In terms of procedure, Wray and Lewis (1998) stress the importance of beginning with discussion and teacher modelling before embarking on joint teacher–pupil construction and finally individual, writing-frame scaffolded pupil writing. They also stress the importance of the situatedness and context-embeddedness of

Opening paragraph	
What is your main argument?	
Arguments	
What is the most important point you want to make?	
What supporting evidence can you add?	
What is your next point?	
Supporting evidence? Details?	
Continue in this way with any other points you want to make.	
Conclusion	
Remind the reader what your main point is and ask them to support you.	

■ **Figure 10.5** A persuasive writing prompt sheet

Source: Wray and Lewis, 2000: 11.

Task 10.2 WORKING WITH WRITING FRAMES

Using some sample L1 English writing frames, for example those provided by Wray on his personal homepage at www.homepages.warwick.ac.uk/staff/D.J.Wray/Ideas/ frames.html, develop some example in your TL. Remember the point about the importance of context and do so with a particular group, topic and 'genre' of writing (see above) in mind.

the activity, rather than treating work with writing frames as an isolated study skill activity.

Importantly, Wray and Lewis are the first to acknowledge that as pupils' knowledge of form increases (2000: 7), so the use of writing frames should be reduced and replaced by other types of scaffold (see e.g. Figure 10.5).

FREE EXPRESSION THROUGH WRITING

A common frustration in FLs learning is the inability to express oneself freely without resorting to translation. Pupils should be encouraged to 'experiment' with and exploit known language by prompting them to write short poems, jokes and slogans within most topic areas. Short stories and the production of texts based on 'my ideal . . .' allow pupils to use their imagination. You need to gauge the extent to which work of this nature is corrected: accurate language production needs to be reinforced, yet at the same time individual and personal use of the TL should not be discouraged.

In the literature, product and process approaches to writing tend to be distinguished. The British Council website offers a useful comparison between the two with pupils having have more freedom on how to approach the task in a process-based approach with writing being treated more as a creative act leading to a more open-ended outcome. For specific approaches to process writing, see e.g. www.teachingenglish.org.uk/articles/approaches-process-writing.

Process writing	Product writing
■ text as a resource for comparison	■ imitate model text
■ ideas as starting point	■ organisation of ideas more important than ideas themselves
■ more than one draft	■ one draft
■ more global, focus on purpose, theme, text type, i.e. reader is emphasised	■ features highlighted, including controlled practice of those features
■ collaborative	■ individual
■ emphasis on creative process	■ emphasis on end product

■ **Figure 10.6** A comparison of process and product approaches to writing

Source: www.teachingenglish.org.uk/articles/product-process-writing-a-comparison

Task 10.3 **PRODUCTIVE LANGUAGE SKILLS – SPEAKING AND WRITING**

■   Observe a range of FLs teachers at your placement school. How do they encourage pupils to repeat new words and phrases? Use the grid in Figure 10.5 to help you record your findings. Which strategy works with which learner types?

■   Pupils need a lot of confidence to speak to each other in the TL. With reference to Figure 10.6, what forms of support are provided in pair and group work? Which work best with which learner types?

■   The table in Figure 10.9 consists of three columns: learner types, activity types and support.

Which activities are most suitable for which learner type and what support is required?

Match up the items in the three columns. Base your choice on the classroom observations you have already carried out.

Follow up this task by including different activity types in your planning; then evaluate them.

For a range of classes devise differentiated writing tasks and discuss them with your mentor or the respective class teacher.

Strategy	Group				Group				Group				Group				Group			
Teacher's initials																				
Whole group																				
Individuals																				
Small groups																				
Competition																				
Teacher changes voice																				
Teacher changes pace																				
Teacher changes pitch																				
Use of gestures																				
Use of visual aids																				
Others . . .																				

■ **Figure 10.7** Strategies for repetition

Support	Comment
Visual stimulus	
Written stimulus (English)	
Written stimulus (TL)	
Props	
Model examples	
'Structure' tables	
Scripts (complete or incomplete)	

■ **Figure 10.8** Support strategies for oral language production

Learner types	Activity types	Support strategies
Beginners	Reporting facts	Fishing lines*
Weak intermediates	Substitution	Alternative answers
Strong intermediates	Selection of correct forms	Model answers
Advanced learners	Joining halves of sentences	Rules and structures
Others – please list	Gap filling	Switchboards
	Labelling	Closed questions
	Answering in sentences	Open questions
	Drill exercises	Tables of facts and figures
	Scripting	Pictures
	Free expression	Symbols
	Discursive writing	Flow charts
	Other – please list	Others – please list

■ **Figure 10.9** Matching learner types, activity types and support strategies

* Fishing lines are drawn on to a sheet to join two ideas; these may be presented as a tangled web, forming a puzzle.

CREATIVITY AND IMAGINATION

Imagination and creativity can be seen to permeate all FLs work. In Miller's words: 'in the modern languages classroom . . . teachers are required, day after day, to involve their pupils in a collective suspension of disbelief' (Miller, 1995: 1).

Traditionally, teachers require verbal responses. However, you might also occasionally, and where appropriate, consider other communicative tools such as:

■ drawing
■ modelling
■ composing music
■ dance
■ movement and/or
■ poetry.

Allowing such a range of responses over a period of time enables the expression of new ideas to be generated in ways, which mirror the human means of perception, i.e. through various senses.

Goleman (1996) stresses the need to assist pupils in the development of their emotional intelligence, which means that opportunities need to be built into the learning process to allow pupils to respond and therefore to understand, express, and use feelings and intuition.

One of the challenges for FLs teachers lies in incorporating into lessons suitable material and activities at appropriate moments. By far not all language use is purely transactional and much is to be gained from the building of personalised patterns and structures. A multi-sensory approach allows for learning to be channelled in ways other than through verbal presentations. Songs, poems, puzzles, games, the creating of cartoons, artefacts and models can all enhance the learning process, appealing to pupils by adding variety and by catering for the diversity of their preferred learning styles.

The process of learning is not and should not be mechanistic. Language offers the opportunity for play, experimentation and even expression through means other than language. The stimulus for comprehension is often the context, and the incentive for communication may be different from the need to communicate for transactional purposes. Poetry, for example, allows for the close analysis of language.

Some published recorded material such as *Un kilo de chansons* (Kay, 1978) contains the continuous rhythmic repetition of simple phrases, set to music. Rap music can provide similar opportunities as can other material available via the Internet. To allow pupils to record their own songs to a simple rhythm and to add basic musical accompaniment can be an effective way to link in with youth culture and pupils' interests.

Encouraging FL production in relation to pupils' music preferences can provide a rich source of motivation. For example, pupils can write about their favourite bands, research music bands from the target culture and write about them, their 'sound', lyrics and lifestyle.

It used to take a long time to produce puzzles in the form of word searches, crosswords or word snakes. Now these can be produced quickly and easily online. Pupils themselves can occasionally be asked to develop such activities and challenge peers to complete them. The production of personalised language forms, which actually serve a purpose, can lead to a feeling of ownership and achievement and can be used with beginners as quick and rewarding introduction, revision and memorisation activities.

For more sophisticated tasks, the Internet is a great source for ideas and stimulus material for language production, e.g. news or events such as concerts, which they can be asked to describe, summarise, respond to, analyse, critique, report on, etc.

Advertisements often make minimal use of language, yet communicate messages through imagery and symbolism. To develop advertisements of their own allows pupils to put limited language skills to good use within a sophisticated context. By exposing pupils to a variety of examples, they can observe how meaning is represented and how sentences are structured, etc.

Language is often the means by which instructions and explanations are communicated. Success can be measured in terms of how well such instructions have been understood and acted upon. To ask pupils to give instructions in the process of making a product such as a meal, model or artefact is a demanding exercise, yet it can be motivating in that TL use can be seen to have an impact on the listener as well as a concrete outcome.

Hanauer (2012), whose work we already discussed in Chapter 3, shows how poetry writing in the FLs classroom can be an effective part of meaningful literacy teaching. To counter the scepticism he regularly encounters when arguing the case for the use of poetry in introductory language classes, he analysed the corpus of student-generated poems in his introductory ESL class over a period of six years comprising some 844 examples according to a range of recognised linguistic, textual and literary measures (pp. 111–112) and found that the poetry his students had generated was short, used predominantly first person singular and high frequency vocabulary, used poetic features such as visual and auditory imagery, some rhyme and alliteration, as well as some figurative language and a comparatively high level of emotive lexicon.

SUMMARY

Both FLs student teachers and pupils should recognise the importance of sequencing activities and integrating FLs skills within a communicative framework. Each FL skill must be developed equally in order to allow pupils to generate language in 'authentic' situations and in an independent way. Moreover, creativity is an important and integral part of FLs work.

FURTHER READING

O'Brien, T. (2004) Writing in a foreign language: teaching and learning. In *Language Teaching*, 37(1): 1–28.
  This state-of-the-art article provides a rationale for the focus on writing in foreign language classrooms and goes on to provide an overview of relevant cognitive and social frameworks underpinning models for foreign language writing.

Pachler, N. and Redondo, A. (2014) *Teaching Foreign Languages in the Secondary School: A Practical Guide* (2nd edn). London: Routledge.
  This book provides a good source of further thoughts concerning the issues introduced in this chapter as well as for most of the other chapters in this publication.

Richards, J. (2008) *Teaching Listening and Speaking: From Theory to Practice.* Cambridge: Cambridge University Press. Available online at: www.cambridge.org/ other_files/downloads/esl/booklets/Richards-Teaching-Listening-Speaking.pdf
  This booklet explores approaches to the teaching of listening and speaking in the light of research in the field of applied linguistics.

CHAPTER 11

TEACHING AND LEARNING GRAMMAR

INTRODUCTION

The ability to use language grammatically correctly is a key component and an integral part of effective communication in the TL. This chapter is based on the premise that the development of communicative competence is a key goal for FL teaching and learning. Importantly, following Canale and Swain (1980), we consider communicative competence to encompass sociolinguistic, discourse, linguistic and strategic competence (see also Pachler, 2000). Therefore, this chapter deals with grammatical competence as a subset of communicative competence.

FLs methodology is characterised by considerable changes in the importance afforded to grammar over time. And many commentators readily acknowledge that grammar teaching remains a hotly contested aspect of FL teaching and learning. Research findings, although not conclusive, are able to support certain pedagogical recommendations around the need for 'some focus on form . . . for many learners to achieve accuracy as well as fluency in their acquisition of a second or foreign language' (Celce-Murcia, 1991: 462; see also Ellis, 2006).

Until the late 1970s and early 1980s, the so-called grammar translation method prevailed in England, which was in part linked to FLs teachers' eagerness to assert equality of status with classical languages. In the grammar translation method, TL structures are typically arranged according to perceived usefulness and in increasing order of supposed complexity with new grammar rules being introduced and explained in the mother tongue, exemplified in the TL and practised through translation out of and into the TL (see Allford, 1999: 232). The grammar–translation method can be seen as an expression of FLs teachers' perceived need to justify the position of their subject on the curriculum by stressing the potential for analytical thinking and the training of the mind FL learning affords. Focus on language forms in grammar-translation often came at the expense of learners' ability to communicate effectively in speaking.

Examinations and their syllabuses/specifications, i.e. the General Certificate in Education O-level and the Certificate in Secondary Education in England, reflected the emphasis on grammar and accuracy. The nature of this approach, and of the examinations accompanying, is widely judged to have contributed to a lack of pupil motivation to study FLs at Secondary level in England.

In the mid 1980s the General Certificate of Secondary Education (GCSE) was introduced in England and Wales. It emphasised communication in a narrowly defined number of topics with clearly specified linguistic items/phrases, functions and structures at the expense of accuracy. The pendulum swing from great emphasis on form to great emphasis on meaning led to the publication of two consecutive National Curriculum documents in the 1990s in England which put little emphasis on grammar.

In recent years, grammar has seen something of a renaissance. Pressure from the grass roots has led to changes, with many FLs teachers holding fairly strong beliefs about the value of grammar (see e.g. Mcrory, 2000). Klapper points to a common misinterpretation of communicative language teaching and stresses that true communication denotes a high level of development predicated on a solid grasp of structure and lexis (see Klapper, 1997: 27). While grammar-related aspects of the TL are still in the main seen as a means to an end, they do now tend to feature explicitly in curriculum requirements and examination specifications. The 2011 *Subject Criteria for Modern Foreign Languages* (Ofqual, 2011; www.bit.ly/gcse-criteria-mfl-2011), for example, governing examinations for pupils aged 16 in England at the time of writing, require an ability to 'understand and apply the grammar of the language' (p. 4) as outlined in an appendix and the same document specifies (p. 5) that for speaking and writing 'at least 10 per cent of the total marks must be allocated to knowledge and accurate application of the grammar and structures of the language' (p. 5). The appendix features a list of grammar items for each of French, German and Spanish, indicating also the expectation of productive or receptive use. For basic French, learners are, for example, expected to know what nouns are as well as gender and singular/plural forms. For articles they need to be able to distinguish definite, indefinite and partitive, including use of *de* after negatives, etc.

At a more advanced level, the teaching of grammar had tended to remain an explicit integral part of requirements and the trend to strengthen the focus on grammar at beginner and intermediate levels can also be seen as an attempt to avoid a further increase in the gap between the two. The most recent criteria for advanced level language study in England published by Ofqual in 2011 (www.bit.ly/gce-criteria-mfl-2011) have as one of their assessment objectives the requirement to 'show knowledge of and apply accurately the grammar and syntax prescribed in the specification' (p. 5) to which 25 per cent of the overall marks are allocated. As with the specification at beginner and intermediate level, the advanced level specifications feature a detailed appendix with a differentiated list of structures to be covered for French, German and Spanish.

Table 11.1 sets out in broad terms the grammatical transition from beginner/intermediate (learners aged 16) to advanced level (learners aged 18) grammar requirements of examination specifications in England.

Increase in complexity is clearly not only evident at the grammar level but also in terms of the topics to be studied and the degree of cognitive and linguistic sophistication, including breadth and specialisation of vocabulary.

Table 11.1 Bridging the gap to post-16 – functions

Beginner/Intermediate	Progression	Advanced
Listening		
Understand specific details. Extract relevant information. Identify themes or points of view. Draw conclusions and relate ideas expressed by others. Follow instructions.	*State a personal reaction to a specific series of events.*	Recognition of the mood and emotions being expressed. Understand and participate in personal conversations, group discussions and debates. To extract key information to enable summary and oral and written responses.
Speaking		
Respond to closed and structured questions. Elicit information. Convey factual information. Respond to visual stimuli. Elicit and convey agreement and disagreement. Request basic services and products.	*Report on an event to more than one audience.*	To express full meaning by conveying facts, mood and emotion. To respond to other speakers in an appropriate register and tone. To initiate and sustain extended conversations and discussions. To elicit further detail by focused questioning. To express and justify opinions.
Reading		
Understand instructions. Extract relevant information from authentic texts. Identify themes or points of view. Draw conclusions. Relate ideas and themes contained within a text.	*Summarise the main arguments within a text, with support and guidance.*	Recognition of mood, emotions and appropriate register. To understand and respond critically to extended fictional and non-fictional texts. To recognise and react to themes, arguments, images and ideas expressed within authentic texts. To analyse and respond to arguments and points of view.
Writing		
Respond to given stimuli. Convey information. Express simple feelings and opinions. Report on real events.	*Respond by countering arguments presented in a short, authentic text.*	To summarise information and to expand upon detail. To translate and transcribe. To express ideas in a creative way. To generate and manipulate original language forms to develop coherent arguments and creative texts. To handle grammar and syntax implicit in all of the above.

As of late the question is no longer whether or not grammar should be taught, but instead how, why and when. As a student teacher, learning how to teach grammar effectively is a crucial aspect of your development as a successful teacher of FLs. Halliwell (1993: 17), for example, points out the value of learning grammar as opposed to acquiring the language. She sees learning as a conscious process and it seems quicker to her than acquisition through immersion. However, building language forms around grammatical rules independently of communicative needs can be argued to serve no real purpose.

The communicative context determines the form of the message conveyed by a speaker or writer. Grammatical accuracy can be argued to be secondary if the message is understood. Nevertheless, pupils need a grammatical base in order to be able to generate language of their own as opposed to merely reproduce set phrases of others. Communicative competence and linguistic competence should, therefore, not be seen as separate entities (see Miller, 2002).

Learners should not be inhibited in terms of communicative competence due to an adherence to a strictly linear approach to learning grammar, i.e. from simple to complex. Lightbown and Spada (1993: 114), for example, note that 'it is neither necessary nor desirable to restrict learners' exposure to certain linguistic structures which are perceived as being "simple"'. As Grauberg (1997: 99) rightly points out, even the simplest exchanges require complex language. See DeKeyser, 2005 for some insights in to what makes learning grammar difficult. To empower learners to operate in the present tense only, for example, can be seen to 'strand them linguistically' (see Jones, 2000b: 149). Yet sequencing of grammar learning can be seen to be necessary to enable learners to build up patterns and structures incrementally.

To teach learners certain grammatical features as set phrases can be seen to be legitimate in so far as it can stand pupils in good stead (see the discussion of chunking in Chapter 3; see also Ellis, 2006). However, this should not be done at the expense of the development in pupils of an understanding of language and of an ability to generate language of their own. A more beneficial long-term strategy seems to us to be to pay specific attention to language with transferable value, such as the key verbs, lexical items, pronouns, adjectives, adverbs or gender markers.

This chapter focuses on the need for you to address the development of grammatical awareness, knowledge and understanding in pupils in a well-planned and structured way within the context of communicative processes. We suggest that grammar should not be presented in isolation but as part of a coherent framework and that it should not be left to pupils to absorb grammar by osmosis.

To underline that this can be achieved in a number of ways, we want to offer the following definition of grammar teaching here:

> *Grammar teaching* involves any instructional technique that draws learners' attention to some specific grammatical form in such a way that it helps them either to understand it metalinguistically and/or process it in comprehension and/or production so that they can internalize it.
>
> (Ellis, 2006: 84)

OBJECTIVES

By the end of this chapter you should:

■ understand some of the important issues concerning the teaching and learning of grammar in the Secondary FLs curriculum;

■ appreciate the need for a structured approach to the teaching and learning of grammar;

■ be aware of one possible framework for and be able to make informed choices about the teaching and learning of grammar as part of the development of communicative competence.

Task 11.1 KEY ISSUES IN GRAMMAR LEARNING AND TEACHING

The following are what may be considered key issues involving grammar in language learning and teaching:

■ Terminology/metalanguage: should we use it at all? If so, in the TL? In English? In both?

■ Explicit instruction/implicit learning/both?

■ Do you favour the systematic introduction of structures/more ad hoc (when the need arises)/a balanced approach?

■ What is the role of practice with drills/exercises?

■ Should 'rules' be taught? If so, how and when? In what format? In which language?

■ What about grammar for recognition? Grammar for production?

Reflect on the issues listed. What are your initial thoughts on them *before* you read the rest of the chapter?

PEDAGOGICAL GRAMMAR

Definitions of the word 'grammar' are manifold: they range from a 'theory of language' to a description of the (syntactic) structure of a particular language'. Of these grammars, work by applied linguists on what they call 'pedagogical grammar', which focuses on language teaching, syllabus design and the production of teaching material, is of particular interest to FLs teachers (see Mitchell, 2000).

At beginner and intermediate level it is particularly difficult for the FLs teacher to strike the right balance between accuracy and meaning. To what extent should FLs teachers tolerate errors when encouraging communication? While perfect grammatical accuracy is not necessary for communication to take place, it can be argued that, in order to operate effectively as a TL speaker or writer, we have to understand – at least to some extent – the possibilities that grammar affords us. The ability to recognise linguistic patterns and to make use of, and apply grammatical rules aids communication rather than inhibits it.

Examination success tends to require awareness, knowledge and understanding of grammatical features. Careful preparation of pupils in examination techniques and familiarisation with past examination papers as well as standard 'grammatical' paradigms and standard role plays and letters to be adapted by pupils according to context is one option, and can be a successful strategy for gaining good examination results. However, does this approach foster 'real' learning?

To some extent grammatical understanding can be seen to provide FL learners in classroom-based settings with a shortcut. The limited curriculum time available, often not more than 10 per cent, coupled with the acquisition-poor nature of classroom-based learning do not tend to allow for natural acquisition. Grammar can be seen as a tool enabling TL use, and the use of specific and technical terminology, i.e. metalanguage, offers learners access to reference material. The teaching and learning of grammar to beginners and intermediate-level is neither undesirable nor inappropriate. In order to be beneficial, it does, however, need to be structured carefully and a range of issues need to be taken on board during the planning process as, for example, Jones (2000b: 151–153) notes (see Figure 11.1). Both under- and over-emphasis on grammatical structures can lead to frustration and can militate against free expression. The exact nature of the teacher's methods will depend, among other factors, on her personal teaching style, pupils' individual needs and differences, the coursebook followed or the general approach adopted by the whole school in terms of language work (see Everett, 2005, for some ideas for making grammar more permanently a part of pupils' language production).

Based on his review of the available research, Ellis (2006: 102–103) offers the following ten beliefs about grammar teaching, acknowledging that many of them remain contested:

1   The grammar taught should be one that emphasises not just form but also the meanings and uses of different grammatical structures.
2   Teachers should endeavour to focus on those grammatical structures that are known to be problematic to learners rather than try to teach the whole of grammar.
3   Grammar is best taught to learners who have already acquired some ability to use the language (i.e. intermediate level) rather than to complete beginners. However, grammar can be taught through corrective feedback as soon as learners begin to use the language productively.
4   A focus-on-forms approach is valid as long as it includes an opportunity for learners to practise behaviour in communicative tasks.
5   Consideration should be given to experimenting with a massed rather than distributed approach to teaching grammar.
6   Use should be made of both input-based and output-based instructional options.
7   A case exists for teaching explicit grammatical knowledge as a means of assisting subsequent acquisition of implicit knowledge. Teaching explicit knowledge can be incorporated into both a focus-on-forms and a focus-on-form approach. In the case of a focus-on-forms approach, a differentiated approach involving sometimes deductive and sometimes inductive instruction may work best.

8   An incidental focus-on-form approach is of special value because it affords an opportunity for extensive treatment of grammatical problems (in contrast to the intensive treatment afforded by a focus-on-forms approach).

9   Corrective feedback is important for learning grammar. It is best conducted using a mixture of implicit and explicit feedback types that are both input based and output based.

10   In accordance with these beliefs, grammar instruction should take the form of separate grammar lessons (a focus-on-forms approach) and should also be integrated into communicative activities (a focus-on-form approach).

---

1   Selection

Within the overall schematic picture of a typical five-year learning programme, the teacher needs to select structures that will be useful in terms of transfer value as regards other structures and other contexts in order to maximise their generative capacity for the learners. In other words, it is useful to teach structures that can be used elsewhere, in different language use. . . .

2   Sequencing

It is the role of the teacher to help the learners to make the connections through a mixture of inductive and deductive approaches, with extensive exposure and opportunities to practise making the link. . . .

3   Recycling

Whilst the constraints and needs of classroom learning necessitate some drilling of discrete items as an aid to internalisation, it is helpful to the learners to be shown how a structure learnt in one context may be recycled in another one. . . .

4   Moving from 'form' to function

This involves a shift from 'skill-getting' to 'skill-using' and envisages the learner moving from a stage of very conscious attention to the language form to a more unconscious use for real communication purposes. . . .

5   Grading of input

It is sometimes useful to restate a very obvious principle such as this assertion that, as well as a sufficient quantity of examples, teachers need to present appropriately graded examples to the pupils. In this way, the first examples will be easier, straightforward and contradiction-free and thus susceptible to helping the learners to infer the pattern(s) and thus to be able to test their hypotheses. . . .

6   Use of terminology

Unfortunately, the issue of grammatical terminology has become . . . something considered so abstract as to be beyond pupils' comprehension. This (can be seen as) a little condescending. It is the quality and timing of a presentation and explanation of a grammatical structure that is important and not the terminology per se. As Carter cogently argues: 'It is not taught for its own sake but to provide an economic and precise way of discussing particular functions and purposes' (Carter, 1997: 24).

■ **Figure 11.1** Some issues associated with teaching and learning grammar

Source: Jones, 2000b.

Ellis stresses the fact that they are open to challenge, but for us they constitute a serious proposal to replace traditional approaches to the teaching of grammar , which are unlikely to result in the implicit knowledge required for fluent and accurate communication.

Swan (2006) proposes a general approach to FL teaching that features grammar as an integral part and that he captures in a matrix comprising input and output, distinguishing three types for each: extensive, intensive and analysed, see Figure 11.2.

	Extensive	*Intensive*	*Analysed*
Input	Quantity of language learners are exposed to which is roughly 'attuned' to their level of development	A small, but carefully selected sample of language which learners 'can internalise, process, make their own and use as bases for production' Detailed study of text, learning by heart	'Information about the workings of particular aspects of the language, presented implicitly or explicitly' (rules, examples, lists)
Output	Quantity of language Free speech and writing	Controlled practice recycling input received	Rehearsing and trying out structures; practising of analysed language patterns Exercises

■ **Figure 11.2** A balanced programme

Source: based on Swan, 2006.

FOUR STAGES OF DEVELOPING GRAMMATICAL AWARENESS

We outline four stages of developing grammatical awareness here (see Figure 11.3). They are intended to link the teaching of grammar to the 'presentation–practice–production' paradigm discussed in Chapter 5.

No	Stage
1	Input
2	Explanation
3	Habit-forming
4	Communicative application

■ **Figure 11.3** Four stages of grammar teaching and learning

Stages 1–4 are not meant to promote curriculum planning based on grammar-orientated objectives alone. Instead, a structured and graded approach of developing linguistic understanding is advanced, which is closely linked to other objectives, such as semantic knowledge across different contexts or functions (e.g. expressing likes and dislikes, asking for, refusing, etc).

> Research findings . . . challenged the traditional grammar-based course by suggesting that learners acquired particular structures in an order which was psychologically determined but not susceptible to explicit instruction. Acquisition took place in stages and the notion that a learner had fully acquired a structure after a period of instruction was naive. Learning did not occur in linear and progressive fashion but was an organic process characterised by backsliding, leaps in competence, interaction between grammatical elements, etc.
>
> (Heafford, 1995: 10)

This notion of an 'organic' nature of language development has implications for teaching and learning. Turner, for example, advances the view that a purely thematic, topic-based approach to planning and syllabus design with an unsystematic and disorganised presentation of the grammatical system (e.g. categories of words, the notion of tense, syntactical considerations including cases, the gender of nouns and the notion of agreement, the mood of verbs, etc.) is unhelpful to pupils. Based on work by Brumfit, she proposes a graded, spiralling approach based on grammatical aspects of a language in conjunction with semantic aspects (the meaning of words and sentences) underpinned by the criterion of 'usefulness to the pupil' (e.g. what does the pupil need to do well in the standardised examination?) with a view to providing a 'tool for learning' (e.g. what helps the pupil in becoming an effective language learner?) (see Turner, 1996: 17–18). 'Organising the grammatical core in conjunction with the topic areas means that structures are always contextualised and related to language use' (Turner, 1996: 18). For example, the topic of 'directions' could be seen to lend itself well to the teaching of imperatives (the command form).

As could be seen already, the role of grammar in FL teaching and learning is complex. Teachers' decisions need to take into account what is known about the FL learning process. Pachler (see 1999c: 97) identifies four broad stages of learning grammar.

■ *Noticing*

The identification that language forms patterns and the labelling, in the learners' own words, of these patterns. (This is where the teacher's carefully planned presentation of the grammar can play a key role, e.g. by intelligent use of digital technologies to enable more 'noticing' of the forms and changes).

■ *Integrating*

The process of identifying and labelling through personal rule formation needs to be related to existing grammatical knowledge.

■ *Internalising*

Learners need to apply their own rules in order to manipulate language forms for their own purposes. This completes the process of committing the form to the long-term memory.

■ *Proceduralising*

Use of the structure becomes 'automatic' through regular usage in a range of contexts. From this follow important pedagogic questions, such as: to what extent should these processes be made explicit to learners? How can they be taught?

1 The input stage

Two main approaches to providing input can be distinguished: an *inductive* approach, where linguistic structures are introduced through examples from which to develop (personal) rules; and a *deductive* approach, where the pupil is provided with a grammatical rule or pattern followed by examples before putting it to use.

Both methods have a legitimate place in FL teaching and learning. Grammar is highly conceptual, which appeals to some pupils more than others. Certain aspects of language are difficult to explain. Why, for instance, is the word 'table' feminine in French and masculine in German, and why has it no grammatical gender in English? To accept certain concepts as given and to apply some rules in a mechanical way without trying to understand them seems on occasion to be a sensible way forward. Nevertheless, having understood a grammatical concept, for instance gender, many pupils are able to work out a rule, such as for adjectival agreement, from a set of carefully constructed examples.

Some pupils can get a sense of security from understanding language patterns and rules. Forth and Naysmith (1995: 78) distinguish

■   *'external' rules:* 'the kind of statements, diagrams, tables, etc., which we can find in coursebooks, grammar reference books or which we as teachers provide'; and

■   *'internal' rules:* 'the learner's own intuitive, informal hunches of how elements of the language might work'.

While they stress that there is 'no one, single approach to the presentation and use of grammar rules in the classroom' (Forth and Naysmith, 1995: 80), they posit that learners should be encouraged to reflect on how they themselves use rules and what works for them. Teachers should encourage learners to challenge grammar rules, for instance, by:

■   asking pupils to change or modify rules presented in their course books so that they are clearer and more accessible;

■   asking pupils to add their own examples;

■   asking pupils to re-present rules in the form of classroom poster-displays perhaps with the addition of pictures or diagrams.

(Forth and Naysmith, 1995: 80)

Input is concerned with the selection of material and of a suitable approach. One possible consideration is for items, which can be seen to be of future use and are, therefore, 'transferable', to be explicitly taught, especially in the early stages of learning. Such items need to be readily understood by all learners and the teacher needs to be sure that they are relatively simple to understand. Ellis (1994: 91), referring to research by Green and Hecht (1992) on what constitutes easy-to-learn rules, lists the following features:

- those that refer to easily recognisable categories;
- those that can be applied mechanically;
- those that are not dependent on large contexts.

Task 11.2 GRAMMAR RULES

Write a rule for the English use of 'yet' and 'still' as in 'I've not been to London yet' and 'I've still not been to London'.
Then consider these questions:

- How did you go about approaching this task?
- When is it useful to resort to a rule and when does it help to refer to examples?

The selection of grammatical items to be covered within units of work is not simple. Some topics lend themselves more easily to new grammatical input than others (e.g. the topic 'Around town' for the teaching of the imperative). However, the selection of grammar points to be covered requires the consideration of more complex questions, such as:

- which items need to be 're-cycled' from previous units covered?
- which items meaningfully build on existing knowledge?
- which items should not be explained in full at this stage, but will require revisiting at a later date?
- which items can be treated as lexical items at this stage?

Coursebooks tend to include suggestions concerning grammar items to be covered. Where possible, account needs to be taken of prior learning and how certain grammatical concepts link with what has come before. Also, extension activities for more able learners are important in so far as the decision to treat certain grammatical structures as lexical items/phrases at a particular stage of learning may not be appropriate for all learners.

Learners need to be prepared for the demands of new language features. Also, they need to be trained to identify patterns, structures, exceptions to rules, etc. and be able to learn from the teacher's corrections. You need to be aware of possible misconceptions and difficulties pupils might have, which might impact upon their motivation.

Personal details and daily routine	
Language functions	
Be able to: 1 Exchange details about the family. 2 Introduce people. 3 Describe and understand appearance. 4 Describe places and buildings. 5 Talk about chores. 6 Describe daily routine at home.	
Core language	*Extension*
Names of members of immediate family Description: hair, eyes, height, weight Name of rooms Household chores Routines	Other relatives Description of personality Other accommodation More complex routines and chores
Grammar	
Key activities	
Letter to penfriend Design ideal home Identikit pictures	

■ **Figure 11.4** Grammar and the unit of work

Grauberg (1997: 104) stresses the importance of the text on which introductory work is based. In his opinion it should:

- ▨ deal with a topic of interest to the learners;
- ▨ build on lexical and grammatical knowledge acquired earlier;
- ▨ at the same time have the attraction of novelty;
- ▨ feature a context, which lends itself to varied and interesting practice where form and function are brought out clearly without distortion to normal use.

In our reading of Grauberg we interpret 'text' very broadly as any type of stimulus material, be it written or spoken.

Rutherford (1987) advocates a process of 'consciousness raising', focusing the learner's attention on features of the TL, which are deemed by the teacher to be significant at a given stage of learning. This might well involve a degree of comparison with the mother tongue, the breaking down of larger items into component parts, etc. in order to sensitise the learner to the structure of the TL.

Hawkins (1984) conceives of grammar learning as a voyage of discovery and argues against a prescriptive model. The recognition that different learners will respond to different approaches requires teachers to understand a wide range of techniques and to develop strategies to suit specific learner characteristics.

The discussion of the inductive and deductive methods below is intended to provide a framework within which a range of strategies for grammar teaching can be categories and consequently better understood.

THE INDUCTIVE APPROACH – AN EXAMPLE

Pupils need to be made aware of the concept of gender early on. In German, for instance, the awareness of this concept should precede the introduction of the case system. The teaching of the accusative case can be done meaningfully in the context of the topic of 'family and pets'. The assumption in this example is that the new vocabulary has already been introduced and that the teacher follows a policy of discussing new grammar items within the context of familiar vocabulary.

Pupils could be presented with a number of sentences, such as those in Figure 11.5.

The pupils are then asked to sort these sentences according to categories of their own choice. Some pupils will choose the categories according to whether the object is a person or an animal. Clearly from the examples given, pupils would not be wrong to apply such categories. The purpose of the inductive approach is for pupils to make up and apply rules of their own, which fit the examples provided. As the examples given in Figure 11.5 are ambiguous and allow for different

Ich habe einen Bruder.	Ich habe ein Kaninchen.
Ich habe eine Schwester.	Ich habe eine Katze.
Ich habe ein Meerschweinchen.	Ich habe einen Wellensittich.

▨ **Figure 11.5** The accusative case in German

interpretation, the FLs teacher needs to provide further examples in a structured way that lead the pupils to the intended focus. Eventually, the majority of pupils should choose the categories: '*einen*', '*ein*' or '*eine*'.

In groups, pupils are then asked to discuss (in English) the ways in which they have categorised the sentences and why, and to attempt to generate a rule, which is subsequently discussed in a plenary. An example of one such rule could be: 'If you have something masculine you add '-en' to '*ein*'. If it's feminine, stick with the normal '*eine*' and for neuter stick with '*ein*'.'

At this stage it is sufficient for the FLs teacher to say that the inflections occur after '*haben*'. Once the concept is familiar, a more formal explanation of the accusative case can be attempted. In this approach new metalanguage is not introduced until the learner has demonstrated an understanding of the concept through the use of language familiar to her at the point of input.

In another example the inductive approach can be used to teach the perfect tense in Spanish. Pupils are asked to read the penfriend letter in Figure 11.6 and underline or highlight any linguistic patterns they seem to notice. In this example, it is the auxiliary '*haber*' in the present tense plus the respective past participle. The teacher then elicits pupil observations in the TL and collects them on the board. The grammatical rule that infinitives ending in '-ar' form the past participle in '-ado', those ending in '-er' and '-ir' in '-ido' is subsequently explained in the TL by drawing parallels to the similarities and differences in the English language. In this way, appropriate use is made of English for comparing and contrasting with the mother tongue.

Albacete 7 de septiembre

Querida Alison:

¿ cómo estás? He vuelto al colegio hace una semana y he empezado mis clases. Lo he pasado muy bien este verano ¿ y tú? He viajado a la costa de Valencia con mi familia y he ido a la playa todos los dias por las mañanas donde me he bañado y donde antes del almuerzo hemos jugado mucho al balónvolea con amigos nuevos que he conocido allí.

Me he puesto muy morena. Mi hermana y yo hemos ido a la discoteca por las noches y hemos disfrutado mucho. Mis padres han ido al restaurante todas las noches y han comido comida típica de la región. También hemos visitado pueblos famosos como Elche y sus museos.

He recogido mis fotografias del laboratorio esta mañana y estoy muy contenta con el resultado. He seleccionado cuatro fotos para mandarte para que puedas ver lo bonita que es la costa del este de España.

De momento nada más.

En tu carta, háblame de tu verano, por ejemplo: ¿has estado de vacaciones? ¿has visitado a tus amigos? ¿has viajado?

Recuerdos a tu familia y espero recibir tu carta pronto.

Con cariño, tu amiga
Sonia

■ **Figure 11.6** Introducing the Spanish perfect tense

Task 11.5 **THE INDUCTIVE APPROACH**

Try to think of other examples for the inductive approach appropriate for your first foreign language and discuss it with your mentor or another teacher you regularly work with.

THE DEDUCTIVE APPROACH – AN EXAMPLE

For many pupils the concept of grammatical gender is difficult to conceptualise. One possible way of introducing the definite article to pupils is by providing them with a table such as the one in Figure 11.7.

THE					
le	=	masculine	*le* chat	=	**the** cat
la	=	feminine	*la* souris	=	**the** mouse
les	=	plural	*les* chiens	=	**the** dogs
l'	=	before a vowel (**a, e, i, o, u**) or **'h'**	*l'*araignée *l'*hôtel	= =	**the** spider **the** hotel

■ **Figure 11.7** The definite article in French

Pupils are then asked to complete the exercise in Figure 11.8 by referring to the table in Figure 11.7.

1 .... *cheval* (m)	2 .... *cahier* (pl)	3 .... *torture* (f)
4 .... *lapin* (pl)	5 .... *prénom* (m)	6 .... *soeur* (f)
7 .... *hôpital* (m)	8 .... *stylo* (pl)	9 .... *jour* (pl)
10 .... *anniversaire* (m)	11 .... *poubelle* (f)	12 .... *animal* (m)
13 .... *frère* (pl)	14 .... *éléphant* (m)	15 .... *femme* (f)
16 .... *homme* (m)	17 .... *serpent* (pl)	18 .... *table* (f)

■ **Figure 11.8** Practising the definite article in French

Pour formuler le **passé composé** vous avez besoin de:			
un sujet	**un verbe auxiliare**		**un participe passé**
je tu il/elle nous vous ils/elles	avoir ai as a avons avez ont	être suis es est sommes êtes sont	stem + i é irregular u
Alors, choisissez le verbe.			
Est-ce que c'est un verbe réfléchi?			
oui		non	
■ utilisez être comme auxiliare ■ n'oubliez pas le 'me/te/se/nous/vous' entre le sujet et le verbe		C'est un verbe MRS TRAVENDAMP RDR?	
		oui	non
		utilisez 'être' comme auxiliare	utilisez 'avoir' comme auxiliare
ajoutez l'accord au participe passé: f. sg.: -e m. sg.: - f. pl.: -es m. pl. -s			n'ajoutez pas l'accord au participe passé

■ **Figure 11.9** The perfect tense in French

The deductive approach to grammar teaching can, for instance, also be used in the context of the perfect tense in French. This can be a stumbling block for pupils and for them to devise a comprehensive rule can be too difficult. Pupils should be able to produce a series of rules, which the teacher might want to pull together. The flow chart in Figure 11.9 gives an example of such a structure, which can help pupils to generate many sentences. Such an approach may be suitable for more able pupils preparing for their GCSE examination.

Although this chart is not all-encompassing – it does not take account of reflexive verbs with indirect reflexive pronouns, which require no agreement – it can provide a useful point of reference assisting pupils in generating TL utterances and can be taught in stages. The columns allow coverage of '*avoir*' verbs in isolation from the '*être*' and reflexive verbs. The need for past participle agreement can be added to the column as learners progress.

One way to help pupils remember which verbs take *être* in the perfect tense is to present a mnemonic. The first letters of the following verbs spell out MRS TRAVENDAMP RDR: *monter, rester, sortir, tomber, revenir, arriver, venir, entrer, nâitre, descendre, aller, mourir, partir, rentrer, devenir, retourner.*

Task 11.6 **INDUCTIVE OR DEDUCTIVE APPROACH?**

1   Focusing on the scheme of work for one particular year group, make a list of three to five grammar points for each approach. You might find it useful to look at the grammar summary of the coursebook.

2   In your opinion, which grammar points lend themselves to an inductive approach and which to a deductive one?

---

2 The explanation stage

The high level of complexity of language can tempt FLs teachers to provide quite detailed explanations of grammatical concepts. The exploration of concepts might on occasion seem easier to achieve through the medium of English than that of the TL as the process of learning might be accelerated in this way by focusing pupils' attention on linguistic structures in a conscious manner. However,

> central to the language learning process must remain 'exposure, exposure and more exposure', that only through the constant engagement of receptive skills can learners begin to get a feel for a language, to sense nuances of meaning, to produce spontaneously.
>
> (Heafford, 1995: 12)

Heafford also suggests (1995: 12) that 'we need to experiment with various forms of formal grammar teaching to see which approaches least compromise exposure to the target language and which most help accuracy'. Careful selection of TL forms used by you as part of general classroom talk serves to reinforce rules and patterns taught in an explicit manner, although there may be some carefully selected use of English. Pachler (1999c: 102) notes that it is important for FLs teachers to provide rich and varied but carefully considered input, which can be exploited by:

■   focusing pupils' attention on noticing new structure;
■   providing activities to use new and old structures to formulate personal meaning;
■   assisting learners to reflect on learning and their own use of language.

For some strategies for teaching grammar in the TL, see Chapter 8. Where there are pedagogically sound reasons for using planned English, this should be considered where it moves pupils' learning on. It may, for example, be helpful to have occasional short whole-class episodes, where new grammar points are discussed and any misconceptions explored.

USE OF METALANGUAGE

The choice of whether or not to use metalanguage such as 'verb', 'noun', 'adjective' remains a question of professional judgement of individual teachers within a coherent departmental approach. You have to decide in line with the approach taken by your placement school to what extent to use metalanguage. The aforementioned appendices to the subject specifications for learners at 16 and 18 provide some guidance.

Cornell (1996: 28) suggests that by the time they study FLs as a subsidiary part of their degree programme, students should understand and use the following terms and concepts:

- the 'word classes' or 'parts of speech' (noun, verb, adjective, etc.);
- the main sentence constituents (subject, direct object, indirect object, clause);
- the concept of tense;
- for German, the nomenclature of the case system;
- miscellaneous terms that would include, for example, relative pronoun, reflexive pronoun/verb, subjunctive, imperative, modal verb, auxiliary verb, past participle, active/passive, but not that many more.

By introducing new linguistic structures through unfamiliar terminology FLs teachers run the risk of pupils struggling with concepts at a level one step removed from the linguistic phenomenon itself. On the other hand, using 'pupil friendly' terms may deny pupils maximum use of reference material in support of their learning. The use of terminology such as 'doing words' and 'describing words' has some place in the learning process and pupils should not necessarily be discouraged from using their own terms. Making some selective, carefully planned and well-targeted use of the mother tongue when discussing and reflecting on grammar can help pupils develop personal terms and rules. Metalanguage can be introduced once a concept is understood by pupils.

Task 11.7 **GRAMMATICAL CONCEPTS**

Figure 11.10 shows some grammatical concepts in alphabetical order.

- In what order do you think they should be first introduced?
- Ask your mentor or another colleague you work with frequently/peer to place them in an order. Do you both agree?

---

3 The habit-forming stage

The role of the FLs teacher does not end with the explanation of concepts contained in Figure 11.10. Explanation is useful if learners are to proceed to using structures and to developing good language habits. Accurate use of the TL by pupils should be one of the aims of FLs teachers with the ultimate goal of pupils reaching a point when language forms 'sound' or 'feel' right or wrong. A first notion of an intuitive 'feel' can be worked towards by habitual use of the TL. The process of developing a 'feel' for correct language forms requires a lot of practice and FLs activities need to serve a purpose beyond the generation of accurate language as an end in itself.

Ranking	Concept
	Adjectival agreement
	Definite and indefinite articles
	Expressions of quantity
	Gender and number
	Imperative
	Negatives
	Perfect tense
	Present tense
	Transitive and intransitive verbs

■ **Figure 11.10** Sequencing grammatical concepts

	comer	al baloncesto	a las . . . y media
	disfrutar	a la playa/a la montaña	antes
he	empezar	a Málaga/Francia/América	antes del almuerzo
has	estar	de vacaciones	dos semanas
ha	ir	el museo/la discoteca	durante las vacaciones
hemos	jugar	estupendo/guay/muy bien	en el verano
habeis	pasar (lo)	fotografias	esta mañana
han	seleccionar	las clases	por las mañanas
	viajar	pueblos famosos	por las noches
	visitar	comida típica	

■ **Figure 11.11** Practising the Spanish perfect tense

In a further example, the introduction of the perfect tense in Spanish in Figure 11.11 is followed up by the habit-forming activity in Figure 11.12. Pupils are given a combination table based on the language used in the penfriend letter. Their task is to generate as many grammatically correct sentences in the perfect tense as possible. Pupils have to use the correct form of the past participle. At the same time they have to find the correct complement to the verb. The use of an adverb(ial) of time can be made optional. Differentiation can, therefore, be built into this activity by outcome, i.e. the number of sentences pupils generate, or by task, i.e. the number of variables pupils are asked to combine. For a fuller discussion of differentiation, see Chapter 13.

Ich	bin	mit Klara in die Stadt	**gegangen**
Wir	sind	um 16 Uhr	**angekommen.**
Sie	hat	eine rote Hose	**getragen.**
Du	hast	Pommes Frites	**gegessen.**
Sie	haben	eine Tasse Tee	**getrunken.**
Ihr	habt	einen tollen Film	**gesehen.**
Er	ist	mit dem Bus	**zurückgefahren.**

■ **Figure 11.12** The German word order

Another example of a habit-forming activity is given in Figure 11.13. German word order in the context of the perfect tense can be practised by writing a number of sentences on card, mixing up the cards and asking pupils (in pairs or groups) to reconstruct correct sentences.

As an extension to this activity, adverb(ial)s of time can be added, such as: *gestern, vor zwei Tagen, am Abend, um 10 Uhr, letzte Woche, zu Mittag* or *am Vormittag*. This allows pupils to practise the positioning of adverb(ial)s of time, including the inversion of subject and auxiliary verb. To differentiate the activity further, the sentences could add up to a story for pupils to recreate.

The application of rules is easier for some pupils than for others. There is a need to grade activities to cater for the different needs of pupils. In this way, should one level prove too difficult, pupils can attempt the preceding one or pupils can quickly move on to the next level if they find one too easy. The levels can be set in a variety of different ways. An example of this is given in Figure 11.13, which shows one way of practising present tense verb endings in German in the context of 'hobbies, pastimes and weather' by referring to a 'rule' or paradigm, in this case a conjugated verb in the present tense.

The assumption is that pupils have been informed that the exercises are designed to enable them to conduct a survey of who does what and in which weather conditions. First, pupils select the correct ending from a given list. Second, they apply the 'rule' in given examples and third, they use the rule to generate language of their own.

Activities of this type bridge the use of grammatical 'rules' or paradigms and their communicative application by preparing pupils for a survey, e.g. of what pastimes pupils pursue in different weather conditions.

It is crucial that you consider the length of time required for pupils to master particular grammatical concepts. This will, of course, vary from pupil to pupil. Input and explanation stages may occur on several occasions as understanding develops. Opportunities for practice must be introduced on a regular basis and the revisiting of grammatical features needs to be well planned. The principles in Figure 11.14 may help.

4 Communicative application stage

A key feature of communicative language teaching is the emphasis on the message as opposed to the linguistic form, on conveying meaning rather than demonstrating

Die Regel			
ich	spiel e	wir	spiel en
du	spiel st	ihr	spiel t
er/sie/es	spiel t	sie	spiel en

Teil 1	
Schreibe den richtigen Satz!	
1 Meine Schwester spiel e / t / en gern Fußball.	
2 Mein Freund schwimm st / t / e im Hallenbad.	
3 Mein Bruder und ich tanz e / t / en im Club.	
4 Ich geh st / en / e oft in die Stadt.	
5 Sie schreib e / st / t viele Briefe.	
Teil 2	
Schreibe einen ganzen Satz!	
6 Mein Vater (kochen) das Abendessen.	
7 Wir (wollen) etwas trinken.	
8 Ich (suchen) meine Kleidung.	
9 Sie (spielen) gern Volleyball.	
10 Ja natürlich, Ich (schwimmen) besonders gern.	
Teil 3	
Was macht man, wenn. . .? Erfinde eine Antwort.	
11 Was macht sie, wenn die Sonne scheint?	Sie geht ins Schwimmbad, wenn die Sonne scheint.
12 Was machst du, wenn es regnet?	. . .
13 Was machen wir, wenn es schneit?	. . .
14 Was macht er, wenn das Wetter schlecht ist?	. . .
15 Was macht ihr, wenn es sehr schön ist?	. . .

▪ **Figure 11.13** Practising present tense verb endings in German

- ▨ Learners cannot learn (or 'acquire') a grammatical structure unless they are exposed to *multiple examples* of it.
- ▨ Each of those examples must occur in the *context of a plausible speech act*. Knowledge of rules in isolation from any context will promote the use of Anglicisms since the only links that learners will be able to create between abstract syntactic system and speech act will be the ones that operate in their own language.
- ▨ Learners must understand how *grammatical choices* can correspond to the expression of *social and interpersonal relationships*. The most obvious example of this is the choice between familiar and polite forms, but these correspondences operate across much wider areas of the language.

(Based on: Miller, 2002: 141–155)

■ **Figure 11.14** Principles of grammar teaching

Task 11.8 **THE DEVELOPMENT OF GRAMMATICAL CONCEPTS**

We suggested above that some topics lend themselves better to the introduction and practice of certain grammatical concepts than others. Consider which topics lend themselves particularly well to the teaching of certain grammatical concepts.

- ▨ Choose three to five grammatical concepts from Figure 11.10 and consider through which topic they might meaningfully be introduced.
- ▨ Reflect on how long it will take learners to master the concepts and their application, and consider the principles of grammar teaching in Figure 11.14.
- ▨ Identify other topics in which practice of the structures could be included.

knowledge about language. While we deem the conveying of meaning to be central to FL teaching at beginner and intermediate level, we recognise the need for systematic coverage of the grammatical system linked to thematic progression. From pre-communicative language practice, including implicit and explicit manipulation of linguistic patterns and structures pupils need to be moved on to communicative application.

Marking and error correction are important in the language learning process. They tend to be discussed as 'recasts' in the research literature. Constructive feedback on pupils' TL production can reinforce accurate use and is an important tool in moving pupils from pre-communicative to communicative language use. Beaton (1990: 42–43), for instance, suggests that '(when) errors are corrected, it goes without saying that revision of the correction is essential. . . . there needs to be an incubation period in which the learner acquires a feel. . .' Work featuring a considerable number of mistakes and errors is a clear sign that the pupil is not ready to progress to the stage of using language in 'authentic', communicative situations. Pupils' readiness to progress to communicative situations, therefore, needs to be carefully

A	*am Morgen*	*am Nachmittag*	*am Abend*
Freitag	zur Schule gehen mit dem Bus fahren Erdkunde haben		Hausaufgabe machen Kassetten hören mit dem Computer spielen
Samstag		in die Stadt fahren einkaufen gehen neue Schuhe kaufen	
Sonntag	zur Kirche gehen Großmutter besuchen Kaffee trinken und Kekse essen	zum Park gehen Fußball spielen angeln gehen	
B	am Morgen	am Nachmittag	am Abend
Freitag		in der Kantine essen mit Freunden plaudern Deutsch haben	
Samstag	im Bett bleiben um 11 Uhr Frühstück essen die Zeitung lesen		zu Hause bleiben fernsehen um 10 Uhr ins Bett gehen
Sonntag			Hausaufgaben machen ein Buch lesen Briefe schreiben

■ **Figure 11.15** *Was hast du am Wochenende gemacht?*

monitored. You need to consider the nature of feedback carefully. It is important to strike the right balance between providing constructive support and demotivating pupils through over-correction. For a more detailed discussion of marking and error correction, see Chapter 15.

Once comfortable with certain structures, pupils should be given opportunities to apply these language forms meaningfully. The use of the TL for a perceived purpose and with success can lead to a sense of achievement. One example is the information-gap activity in Figure 11.15, focusing on the German perfect tense. Another example of the communicative application stage is, for instance, an activity known as the 'alibi game', which is useful when reinforcing the perfect and imperfect tenses as well as question forms in any FL. (For other examples of the 'alibi game', see Langran and Purcell, 1994: 24 or Miller, 1995: 7.)

The teacher sets the scene in the respective TL: 'The crown jewels have been stolen from the Tower of London over the weekend. Two suspects have been arrested when they were seen in the vicinity around the time the theft has occurred.' Two pupils are asked to play the role of the 'suspects'. Any number of paired pupils can act as 'suspects'. The 'suspects' have to prepare a story between them, which will serve as their alibi. The rest of the pupils are tasked with formulating questions, which they will ask the two 'suspects' in turn. The aim is to extract information, which shows that the two 'suspects' are making inconsistent statements. Once familiar with the format of activity, pupils can be asked to work in groups supported by the teacher and the foreign language assistant, who circulate from group to group so that pupils get a number of opportunities for language production.

Once an alibi has been thought of and questions have been devised, the first pupil is 'questioned' and peers note the responses. Afterwards the second pupil is 'questioned' and the questioners note the information provided. The questioners are required to use the information extracted to compile a report and a recommendation for 'prosecution'. The activity requires pupils to extract and use information through the medium of the TL and allows for repetitive practice of a particular linguistic form. At the same time pupils are generating their own forms of language.

Task 11.9 **TASK 11.1 REVISITED: KEY ISSUES IN GRAMMAR LEARNING AND TEACHING**

■ Terminology /metalanguage: should we use it at all? If so, in the TL? In English? In both?

■ Explicit instruction/implicit learning/both?

■ Do you favour the systematic introduction of structures/more ad hoc (when the need arises)/a balanced approach?

■ What is the role of practice with drills/exercises?

■ Should 'rules' be taught? If so, how and when? In what format? In which language?

■ What about grammar for recognition? Grammar for production?

SUMMARY

Grammar is an important aspect of the FL learning process and you need to use your professional judgement and take on board theoretical considerations when deciding on your personal approach to grammar teaching. Teachers and learners need to be aware that grammar is not assimilated instantly, nor can it be presented in an oversimplified, linear fashion. Learners need time to become accustomed to what they notice about the TL and transform it to personal use.

Grammar can be taught and learnt explicitly and implicitly. Either way, successful learning is, at least in part, dependent on the teacher's skill in planning, presenting and enabling practice as well as opportunity for personalisation of language forms. There are no hard-and-fast rules governing the teaching and learning of grammar, but a carefully structured and thought through approach can be seen to be helpful. In this chapter we presented a possible framework aimed at helping you develop a coherent approach to the teaching of grammar.

It is important to remember that, in the context of FL teaching and learning in the Secondary school, grammar should not be taught in isolation from communicative objectives. At the same time, pupils should not be left to assimilate and absorb information without the support and guidance of the FLs teacher.

FURTHER READING

Batstone, R. and Ellis, R. (2009) Principled grammar teaching. In *System*, 37: 194–204.
This paper focuses on the relationship between grammatical forms and meaning, and discusses the conditions that support learners in making the necessary connections between them.

Ellis, R. (2006) Issues in the teaching of grammar: an SLA perspective. In *TESOL Quarterly*, 40(1): 83–107.
This paper considers eight key questions pertaining to grammar teaching with reference to findings from research in second language acquisition exploring whether grammar should be taught, and if so what grammar, when, and how.

CHAPTER 12

TEACHING AND LEARNING CULTURE

INTRODUCTION

The ability to understand the cultural context of FL use is a key aspect of effective communication in the TL and cultural components have played an increasingly important part in FLs curricula. The conceptualisation of culture, however, has changed over time and varies in different jurisdictions, as does its assumed relationship with the language component.

As Scarino (2010: 324) points out, historically the cultural 'component' has tended to be covered separately from, and subordinate to, the language component and has frequently comprised

> a generalized body of knowledge about the target country and its people, ranging from literature and the arts (high culture) to aspects of everyday life. Although this body of knowledge was intended to enrich students' understanding of the target language, it remained external to and separate from the students' own first language(s) and culture(s). It was not intended that students would engage with this cultural knowledge in such a way that their own identities, values, and life-worlds would be challenged and transformed.

Significant changes to society in recent decades as a result of globalisation, internationalisation and migration have considerably changed the linguistic and cultural make-up of many parts of the world, in particular in urban areas, as well as the need for cultural knowledge, understanding and skills. The increasing diversity of languages spoken, and the related cultural practices being in evidence in many societies, captured frequently through labels such as 'multiculturalism' and 'multilingualism', requires of us as FL teachers to review, and possibly revise, our perspectives on the role of culture in the language curriculum. For us as educators it raises questions about culture in the curriculum more widely.

The affordances of digital technologies, coupled with their increasing normalisation in everyday and working lives, add an additional dimension – for example, in relation to the world increasingly becoming a 'global village', a phrase coined by the Canadian philosopher and communication theorist Marshall McLuhan in the 1960s in the context of his vision about the impact of electronic media on visual culture.

One of the terms we use here because of its rootedness in a broader educational purpose of FLs learning (see e.g. Byram, 2010: 317–318) is 'cultural awareness'. We understand it to be more than simply the identification of different cultural characteristics or knowledge about the countries where a particular TL is spoken. For us it involves the understanding and appreciation of different ways of life. The curriculum requirements for England and elsewhere have tended to imply a particular approach to the teaching of culture based around the notion of awareness and linked to ethnographic methods such as the use of 'authentic' materials and contact with native speakers. They aim to enable pupils to identify with, recognise and draw comparisons between their own culture and the cultures of the countries where the TL is spoken. While a lot can be achieved in the FLs classroom, cultural awareness is often more meaningfully developed outside of it. Importantly, the pupils' point of view and their experiences should be taken as a starting point and not necessarily specific aspects of the target culture (see e.g. Pachler, 1999b: 84 and Jones, 2000a).

We will use Levy's paper (2007) here to help us understand the complexity of the culture concept. He outlines the following five perspectives on culture:

- culture as elemental;
- culture as relative;
- culture as group membership;
- culture as contested;
- culture as individual (variable and multiple).

We consider such an understanding of the complexity of the concept of culture as essential and ask you to bear it in mind every time you come across terms such as 'target culture(s)' or 'culture(s) of the country/countries where the TL is spoken' in this chapter as they are invariably shorthand labels. To illustrate Levy's point, we briefly expand here only on the discussion of culture being relative. By this, Levy means that a culture can only be understood in relation to another, and a discussion of culture invariably includes generalisations, which is problematic in terms of an ability to reflect the complex realities and can lead to oversimplification (p. 107).

In this chapter we discuss possible approaches to the teaching of culture, particularly at beginner and intermediate level, and describe activities that require and enable pupils to use the TL inside and outside the classroom. For a detailed discussion of culture, see also Holmes, 2014.

In order to enhance their value, activities involving TL use and the development of cultural awareness outside the FLs classroom should relate to, build on and extend work carried out in FLs lessons. Importantly, they need to be planned carefully and pupils need to be prepared well for them.

OBJECTIVES

By the end of this chapter you should:

- understand the rationale for and some important issues of the teaching of culture in FL teaching;

- be aware of a range of possible teaching strategies and approaches to enable pupils to develop cultural awareness and intercultural (communicative) competence in FLs;
- recognise the value of educational activities outside the FLs classroom;
- understand what is involved in organising a range of learning opportunities outside the FLs classroom.

TEACHING CULTURE: WHY?

The Council of Europe marked the celebration of the fiftieth anniversary of the European Cultural Convention with the publication in 2006 of a document called *Plurilingual Education in Europe*. This convention commits signatory states to promote the teaching and learning of each other's languages. The Council of Europe language education policies, according to the document, aim to promote:

Plurilingualism:

All are entitled to develop a degree of communicative ability in a number of languages over their lifetime in accordance with their needs.

Linguistic diversity:

Europe is multilingual and all its languages are equally valuable modes of communication and expressions of identity; the right to use and to learn one's language(s) is protected in Council of Europe Conventions.

Mutual understanding:

The opportunity to learn other languages is an essential condition for intercultural communication and acceptance of cultural differences.

Democratic citizenship:

Participation in democratic and social processes in multilingual societies is facilitated by the plurilingual competence of individuals.

Social cohesion:

Equality of opportunity for personal development, education, employment, mobility, access to information and cultural enrichment depends on access to language learning throughout life.

(p. 6)

These policy aims provide clear evidence of the importance of language and culture in the modern world around social cohesion and individual agency. They also clearly signal the political desire for a move away from linguistic specialisation towards the development of diverse and individualised linguistic repertoires comprising different levels of proficiency in different languages, as well as linguistic varieties and their interrelationships depending on specific contextual factors:

A plurilingual person has:

- a repertoire of languages and language varieties
- competences of different kinds and levels within the repertoire

Plurilingual education promotes:

- an awareness of why and how one learns the languages one has chosen
- an awareness of and the ability to use transferable skills in language learning
- respect for the plurilingualism of others and the value of languages and varieties irrespective of their perceived status in society
- a respect for the cultures embodied in languages and the cultural identities of others
- an ability to perceive and mediate the relationships which exist among languages and cultures
- a global integrated approach to language education in the curriculum.

(p. 7)

In the US, in response to a perceived 'language deficit' and with particular reference to higher education, the Modern Language Association published a report on culture teaching and learning in 2007. The report sought to respond to the perceived language failures widely discussed in the media in the context of US military interventions around the world, e.g. in Afghanistan and Iraq, in the course of which the need for greater cultural understanding became evident. The report identifies 'deep translingual and transcultural competence' as the key goal for FL study.

> The idea of translingual and transcultural competence . . . places value on the ability to operate between languages. Students are educated to function as informed and capable interlocutors with educated native speakers in the target language. They are also trained to reflect on the world and themselves through the lens of another language and culture. They learn to comprehend speakers of the target language as members of foreign societies and to grasp themselves as Americans—that is, as members of a society that is foreign to others. They also learn to relate to fellow members of their own society who speak languages other than English.
>
> This kind of foreign language education systematically teaches differences in meaning, mentality, and worldview as expressed in American English and in the target language. Literature, film, and other media are used to challenge students' imaginations and to help them consider alternative ways of seeing, feeling, and understanding things. In the course of acquiring functional language abilities, students are taught critical language awareness, interpretation and translation, historical and political consciousness, social sensibility, and aesthetic perception. They acquire a basic knowledge of the history, geography, culture, and literature of the society or societies whose language they are learning; the ability to understand and interpret its radio, television, and print media; and the capacity to do research in the language using parameters specific to the target culture.

(MLA, 2007: 3–4)

Task 12.1 **EXPLORING DIFFERENT POLICY AIMS**

Compare the approach taken by the Council of Europe and the US Modern Language Association with the aims of the curriculum framework governing your practice such as the draft 2013 National Curriculum (see Chapter 1 for details).

How does the conceptualisation of language and culture in the Council of Europe aims compare with that of your curriculum framework? What similarities exists? What differences can you detect? And, what are the implications for your practice?

In addition to such overtly political drivers for culture policy we can also identify rationales that link much more to the individual learner and his/her (immediate) social context, namely identity and social milieu. As can be seen in a range of educational contexts (see e.g. Pachler *et al.*, 2010), personal notions of relevance and their link to cultural practices influenced by socio-economic factors can be seen to be increasingly important in defining and helping to understand learner motivation in relation to their identity.

Scarino (2010) notes that an intercultural orientation towards FL teaching 'seeks the transformation of students' identities in the act of learning' by getting them to 'decenter from their linguistic and cultural world to consider their own situatedness from the perspective of another' (p. 324). In such an approach, culture becomes 'not only . . . information about diverse people and their practices but also, and most importantly, . . . the contextual framework that people use to exchange meaning in communication with others and through which they understand their social world' (p. 324). Unsurprisingly, as Scarino is one of the authors, her conceptualisation reflects that of the Australian Government (2003), which uses the term 'intercultural language learning' as their frame of reference. This, the authors, (p. 50) view as involving the development of an understanding of the learners' own language(s) and culture(s) in relation to an additional language and culture:

> Learners engaged in intercultural language learning develop a reflective stance towards language and culture, both specifically as instances of first, second, and additional languages and cultures, and generally as understandings of the variable ways in which language and culture exist in the world. An individual's multiple sociocultural and linguistic memberships, specifically and generally in this world, provide a variable perspective on identity with multiple possibilities for bridging across and interrelating with other variably constructed identities.

Perry and Southwell (2011) conceptualise the attributes and skills that make a person successful in intercultural interactions increasingly necessary in a multicultural and globalised world as 'intercultural competence', which they define as 'the ability to effectively and appropriately interact in an intercultural situation or context' (p. 453). They see it related to four dimensions: knowledge, attitudes, skills and behaviours (p. 455) and view intercultural competence to build on intercultural understanding, which they consider to comprise both cognitive and affective domains. The affective domain, they note, can be viewed as intercultural sensitivity, and to be determined by dispositions towards wanting to understand, appreciate and accept cultural differences as well as experiences of cultural differences (p. 454).

Byram (see e.g. Porto, 2013: 4) identifies the following dimensions of culture knowledge, skills and attitudes:

- *savoir être* (for instance, attitudes of curiosity and inquisitiveness);
- *savoirs* (knowledge of different aspects of life in a certain society, such as work, education, traditions, etc.);
- *savoir comprendre* (involving the skill of interpreting and relating those *savoirs*);
- *savoir apprendre/savoir faire* (involving the skills of discovery and interaction);
- *savoir s'engager* (involving critical cultural awareness).

Perry and Southwell consider intercultural communication to be an aspect of intercultural competence which, drawing on Lustig and Koester (2006), they see occurring 'when large and important cultural differences create dissimilar inter-pretations and expectations about how to communicate competently' (p. 456). This has implications for FLs teachers and their orchestration of the classroom environment in that, in order to be able to develop intercultural (communicative) competence in learners, particular contexts and associations between individuals appear to be necessary.

Porto (2010) frames her discussion of culture within an educational view of FLs learning which, she argues, focuses on the development of learners as individuals (p. 46):

> This development takes place when human beings reconcile new and challenging ideas with their pre-existing beliefs and values through diverse reading and writing experiences in the foreign language, which lead to the multifaceted development of the self . . . Seen in these terms, foreign language education encourages learners to create, maintain, and/or develop their unique identities.

And identity matters, she continues, because it frames the way learners make sense of, and act in the world, including their literacy practices. She concludes from her discussion of the concept of identity that it is important for FLs teachers to 'make connections with their students as individuals, while understanding the sociocultural and historical contexts that influence their interactions' (p. 47) and she goes on to discuss a range of tasks she uses with her classes (pp. 48–52).

Van Leeuwen (2009) offers an interesting variation on the theme of identity by discussing the concept of 'lifestyle' and how it links to identity. Hall (2011), while acknowledging the importance of the roles of the groups and communities to which we belong, also notes the agency of the individual. He explains how such forms of expressions are 'subjectively experienced as individual and personal choices from the wide range of semiotic resources made available by the market' (p. 214), which includes discourse conventions that also have a regulatory function: 'A given colour, or length of skirt, or linguistic expression can be "in one year and 'out' the next", so that we must constantly monitor media, compare notes with friends and colleagues, and update the consumer goods and semiotic practices that signify our identities' (p. 219). By communicating with and through the semiotic resources at our disposal – which include but go beyond language – we represent and construct a particular identity.

The target culture can be seen as inextricably linked to the TL (see e.g. Byram and Morgan *et al.*, 1994). In order to understand language and its use fully, an awareness and knowledge of culture are important (see Pachler, 1999b: 78). While it is possible to teach the culture(s) of a country in a way that is divorced from its language(s) – and in the past coursebooks have tended to provide English accounts of aspects of the way of life of the target culture(s) such as cultural facts, figures and habits – this is not appropriate in view of the conceptualisations of culture discussed above.

To place language learning within a cultural context is to make both the TL and the target culture(s) more accessible and understandable, while not reducing its complexity and potential challenge unduly. The task for the FLs teacher is to some extent to re-create and simulate the cultural environment, and to create a purpose for realistic language use within that environment while ensuring that learning activities are not contrived.

In the process of understanding that there are other ways of speaking and being, learners invariably will need to confront some of their (negative) stereotypes. Stereotypes are not necessarily a bad thing; they can be seen as a strategy to simplify perceptions of other peoples (see Byram 1989: 70). There is, however, a danger that, by exaggerating the typical in the target culture(s), the perception pupils have of the ways of living and communicating in the target cultures(s) become distorted (see Byram 1989: 16; Byram and Risager, 2002). FLs teachers, therefore, need to guard against the use of negative stereotypes, as well as engage in awareness raising about the use of (negative) stereotypes (see also Pachler with Reimann, 1999).

Task 12.2 **PUPIL QUESTIONNAIRE**

Devise a questionnaire for pupils in different year groups to elicit their views on typical characteristics of native TL speakers.

Ascertain reasons for their perceptions about TL speakers and provide opportunities for pupils to explore, through discussions with you, their understanding and how they came to form it. Where do pupils get their ideas from?

What can/should you do to take pupils forward in their cultural understanding and break down possible (negative) stereotypes? How can you actively engage them in that process?

Coursebooks can vary enormously in the representation of the cultures of the countries where the TL is spoken. Many coursebooks provide a (superficially) multicultural picture. However, coursebooks tend to date quickly. This ephemeral nature of presenting culture in print requires you to use supplementary, up-to-date authentic materials, such as articles and pictures from the Internet, magazines and newspapers, or audio and video recordings of programmes concerned with current issues.

Among many other criteria, coursebooks can be evaluated against a number of culture-related criteria (see e.g. Meijer and Jenkins, 1998); they include:

- ■ functionality, e.g. does the coursebook concentrate on facts and knowledge about the target cultures?
- ■ target audience, e.g. are materials selected in accordance with the likely interests of the target audience?
- ■ diversity, e.g. does the coursebook take account of intracultural differences?
- ■ realism, e.g. is the representation of culture in the coursebook authentic? Are (negative) stereotypes in evidence?
- ■ intercultural approach, e.g. are attempts made to make comparisons between home and target countries?
- ■ choice, e.g. do learners have the possibility to choose culture-related topics they are particularly interested in?

Task 12.3 EVALUATING THE APPROACH TO CULTURE OF A COURSEBOOK

Evaluate one of the coursebooks in use in your partnership school against some of the above criteria. What approach is adopted and how is the target culture presented?

What supplementary materials could be used to augment an aspect the coursebook doesn't cover very well in your opinion?

TEACHING CULTURE: HOW? H. D. BROWN'S FOUR STAGES OF ACCULTURATION

H. D. Brown's four broad stages of acculturation (see Brown, 1986: 36) are used here are as one way of approaching the teaching of culture. It is not possible to separate the various stages from the natural process of maturation and it is often not possible to clearly separate them from each other. Also, not all need necessarily occur. Nevertheless, they offer a possible conceptual frame for sequencing culture-related activities. In all of them, as FLs teacher, you can play an important role in

No.	Stage
1	Excitement
2	Alienation
3	Recovery
4	Acceptance

■ Figure 12.1 Four broad stages of developing cultural awareness

guiding and encouraging pupils. The four stages do not imply a linear progression. Slipping back and leaping forward are characteristics not only of linguistic but also of cultural development.

For a range of other possible approaches to the teaching about the target culture(s), see Pachler, 1999b: 83–90, or Wintergerst and McVeigh, 2010.

EXCITEMENT

For many young learners the study of FLs is exciting. An introduction to a new culture offers a range of interesting learning opportunities. The study of the target culture(s) from the security of the classroom offers some shelter from the challenge of 'the foreign' or 'the other'. The behaviour and the way of life of others from an outsider's perspective can be stimulating and fun. The challenge to the FLs teacher is to provide ample opportunities for pupils to engage in activities related to the target culture(s). This can be done in a number of ways.

The use of anecdotes and personal stories is a good start and a way of personalising teaching as well as of contextualising the need to make first-hand experiences in order to be able to relate and understand aspects of other cultures that are so different from one's own.

The Internet provides an effective way of accessing relevant authentic material, including visual texts and images for carrying out research into target cultures. For example, the Goethe-Institut offers some interesting resources (www.goethe.de), as do the Institut Français (www.institut-francais.org.uk) and the Instituto Cervantes (www.hispanismo.cervantes.es). A great amount of cultural information and awareness can be gained by accessing the online versions of national and regional TL newspapers and magazines. Other useful link collections include the webpages of the Sussex Centre for Language Studies (www.sussex.ac.uk/languages/resources).

The Internet is a rich source of information, available at many levels of sophistication and aimed at a range of target audiences. It can be used in a FLs teacher-mediated mode or directly by learners in order to become acquainted with a wide range of cultural aspects of the target countries. Pupils' engagement with the Internet in pursuit of cultural information should follow established principles. For example, and depending on the age of the learners, it is arguably preferable to ask learners to engage with carefully pre-selected URLs that relate directly to specific lesson objectives and fit within a given time rather than carry out free searches. Extension work and differentiated follow-up tasks can build on core activities.

A fundamental methodological consideration is whether to stress cultural similarities or differences at an early stage. Research suggests that attention should initially be given to similarities as 'doing so can undermine the human tendency to exaggerate and generalise differences (Pachler, 1999b: 85).

Similarities between the pupils' own way of life and that in TL countries can be accentuated, for example, at a very early stage by using images from various sources.

Engaging with food is a popular and basic but effective way to enable discussion. From there move to other aspects of the different ways people in the target culture might go about their daily lives and explore this in ways that are of interest to pupils as young people with their own likes and interests, e.g. specific

Task 12.4 STRESSING CULTURAL SIMILARITIES

What ways of stressing the similarities, rather than the differences, between home and target cultures at an early stage of FL teaching and learning can you think of?

popular sports, music, daily 'going about habits' like transport to school, friendships, times for school and leisure, etc.

Often, food is the extent of first-hand classroom experiences for young pupils with culture. This is limited as young people tend not to be as interested in food or cooking as adults are. If, however, some pupils are interested in cooking you might want to liaise with relevant colleagues in the school with a view to including a cultural aspect to a cooking session, and include appropriate lexical and syntactical information.

In this way you can develop the cross-curricular dimension of culture. Subjects in which aspects of the target culture(s) are being taught include Geography, where pupils often study a European country other than the UK with a focus on geographical questions such as 'What/where is it?', 'What is it like?', 'How did it get like this?', 'How and why is it changing?', 'What are the implications?'. Such questions, normally explored through the medium of English, can be meaningfully linked to aspects of FLs work and provide opportunities for the FLs teacher to feed into other subject areas.

Task 12.5 CROSS-CURRICULAR LINKS

Examine the curriculum requirements for Geography.

■ Find out what aspects of the target culture(s) can be found and where links are possible.

■ Through discussion with teachers of Geography find out more about when and how these aspects are taught.

■ Make up a quiz drawing on knowledge of the target culture(s), incorporating details from the Geography curriculum requirements. Use the results of the quiz as a basis for cross-curricular and cultural discussion.

'Science across the World', facilitated by the Association for Science Education and available online at www.scienceacross.org, allows pupils to compare their work on scientific topics with peers across Europe and the wider world. A range of resource units in a number of languages is available, providing stimulus material, teachers' notes and activity sheets on topics such as acid rain, using energy at home, renewable energy, drinking water, food, global warming or domestic waste. Work on these units can meaningfully combine learning objectives relating to Science as well as FLs.

Health and food, for example, are topics of concern for all pupils and ideal topics to explore, e.g. what a healthy diet or a good fitness regime might look like as well as the interrelationship between the two. They can compare their own habits with those of their counterparts in the target country and link the rationale as in Task 12.6. The topics also lend themselves to the use of a range of data collection activities requiring communication among students as well as the use of varied representational forms such as charts, tables, diagrams or mind-maps.

Task 12.6 **EATING HABITS – A COMPARISON (BASED ON *SCIENCE ACROSS THE WORLD*)**

Compare the information from a school in a country where the TL is spoken with that from your class.

1   Compare:

a) the pattern of daily life: when other pupils get up, start school, etc.;
b) who chooses and prepares the food;
c) what is eaten for breakfast;
d) snacks and sweets eaten;
e) arrangements for meals during the school day.

2   Do pupils in the target country think that eating a good breakfast is important?
3   What do you think is responsible for the similarities and differences in the foods eaten by pupils in the target country?
4   Did you learn about any traditional beliefs about foods? Can they be explained by science?
5   Are eating habits in both countries changing? If so, how?
6   Do you think that most pupils eat a balanced diet?
7   Are pupils concerned about the links between diet and disease? If so, do their concerns differ in the two countries?
8   Compare food labels from the two countries. How is the nutritional value of food shown? Do the same foods contain the same ingredients?
9   What suggestions can you make for improving the diet of your class?

Consider how these tasks could be linked to your FL department's unit(s) of work on food and drink and illness:

■   By talking to your mentor or an interested class teacher as well as a teacher from the Science department, explore which of these activities could be carried out in FL lessons and which in the Science lesson?
■   How could they be translated into the TL and how can the contents be covered in the TL?

ALIENATION

The greater the personal involvement with another culture, the more differences become apparent. Dealing with alternative ways of life can be threatening and challenging. Goal-orientated and purposeful personal contact with TL speakers as well as appropriate activities, such as educational visits to the target culture(s), can foster the understanding of certain differences in context and reduce the potential threat by engaging pupils in reflecting on and discussing perceived differences between cultures.

Task 12.7 PERSONAL AWARENESS RAISING

List ten items you would choose to represent the culture of your home country and ten items you would choose as representative of the culture of a country where the TL is spoken. What influenced your choice?

What differences are there between your two lists and what do they tell you about the cultural differences between the two countries or your own perceptions about these differences?

Then, consider how each of these differences could be addressed in the FL curriculum.

Taylor and Sorenson (1961) developed the concept of 'culture capsules' as one way of addressing cultural differences around a brief (multimodal) description of a particular aspect of the target culture followed by contrasting information from the learners' native culture.

Figure 12.2 illustrates how pupils might be given an opportunity to reflect on cultural differences around controversial topics. This should include a discussion and/or debate format and require them to use the TL. The activity involves them in reading information, allowing them to demonstrate their understanding and to express opinions on a controversial topic that divides opinion even in the target countries. Work on the activity can be meaningfully extended through letter or e-mail exchanges with pupils in partner schools to elicit information by asking questions that can lead to display work. The text provides opportunities for reading for gist, reading for detail, reading aloud in small groups, silent individual reading, reading in pairs with the assistance of a dictionary, etc. Understanding (lexical, syntactical and cultural) can be developed through comprehension questions, be they open questions, differentiated questions; written and/or oral, in class or for homework.

Critical incidents are another useful technique in which learners are given a vignette containing an example of cultural miscommunication which they then discuss with a view to identifying how it might have been pre-empted. Role play can be a useful extension of such analytical and reflective work. For a description of critical incident development, see e.g. Jackson, 2002 and Kilianska-Przybylo, 2009.

Many schools organise visits abroad, which can be used to encourage pupils to investigate familiarities and differences of their own and the target culture. The relationship between language learned and its potential use should be highlighted by the provision of structured activities when abroad.

LAS CORRIDAS DE TOROS – INFORMACION DE FONDO

Torear es considerado como un arte y no un deporte. La tradición de las corridas de toros se remonta a más de trescientos años. La crianza de toros salvajes adecuados para llevar a las plazas de toros es normalmente llevada por ciertas familias que viven del mundo del toro y de las corridas. Torear y criar toros salvajes se pasa de padre a hijo.

Hay toreros que desde que son niños estan en las plazas y torean a vaquillas (toros pequeños). Ellos ven y viven el mundo de los toros desde muy pequeños en casa y así, cuando pueden, ellos van a torear también.

No sólo hombres pero también mujeres y niños torean en las plazas.

Hay **corridas de toros** y **novilladas**: las corridas de toros consisten en torear seis grandes toros de entre seiscientos y setecientos kilos de peso. En las novilladas se torean a toros pequeños de trescientos a cuatrocientos kilos de peso. Toreros jóvenes empiezan con novilladas y luego pasan a torear toros grandes.

Otro tipo de toreo es el **Rejoneo** que es torear y matar al toro montado a caballo; estos se llaman rejoneadores y son magníficos jinetes.

Los toreros visten el **traje de luces** que es muy especial y de un color favorito del torero. Lleva una **montera** sobre la cabeza y una **coleta** de pelo detrás. Cuando el torero se jubila, se corta la **coleta** y así pues esto es una expresión española. Por ejemplo cuando una deportista abandona el deporte se puede decir: ella 'se corta la coleta'!

Los toreros son muy religiosos y antes de cada corrida se toman unos minutos para meditar y rezar.

También son muy supersticiosos y llevan algun detalle para tener buena suerte.

Todas las personas conectadas con los toros como toreros, rejoneadores, criaderos y otros hablan de su respeto y amor a los toros. Ellos admiran a un animal tan bravo y valiente. En las corridas, los toreros se enfrentan al toro para arriesgar su vida y jugar con la idea de la muerte. El toro va a morir y el torero puede morir también!

Si un toro es muy valiente, el torero le puede perdonar su vida reconociendo así su valor.

El torear es una tradición muy española y es un espectáculo muy popular con españoles y extranjeros que visit an Espanã.

En Portugal, sur de Francia y en algunos países de Sudamérica también hay corridas de toros pero no matan al toro. En España matan a los seis toros de cada corrida todas las tardes de la temporada taurina.

LA SITUACION MAS RECIENTE

La prensa CARACOL informó en Julio de 2010 que:

El Parlamento de Cataluña prohibió hoy las corridas de toros en esa región del noreste español a partir del 1 de enero del 2012.

Con 68 votos a favor, 55 en contra y 9 abstenciones la Cámara regional catalana dio hoy luz verde a la Iniciativa Legislativa Popular (ILP), avalada por 180.000 ciudadanos, que pedía la prohibición de la lidia, considerada una de las señas culturales de España.

Se trata de la segunda región española que prohíbe los festejos taurinos, después de que las islas Canarias (en el Atlántico) fue la primera en España en prohibir las corridas de toros, merced a la una ley regional de protección de animales, aprobada en 1991.

La supresión de las corridas de toros afectará, a partir del 1 de enero de 2012, sólo a la plaza de Toros Monumental de Barcelona, coso fetiche del diestro español José Tomás.

La noticia ha generado una gran expectación social, política y mediática, y la atenta mirada desde países con tradición taurina como Ecuador, Colombia, Francia, México, Perú, Portugal o Venezuela.' (Adapted from www.bit.ly/prohibidas-las-corridas)

■ **Figure 12.2** Las corridas de toros

Vocabulario			
la crianza de toros	The breeding bulls	Montado a caballo	On horseback
se remonta	it has existed since	matar al toro	to kill the bull
las plazas de toros	bullrings	jinetes	horse riders
toros salvajes	wild bulls	Traje de luces	bullfighter's costume
vaquillas	young bulls	montera	bullfighter's hat
novilladas	bullfights with young bulls	coleta	bullfighter's hair worn as a pony tail
morir	to die	'se corta la coleta'	s/he retires
rejoneo	bullfighting on horseback	temporada taurina	bullfighting season

Tareas de varias difficultades y destrezas

Lectura individual o en parejas:

Ejercicio 1: ¿verdad? ó ¿mentira?

		¿verdad?	¿mentira?
1	Torear es un deporte.		
2	Todos los toreros son hombres.		
3	'Se corta la coleta' significa empezar una profesón.		
4	Rejoneo es torear montado a caballo.		
5	Las corridas de toros son un espectáculo reciente.		
6	Los toreros son muy religiosos y superticiosos.		

Encuesta

Ejercicio 2: Trabajo Oral A. en parejas y 2 en grupos de cinco personas

Pregúntale a cinco compañeros de clase:	1	2	3	4	5
1 ¿Crees que la tradición es importante?					
2 ¿Crees que las corridas son un espectáculo emocionante?					
3 ¿Te gustaría ver una corrida de toros?					
4 ¿Opinas que las corridas son crueles para el toro?					
5 ¿Te parece que las corridas se deben abolir?					
6 ¿Crees que las corridas sin matar al toro son acceptables?					
7 ¿De qué modo afecta el reciente voto a la fiesta taurina? ¿Crees que seguirá siendo tan popular?					

■ **Figure 12.2** *continued*

Ejercicio 3: ¿a favor? ó ¿en contra?	
Cuántas personas están a favor?	...................% está a favor de las corridas.
Cuántas personas están en contra?	...................% está en contra de las corridas.

■ **Figure 12.2** *continued*

RECOVERY

A positive response to discussions about perceived differences can be a sign of recovery. First-hand experience of the target culture(s), the productive use of personal knowledge, skills and understanding through displays or presentations for the benefit of others can lead to a familiarisation with the target culture(s). Recovery can be worked towards, for instance, by engaging pupils in 'experimentation' with the target culture(s) and comparison with their own culture. At this stage of developing cultural awareness, cultural similarities might once again be accentuated.

A useful activity (adapted from Jones, 1995: 27–34) comparing two cultures is to ask pupils to put into a shoe-box ten items they feel represent their own culture. The scenario is that this will be buried for future generations to find. A brief written or taped explanation should accompany the artefacts. A similar exercise is then undertaken, except this time the 'time capsule' should contain ten articles representing the culture(s) of a country where the TL is spoken. The selection of artefacts should stimulate meaningful discussion about the TL culture in question, particularly in relation to the perceived 'home' culture.

Gerhard Neuner and Hans Hunfeld suggest the use of what they call 'universal experiences of life' as a basis for intercultural comparison. They list a number of such experiences loosely translated from German here (see Neuner and Hunfeld, 1993: 112–113):

■ fundamental experiences, e.g. birth, death, living;
■ personal identity, e.g. personal characteristics;
■ social identity, e.g. private self, family; neighbourhood, local community, nation;
■ partnership, e.g. friendship, love;
■ environment, e.g. house and home; local area, nature, civilisation;
■ work, e.g. making a living;
■ education;
■ subsistence, e.g. food, clothing;
■ mobility, e.g. traffic;
■ leisure and art;
■ communication, e.g. media;
■ healthcare, e.g. health, illness, hygiene;
■ ethics, e.g. morals, values, religion;
■ events, e.g. past, present, future;
■ spirituality, creativity, imagination, emotions, memory, etc.

(Multimodal) (Critical) Discourse/Text analysis is another useful technique in culture teaching and learning normally associated with sociolinguistics which looks beyond what is said and how it is semiotically represented, and takes into account the socio-political context and cultural practices within which something is said. Ostensibly, it focuses on the systematic analysis of (multimodal) text comprising the written word and/or the spoken word and/or still/moving images according a set of criteria drawn from the literature in culture teaching and learning. Here are some possible questions about multimodal artefacts: Who and what is being depicted and how? What are the key themes and what perspective has been chosen to represent them? What communicative actions are in evidence and what characterises them? What is the relationship between the subjects and objects? What dynamics are in evidence and/or implied? What can be said about the wider context? What semiotic resources are being used and how are they orchestrated? What rhetorical and design principles are at play? What can be said about power relationships and aesthetics of the ensemble? For guidance on discourse analysis, see e.g. Gee, 2010 and Kress, 2010a.

Task 12.8 CULTURAL COMPARISON

Examine the scheme of work at your placement school and try to match the 'universal experiences of life' listed above to particular topics.

Then, devise a number of activities comparing pupils' own culture with the target culture(s) for a particular class you teach for one of these areas. For guidance you might want to have a look at how available coursebooks approach the topic of 'education' and how they compare 'school life' in England to the target culture(s).

ACCEPTANCE

Acceptance is more than tolerance. Some, particularly more advanced, learners can be seen to embrace certain aspects of the new culture. Participation in, and interaction with the target culture(s) through communication in the TL can help to develop the ability to analyse and critically appraise 'otherness'.

For pupils of appropriate maturity taking part in an exchange can present an invaluable experience. Preparation for and follow-up to an exchange is important. Pupils could present an account of their stay – individually or collaboratively – for the benefit of parents and other interested parties. The identification of positive experiences and the public appreciation of the specific TL culture can not only be a motivating factor for the pupils themselves, but also a source of reassurance for other pupils less advanced in the process of acculturation.

PRINCIPLES FOR INTERCULTURAL LANGUAGE LEARNING

The Australian Government sets out some useful guidance on curriculum design and classroom interaction to promote effective intercultural language learning (see Liddicoat *et al.*, 2003: 47–51). It centres around the principles of active construction, making connections, social interaction, reflection and responsibility. We include the guidance on one of the areas – making connections – here by way of illustration.

> ## Task 12.9 **ENCOURAGING ACCEPTANCE OF THE TARGET CULTURE(S)**
>
> Look through the departmental scheme of work and note classroom activities requiring use of the TL to collect information – for instance, surveys.
>
> Consider how such activities could be extended to include communication with a parallel class in the partner school abroad.
>
> Through discussion with your mentor or another interested class teacher, investigate the possibility of setting up such a project.

■ **Table 12.1** Principles for intercultural language learning

General principle	Application in languages learning	Elaboration
Making connections		
Learning is based on previous knowledge and requires challenges to initial conceptions that learners bring. The challenges lead to new insights through which learners make connections, to reorganise and extend their existing framework of knowledge.	Comparing languages and cultures and drawing connections and building the relevant bridges between home and target language and culture. Comparing existing knowledge of language and culture against new input.	Learners: ■ develop ways to rethink their initial conceptions, to transform themselves (identity) and their knowledge; ■ combine learning of language and culture with learning across the curriculum; ■ develop a growing understanding of language, culture, and values and their interdependence. Teachers: ■ begin tasks with understanding that learners bring from home or their local community; draw upon the diversity of their learners; ■ provide scaffolding through interactive questioning, instruction, resources, technologies; ■ offer alternative explanations; ■ encourage learners to observe, predict, compare, explain, integrate, inquire; ■ encourage interaction and connections across texts and contexts; ■ show learners how bridges are made.

Source: Liddicott *et al.*, 2003: 47.

Task 12.10 **PRINCIPLES FOR INTERCULTURAL LANGUAGE LEARNING**

Download the Australian Government report on intercultural language learning from www1.curriculum.edu.au/nalsas/pdf/intercultural.pdf and look in particular at pp. 47–51. What activities and tasks do these guidelines imply? Using one or more of Neuner and Hunfeld's (1993) universal experiences of life, devise a series of activities drawing on as many of the principles outlined by the report as possible.

ONLINE INTERCULTURAL PROJECTS

Most schools have links, sometimes even established partnerships, with educational institutions abroad and many encourage exchanges at an individual level. Useful resources in this context are www.etwinning.net, www.epals.com and www.schools online.britishcouncil.org (see Pachler, 2007 for details on the use of the Internet for project work; see also www.goethe.de/ins/ie/prj/scl/enindex.htm, a Goethe-Institut online resource in English for school projects; and O'Dowd, 2007, for online intercultural exchange projects). Cultura is a well-known web-based, intercultural project connecting students in different countries underpinned by a sound peda-gogical design. For details, see www.cultura.mit.edu and Furstenberg *et al.*, 2001).

Online projects can provide useful opportunities for realistic and meaningful communication. For example, survey work carried out in the classroom or the local community can be extended through a series of e-mail exchanges to which a number of lessons is dedicated. Pupils can share, compare and analyse their findings with (those of) pupils in a partner school.

When considering the use of e-mail or the Internet in FL teaching it is important to ensure they are properly embedded in the scheme of work. Experience suggests that personal contact with a colleague tends to be an important factor in ensuring the success of work involving partner schools abroad. Successful projects tend to have very clear aims and objectives and a clearly defined thematic structure and timeframe. It is advisable to divide classes into smaller groups, who in turn communicate with small groups in a partner school. This way the teacher can ensure all pupils can get actively involved and flexibility in the development of topics is allowed for.

Project work might comprise the following phases:

Preparation: co-ordination between teachers in both schools
Phase 1: pupils introduce themselves, their schools, their environment in writing and pictures.
Phase 2: questions and answers, exchange of information.
Phase 3: exchange of detailed answers based on research; follow-up questions.
Phase 4: analysis and comparison of results.
Phase 5: (joint) presentation of results (e.g. compilation of a display, brochure, newspaper, video/audio recording or webpages), summary of learning outcomes, project evaluation, goodbye letters.

Each group should be required to keep a log or learner diary in which they reflect on their work, note new vocabulary and structures, etc. From time to time group work needs to be supplemented by plenaries, during which the teacher provides necessary input – for example, on strategies for working independently – revises previous learning outcomes relevant to the project and during which pupils are required to report on the progress they have made. This way the teacher can ensure that pupils stay on task. The teacher also needs to be available throughout to clarify any difficulties, questions and misconceptions pupils might have. Decisions will need to be taken – for instance, whether pupils' messages have to be checked by the teacher before they are sent and to what extent redrafting by the teacher is required. Alternatively, pupils in the partner school could be asked to provide diagnostic feedback for each other. A further important consideration concerns the use of the TL. Where possible, pupils should be encouraged to use the TL during group work to communicate with each other and with peers in the partner school. Experience suggests, though, that the mixing of languages might at times be required and necessary to ensure maximum outcomes (see e.g. Butler and Kelly, 1999).

Projects can be meaningfully linked to controversial topics, about which pupils have an opinion which they are keen to communicate, as well as to real-life experiences of pupils, such as their reading, listening and viewing habits, school-life, hobbies and pastime, family life, etc.

Task 12.11 **PLANNING AN ONLINE PROJECT**

Drawing on the guidance given above (see also Pachler, 2007), develop an online project in conjunction with your mentor or an interested class teacher, which relates to a relevant topic in your placement school's scheme of work. You might want to use the following framework when planning your project:

- preparation required;
- age-range;
- objectives (linguistic and cultural);
- activities and time-scale;
- useful links and resources;
- methodological considerations.

EDUCATIONAL VISITS, EXCHANGES AND WORK EXPERIENCE ABROAD

Study abroad, as extended visits tend to be called in the literature, have been very popular for a long time and the last two decades or so have seen a considerable increase in the amount of research investigating its efficacy and impact. Due to lack of space we can only explore this literature briefly here, which reports inconsistency and variation of outcomes (see e.g. Wang, 2010). One qualitative study, which we want to look at, is Spenader (2011) who investigates the relationship between acculturation and language learning through the case studies of four learners. She concludes that higher levels of acculturation are associated with higher levels of proficiency and personality features, such as integrative dispositions and assertiveness, are also found to have an impact. She also discusses some implications for the design of study abroad programmes, in particular the need for compatibility between the sojourner and the hosts, with the latter needing to show an active interest in the learner and provide her with meaningful relationships and adequate opportunities for interaction. In this context, recent work by Shively (2010) is of interest, which explores the role of the study of pragmatics in preparing students to learn language and culture in study abroad. Ongoing formal instruction was found by Spenader not to be a necessary condition for reaching high levels of proficiency and learner assertiveness about risk-taking behaviours, and using the target language impacted positively on language proficiency. In addition, the study found that humour may have a positive influence on language learning in that it fostered relationship building with host nationals. Amuzie and Winke's study (2009) found a relationship between study abroad and learner beliefs.

Many FLs departments are eager to provide opportunities for pupils to visit countries where the TL is spoken. Pupils who have (had) such an opportunity can have an increased interest in the subject and the TL as a means of finding out more about the respective countries and cultures. As could be seen, in some cases first-hand experience of the target culture(s) can lead to (a positive disposition towards) acculturation. Some pupils, however, can get frustrated and demotivated as the result of a 'culture shock'. Negative experience might lead to estrangement, anger and hostility. Teachers involved in visits and exchanges should, therefore, not take anything for granted. Some pupils will have experience of travelling, others may never have stayed away from their own homes. Some pupils will have a good general knowledge base, whereas others may even be unaware of the geographical location of the country in question. School visits should be accompanied by meaningful linguistic and cultural awareness tasks, which can be of a cross-curricular nature.

Shively (2010: 110), drawing on Martínez-Flor and Usó-Juan, 2006, proposes the 6R approach to the teaching of pragmatics (see Table 12.2), which could form part of the preparatory work for an educational visit or exchange.

FLs departments in many Secondary schools offer their pupils visits to a country where the TL is spoken. Three main types of activities are distinguished here: visits, exchanges and work experience placements. The type of visit undertaken by pupils tends to reflect their linguistic, social and cultural development. While on visits, the exposure to the target culture and the TL tends to be tightly structured and controlled, and the pupils tend to remain in close contact with their English-speaking peer group throughout their stay abroad, the number of opportunities to interact with native speakers and their way of life increases on exchanges. These are in the main organised around the pupils' stay with exchange partners, whom they may know already from previous visits, letters and/or e-mail links and whose families tend to act as an interface between the 'otherness' of life in the foreign culture and the 'universal' features of life at home. Work experience placements abroad often present the greatest challenge to pupils, and tend to depend on adequately developed personal, social and linguistic skills in pupils who need to cope, frequently independently, with the vocational and occupational demands made by TL interactions in the 'world of work'.

■ **Table 12.2** 6R approach to the teaching of pragmatics

Steps in teaching pragmatics	Summary of what is taught in each step
Step 1: Researching	Learners are taught what pragmatics is and the specific phenomenon to be taught (e.g. requests, apologies, refusals). Then students collect pragmatics data samples in their L1.
Step 2: Reflecting	Learners analyse their L1 pragmatics data through guidance from the instructor. This stage raises learners' awareness about social factors (e.g. age, gender, social status) and setting that influence pragmatic behaviour.
Step 3: Receiving	Learners receive explicit instruction about how the pragmatic feature being taught is realised in the L2. For example, learners may be shown a range of possible strategies used to perform requests in the L2 and may be asked to compare request performance in L1 and L2.
Step 4: Reasoning	Learners analyse the L2 pragmatics data and identify social and situational factors, as well as the speakers' intentions (awareness-raising activities).
Step 5: Rehearsing	Learners put into practice their knowledge about the pragmatics feature being taught by participating in communicative activities, which ideally move from more controlled to more free.
Step 6: Revising	Learners receive feedback and further guidance on their pragmatic performance in the communicative activities.

Source: Shively, 2010: 110.

If the opportunity arises, you should try to observe the various tasks involved in preparing and planning visits and exchanges at their placement schools. Many valuable lessons can be learned from teachers with relevant experience. We would strongly recommend you work in tandem with experienced FLs teachers on planning visits and exchanges and to take on responsibility for some of the tasks involved only gradually.

Visits and exchanges can help to make both the TL as well as the target culture(s) more accessible to pupils and can be motivating. They provide valuable opportunities to find out more about the target culture(s) and can help to illustrate that the TL can be used effectively for communication. Also, visits and exchanges can enrich pupils' general knowledge base by giving them an opportunity to experience first hand the excitement of travelling, meeting new people and finding out about their way of life. One key element of successful visits and exchanges is having clearly delineated aims and objectives. Both staff and pupils need to be aware what the benefits and reasons for carrying out such an activity are.

When organising exchanges, finding a suitable partner is another essential prerequisite. Often, personal contacts with teachers abroad are most effective. To establish good channels of communication is equally important. Preparatory visits can provide useful information.

Fisher and Evans (2000) make the following practical suggestions based on their research study into the effects of school exchange visits on attitudes and proficiency in language learning:

■ prepare pupils for the kind of language they will need when staying in the family, for example, including a range of expressions of social convention in the scheme of work and continuing to focus on the sometimes neglected area of pronunciation;

■ offer guidance to parents about the value of linguistic support for the exchange pupil staying with their family and offer suggestions as to the amount and nature of the correction and encouragement they give;

■ offer guidance to parents on ways of helping pupils settle in – for example, using photographs as a prompt;

■ consider arranging the exchange schedule to include a weekend with the family straightaway;

■ seek to develop pupils' cultural awareness before visiting the country, with an emphasis on 'the acquisition of ways of investigating and observing' (Snow and Byram, 1997: 31) to prepare pupils better for their stay;

■ discuss 'language-gathering' strategies, encouraging pupils, for example, to keep diaries or log-books of all new language they use;

■ be encouraged to look for evidence of linguistic progress in the pupils on their return and to build on this in their subsequent teaching;

■ encourage pupils to maintain contact with their partner through correspondence and e-mail;

■ use the exchange experience to contribute to an overall ethos within the department of promoting language learning as part of a real communicative experience.

Task 12.12 **AIMS AND OBJECTIVES OF VISITS AND EXCHANGES**

Where possible, find out what the aims and objectives of the visits and exchanges organised by your placement school are – for instance, by asking appropriate members of the FLs department or by having a look at some documentation used in a recent visit.

It is important to fully understand, cover and comply with all legal responsibilities and requirements and abide by school, Local Authority (LA) and/or any other regulations and guidelines. These cannot be covered in this chapter. They must be considered fully in the planning of any such activity in conjunction with senior colleagues in school. Activities beyond the classroom should not be taken on lightly. Useful guidance is inter alia from the government at the time of writing at: www.bit.ly/dfe-health-and-safety. There are many issues to consider when organising, or accompanying, a trip or visit.

Task 12.13 **ISSUES TO CONSIDER WHEN ACCOMPANYING/ORGANISING TRIPS**

Familiarise yourself with the guidance and find out what you can on the following issues:

- insurance implications;
- parental/guardian consent;
- ground rules;
- being *in loco parentis*;
- supervision ratios;
- necessary travel and medical/emergency documentation;
- transport/drivers;
- financial issues – pre- and during the trip (charging for the trip and spending money on it);
- emergency procedures;
- other.

HOSTING EXCHANGE PARTNERS

The hosting of exchange partners is also not as simple as it may at first appear. Before the visitors arrive, the teacher in charge of the exchange has to ensure that visitors and hosts are appropriately matched. For this purpose, a pro forma could be devised. The following information, provided by parents and the pupils themselves, might be useful: name, sex, age, a passport photograph, number of brothers and sisters and their ages, pets, personality, hobbies, whether they would prefer a boy or girl with similar or different characteristics to themselves.

Task 12.14 **MATCHING PUPILS**

You have been asked by your head of department to match up the Spanish and English participants on the annual Spanish exchange.

- Design a checklist, including all the relevant details and information you will need to know about individual pupils to enable you to match them.
- How does your list compare with the criteria used by your placement school?

The teacher with responsibility for exchange visits might want to try to help the visiting members of staff – for instance, by organising excursions to local places of interest. Planned excursions for visitors and hosts can provide useful opportunities for the TL to be used in authentic situations. Many schools insist that during such journeys pupils have to sit next to their own exchange partners. This can avoid divisions by nationality and create opportunities for interaction. It is well worth considering visits to places familiar to the British pupils and to provide activities, which necessitate – through collaboration – communication and explanations between the visitors and the hosts. See Turner, 2001, for some very useful ideas and advice on working with exchanges.

In order to give the exchange a suitable profile, it is important to involve the senior management of the host school. A formal welcome in an assembly serves at least two purposes: first, it demonstrates courtesy and second, it introduces the exchange partners to the unique experience of school assemblies and the ethos of the school as a whole. A reception or welcome party is often an integral part of a successful exchange visit. At such an occasion host families could be introduced to visiting pupils and visitors, and hosts can get to know each other in an informal atmosphere.

There are also arrangements to be made for when the foreign pupils visit and take part in life at the school. There, visiting pupils can shadow host pupils and accompany them to lessons. Clearly, colleagues have to be asked if they are happy to have in some of their lessons visiting pupils who could, for instance, be used for cross-curricular work.

Parents might wish to become involved in the exchange by providing 'family' days where they put on further excursion on free days at weekends. It might be useful to provide a list of possible venues and activities to support parents in arranging days out for their visitors. Often parents are happy to organise social events during the exchange at their own homes.

There is always the risk of some pupils feeling homesick. Providing a list of telephone numbers of all participating families can allay some concerns, and allow visiting pupils and their hosts to network among each other if necessary. Approval to distribute telephone numbers in such a way needs to be sought from all concerned. It might be appropriate to remind parents that while visiting pupils are in their homes, they are responsible for them, which includes, for instance, determining meal- and bedtimes.

PUPILS AS ETHNOGRAPHERS

While on a trip or exchange, learners require a focus for their learning, both linguistically and culturally. This is usually provided in the form of a quiz, or a set of tasks/activities for pupils to complete while in the TL country, often preceded by a preparatory task or series of activities where the pupils are familiarised with their destination, etc. and prepared linguistically as appropriate. These are very useful approaches and can perhaps be the starting-point for something a little more ambitious, where pupils take on the role of 'researcher' and thereby not only assume more responsibility and independence for what they investigate, but also do so in a way more personal to them and their reactions/priorities, as well as those of their TL country environment and experience. Tasks intended for the whole group are of necessity generic and can sometimes result in 'facts and figures' approaches (for example, 'How high is the church spire? When was it built?, etc.).

Roberts *et al.* (2000) outline how (initially) university students – although they do also refer to upper Secondary pupils – can become 'ethnographers' in their work during stays in a TL country. Ethnography is a methodological approach in research where the researcher lives (or spends substantial time) with the subjects of his or her research and learns as much as possible about that particular way of life; this research approach was used extensively by anthropologists – for example, to study the lives of tribal people and has been extended by sociologists to research into particular social groups (including teachers).

Roberts *et al.* (2000) argue that learners who have an opportunity to stay in the TL country can be trained to do an ethnographic project while abroad. This would involve them studying the local people as they interact with their environment and culture. This is obviously on a much larger scale when the 'ethnographer' is a university student spending a year abroad to that of a pupil on a trip or exchange. However, many of the ideas are still applicable: learners could be asked to:

- Keep a diary (in L1 and TL where possible and appropriate) of what they do and their reactions/responses. Some key language/examples could be provided or a framework.
- Using digital photographs (or video), certain events (within the home, at school, in town, etc.) could be recorded and annotated (how different/similar is this to my life? What is different exactly? What do I think of this?).
- Using audio technology (mobile phone, etc.) music examples could be brought back and a similar 'review' conducted.
- Realia (posters, tickets, etc.) could be collected and commented on.
- Each learner could be encouraged to investigate something that particularly interests them, e.g. cooking/eating out, sport (of a particular type), facilities for young people, dance, music, theatre, education, family life, media (newspapers, TV, Internet, etc.).
- Learners could then 'package' their research into an output of their choice and 'disseminate' it (to the class, to staff, to parents, to the exchange school, etc.).

The issue of TL and the mother tongue is obviously a challenging one but, as already noted, the purposes of a TL experience (whether at home or abroad) are not only linguistic. Many linguistic advantages will occur alongside investigations into other (cultural) issues and, from a learners' perspective, an approach involving L1 as well as the TL enables them to work at a far more sophisticated level on content than otherwise. Learners should, nevertheless, be encouraged to work subsequently in the TL where possible on the comments they have already made in L1.

Visits within their own country can also provide pupils with opportunities to gain meaningful cultural information about other cultures related to, and including the target culture(s). For example, visiting exhibitions where artefacts can be seen that are cultural representations of ideas, values, traditions and religious beliefs. The British Museum, for example, offers a permanent Islamic exhibition where connections to the Spanish language, architecture and historical events, can be made. Another exhibition about the theme of 'death' as seen through the eyes of a range of cultures, including a number of South American countries, can also offer pupils a chance to explore ideas and beliefs with reference to the cultural development of those countries throughout their history up until today. In the process, pupils can perceive some fundamental differences to their own outlook to the world. By combining travel to the target countries and visiting places of learning within their own, teachers can enable pupils to experience acculturation of new and not so different ideas that can help to secure some cultural maturity and ultimately learning about the world.

THE FOREIGN LANGUAGE ASSISTANT (FLA) AS A CULTURAL RESOURCE

Working with FLAs or other native speakers can present a very valuable opportunity to enhance FLs work across all stages of cultural awareness. Therefore, if the support of an FLA is available, this should be maximised. Useful guidance on how to work with the FLA is, for instance, available from the National Association for Language Advisers (NALA) and the British Council (see www.britishcouncil.org/languageassistant; NALA/Central Bureau 1992; Page, 1997; Rowles *et al.*, 1998). There might be occasions when you have the opportunity to work with FLAs during your programme of teacher education and some student teachers may have worked as FLA themselves. In any event, you need to be aware of the potential of working with FLAs and how to maximise this resource in preparation for your work as qualified FLs teachers.

FLAs are, in the main, used by departments to allow pupils to come into contact with native speakers of the FL(s) they study, to provide a direct link to the culture(s) associated with the TL as well as more specifically to provide opportunities for pupils to speak and to prepare them for their oral examinations. One of the advantages of FLAs is the fact that they tend not to be that much older than the pupils themselves and potentially, therefore, constitute a resource regarding the particular areas of their interests.

The NALA/Central Bureau guide on working with FLAs (1992: 11–12) provided a range of valuable ideas and suggests a number of different ways in which the cultural dimension can be portrayed with the help of the FLA which still apply:

- straightforward – and probably simple and concise – presentations by the FLA on an aspect of their background, followed or preceded by questions from the pupils;
- role play, whereby the FLA portrays national figures, professions, members of society within their country;
- establishing differences and similarities by questioning pupils closely about their own culture and encouraging them to articulate their views on what they understand to be characteristic of other countries;
- data collection and project preparation with the FLA working with particular groups on specific cultural dimensions, e.g. music, sport, leisure, the media;
- working on European awareness projects with other departments within the school;
- collecting newspapers and magazines throughout the year and keeping an ongoing survey of, for example, sport results, major events, local incidents, political happenings, leisure and arts activities;
- joint FLA/pupil compilation of 'A day in the life of a pupil/commuter/shop-keeper/lorry driver, etc.' as perceived in both countries;
- using maps and historical viewpoints from the FLA's own country to obtain comparative viewpoints;

- using magazines and the press for cultural update but also for predictability exercises where issues are ongoing;
- discussing not only habits and customs but also attitudes (e.g. towards racism, class, religion, poverty, leisure).

Morgan and Neil (2001: 80–82) suggest the following advantages of working with and team teaching with an FLA.

Main advantages:

- a genuine communicative partner and native speaker model;
- an additional source of the target culture often allowing for stereotypes to be challenged;
- an extra 'teacher'.

Considerable advantages to team teaching with the FLA:

- the teacher–pupil ratio is improved;
- the TL can be modelled in an authentic way (role plays, for example);
- pupils, particularly for advanced study topics, can have the benefit of different cultural inputs and viewpoints from two sources of instruction;
- the 'team' can in itself act as a good model for pupils in terms of how to operate collaboratively.

Task 12.15 **WORKING WITH THE FLA**

Through observation, note what classroom activities have been made possible by the presence of an FLA.

Scrutinise a number of lesson plans of your own and identify opportunities that would enhance pupils' learning if an FLA were available.

SUMMARY

Pupils need to develop cultural awareness and intercultural (communicative) competence as an integral part of their FLs learning – for example, for linguistic and educational reasons. The FLs teacher plays an important part in facilitating its development as relevant activities require in-depth knowledge and understanding of the target culture(s) as well as very careful planning and structuring.

In this chapter we presented a possible framework for developing cultural awareness, making use of a range of learning opportunities inside and outside the FLs classroom, including first-hand experience of the target culture.

In developing the cultural component, particularly outside the FLs classroom, thorough preparation is vital in order to safeguard the welfare of pupils and to ensure success. It is imperative that teachers give due consideration to relevant legislation, regulations and guidelines.

FURTHER READING

Furstenberg, G., Levet, S., English, K. and Maillet, K. (2001) Giving a virtual voice to the silent language of culture: the Cultura project. In *Language Learning & Technology*, 5(1): 55–102. Available online at www.llt.msu.edu/vol5num1/furstenburg/default/pdf

This paper reports on an important curricular initiative using digital technologies, the Cultura project, which aimed to develop students' cultural attitudes, concepts and beliefs, as well as ways of interacting and looking at the world.

Levy, M. (2007) Culture, culture learning and new technologies: towards a pedagogical framework. In *Language Learning & Technology*, 11(2): 104–127. Available online at: www.llt.msu.edu/vol11num2/pdf/levy.pdf

This paper explores the contribution of digital technologies to the learning and teaching of culture with reference to culture as elemental, relative, group membership, contested and individual.

Pachler, N. (1999) Teaching and learning culture. In Pachler, N. (ed.) *Teaching Modern Foreign Languages at Advanced Level.* London: Routledge, pp. 76–92.

This chapter in a book about the teaching and learning of foreign languages at advanced level examines the pedagogical literature about culture and discusses a range of approaches to and strategies for the teaching of culture.

PART

3

LEARNER RELATED

PUPIL DIFFERENCES AND DIFFERENTIATION

INTRODUCTION

It is fundamentally important for teachers, be they FLs teachers or not, to recognise that pupils are individuals with different needs. No group of pupils is ever homogenous. Differences in areas such as gender, interest, self-concept, self-esteem, self-efficacy, social class, ethnic and cultural background, first language, ability, motivation, aptitude, age, previous attainment/experience, learning difficulties, etc. can influence pupils' degree of progress, achievement or participation in FLs work inside and outside the classroom.

According to Dörnyei and Skehan (2003: 589) aptitude and motivation have been shown to be among the most consistent predictors of success in second language learning. And despite inherent problems with the perception of the construct 'aptitude' being relatively stable and, therefore, difficult to overcome and of learners with low aptitude being at a distinct disadvantage, they posit that aptitude may well be an important issue, particularly in a cognitive perspective on SLA.

Another deals with cognitive and learning styles, which refers to certain predispositions around information processing and approaches to learning. Dörnyei and Skehan (2003) conclude that while construct learning styles may be more inherently attractive than aptitude because it implies a range of choices and preferences, each with respective strengths and weaknesses, the construct suffers from a number of basic theoretical shortcomings such as a precise lack of definition and, for them, does not deserve to be afforded a high research priority. The psychologists Riener and Willingham (2010) are even more sceptical; they argue that 'there is no credible evidence that learning styles exist' (p. 33). They accept that learners are different from each other, for example in terms of ability, interests, background knowledge or learning difficulties; that these differences impact on learners' performance; and that teachers should take these differences on board. However, Riener and Willingham take issue with the claim that 'learners have preferences about how to learn that are independent of both ability and content and have meaningful implications for their learning' (p. 34). While the authors acknowledge that students do have preferences about how they learn, they argue that these have not been found to make a measurable difference under controlled conditions. They further argue that evidence and experimental support for changing mode of instruction to match preferred learning styles of students has not yet been found.

One prominent strand of SLA research in recent decades has been that of learning strategies, which focuses on the active contributions learners can make to the efficacy of their endeavours. For an in-depth discussion of research on learning strategies, see e.g. Cohen and Macaro, 2007. Dörnyei and Skehan (2003) point out certain weaknesses of learner strategy research, namely the lack of 'theoretical soundness of the concept' with definitions offered by different writers being 'rather inconsistent and elusive' (p. 608). On the basis of their comparison of different strategy systems available in the literature, they delineate the typology in Figure 13.1 but stress the importance of resolving the conceptual ambiguities. They also indicate a preference in the educational psychology literature for the more versatile concept of 'self-regulation' which has become prominent in the assessment for learning literature (see e.g. Nicol, 2007).

One important implication of the above for us as FLs teachers is to become aware of the learning preferences in our teaching environment, to consider what, if any, strategies to use, when, why and how, as well as how to engage our learners into processes of reflecting on and monitor their own strategy use.

An EPPI Review (Hassan *et al.*, 2005) suggests that strategy training constitutes an effective intervention but that a number of conditions apply, that no direct comparisons between different types of interventions have been made and also that longevity of benefits has not yet been measured.

Mercer (2008) offers a useful definition of, and distinction between self-esteem, self-concept and self-efficacy. She notes that self-esteem is a comparatively global construct that is linked to the value system of the individual learner. Self-efficacy for her has more of a cognitive focus and relates to the perceived capability to perform a particular task in a specific domain. And self-concept, she notes, comprises cognitive and affective elements, and is comparatively less context-dependent.

In any given class there is normally a combination of factors pertaining to individual differences, which is one of the reasons why teaching is a highly complex process. In order to minimise differences in classes, some schools operate a setting

- *cognitive strategies,* involving the manipulation or transformation of the learning materials/input (e.g. repetition, summarising, using images);
- *metacognitive strategies*, involving higher-order strategies aimed at analysing, monitoring, evaluating, planning and organising one's own learning process;
- *social strategies*, involving interpersonal behaviours aimed at increasing the amount of L2 communication and practice the learner undertakes (e.g. initiating interaction with native speakers, cooperating with peers);
- *affective strategies*, involving taking control of the emotional (affective) conditions and experiences that shape one's subjective involvement in learning.

■ **Figure 13.1** Four main classes of learning strategies

Source: Dörnyei and Skehan, 2003: 608.

policy, where some departments – usually including FLs – group pupils according to certain criteria but particularly attainment. In a school where setting takes place, pupils can be in different sets in certain subjects like FLs, Mathematics and English. Other schools adopt a streaming policy. On entry they place pupils into (attainment) groupings across the whole curriculum, with pupils being taught in the same group in all or most subjects of the curriculum. This happens often on the basis of test scores in English and Maths, and/or information passed on from the pupils' Primary schools. Commonly used tests are MidYIS and Yellis, developed by the University of Durham. Nevertheless, FLs classes, be they setted, streamed or mixed ability, invariably contain pupils, for example, with different ability levels, interests and backgrounds. For a discussion of mixed-ability grouping (in FL teaching) see Ainslie and Purcell, 2000, Redondo, 2000 and Hallam and Deathe, 2002.

As a FLs teacher, you need to ensure that all pupils can participate, become involved in lessons and have valuable learning experiences of equal worth. Individual differences should be catered for by building classroom practice on the notion of equality of opportunities in education – that is, helping all pupils to realise their full potential or to maximise their aspirations. To achieve this, three issues are of particular importance: setting suitable learning challenges, responding to pupils' diverse learning needs, and overcoming potential barriers to learning and assessment for individuals and groups of pupils (see e.g. DfEE/QCA, 1999: 20–3). The notion that pupils respond consciously or unconsciously to the expectations of the teacher, be they explicitly stated or implied, is generally accepted. From this follows that high teacher expectations in terms of achievement and behaviour of pupils can help pupils fulfil their potential. Differentiation, which is discussed in detail in this chapter, aims at maximising the potential of pupils by building on their prior learning and taking into account their individual differences.

Catering for the full range of differences in and individual needs of pupils, and helping all pupils maximise their potential is very challenging. It requires the recognition of pupils' individual differences and needs, familiarisation with their backgrounds and the identification of appropriate teaching strategies and activities (see also Peacey, 2013: 285–304).

Booth *et al.* (2000) provide explicit guidance at all levels of provision (see in particular Section C1 entitled 'Orchestrating learning', pp. 75–88). They encourage teachers to audit their own practices in terms of the following: whether

- lessons are responsive to pupil ability;
- lessons are made accessible to all pupils;
- lessons develop an understanding of difference;
- pupils are actively involved in their learning;
- pupils learn collaboratively;
- assessment encourages the achievements of all pupils;
- classroom discipline is based on mutual respect;
- teachers plan, teach and review in partnership;
- teachers are concerned with supporting the learning and participation of all pupils;
- learning support assistants are concerned with supporting the learning and participation of all pupils;
- homework contributes to the learning of all.

We believe in the entitlement of all pupils to study a FL and this chapter is intended to provide guidance for you on how to make support available to pupils who experience possible barriers to foreign language learning. See Pachler and Redondo, 2005 for a collection of papers on inclusion in FLs.

OBJECTIVES

By the end of this chapter you should be able to:

■ appreciate the importance of getting to know your pupils as individuals with a view to catering for their different needs;

■ consider strategies for addressing these needs.

ENTITLEMENT

George (2005), writing against the background of US educational policy debate of the early 2000s, makes a strong argument for what he calls 'the heterogeneous classroom' which provides a learning environment consistent with democratic goals preparing learners for real-life situations in a diverse nation. One key characteristic of this heterogeneous classroom, in addition to diversity, for him is differentiated instruction, 'the adaptation of classroom strategies to students' different learning interests and needs so that all students experience challenge, success, and satisfaction' (p. 189).

You need to ensure that you make the full programme of work defined by the statutory framework accessible to all pupils, as 'the right to share the curriculum . . . does not automatically ensure access to it, nor progress within it' (NCC, 1989: 1). In order to achieve this, individual differences in pupils need to be identified and pupils' individual needs assessed. Only then can the process of *addressing* pupils' individual needs begin in order to maximise the rate of progress and to enhance the degree of participation.

Four important principles of equality of opportunity in making the full programme of work available to pupils are *entitlement, accessibility, integration* and *integrity* (see DES/Welsh Office 1991: 56–57). According to these principles:

■ all pupils have a right to participate in the study of FLs;

■ the FLs student teacher needs to ensure that activities are planned and delivered in a way that allows all pupils to become involved in the FL learning experience and that the individual needs of pupils are catered for;

■ pupils with special educational needs (SEN) should participate in FLs activities alongside pupils without SEN, where possible without substantial alteration of the programme of work or where necessary with modifications to it;

■ activities need to be of equal worth and not patronising or tokenistic to the pupils concerned.

Such general aspects of policy statements need to be of concern to you, particularly if you view FL learning as an entitlement for all pupils and believe that it is an essential element of a broad and balanced curriculum. These general aspects of education policy can be particularly helpful when the need arises to argue the case for FLs which, sadly, is often necessary.

Task 13.1 **FLs FOR ALL?**

Do you believe that FLs should be taught to all pupils, throughout their compulsory schooling? If so, list arguments in support of FLs for all in the curriculum. If not, outline your reasons against.

In your opinion, what would the implications of 'languages for all' be for FLs teachers?

How do you view the inclusion of FLs for pupils aged 6–11 learners? What are the implications for FL learning at 11–16?

DIFFERENTIATION

The notion of 'differentiation' is a key strategy in catering for differences in a group of learners. It is based on the principle of helping individual pupils achieve to the best of their ability by planning learning experiences that take into account their individual characteristics, particularly in terms of ability and interest, as well as their prior learning.

Differentiation requires careful and thoughtful planning. You need to adapt the way in which the subject matter is presented at the input/presentation stage – for instance, by using a range of visual aids and by varying the presentation of new lexical items and structures. At the practice and exploitation/production stages you need to offer pupils opportunities to interact with the subject matter at different levels and in different ways. Allowing pupils to talk/write about themselves in the course of their FLs work and enabling them to relate their own experiences to the way of life of people in the target culture(s) can make the study of FLs relevant to pupils and the TL a vehicle for self-expression. In this way, pupils can draw on their different experiences for the purposes of MFL learning.

Apart from an awareness of pupils' individual differences, you need to anticipate what difficulties might arise from the subject matter and skills to be taught – for instance, whether the pronunciation, orthographic conventions, linguistic structures or semiotic boundaries are different from those in the mother tongue(s) of pupils and, therefore, need particular attention or whether the types of activities, material or interaction modes might pose certain difficulties. In preparing a lesson or unit of work, you need to consider strategies to provide reinforcing support for some pupils while stretching others.

In its non-statutory guidance to FLs teachers, the National Curriculum Council suggested the differentiation of FLs work according to three categories (see NCC, 1992: E3). Despite its early publication date, this model is still relevant and applied widely today:

Task 13.2 **PUPIL PERCEPTIONS OF A UNIT OF WORK**

Following the completion of a unit of work, or a short series of lessons, depending on the stage of your placement, issue the pupils with a brief questionnaire asking them to identify what they found easy, difficult and/or enjoyable within the unit. You will need to remind pupils of the tasks and activities undertaken in the unit of work. How can this information be used to inform future planning and the differentiation of work?

Discuss the findings with your mentor or a class teacher you work with closely.

- **core:** language items and structures as well as tasks, which all pupils are expected to master;
- **reinforcement:** tasks for those pupils who need more practice in order to achieve the planned core outcomes;
- **extension:** language items and structures as well as tasks for those pupils capable of carrying out more advanced and complex work than their peers.

Similarly, learning outcomes are often categorised as those elements which *all* pupils will cope with, those which *most* will manage and those which only *some* may achieve.

Figure 13.2 shows an example of how the first three categories can be applied to the planning of a unit of work in order to cater for the needs of all pupils in the class. It follows the approach to planning suggested in Chapter 7. On the basis of differentiated learning objectives the unit of work 'In the restaurant' identifies a range of activities building on what pupils already know and covers a number of learning opportunities at various levels in order for the full attainment range to be challenged.

Task 13.3 **CHALLENGE IN FLs TEACHING AND LEARNING**

What does 'challenge' look like in FLs lessons? What can help increase the challenge?

Below are some ideas where the challenge may be increased. Can you think of similar ways of helping increase the challenge?

- Requiring learners to introduce other elements to the work they are producing, e.g. sometimes/often/never/, etc.
- Taking away support, e.g. book or OHT when pupils practise a role play.
- Adding a challenging element: cognitively (getting them to think), emotionally (adding an extra dimension to the task), linguistically, (un-)predictability, spontaneity . . .
- *Using* opportunities for pupils to think and be independent *or* providing more support where required.

In a unit of work the various activities are normally cross-referenced to the specific coursebook, worksheets or other resources available to, or used by, the department to make individual lesson planning easier. This is not possible here but needs to be done in any planning you carry out.

In this unit of work, as in the model outlined above, all pupils are expected to complete the core activities. At appropriate times in the unit some pupils are set reinforcement activities consolidating core learning objectives, while others will be able to work on extension activities in order to gain a deeper knowledge and understanding, and develop additional skills. As Figure 13.3, adapted from Convery and Coyle, 1993: 3–5 illustrates, this can be done in a number of ways.

Figure 13.3 shows some examples of how the types of differentiation identified in Figure 13.2 relate to the unit of work 'In the restaurant'.

Those pupils who complete the core tasks more quickly can be set additional extension activities, allowing pupils who need it more time to complete the task. For instance, the core task of writing descriptions of types of food/meals can be followed by the extension task of researching and describing traditional English dishes in the TL.

Pupils can be given the same task(s) but different stimulus material, for instance to extract meaning (categorise food into starters, main courses and desserts) from authentic texts (from different menus). This is an example of differentiation by text.

Alternatively, pupils can be given the same stimulus material but differentiated tasks to complete. Pupils can, for instance, be asked to listen to a dialogue in a restaurant. Some pupils can focus on word recognition by choosing items of

In the Restaurant	
Number and length of lessons: 5 x 70 minutes	
Learning objectives	
Core ■ To be able to read and understand a menu ■ To be able to understand the waiter/ waitress ■ To be able to pay the bill	*Extension* ■ To be able to ask for clarification of what items on a menu are ■ To be able to complain about the quality of food provided ■ To be able to question the bill ■ To be able to ask to pay by cash or card
Main language items/structures	
Core Common items of food and meals Common restaurant phrases and structures	*Extension* *Kann ich mit . . . bezahlen?* *Es gibt ein Problem.* *Mein Essen ist kalt/nicht gut, etc.*
Main materials and resources	
Visual aids (digital technologies, flashcards), authentic menus, recordings of short dialogues, transcripts of recordings	

■ **Figure 13.2** Sample unit of work plan

Main activities
Core: ▨ Visual aids to present items of food. ▨ Categorise food into starters, main courses and desserts. ▨ Listening activity extracting details of food ordered. ▨ Structured pair work: ordering food. ▨ Open-ended role play in a restaurant. ▨ Reading exercise from menus with unfamiliar foods, matching with descriptions. ▨ Writing descriptions of types of food/meals. Reinforcement: ▨ Compile vocabulary list of basic foods. ▨ Categorise dishes contained on samples of menus. ▨ Decipher recorded dialogues from jumbled transcripts. ▨ Use gapped text of recorded conversations as a prompt for pair work. ▨ Prepare open-ended role play in pairs/groups. ▨ Use reference material and drill exercises to practice. ▨ Match items of unfamiliar foods with descriptions. Extension: ▨ Provide additional vocabulary to learn. ▨ Rework recorded dialogues from details extracted from tape. ▨ Conduct pair work without scripts but with visual prompts; insist that 'extension' vocabulary and phrases are incorporated. ▨ Prepare open-ended role play but in groups which will perform together; ask all the waiters and all the customers to prepare together; pupils will not know exactly what peers will say. ▨ Research and describe traditional English dishes in the TL. Homework: ▨ Note and learn vocabulary. ▨ Complete drill exercises reinforcing common vocabulary and phrases. ▨ Write the scripts of dialogues. ▨ Produce a full menu in German. ▨ Prepare for end of unit goal.
Assessment opportunities
Continuous: ▨ Peer assessment of pair work. ▨ Take in marks for listening. ▨ Mark drill exercises, menu, transcripts. ▨ One-to-one assessment of role plays. Summative: ▨ In mixed ability groups write and act out a short play to be video-taped: a family is celebrating exam success, but all goes wrong in the restaurant. ▨ End-of-unit test covering listening, reading and writing.

■ **Figure 13.2** *continued*

Differentiation type	Description
Text	Level of difficulty/type of stimulus material.
Task	Level of difficulty of what learners are asked to do with the stimulus material; number of tasks.
Outcome	Quantity and quality of performance/attainment expected from pupils.
Support	Amount of teacher time/access to reference material, etc. available to pupils.
Interest	Opportunity for pupils to choose tasks, stimulus material, medium, etc.

■ **Figure 13.3** Some types of differentiation

food/dishes they have heard from a list, while others also write down additional items they hear, which are not included in the list.

Differentiation can also come via open-ended tasks, for instance, producing a menu. This is differentiation by outcome. It allows for differences in quantity as well as linguistic difficulty of work produced such as the use of core vocabulary by some pupils and extension vocabulary by others. It also allows pupils to bring their own interest to the task, for instance by including their favourite dishes.

Different levels of support constitute another possibility. The amount of time the teacher spends with individual, pairs or groups of pupils or the access to reference material can vary. Pupils can be asked to perform a role play in a restaurant by producing a script with the help of a gapped text, from visual clues, by working simply from a scenario or by making use of help from the foreign language assistant (FLA).

When differentiating by interest you might allow pupils to choose from a range of stimulus material or activities – for instance, pupils could choose one of a number of menus or select from a range of scenarios for pair or group work. They might assume different roles in pair or group work – for instance, play the waiter or the client, or invent things that may go wrong to add spontaneity to dialogues, such as the waiter bringing the wrong order or there being a hair in the soup, which necessitates the inclusion of language associated with complaints.

When differentiating programmes of work, you need to ensure that reinforcement and extension activities are of equal worth and that pupils who are working on reinforcements activities do not feel belittled in their capability.

In the remainder of this chapter we discuss a number of pupil differences and identify a range of different teaching strategies to cater for them. The differences discussed are:

■ gender differences;
■ pupils with English as an Additional Language (EAL);
■ pupils with SEN;
■ exceptionally able pupils;
■ pupils with motivational difficulties.

Task 13.4 DIFFERENTIATED LESSON PLANNING

Following the guidelines for lesson planning given in Chapter 7, plan a number of differentiated lessons for a beginners class you have already worked with/observed and therefore know the range of individuals within the class. You may wish to use the unit of work in Figure 13.2 as a point of reference.

▨ For every key activity, consider what form of support you can provide for pupils. How can you cater for pupils' different needs? And how can support be phased out gradually?

▨ Consider the means by which a task can be presented to pupils of different abilities. Will the inclusion of illustrations help? How many examples will you provide? What size print will you use on materials?

▨ Devise follow-on activities, which enable pupils who finish sooner than others to extend their knowledge, skills and understanding within the given topic area. How will you reward the completion of this supplementary work without it feeling like 'just more work'?

▨ Also devise suitable reinforcement activities for those pupils who are not (yet) ready to carry out extension work, but where challenge is still present.

▨ Discuss these lesson plans with your mentor or the respective class teacher.

▨ Ask if you can teach the lessons you have planned with the respective teacher observing and providing feedback on what worked well, what did not work so well and how you could improve (in) these areas.

The various teaching strategies identified in this chapter need to be seen in the context of differentiation.

GENDER DIFFERENCES

The realisation that there are certain differences between boys and girls is clearly important. Clark and Trafford (1996) report a range of research findings which you may want to take into consideration in your planning. These remain valid today and are shown in Figure 13.4.

It is important for you to consider and use effective strategies to address these research findings and thereby cater for gender differences in FLs. Field (2000) warns against a simplistic approach to gender differences and suggests that teachers need to bear in mind gender-related matters, which include maturational rates, motivational factors, teaching and learning styles, parental support and attitudes, concentration spans and behavioural matters. You should guard against adopting 'boy friendly' and 'girl friendly' approaches to redress any perceived imbalances, but instead to draw on a broad understanding of gender-related issues to inform planning and teaching methods (see Barton, 2002a and 2002b, and Harris, 2002 for some perspectives on these issues).

Research findings	Implications for planning
Differences in the perception of usefulness, enjoyment and difficulty of FLs between girls and boys.	When planning programmes of work, are the perceived interests of boys and girls taken into account, e.g. in the choice of types of sports to be taught in the context of the topic 'hobbies'?
Boys tend to have a less conscientious approach towards their work and mature later than girls.	Are accuracy and communication being encouraged equally?
Boys tend to do better than girls at problem-solving whereas girls tend to be better at verbal reasoning.	When planning programmes of work, are different learning styles being catered for, e.g. are various types of activities being used?
Boys tend to be more demanding of time and attention from the teacher than girls.	Are boys and girls given the same amount of teacher attention? Is there a gender balance in who is asked to answer questions in class?
The presentation of girls' work can be 'seductively' better than that of boys.	Is presentation but one of a number of assessment criteria such as effort and accuracy?
Girls tend to be less obviously disruptive than boys, less confident about speaking than boys but more concerned about 'getting it right'.	Are boys and girls equally encouraged to carry out oral work and perform role plays in front of the whole class?
Boys tend to give less attention to lesson and coursework and more to revision and examination work.	Are both formative/continuous and summative assessment used? Are learning and revision strategies being taught explicitly?

■ **Figure 13.4** Gender differences

Task 13.5 **GENDER DIFFERENCES**

Observe a number of FLs lessons focusing on the participation rate of boys and girls, both during whole-class activities and pair/group work.

Devise (a) tally sheet(s), which help(s) you in recording, for instance, how often boys and girls put up their hands or make a contribution to a lesson. Also note which strategies the teacher uses to encourage equal participation by boys and girls, such as targeting questions to specific pupils.

Then discuss with your mentor or a relevant class teacher possible strategies for ensuring equal participation of girls and boys, referring to Figure 13.5 as appropriate.

- Boys see FLs as different from other curriculum subjects and as making distinct demands. Differences relate in particular to:

  - the central position of the teacher in language classrooms (as a model for language and culture, enthusiast, manager and teacher);
  - classroom interaction being predominantly dependent on understanding and using another language;
  - the volume of learning in FLs that is based on language, rather than content;
  - the emphasis on accuracy in FL learning and the relative absence of opportunities to explore 'ideas';
  - the complex and cumulative nature of FL competencies, of having to persevere and the consequent difficulties of 'catching up' for those who fall behind;
  - the importance of particular working practices on which successful performance depends;
  - the elusive nature of FLs as a subject and the lack of 'reality'/'relevance' that it has for some boys.

- Having a teacher whom boys would judge to be 'good' is an important dimension of engagement, especially in a subject where classroom work tends to be strongly teacher-centred.
- Boys respect and want teachers who can make learning in FLs exciting and engaging and who can also maintain an orderly and purposeful classroom. 'A good teacher', in boys' eyes, is one who respects individuals, who can engage pupils over the span of the lesson and across lessons, vary pace, find ways of involving them actively in their learning, find opportunities for some degree of choice, sustain an orderly and purposeful atmosphere, and have fun. 'Having a laugh' is not inconsistent with orderliness; what boys dislike are lessons where 'a bit of fun' escalates and the teacher is unable to get the class back on track.
- Neither boys nor girls see FLs as strongly gendered (earlier research showed a stronger link between the subject and its gendered image).
- Boys seem less concerned about whether a teacher is male or female than about the quality of the teacher.
- 'A good FLs lesson' is one in which there is a clear and explicit reason for all the activities which a teacher organises; this will include answers to why choral repetition, why pair work, why listening tasks, why writing and how these activities help learners learn and make progress in the FL.
- Boys recognise their own underperformance and can suggest reasons for it. Some believe that their individual performance can be improved if, for example, they have more ownership of content, task and strategy. A few see trying to improve as futile. For some, the potential for underperformance may have its seeds early on in their FL learning in school.
- Because the pedagogy of FLs is so teacher-centred, boys who are underperforming tend to see the teacher as responsible for the difficulties they have in their learning.
- Where boys fall behind in a FL and feel lost or disoriented, 'messing about' is a way of responding; given the distinctive nature of FLs, the subject appears to be particularly vulnerable to such a situation.
- Because of the cumulative nature of learning in FLs, underachievement, once established, is difficult to correct. Boys become caught in a downward spiral and can feel excluded; strategies for helping them to catch up and keep up seem to be particularly important for FLs classrooms.
- Learning a FL is, for some boys, an 'unreal' experience; the reality factor increases when pupils meet and can communicate with native speakers within school or on visits to other countries or cultural centres.
- Learning a FL is seen as 'hard' by many boys. The task of learning a second FL in school is not necessarily experienced as easier since the second language's structure and conventions are usually perceived as different.

■ **Figure 13.5** Boys' attitudes to FL learning   Source: Based on Jones and Jones, 2000: 46–47.

PUPILS WITH ENGLISH AS AN ADDITIONAL LANGUAGE (EAL)

This is a very interesting debate for FLs teachers, where the majority of the lesson is normally conducted in the TL. Clearly, a pupil's own language competence is important when learning a new language, and competence in a range of languages may be very advantageous if links are encouraged. EAL learners will have another language as their L1 – this could prove fruitful in the FLs classroom.

Task 13.6 LEARNERS WITH EAL

From your observations, discussions and readings, consider the following questions:

■ How might pupils with EAL be *disadvantaged* in FLs classes?
■ How, conversely, might they be *advantaged*?
■ What steps can you as the teacher take to *maximise their learning*?

Obtain some written FLs work completed by a EAL learner.

■ What feedback would you give this pupil?
■ What characteristics do you notice?
■ Are these different because the pupil has EAL?

EAL was defined on the now defunct Multiverse website (www.bit.ly/multiverse-eal) as:

> English as an Additional Language (EAL) is the expression used in the UK to refer to the teaching of English to speakers of other languages. Current statistics indicate that almost 10% of pupils in maintained schools are learning English as a second, third, or indeed fourth, language, in addition to the language spoken in their families and over 300 languages are spoken by pupils in UK schools. The term is now preferred to English as a Second Language (ESL) as it indicates that pupils may use two or more languages other than English in their every day lives; it also suggests that learning English should be viewed as adding to a pupil's language repertoire, rather than displacing languages acquired earlier. The term 'bilingual' is also commonly used to describe children learning EAL; this is sometimes used to focus less specifically on the learning of English and more on the wider issues that concern children brought up in more than one language.

The National Association for Language Development in the Curriculum (NALDIC), the professional association of teachers specialising in EAL which offers a wide range of online resources about EAL (www.naldic.org.uk/eal-teaching-and-learning), stated:

> Pupils learning EAL share many common characteristics with pupils whose first language is English, and many of their learning needs are similar to those

of other children and young people learning in our schools. However, these pupils also have distinct and different needs from other pupils by virtue of the fact that they are learning in and through another language, and that they come from cultural backgrounds and communities with different understandings and expectations of education, language and learning.

The challenge for you as student teachers is to take into account, and build on the linguistic and cultural understanding, skills and knowledge that pupils bring to the classroom. In the FLs classroom, with the TL as the main means of instruction, interaction and assessment, weaknesses some pupils may experience in their command of English need not necessarily be a disadvantage. Linguistic skills in languages other than English can offer a basis for comparative and contrastive language work for the whole class.

Some schools (have) run language awareness programmes with aims such as '(to bridge) the "space between" the different aspects of language education (English/foreign language/ethnic minority mother tongues/English as a second language/Latin)' (Hawkins, 1987: 4). Such programmes might, for instance, include an examination of which languages are spoken in (particular parts of) the world, what families of languages there are and how languages are 'related' to one another. This might help pupils in the application of language learning strategies such as the use of cognates. Also, work might be carried out on an awareness of the diachronistic dimension of language development through the comparison of, say, the TL and English on the basis of a few words or phrases. Pupils could be shown how particular words have changed in form or meaning over a period of time. This might help them appreciate that form and function of language are determined by their use and that language evolves over time. From this, pupils might gain an appreciation that certain features of the TL, such as different grammatical genders, which they might perceive as 'idiosyncratic', were at one time also characteristic of the English language. A valuable resource in developing such programmes is Crystal's encyclopedia of language (see Crystal, 2003). Language awareness programmes should build on the understanding that pupils are developing during their time in Primary school, in particular work on metalinguistic understanding and writing frames.

FLs departments can be seen to have a key role to play in the development of a whole-school language policy. Mother tongue and FLs teachers might work collaboratively and follow a clear and consistent policy to assist pupils in their language development (see e.g. Kingman, 1988: 69).

FLs learning can be beneficial for pupils in terms of developing general language skills, including summarising, redrafting and varying language to suit context, audience and purpose. Beyond functional aspects of FL teaching and learning, there is also the need to become familiar with the structure of the TL. All these activities can be seen to reinforce work carried out in English and be beneficial in terms of the development of pupils' understanding of and ability to use language. The skills of paying attention to detail and of producing accurate spoken or written utterances are transferable from one language to another. In the TL, sounds or patterns can normally not be taken for granted because they are, in the main, unfamiliar. Pupils have to pay attention to every letter and sound, which can be easier in the TL because the amount of input tends to be finite/limited. This attention to detail can be a valuable skill for pupils with difficulties in writing and listening to their mother tongue/English.

Task 13.7 **LITERACY AND FLs WORK**

Carry out some observations of L1 lessons.

Drawing on your reading and observations of English lessons as well as on any experience in a Primary school, what specific examples of literacy-related FLs work can you think of?

PUPILS WITH SEN

Many classes include pupils who have 'learning difficulties significantly greater than those of the majority of children of the same age'. They are referred to as pupils with SEN. The Warnock Report (1978) came to the conclusion 'that services should be planned on the basis of one child in five requiring some form of special educational provision at some stage' (HMI, 1992: 1). This led to the recognition by the 1981 Education Act of the value of the integration of pupils with SEN into mainstream schools where possible.

The following categories of learning difficulties have been identified:

- a physical disability;
- a problem with sight, hearing or speech;
- a mental disability;
- emotional or behavioural problems;
- a medical or health problem;
- difficulties with reading, writing, speaking or mathematics work.

(DfE/Welsh Office, 1994: 6)

The revised SEN Code of practice was published in 2001 (www.bit.ly/2001-sen-code). This has important implications for the work of all teachers, including those of FLs. Subject teachers have an important role to play in the identification and support of pupils with SEN. Where an individual education plan (IEP) is drawn up, subject teachers need to familiarise themselves with it. IEPs tend to set out short-term targets, teaching strategies, provision to be made, review points and success criteria. Subject specialists need to liaise closely with the school's special educational needs co-ordinator (SENCO) as well as, on the basis of knowledge of the nature of a pupil's learning difficulties, help to achieve the specified targets or learning objectives in class.

Task 13.8 **IDENTIFYING PUPILS WITH SEN**

During your work at your placement school, enquire about the procedures in place in the FLs department concerning the identification of pupils with SEN. Discuss similarities and differences with the procedures identified by a peer from another school.

A report from CILT and the NCC (NCC, 1992: 1) notes that pupils with SEN can benefit in three main aspects of FLs work, i.e. in terms of:

■ linguistic development;
■ social development;
■ cultural awareness.

The findings of this project clearly underline the principle of entitlement to the study of FLs for all (see also McKeown, 2004).

Work by Leons *et al.* (2009) and Ganshow and Sparks (2000) in the US shows that learners with learning difficulties tend to have problems at the phonological/orthographic level and with understanding the rule system.

> Weaknesses in phonology affects a student's ability to process the sounds of the language. Weaknesses in morphology results in students having poor appreciation of word roots, tenses, and inflections. Weakness in syntax means that students lack an understanding of grammar and how word order affects meaning.
>
> (Leons *et al.*, 2009: 43)

Summarising over a decade of personal research, Ganshow and Sparks (2000: 92–94) offer the following six statements:

1 At-risk learners' learning problems are primarily language-based; anxiety might accompany the learning problem but is not likely to be the cause of the FL learning problem.

2 At-risk learners have difficulties understanding and using the rule systems of language.

3 At-risk learners have their main difficulties at the phonological: orthographic level.

4 At-risk learners lack metacognitive skills, i.e. ability to reflect on language and to use self-correction strategies without explicit instruction.

5 At-risk learners appear to benefit from direct, systematic, multi-sensory instruction in the rule systems of language: phonological: orthographic; grammatical: syntactic; semantic; and morphological (prefixes, suffixes, roots).

6 In our studies to date, at-risk high school and college learners classified as LD and at-risk learners not classified as LD (i.e. individuals who have extensive difficulties learning a foreign language) have shown no significant differences in IQ, native language skills, FL aptitude, FL grades and overall grade point average.

For more information and advice about working with pupils with SEN, see also the website of the National Association for Special Educational Needs, available at www.nasen.org.uk.

SOME TEACHING STRATEGIES

FLs teachers use a wide range of strategies in order to cater for pupils' individual differences. There is no specific methodology for teaching pupils with SEN. The strategies described here tend to be considered to constitute good practice in FL teaching and learning generally. Since we feel that they can be particularly useful when teaching pupils with SEN, we discuss them here.

Consistency in approach

Teachers of FLs often aim for consistency in approach in their teaching because familiarity with the format of material, types of tasks used and with classroom routines can increase the accessibility of the content of work for pupils. Using certain 'stock' types of activities can be reassuring to pupils. It can help minimise the amount of TL instruction needed and allows pupils to carry out their language work without apprehension about not knowing what to do.

Greeting pupils in the TL on entry to the classroom and expecting pupils to make a TL utterance in response or when calling the register can serve to reinforce a sense of purpose of TL use for pupils. It also provides a regular opportunity to reinforce key linguistic items and structures.

Planning in terms of small, achievable steps

Reducing the content of work to a manageable size and breaking it down into small, achievable steps are also often used. Memorising new words and phrases is an important skill in FL learning. Manageability of the number of new lexical items the FL teacher introduces at any one time or the number of items pupils have to remember in order to complete a task successfully can be particularly useful for pupils with SEN. This can help them gain a sense of security and achievement as well as break down possible affective barriers towards the TL.

Using praise

Praise for effort and/or achievement is one form of feedback, as are constructive comments when marking pupils' work. For marking, error correction and feedback, see Chapter 15.

Many teachers have adopted systems of praise and encouragement, which are attractive to pupils and make them want to achieve. 'Small' steps of progress made by pupils with SEN deserve equal praise as the 'bigger' steps of progress made by pupils without SEN. As Black and Jones explain (2006: 4), this necessitates knowing exactly where the pupils are in their learning.

> Effective learning demands an alternation of feedback, pupil to teacher and from teacher to pupil. Thus the starting point for a classroom activity may be a question formulated by the teacher to ascertain the pupils' existing understanding of a topic. This implements a first principle of learning, which is to start where the learner is, rather than to present strange new ideas to overlay the old and cause confusion.

Planning in terms of multidimensional progression

The NCC non-statutory guidance for England and Wales suggested that progression should be built into FLs work in a number of ways (see Figure 13.6).

Task 13.9 **PRAISE AND ENCOURAGEMENT**

▣ Find out what system of reward and praise are used by the FLs department at your placement school.

▣ Talk to a student teacher placed in a different school and find out what reward and praise system she uses.

▣ Compare the two systems for pupils with SEN in particular.

From		To
concrete	ideas	abstract
simple	aspects	complex
specific	themes	general
factual	topics	non-factual
classroom	experiences	wider
familiar	contexts	unfamiliar
less	controversial aspects	more

▣ **Figure 13.6** Multidimensional progression

Source: Adapted from NCC, 1992: D2.

Figure 13.6 has clear implications for unit of work and lesson planning, which can be explored in Tasks 13.10 and 13.11. For multidimensional learning objectives, see also Chapter 7.

Task 13.10 **PLANNING FOR PROGRESSION IN FL TEACHING – I**

Look at the scheme of work for beginners and intermediate classes in your FLs department at your placement school.

▣ Make a note of how many times certain topics, for instance free time or holidays, are taught across different year groups.

▣ Discuss with your mentor or a class teacher with whom you work closely what is taken for granted when a given unit of work, e.g. free time or holidays, is revisited and how much revision of material covered previously is necessary.

▣ Now try to relate the different approaches in how topics are covered to the continuum in Figure 13.6. How is progression from concrete to abstract, from simple to complex, from specific to general, from the classroom to the wider world or from the familiar to the unfamiliar, etc. built in?

Task 13.11 **PLANNING FOR PROGRESSION IN FL TEACHING – II**

Look at a scheme of work for any year group of the FLs department at your placement school.

■ Note how two consecutive units of work build on existing knowledge and skills.
■ Discuss with your mentor or a class teacher with whom you work closely what is taken for granted at the beginning of the new unit of work and how much revision of linguistic items and/or structures covered in previous units is necessary.

Your findings for this task are likely to vary considerably, according to which units of work you choose and at what stage of the linguistic development of pupils they come. Therefore, carry out this task with a number of different units across different stages of the learning process.

Creating a non-threatening learning environment

For pupils who are not so confident in speaking, opportunities should be created to practise in pairs or small groups with the teacher or the foreign language assistant (FLA) rather than in front of the whole class. This can avoid feelings of insecurity about perceived incorrect TL production. Extended periods of practice of a small amount of TL can also help pupils in this respect, as can short bursts of pair work (paired practice of a few new words) or a timed period (e.g. a strict 30-second slot with a countdown perhaps on the projection screen/interactive whiteboard) where all the class practise individually to themselves the one new phrase or question.

Clarity of presentation and using clear instructions

For pupils with difficulties with reading, worksheets and other writing, e.g. on the board or PowerPoint, need to be clearly legible and sufficiently big. Visual support as well as uncluttered presentation of material are also important. The board and screen should be visible from all angles of the classroom. All of this can be particularly important, of course, for pupils with visual difficulties. Pupils with difficulties with hearing should be encouraged to sit in a position that allows them to lip-read if necessary.

Instructions in the TL should be clear and precise and, where possible, be accompanied by visual support, e.g. the word 'listen' in the TL can be used together with a symbol of a tape or a mime, i.e. the teacher pointing to her ear. Symbols and instructions used by the coursebook should be the same as those used on worksheets as well as assessment material in order to avoid confusion. Familiarity with 'stock' types of tasks can also help to keep instructions manageable.

Presenting new language with the help of visual support

New language forms can be presented through reading and listening activities. Pupils with SEN are more likely to have difficulties with the highly conceptual nature of FL learning. Visual support in the form of pictures and flashcards as well as real objects such as, for instance, fruit can make non-abstract language more immediate and accessible. The visual support material can subsequently be used effectively as stimulus material for language practice and production.

Creating opportunities for non-verbal responses

Equally, the opportunity for pupils to respond physically to stimuli – for instance, by miming, making gestures, ticking boxes – can help them overcome difficulties in speaking and writing. By agreeing physical responses with a class – for instance, what mime to use for *'juego al tenis'* ('I play tennis') – pupils are given an opportunity to contribute to the lesson content. Pupils could be asked to stand up, put up their hand or hold up a word card when they identify a specific word or phrase in a listening text.

Planning in terms of tangible and practical outcomes

Tangible and practical outcomes and 'products' of the learning process, such as a project booklet building on drafting and redrafting, a collage for display purposes or the focus on the process of learning, such as carrying out simulation tasks, can help pupils in breaking down real and perceived difficulties with the linguistic content. The NCC non-statutory guidance for England and Wales offered many suggestions concerning 'concrete goals' and considers them as essential elements in the planning of units of work (see NCC, 1992: G1–13).

Recycling small amounts of language

Because of the importance of the ability to memorise linguistic items and recall them, which pupils with SEN are more likely to have difficulties with, the key to successful FL learning for pupils would appear to lie in presenting new language in different guises, 'recycling' small amounts of language in many different ways, yet in familiar types of tasks, to engage pupils in the process of carrying out activities without being aware that they are repeatedly practising the same language content.

EXCEPTIONALLY ABLE/GIFTED AND TALENTED PUPILS

There are some pupils whose individual differences relate to their exceptional ability and who have the potential for exceptional achievement, often in a range of subjects. Another widely used term for these pupils is 'gifted children'. For a discussion of working with very able pupils, see also Jones, 2000.

Clearly, a key consideration in working with pupils of exceptional ability is their identification in order to avoid underachievement and to be able to take remedial action. Early identification of exceptionally able pupils is particularly important as they may display symptoms similar to those shown by pupils with motivational

---

Task 13.12 **PRODUCTION OF A STUDY GUIDE FOR A UNIT OF WORK**

In a collaborative teaching situation, work alongside pupils who have difficulties with FLs.

■ Make a note of the particular difficulties experienced by them. These may include bringing the right equipment, using reference material, maintaining concentration, recalling key vocabulary, understanding instructions and other aspects identified in this chapter.

■ As a result of your findings produce a short 'study guide' for a future unit of work. This guide may include an equipment check, activities such as puzzles and games to reinforce key vocabulary, guidance on how and where to find reference material, a 'skills' profile ('can-do' checklist) and help on what to do if objectives prove too difficult. To assist you with this task, refer to the unit of work plan. The guide might also include guidance on established TL routines.

■ On completion, discuss the guide with your mentor or a class teacher with whom you work with closely.

Assume that the pupils will be able to work with a support teacher.

---

difficulties: they may appear inattentive or exhibit attention-seeking behaviour and underachieve. George (1993: 3) distinguished three characteristics of gifted underachievers:

■ low self-esteem;
■ academic avoidance behaviour;
■ poor study skills, poor peer acceptance and lack of concentration.

The identification of gifted pupils is not a straightforward process. George lists a number of ways of identifying exceptionally able pupils, among them teacher observation, checklists, intelligence tests and achievement test batteries.

Denton and Postlethwaite (1985: 31–32) suggest a non-subject specific checklist as possible means of identification of very able children.

Gifted pupils:

1 Possess superior powers of reasoning, of dealing with abstractions, of generalising from specific facts, of understanding meaning, and of seeing into relationships.
2 Have great intellectual curiosity.
3 Learn easily and readily.
4 Have a wide range of interests.
5 Have a broad attention-span that enables them to concentrate on and persevere in solving problems and pursuing interests.
6 Are superior in the quantity and quality of vocabulary as compared with children their own age.

7   Have the ability to do effective work independently.
8   Have learned to read early (often well before school age).
9   Exhibit keen powers of observation.
10 Show initiative and originality in intellectual work.
11 Show alertness and quick response to new ideas.
12 Are able to memorise quickly.
13 Have a great interest in the nature of man and the universe (problems of origins and destiny, etc.).
14 Possess unusual imagination.
15 Follow complex directions easily.
16 Are rapid readers.
17 Have several hobbies.
18 Have reading interests that cover a wide range of subjects.
19 Make frequent and effective use of the library.
20 Are superior in Mathematics, particularly in problem solving.

A number of checklists of this nature can be found in specialist literature. These can serve as aide-memoires in identifying exceptionally able pupils.

The particular challenge for teachers working with exceptionally able pupils is always to provide work that stretches them and to have high expectations (see HMI, 1992: vii). This is, of course, also an aim for all learners: to provide sufficient challenge to enable them to make progress. For some excellent ideas on getting pupils to think, see Lin and Mackay, 2003.

There are also a number of helpful websites, which offer advice on effective teaching of more able FLs learners, such as the QCA's *Guidance on Teaching the Gifted and Talented in Modern Foreign Languages*, available online at: www.bit.ly/gifted-fl.

Task 13.13 IDENTIFYING EXCEPTIONALLY ABLE PUPILS

What FLs specific knowledge, skills and understanding characterise exceptionally able pupils? Draw up a list of indicators which, in your opinion, signal exceptional ability in FL learning and discuss them with your mentor or a class teacher you work with closely.

SOME TEACHING STRATEGIES

When working with exceptionally able pupils, FLs teachers need to look out for the characteristics described above. Tasks, activities and exercises need to be challenging and stimulating for all pupils, including pupils with exceptional ability (see McLachlan, 2002). There is, once again, no distinctive methodology for working with very able pupils or pupils with exceptional ability. The inclusion of extension work into a programme of study building on differentiated learning objectives is a strategy used by FLs departments to cater for more able and exceptionally able learners in a class. Often it is not so much the quantity of work set than its nature that is important. Below are some suggestions, which represent good practice in FL teaching generally but which may appeal to more able and exceptionally able learners in particular.

Using creativity and problem solving

The language prescribed in GCSE examination specifications tends to be functional and can be perceived as narrow. Therefore, student teachers need to ensure, through careful planning, that there is room for 'risk taking' and 'experimenting' with language as this can benefit more able pupils in particular. Working with language can take the form of manipulation. Pupils capable of higher-level work in particular can gain a lot from exploring and articulating thoughts and ideas.

Conundrums and puzzles allow for the use of language by appealing to pupils' imagination. Also, open-ended tasks in the respective TL can present pupils with a challenge allowing them to use their imagination and to solve a problem in a creative way. One example is known as *'Le jeu des poubelles'*. The teacher places a collection of authentic materials and realia in a bag. These might include menus, bus tickets, food wrappers, receipts, magazines, newspaper articles, personal letters or audio recordings. The aim of the activity is for pupils to adopt the role of a detective. This involves scrutinising the materials and (re-)creating a story featuring an imaginary or real person, who has (supposedly) collected the materials during a period of time in the target country. Outcomes can range from creative prose writing to role plays. Activities like this allow for the use of pupils' imagination. They draw on lexis from various topics and require pupils to make use of reference material.

The development of learning activities for peers on their own or in pairs or groups can also offer a challenge to more able pupils in particular.

Going beyond understanding detail

Examination specifications tend not to go much beyond the identification of details within TL texts. Responding to texts by adapting the meaning of poems and songs or drawing out themes and images portrayed in texts are all higher-level skills. To 'experiment' with language extends beyond the manipulation of grammatical forms and can include the expression of meaning through a range of literary techniques.

Fostering independence

Learner independence is important. More able and exceptionally able pupils are often effective independent learners. You can try to build on this by encouraging more able and exceptionally able pupils to reflect on how they learn, practise and exploit new language. They can then devise activities and provide some input for peers, for instance, from time to time become involved in 'teaching' other pupils. Keeping a 'learning diary' is one way to encourage reflection. Work by Dam (1990 and 1995) demonstrates the value of self-evaluation in the TL, both in terms of the ability to manipulate the language learned and in motivating pupils. Striving towards independent language learning and language use is also a feature of teaching and learning FLs at advance level. For a detailed discussion, see Pachler and Field, 1999.

Focusing on accuracy and nuances of language use

To help them improve accuracy, pupils can be encouraged to carry out language analysis tasks such as the comparison of different language styles and registers. To contrast the language forms used in two newspaper articles covering the same story can, for instance, be a very productive way of addressing how language is used beyond conveying essential facts. Again, some strategies recommended for pupils at advanced level may be appropriate for other 'able' pupils (see e.g. Field, 1999 and Powell, 1999).

Conceptualising

In Chapter 11 we argued that grammar requires conceptual thinking. Invariably, this challenge will appeal to some pupils more than others. To provide pupils with texts and examples, and ask them to draw conclusions about the structure of the TL can be a demanding task. Given the opportunity, some pupils might be able to produce explanations, which can be used by you for teaching certain grammar points to the whole class.

Developing extended cultural awareness

To research particular cultural issues with the help, for instance, of articles from the press, reference material or the Internet can appeal to pupils. The focus is on learner independence and the extension of pupils' general knowledge. It can also help pupils to place FL learning into a wider cultural context.

To provide texts such as short stories, poetry and prose to complement topics covered in a scheme of work with extended reading /reading for pleasure is a possible strategy. Work carried out by pupils on such supplementary material needs to be carefully monitored, and time must be made available for feedback and discussion. The outcomes can be rewarding for both the teacher and the learner. Monitoring of progress might be achieved by the pupil recording her efforts in a learner diary. FLs teachers often build into lesson plans and/or their non-contact time – for instance, at break- or lunchtime – opportunities to discuss progress with pupils. This way a record of the work carried out is kept and the pupils themselves are involved in building up a profile of their achievements.

PUPILS WITH MOTIVATIONAL DIFFICULTIES

One particular challenge for FLs teachers are pupils who display behaviour patterns that are disruptive to the delivery of lessons or those who are indifferent to the tasks planned. Pupils in these categories tend to be insufficiently motivated towards their study of FLs. For a detailed discussion of motivation, see Chambers, 1999; see also Bartrum, 2006 for a study on peer group influences.

Internal as well as external motivation facilitate learning. Internal or intrinsic reasons for wanting to learn could, for instance, be the wish of pupils to tell a pen-friend about themselves, the desire to complete a challenging task or to win in a competitive situation. External or extrinsic reasons for wanting to learn could be

Task 13.14 **WORKING WITH EXCEPTIONALLY ABLE PUPILS**

1   Examine activities in an existing unit of work. Consider which of the following, or any other challenging activity types could be added to stretch exceptionally able pupils:

- research skills;
- creative writing;
- extended reading;
- translation;
- conundrums;
- grammar exercises;
- preparing a presentation.

2   Develop relevant materials and, in collaboration with your mentor or a relevant class teacher, plan how to work with (an) exceptionally able pupil(s) on extension tasks throughout the unit of work.

3   When evaluating the project, consider the impact of your work on the attainment and motivation of the pupil(s).

4   Consider how various of these activities might provide suitable challenge for a wider range of pupils.

the need to pass an examination at the end of compulsory schooling as a means of entry into post-compulsory education. Research would suggest that the more immediate the reasons for wanting to learn and the more they can be determined by the learner, the more influential they are. There are some excellent studies on what it is that FL learners see as their reasons for their perceived success or failure in the subject (see Williams *et al.*, 2002, 2004 and Graham, 2004).

Cajkler and Addelman (2000: 2) list some elements to increase motivation.

Fun is obtained from:

- smiles;
- language games;
- competitions that anyone can win;
- competitions that the 'best' can win;
- friendly jokes and quips;
- puzzles;
- problems to solve;
- making things;
- moving about;
- the unexpected;
- the unpredictable;
- the privilege of relaxing now and then;
- success in learning.

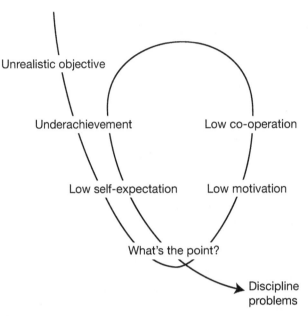

▨ **Figure 13.7** Deane's downward spiral
Source: Deane, 1992: 44.

Motivators include:

- ▨ some kind of reward (time out, a fun activity, a comic to read, etc.);
- ▨ praise by peers;
- ▨ genuine, warm praise by the teacher;
- ▨ a special visitor;
- ▨ an attempt to show that tasks are relevant;
- ▨ a clear understanding of what the task ahead is (notes, target sheets, verbal explanation, work schedules);
- ▨ success in learning.

To make lesson objectives explicit and occasionally to negotiate them with pupils can be motivating. Making objectives explicit is considered to be good and widespread practice as it enables the learners to set targets. Many coursebooks feature unit objectives in the form of a preamble or as a 'can-do' self-check list. The differentiation of objectives and the avoidance of unrealistic objectives are particularly important when working with pupils with motivational difficulties. This is effectively demonstrated by Deane's diagram (see Figure 13.7), which illustrates that to have unrealistic objectives can lead to a 'downward spiral'.

SOME TEACHING STRATEGIES

Below are some additional teaching strategies, which – as the ones already introduced earlier in this chapter – apply to FL teaching generally but might prove to be particularly useful in the context of working with learners with motivational difficulties.

Task 13.15 **THE USE OF EXPLICIT OBJECTIVES**

■ Examine the coursebook used by your placement school for one particular year group from the point of view of whether and how unit objectives are made explicit. Also, observe how the FLs teachers, whose lessons you observe, communicate lesson objectives.

■ Devise an end-of-unit goal for a specific unit of work. Engage pupils in a discussion about what is required to achieve this goal. Make a note of the pupils' comments and then translate these into meaningful learning objectives. This will allow you to measure the value of each planned learning activity by relating it to the agreed objectives.

Target setting

One of the challenges faced by FLs teachers in Secondary schools is the fact that the (externally) accredited assessment of pupils' proficiency tends to take place in the main, particularly in non-modular specifications, only at the very end of pupils' period of study. Because many learners find it difficult to derive motivation from this long-term objective, the content required by the examination specification needs to be broken down into achievable steps and pupils' progress monitored through effective assessment for learning. This way pupils can aim at achieving short-term targets.

Personalised language and purposeful activities

In her book on working with reluctant learners, Alison points out the importance of ensuring that the language pupils are exposed to is 'their own language and that they see a valid purpose in learning it' (Alison, 1993: 15). This is a notion frequently echoed by FLs teachers. For the presentation stage, Alison identifies the strategies of letting pupils find out for themselves what they need to learn and to give them opportunities to show what they already know, while for the practice stage she lists strategies/activities involving speculation, remembering, timing, guessing, the manipulation of objects, competition and the inclusion of pupils' ideas in the lesson.

Emphasis on enjoyment and creativity

Shaw makes a similar suggestion in an account of his experience with reluctant learners, suggesting that pupils should be involved in the production of language where the emphasis is on enjoyment and creativity. He describes a task, which is based on the use of stimulus material from authentic sources – for instance, pictures, short texts or adverts from newspapers or magazines, in English or the TL – as a basis for language production. Pupils are allowed to mix the TL with English. As examples of pupils' work Shaw quotes, for instance: 'uno, dos, tres – I know Shaw's address', 'A man in a dress? Is he inglés? or 'Monumental cities: Vivo en Birkenhead' (Shaw, 1994: 39).

The pacing of lessons and the use of a variety of tasks and material

The pacing of lessons and the use of a variety of tasks and material, which is an important consideration in planning FLs lessons in general, can be seen to be particularly important for pupils with motivational difficulties. Halliwell suggests that there needs to be a balance of 'peace and quiet' as well as 'stimulation and excitement'. In support of this she proposes an important concept for the planning of interactive FLs lessons – namely, the balance of 'settling' and 'stirring' activities (see Halliwell, 1991: 25–26). FLs teachers, she argues, should and do carefully consider whether an activity is 'stirring' – such as oral work, competitions or games – increasing pupils' engagement or whether it is 'settling' – such as copying, labelling or listening – helping to calm pupils and, as a consequence, lessons down (see Halliwell, 1991: 3–4).

Variety in the use of teaching strategies, whole-class work, group work, pair work, independent study, as well as the use of a range of teaching aids such as recordings to the whole class, carousel activities, listening stations, the overhead projector, language games and software, individual technology-orientated work, drama and songs, can help to motivate pupils.

Use of competition

Often, the introduction of a competitive element, which focuses on pooling the strengths of individual pupils in a team or allows pupils to compete against their previous performance or their own targets – rather than on identifying their individual weaknesses for the benefit of a small number of 'winners' for whom the competition serves as motivation – also work well.

The use of vocational contexts

Vocational settings can provide useful contexts for FLs learning. Combining work-related activities with language learning can provide useful contexts for FLs work and can have a beneficial motivational impact. Pupils working through scenarios taken from the world of work are considered to be of motivational value because they are perceived to be relevant to pupils. Both at beginners and intermediate levels the teacher can build in more vocational contexts to the work undertaken in the classroom, whether this aspect is an element of the official external assessment or not.

Task 13.16 **THE USE OF TEACHING STRATEGIES**

With reference to the table in Figure 13.8, observe a number of FLs lessons focusing on what strategies FLs teachers in your placement school use in working with pupils in order to overcome some difficulties commonly experienced by them. Following your observations, discuss with your mentor how you can include these and other suitable strategies in your own teaching.

Pupil difficulty	Strategies observed	Additional strategies identified in discussion with colleagues
Short concentration span		
Poor organisational skills		
Lack of confidence		
Untidy writing		
Weak first language skills		
Isolation from other pupils		
Difficulties with spelling		
Physical/sensory impairments		
Difficulties with memory skills		
Lack of interest generally		
Poor general knowledge and cultural awareness		

■ **Figure 13.8** Catering for individual needs of pupils

WORKING WITH SUPPORT TEACHERS AND TEACHING ASSISTANTS

An important aspect in catering for the different needs of pupils in the FLs classroom is working with support teachers. These might be (peripatetic) SEN specialists, staff specialising in EAL assigned to individual or groups of pupils, teaching assistants or colleagues from within the FLs department providing support with specific groups.

Working in tandem with other adults in the classroom is not always easy for many FLs teachers as it raises a number of important issues such as who is responsible for what aspect of the lesson. Of particular relevance for FLs contexts is the question of what FLs skills a support teacher has. In order to maximise the impact of 'another pair of hands' in the classroom on pupil learning, careful planning of lessons by the FLs specialist together with the support teacher is essential.

As support teachers work very closely with particular pupils they can be intimately familiar with pupils' needs. This expertise can be invaluable, for example, when designing worksheets and other teaching material. Support teachers are often willing to act as a 'model learner' to demonstrate role plays, pair work, games and puzzles. Organising 'carousel' lessons and group work can become easier with help from a support teacher, who can supervise a particularly demanding activity and/or circulate around the classroom. For a detailed discussion of working with other adults in the classroom, see Redondo, 2014a.

Task 13.17 **WORKING WITH SUPPORT TEACHERS – I**

During your work at the placement school, enquire about the nature of support that FLs teachers receive by talking to FLs staff as well as some support teachers. What do they consider to be best practice in collaborative work?

Task 13.18 **WORKING WITH SUPPORT TEACHERS – II**

When working with a support teacher, where possible:

■   design a list of key TL phrases, which will allow the support teacher to help pupils with their productive FLs skills if she is not an FLs specialist;

■   discuss the presentation of material in advance of lessons and adapt existing worksheets; what are the key features and underpinning principles of the changes?

■   consider which support activities the support teacher could use with pupils when a given activity designed for the whole class proves too difficult; a set of very basic activities on numbers, days, dates, personal details, gender rules and other core linguistic items can support her work on the reinforcement of pupils' key linguistic skills.

Task 13.19 **PLANNING A LESSON TAUGHT WITH A SUPPORT TEACHER**

Refer to the sample lesson plan in Chapter 7 (Figure 7.4). Modify this lesson plan by building in the use of a support teacher.

SUMMARY

It is very important to recognise that pupils are individuals with different needs, for instance, due to their ability, gender, interests, motivation, social class, self-concept, self-esteem, ethnic background or creativity and that, therefore, no teaching group is homogenous.

A big challenge for you is to identify individual differences and needs in pupils and to devise strategies to cater for the needs of all pupils in a class.

FURTHER READING

Dörnyei, Z. and Skehan, P. (2003) Individual differences in second language learning. In Doughty, C. and Long, M. (eds) *The Handbook of Second Language Acquisition*. Oxford: Blackwell, pp. 589–630.

This chapter discussed individual differences in second language learning, in particular aptitude, motivation and learning styles.

Pachler, N. and Redondo, A. (eds) (2005) Support for learning: special issue on inclusive approaches to teaching foreign languages. *British Journal of Learning Support* 20(3). NASEN.

The contributions to this special issue of the *BJLS* cover a range of issues across the policy and practice of teaching 'languages for all'.

14 CREATING A MEANINGFUL LEARNING ENVIRONMENT

INTRODUCTION

For the student teacher of FLs faced with the teeming daily realities of school and classroom life on the one hand, and the demands and attractions of new opportunities for teaching and learning on the other, it may be helpful to begin by clarifying three distinct but complementary dimensions of the FL learning environment in school.

1 The classroom as a space for formal instruction

■ The classroom is the main arena in which the TL is taught, information is transmitted, activities are orchestrated and completed, corrective feedback is given and a host of other necessary instructional practices are conducted.

■ For effective teaching and learning to take place within this process, there are at least two important conditions to be met. First, there needs to be good behaviour and discipline within lessons in order that learners are able to focus on the teaching and learning rather than on noisy distractions. Entry and exit from the classroom should be orderly. Younger learners, especially, may need to line up outside the classroom before entering with your permission. Second, good behaviour is usually enabled through the use of clear and consistently applied rules regarding matters such as the completion of homework or misbehaviour in lessons such as calling out or talking during listening comprehension and other activities. Rules are usually accepted by learners if they are seen as part of established routines, especially if the rationale is made clear and if the class can participate in the formulation of the rules.

■ You should ensure a degree of physical tidiness in the room. You cannot expect children to focus on their learning in an orderly way if the classroom is in a state of disorder and disrepair. The pupils should be required to leave the classroom in a tidy state, with chairs pushed in and paper picked up from the floor, and so on. Similarly, you should make a quick check of the state of the room in the few spare minutes you may have before letting the class in.

2 The classroom as a space for informal learning

There are different ways in which the FLs classroom can function as a supportive learning environment for the promotion of FL learning in a school, beyond the didactic, instructional framework described above.

■ The classroom can function as a physically welcoming and supportive hub for FLs activities. This is done through material features such as attractive wall displays of pupils' work, photos of school trips, of partner schools in the target country, of cultural tokens, key classroom TL phrases, resources stores, updated language notices, etc. These stimuli serve several purposes, from spontaneous sources of support during lessons (e.g. posters or phrases can catch the attention of a learner during the lesson and stimulate his or her learning) to more symbolic messages such as an indication that FL learning is important and valued in the school.

■ The classroom can also be the space for out-of-lesson activities such as lunch-time clubs (reading, film, homework, exam revision, conversation practice, learning alternative FLs, etc.) or motivational activities such as 'French breakfasts'.

■ Within lessons, the classroom can be the setting for more flexible learning arrangements (such as carousel activities involving a variety of tasks including digital and analogue resources), active learning through peer and group activities. The classroom thus becomes the space in which orderly but independent movement takes place and supports the FL learning. Such movement can occur with different degrees of freedom, ranging, for instance, from the more controlled movement of dramatised role plays or tasks involving questions or answers pinned around the classroom for pupils to match to more open-ended activities such as oral surveys or project work.

3 The learning environment beyond the classroom

■ Increasingly, the process of FL teaching and learning entails working within a digital environment both within lessons and outside of the classroom.

■ Out-of-school language learning includes trips abroad and school exchanges.

■ Homework has always been a way in which FL learning extends beyond the confines of the classroom but the rationale for the link between homework and in-class learning can benefit from constructive reflection.

The different dimensions outlined above need to be seen as a global framework within which the pupils' FL learning experience can be nurtured and developed. Developing such a culture and context of learning takes time, of course, and requires collective and institutional support. As a student teacher it is important for you to be aware of what the full scope of this potential environment is and how far you can ensure a balance of experiences and opportunities for different modalities of learning for your pupils.

OBJECTIVES

By the end of this chapter you should:

■ have a sense of the value of the three dimensions of the FL learning environment: formal, informal and beyond the classroom;
■ recognise the need to integrate opportunities for learning in these three modes within your planning;
■ have developed an understanding of classroom management issues and how to construct an appropriate learning environment in your lessons and classroom;
■ understand the principles behind the management and use of resources in FLs lessons;
■ reflect constructively about the role of homework;
■ have some knowledge about the impact of school exchanges on pupils' learning and motivation.

THEORETICAL RATIONALE: THE FLs CLASSROOM AS AN ECOSYSTEM

The relentless pace of change and innovation in the technological and educational contexts of contemporary Western schooling environments means that thinking about management of the learning environment requires clarity in distinguishing between a complex set of interconnecting issues. To some extent the conditions for this context are set by external socio-political factors over which the individual teacher has no immediate control. Van Lier (2010: 600), for instance, refers to the 'ecological' nature of this condition as follows:

> The language classroom is not an island unto itself. Whatever happens in the classroom is connected in multiple ways to issues in the school, the family, the community, local educational authorities, government agencies, ideological and cultural pressures of the moment and so on.

However, as van Lier also argues (2011: 390–391), a further influence on the ecology of the classroom is the teacher as promoter of agency:

> I define agency as movement [. . .]. This means physical, social and intellectual movement. There are a number of preconditions to the possibility of movement. For example, physical movement may be hampered by material obstructions; social movement may be obstructed by 'not getting a word in edgeways'; intellectual movement may be obstructed by habitus, indoctrination, fear, or lack of awareness. On the other side of the coin, agency may be enabled by perceptual learning, initiative taking, engaging in discourse, critical reflection, and many other processes that can be fostered in an ethical and moral education.

Wright (2005: 101) explains the 'classroom as ecology' metaphor by describing the classroom 'as a complex and multidimensional system [which] emerges from the dynamic and interaction of learning goals, learning opportunities, learners and learning and teachers and teaching in classroom contexts'. How are you to assume this role in order to create a meaningful learning environment for your pupils? This question is the focus of this chapter.

THE CLASSROOM AS SPACE FOR FORMAL INSTRUCTION

Class management

In our view, good practice in FL teaching in the Secondary school is characterised by a balanced and purposeful use of a range of different types of material and resources. Each of the various types of material and resources has the potential to enhance, support and structure learning. Variety can help you to appeal to pupils' wide range of learning styles and interests.

In order to deploy a range of material and resources to provide the variety of activities required to maintain pupils' interests, you need to establish an agreed code of conduct. This must not be at variance with any school code of conduct and procedures. You must ensure that any classroom rules you implement reflect whole-school/departmental policy as appropriate.

Use of the TL for classroom management purposes demands careful consideration. Wragg (1984: 67) listed the following eleven most common rules used by teachers (see Task 14.1) and you should consider how they can be operationalised in the TL.

Task 14.1 **TYPES OF CLASSROOM RULES**

To what extent are the following types of rules listed by Wragg relevant to the FLs classroom?

- no talking when the teacher is talking;
- no disruptive noises;
- rules for entering, leaving and moving around the classroom;
- no interference in the work of others;
- work must be completed in a specified way;
- pupils must raise their hand – not shout out;
- pupils must make a positive effort in their work;
- pupils must not challenge the authority of the teacher;
- pupils must show respect for property and equipment;
- rules to do with safety;
- pupils must ask if they do not understand.

Consider how these classroom rules might be adapted and presented to pupils through use of the TL. This may include displays with symbols and pictures, role plays and teacher-led presentations. How can these be reinforced through regular use? What rewards and sanctions could be linked to the code?

Establishing and maintaining a code of conduct through rules, routines and procedures demand that you draw on a wide range of presentation and communication skills. All pupils must understand the code and recognise its value as well as the need for sanctions when it is breached. At times, classroom management will require you to use non-verbal communication as pupils may find a TL explanation difficult to follow and may feign non-comprehension as a work avoidance strategy. You must take care to be aware of gestures and postures, which signal different messages in different cultures. Not only do you need to develop and use these skills, you also need to be able to read the body language of pupils to gauge levels of interest, motivation and involvement. Robertson (1989) identifies some aspects of body language that facilitate communication and contribute to the development of positive relationships:

- *body orientation*: your position in relation to pupils helps to determine role definition. While face-to-face on a one-to-one basis can be perceived to be confrontational, sitting side-by-side can lead to higher levels of co-operation. This is relevant for teacher–pupil (helping individuals) and pupil–pupil (e.g. pair work) interaction.
- *bodily posture*: standing straight with the chin held high tends to indicate a wish to dominate (whole-class work). Leaning towards someone with a warm smile can indicate encouragement (question and answer activities).
- *head movements*: nodding is important as it signals permission to speak as well as agreement. Reticent speakers can be encouraged in this way (question-and-answer work).
- *eye contact*: eye contact can be seen as a sign of mutual respect. The higher the interest level in a person/topic, the greater the amount of eye contact tends to be (whole-class teaching).
- *use of voice*: volume, pitch, tone, speed, expressiveness and articulation can convey messages associated with mood, e.g. anger, calm, frustration, control, interest or boredom. It is essential to exaggerate features like these to accentuate the precise meaning of what is being said (as well as to ensure that greater attention is maintained rather than the 'switching off' which may occur with a monotonous voice).
- *hands and feet*: open postures (hands and feet pointing slightly outwards) convey a sense of welcome and calm. 'Inward pointing' represents insecurity.
- *facial expressions*: exaggerated expressions, e.g. smiles, frowns, inquisitive looks, agreement, pleasure, should all be part of your repertoire.

Task 14.2 GIVING BASIC INSTRUCTIONS

Conduct a brief microteaching session with other student teachers on the theme of giving classroom instructions. As the teacher, mime all instructions (coats off, bags on the floor, pens out, books on the table, listen, repeat, copy, etc.). Once your peers have mastered the messages you are conveying, list each instruction and add the simplest form of the TL to the mimes.

Selection and use of material and resources need to be determined by the intended learning outcomes. Effective use of certain material and resources requires particular types of activities and pupil response and the use of certain material and resources in turn affects classroom layout and seating arrangements. The characteristics of each classroom and each group, established practice, the age of the pupils and the types of planned activities all affect your decisions about room layout. The use of particular resources requires focused individual work, the use of reference material, interaction with others through group and pair work or movement around the classroom to support communication (e.g. surveys). You need to consider carefully the seating arrangements that best facilitate different activity types. You should experiment with different classroom layouts. However, you should not do so without consulting the respective class teacher.

Essentially, four types of classroom layout can be distinguished:

1   *Rows*: one advantage of seating pupils in rows is that they are less able to copy and disrupt through inappropriate talk. Sitting in a row assists with concentration and disruptive pupils can be isolated from others in the class. One disadvantage is that the arrangement hinders collaborative and co-operative work. Pupils are unable to see each other's faces to assist them in the communicative process. Also, the sharing of resources and material can be problematic.

2   *The horseshoe*: the teacher can stand or sit in the centre and thereby have ready access to all pupils. Pupils are able to see each other and pair work is relatively simple to organise. However, movement to the corners of the classroom can be difficult. The teacher is almost always face-to-face with pupils, even when assisting individuals with independent work.

3   *Groups of desks*: not all pupils are facing the teacher for whole-class work. Due to the proximity to each other, pupils might be tempted to interfere with each other's equipment. However, this greatly facilitates interaction between pupils for both group and pair work. Movement around the classroom can be eased by careful placement of desks.

4   *Desks placed around the edge of the room*: many computer rooms, for example, require pupils to face the wall, which can prevent distraction by other pupils. Often this provides a large space in the middle of a room, where teachers can work with groups of pupils who require support or extension. This arrangement can also be useful for carousel lessons. However, pupil collaboration for pupils seated around the edge of the room can be difficult, particularly where there is insufficient space between work stations or where there are no swivel chairs. Whole-class explanations require pupils to move their positions.

USE OF RESOURCES: THE COURSEBOOK

For many pupils the coursebook is their first point of contact with the TL and its culture(s). It can offer a form of security in that it organises the language content and conveys messages about the values, attitudes and culture of TL speakers, albeit from the point of view of its writer; the user needs to beware of this:

> One of the functions of coursebooks is to present the language in such a way that it is learned as effectively and quickly as possible. This implies that the coursebook writers have a view on how language is learned and how it is best taught. Although the coursebook may not seek to impose a rigid methodology on learners and teachers, nevertheless the way it organises its material and the kind of activities it promotes can have a profound influence on what happens in the classroom.
>
> (Cunningsworth, 1995: 97)

Recent coursebooks tend to be structured and tailored to suit examination specifications and the statutory requirements such as the use of the TL for instructions and explanations. Many coursebooks and teachers' books cross-reference activities and tasks to the National Curriculum in order to help you in your planning. Frequently, colourful photographs are used and (quasi-)authentic texts to provide cultural detail in an attempt to open up pupils' minds. It could be argued that coursebooks are a quasi-authentic window to the life and culture of native speakers.

Coursebooks can contain brief summaries of the content in terms of vocabulary, structures and grammatical rules linked to particular exercises. Some provide examination practice. The coursebook can help you in sequencing activities to bridge the gap between the known and the new, and provide graded exercises allowing for steady progression and lead towards independent study. It can function as a resource for presenting new language, contain reference sections on grammar and vocabulary, stimuli for classroom activities and self-directed study, as well as support for student teachers (see Cunningsworth 1995: 7; Barnes, 1997).

The coursebook is primarily a resource and learning tool for pupils. It is a resource that enables pupils to work independently from the teacher. This, in turn, allows you to work with individual pupils. When using a coursebook, you need to bear in mind common causes of misbehaviour identified by Davison (2000: 122): 'boredom; an inability to do the work a teacher has set; and effort demanded for too long a period without a break'. You therefore need to ensure that instructions are clear and understood by all pupils. Comprehension checks are essential and they can take different forms. First, TL instructions can be translated by a pupil for the whole class. You can use question-and-answer techniques to ensure comprehension. Visual displays of instructions, particularly when there is more than one exercise to be completed, and demonstrations of the activity by way of an example prior to pupils commencing are very useful. Second, you should not set independent work until whole-class work has enabled the practice of specific language skills and has established a confidence in pupils to undertake the task. Finally, you should set clear time limits for activities, enabling learners to pace themselves. This should, of course, be done as appropriate in the TL. Such an approach helps to establish a routine as well as a secure working environment.

Davison (2000: 126) also points out that a teacher should be 'on hand to give academic help'. Once again, it is crucial to establish routines: raising their hand before talking or using reference material before asking you are widely used strategies. Pupils should be made aware of the need to wait their turn, to ask courteously, where possible in the TL, and not to waste time waiting for assistance while you attend to other pupils but to attempt another aspect of the activity in the meantime.

It would be erroneous to assume that careful plans never go wrong. In particular, during pair, group and/or independent work it is difficult for you to be sure that all pupils are on task and fully engaged all the time. Sometimes you may need to reprimand some pupils. The behaviour, not the pupil, should be criticised and 'quiet words' are often more helpful than whole-class reprimands. Very often positioning yourself near to potential miscreants, stares, using body language and gestures can refocus pupils without creating a hostile and confrontational atmosphere. More serious misbehaviour may require more serious action.

During individual work you need to circulate to assist pupils with difficulties and also to 'police' the activity. Research carried out in the US (see Taylor, 1994: 162) indicates that quick teacher feedback and the close monitoring of individual performance increase the quality of pupils' work. While pupils are working individually using the coursebook, you should monitor the class by looking and walking around the room. When assisting individuals, it is sensible to place yourself so that you can see the majority of the rest of the class. Turning your back to the majority of the class can be an invitation to pupils to display off-task behaviour.

Kyriacou (1991: 53) calls qualities like those described above 'withitness' and suggests that these skills improve with experience. Task 14.3 sets out a step-by-step approach to developing 'withitness'.

Task 14.3 **WITHITNESS**

1   Observe an experienced teacher engaging pupils in independent and individual work. Try to identify signs of misbehaviour.
2   Relate the signs of misbehaviour to possible causes.
3   Identify strategies deployed by experienced teachers, which create the belief that they have eyes in the back of their heads.

Pitfalls and possible problems

No coursebook is perfect. In some, the presentation of new language and structures can appear cluttered. Because of a focus on the introduction and practice of new language in a wide range of topics, there are rarely extended passages. The cultural aspect of a coursebook can date quickly, which can lead to a false impression of the culture of the countries where the TL is spoken. To introduce cartoons and fictional characters in a bid to achieve greater durability by being less susceptible to changes in fashions and trends runs the risk of presenting a stereotyped or even non-TL culture-specific view of life in the target countries. Language is underpinned by the cultural and social context of its use. For commercial reasons, coursebooks tend to be designed for as large an audience as possible. They are, therefore, invariably impersonal and pupils may associate them more with life in the classroom than life in the countries where the TL is spoken. The extent to which coursebooks allow for the 'personalisation' of language through solving realistic problems through authentic communication tends to be limited.

Understandably, coursebooks reflect the writers' own preferred methodology. Grammar, for example, can be presented inductively or deductively but there often tends not to be much of a choice of methods within one coursebook. When using the coursebook as a guide to unit of work and lesson planning, you therefore need to exercise professional judgement according to the learning needs of pupils and make deliberate choices and select those materials best suited to achieving the learning objectives identified for a particular class.

Obviously, too, the coursebook is limited in its coverage of the examination specification. According to Cunningsworth (1995: 55), syllabuses tend to contain the following:

■ forms: structures and grammar;
■ functions: communicative purpose;
■ situations: context of language use;
■ topics.

A coursebook contains a finite set of activities and exercises to cover these four aspects, which can be adequate but may also be either insufficient or ample in number. This means that you need to be either selective or to supplement according to the needs of pupils and the time available. Often and importantly, you also need to grade and sequence the activities in a coursebook to take account of the needs of a particular class.

Unlike in some continental European education systems, coursebooks do not have to be vetted by the respective government ministries for suitability. FLs departments in UK Secondary schools are free to choose coursebooks from competing publishers (or not to choose one at all and to create a tailored set of resources for the department). FLs teachers need to judge the suitability of coursebooks for themselves. Many questions need to be asked about a coursebook:

■ Does the coursebook lend itself to extending an active knowledge of vocabulary and does it stimulate oral work in a variety of contexts?
■ Is the accompanying listening material appropriate?
■ Does the coursebook develop reading strategies through a variety of types of text encouraging the use of a range of reading skills and providing information of real interest?
■ Does it serve as a model of accurate writing in appropriate styles?
■ Is grammar presented as well as recycled in an attractive and meaningful way?
■ Is an accurate cultural impression presented, free of negative stereotyping in terms of class, gender, race, ethnicity, social relationships and personal feelings?

The coursebook is a teaching and learning tool and should be used and adapted to fit a specific learning context rather than simply be followed. Cunningsworth (1995: 137) suggests a useful method to decide whether to adapt an exercise or change it altogether. This method is shown in a slightly modified form in Figure 14.1.

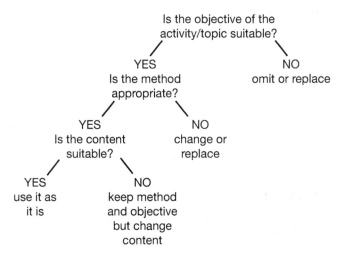

Is the objective of the
activity/topic suitable?

YES — Is the method appropriate?   NO — omit or replace

YES — Is the content suitable?   NO — change or replace

YES — use it as it is   NO — keep method and objective but change content

■ **Figure 14.1** Flow chart for evaluating activities in coursebooks

Source: Based on Cunningsworth, 1995: 137.

Task 14.4 **EVALUATING A COURSEBOOK**

The following task is meant to help you to evaluate a coursebook.

Select a coursebook used by a class you have observed or teach and use the criteria in Figure 14.2 to evaluate it.

Where any responses to these questions are negative, consider in what ways the course material could be supplemented and/or adapted.

(Adapted from Cunningsworth, 1995: 3–4)

No.	Criteria	Evaluation
A	**Aims and objectives**	
1	Do the aims of the coursebook correspond to the aims and objectives expressed in the units of work?	
2	Does the coursebook allow for different teaching and learning styles?	
3	Is the coursebook comprehensive in its coverage of topics?	
B	**Design and organisation**	
1	What components make up the total course?	
2	How is the content organised? (structures, functions, topics, skills)	
3	Are the grading of exercises and progression suitable for all learners?	
4	Is there adequate recycling and revision?	
5	Are there reference sections? (grammar, vocabulary, etc.).	

■ **Figure 14.2** Criteria for choosing a coursebook

C	Language content	
1	Does the coursebook provide material and activities to allow for vocabulary and grammar learning?	
2	Does the material include opportunities for pronunciation work?	
3	Are style and appropriacy accounted for?	
4	Are there examples of language use in a range of contexts?	
D	Skills	
1	Is equal emphasis placed on the development of all four skills?	
2	Are there opportunities for the integration of skills?	
3	Is the content of extended reading passages suitable for learners' interests and the level of the majority?	
4	Are listening materials authentic and accompanied by background information? Are exercises graded?	
5	Are speaking activities designed to equip learners for real-life interactions?	
6	Do writing activities allow for a suitable range of styles?	
E	Topics	
1	Is there enough variety and range of topics?	
2	Will the topics help to expand learners' cultural awareness?	
3	Are women portrayed and represented equally to men?	
4	Are people represented with reference to ethnic origin, occupation, disability, etc.?	
F	Methodology	
1	Is the methodology underpinning the coursebook suitable for the learning environment?	
2	What level of learner involvement is expected?	
3	How broad is the range of activities for presenting new language?	
4	Is communicative competence developed?	
5	Does the coursebook contain advice to learners on study skills and learning strategies?	
G	Teacher's book	
1	Is there adequate guidance for teachers on the use of the coursebook and accompanying materials?	
2	Does accompanying material adequately cover teaching techniques for language items such as grammar and culturally specific information?	
H	Practical considerations	
1	What is the total cost of the coursebook and associated material?	
2	Are the books strong and long lasting?	
3	Are the materials attractive?	
4	Do any of the materials require particular equipment and if so are these available in the department?	
5	Can the course be used without particular materials?	
6	What can and cannot be copied?	

■ **Figure 14.2** *continued*

USE OF RESOURCES: VISUAL AIDS

Visual aids are often used to present new language forms and to promote the practice of the language skills of listening, speaking, reading and writing. They provide a non-verbal link between the actual language used and the idea or concept expressed. Nunan (1989: 195) notes that the use of realia and/or symbolic representation is close to the 'natural approach'. As the link between words and concepts represented by visual aids is in the main arbitrary – with possibly the exception of onomatopoetic words – they can be used to avoid translation. Translation could be considered an obstacle at this early stage of learning as it can slow down and lengthen the process of skill development. An over-emphasis on word-for-word translation can be considered as a hindrance. For more on translation, see Chapters 3 and 8.

In order to facilitate the learning process, visual aids should be clear and instantly recognisable. You need to help the learner progress beyond simple one-word utterances. Visual aids should, therefore, also represent a series of words and phrases rather than just single items. It should be recognisable by all pupils, irrespective, for instance, of their ethnic or social background, but at the same time it should represent the cultural context of the TL where possible. The use of bold colours and simple pictorial representations tend to ensure easy recognition by pupils.

The use of flashcards is usually associated with whole-class work. It requires high levels of pupil concentration and participation. Ground rules need to be clear. You need to make the conditions clear and to establish routines for different activity types. Pupils are required to speak publicly, which demands a non-threatening and supportive atmosphere. Kyriacou (1991: 66) asserts the need for the teacher to appear calm and controlled. Placing flashcards in order, not dropping them on the floor, effectively targeting and sequencing of questions all contribute to this aura. You may well wish to script questions on the reverse side of flashcards or, with PowerPoint, to use private notes screen in 'Presenter View', in order to ensure pace and flow.

Visual stimuli should be made visible to all pupils. The layout of the classroom is important. A horseshoe layout lends itself well to flashcard work, enabling equal access for all pupils and allowing you to approach individuals as a means of securing their attention and targeting questions.

You need to make it a priority to get to know and use pupils' names to be able to target questions. Individual pupils should be asked questions they can answer, to encourage participation. For some this will involve simple repetition and for others the answering of open questions. You should use praise and encouragement freely. Pupils failing to respond should be asked similar questions again at a later stage to demonstrate care and concern for their progress. This helps you to demonstrate that you make good use of pupil responses and that learning outcomes are ensured for all pupils in the class (see Kyriacou, 1986: 105).

A further teaching skill identified by Kyriacou in whole-class teaching activities is the maintenance of pace and flow. Maintaining pace means adjusting activities as pupils seem ready, not necessarily changing resources. Very often activities to follow the use of flashcards and other visuals are slower in pace and calming. Halliwell (1991: 3–4) refers to the notion of 'stirrers' and 'settlers', which can help to maximise pupil participation and prevents the risk of over-excitement.

An important purpose of using visual aids is to illustrate the meaning of new lexical items and to enable the learner to discriminate between key sounds and peripheral detail. Visual aids can motivate pupils to speak by providing non-verbal clues and by creating a context for communication. They can also be used to encourage interaction through pupil involvement. Once pupils are able to discriminate sounds, words and phrases, flashcards can be distributed among pupils and games be played. Learners can give instructions for moving text or images on the interactive whiteboard or a story can be built up step-by-step as images appear in or out of sequence on the screen. You need not direct activities yourself but pupils can be asked to come to the screen or handle the flashcards. Information introduced in this way can offer a recognisable, colourful and attractive context for writing. Pictorial representations can be used to decorate texts and provide clues for gist comprehension as well as the extraction of detail in reading exercises. Similarly, cue cards can be used to focus pupils' attention when carrying out listening comprehension work.

In his discussion of the use of images and pictures in FL teaching and learning, Allford (2000) usefully distinguishes 'convergent' and 'divergent' exploitation tasks. He argues that divergent, i.e. open-ended tasks, should be used where possible to maximise opportunities for spontaneous and meaningful productive language use. Allford stresses that convergent, i.e. closed and often inauthentic tasks, can limit the potential value of images and pictures in the FL learning process. In the use of pictorial images the distinction between learning new language, which may entail a focus on form, and language use, which is suited to essential practice of already familiar language, should not be overlooked.

Pitfalls and possible problems

The use of visual aids can be exciting and stimulating. Visual aids can be very effective tools to encourage repetition and the reproduction of language forms. Therefore, you need to develop the necessary skills for using them effectively. However, you need to bear in mind the need for pupils to make real progress in their learning. Audio-visual course material used in the late 1960s and 1970s followed a set format: learners listened to 'texts' and watched film strips. For each and every unit they listened, repeated and responded to simple questions. The film strip prompted reactions from the learner. The content of each unit of work remained distinct and separate from the previous units. Consequently, learners found it difficult to transfer known language to, and use it in, this new context. You need to be aware that they run the same risk when using visual aids. This is not to belittle the value of visual aids in the language learning process, however.

Over-use of one set of visual aids can be stultifying. Given the limited range within any particular topic, activities need to be changed regularly to maintain pupils' interest. You need to provide ample opportunity for practice, reusing the same language forms within different contexts.

One phrase should be represented by one visual symbol. Consistency is important: to introduce new images for familiar language can be seen to be as ineffective as to introduce new language with known images. Visual aids tend to be used by FLs teachers as a strategy to achieve a number of different purposes such as to increase comprehension, facilitate interaction, avoid translation or increase cultural awareness.

Once able to respond comfortably to visual aids in a teacher-centred activity, pupils can be asked to use small cards depicting similar images for a variety of activities. For instance, a game of 'pairs' can be played providing pupils with opportunities to practise new language. Pupils put the cards upside down on the desk and have to remember where matching pairs can be found.

'Happy families' requires pupils to communicate information to each other. Accurate communication is rewarded by obtaining a card from a peer. Pupils need to complete a set of four to win. For instance, cards depicting four goods, which can be bought from four different shops, can be made into playing cards. The entire pack of sixteen is shuffled and distributed to four players. Player 1 turns to her left and asks Player 2 in the TL for a particular item: '¿*Tienes el queso?*' ('Have you got the cheese?') or the name of the shop where they can purchase certain types of goods '¿*Tienes algo de la carnicería?*' ('Have you got anything from the butcher's?'). If Player 2 has the card depicting the item in question or a relevant card, she must pass it to Player 1. Player 1 will give Player 2 a card of her choice (which she does not feel she needs) in return. If Player 2 does not have a relevant card she will reply: '*Lo siento, no tengo.*' ('I'm sorry I haven't got it'). Player 2 then turns to Player 3 and requests a card. The conversations continue around in this way until one player has a full set and wins the game. In this example, visual aids in the form of cue cards clearly stimulate real communication. Yet the range of language is restricted to suit the language abilities of the players.

Task 14.5 **VISUAL AIDS**

Which visual aids are used by FLs teachers at your school experience school?

1   With reference to Figure 14.3 and through discussions with FLs teachers, find out the purposes for using the aids. Which visual aids fulfil which of the stated purposes?
2   Does the use of visual aids require specific classroom management strategies?
3   Use visual aids in a collaborative teaching situation for a particular purpose, which you should agree on with the relevant class teacher.

USE OF RESOURCES: RECORDED MATERIAL (ANALOGUE AND DIGITAL)

Apart from representing a welcome change from the sound of the teacher's voice, the use of recorded material provides faithful reproduction of authentic speech and examples of relevant vocabulary and grammatical items in quasi-authentic situations. Listening to recorded texts can obviously improve comprehension but it can also stimulate language production. In terms of comprehension it is important to exploit the fact that recordings can be replayed. The recordings are 'faithful' in that each time a passage is replayed it remains the same. The speakers' intonation, pronunciation and accent as well as the accompanying background noise are constant. This allows for the development of comprehension in stages (see Dakin, 1976: 167–168). Learners need to have the opportunity to decipher the sound system independently of the information processing required, to orientate themselves, to

Purpose	Presentation software	Flashcards	Cue cards	OHP	Realia	Displays
To encourage oral presentation						
To aid comprehension						
To present new language						
To increase cultural awareness						
To provide a context for language use						
To enable communication and interaction						
To avoid translation						
Other – specify						

■ **Figure 14.3** Purposes of the use of visual aids

pick out relevant detail and then to confirm that they have constructed correct forms of meaning when listening. Recordings allow you to structure language production and use repetition. Using recordings allows learners to note that different speakers share a phonology despite varying local accents. Indeed, learners need to be aware of the range of regional accents in order to be prepared for future language use.

Recorded material is also a valuable resource as a stimulus for more independent language use. Activities requiring non-verbal responses to record details expressed in passages allow pupils to rebuild 'texts'. Coursebooks nearly always provide transcripts for the passages contained on the accompanying audio material. These allow for the skills of reading and writing to be integrated with listening and for work to focus on the particular language forms used. Activities can be devised using transcripts of recordings: this sort of activity can help reinforce the sound/spelling links so important for language development.

Digital audio recordings can be made available to pupils for use on portable devices such as MP3 players and computers and hand-held digital recording devices allow for easy recording of oral language production. Useful free software packages in this context are Audacity, a free, open source software for recording and editing sounds available online at: www.audacity.sourceforge.net, or PocketVoice, a freeware sound recorder at www.xemico.com/pvr.

The ubiquity of digital video recording devices, such as digital video (DV) cameras and mobile phones, allows for easy production of DV material and resources. And website such as YouTube, as well as streaming of video content by TV stations over the Internet allow for easy access to DV material. However, in view of the use of audio rather than video recordings in examinations, there remains a need to work with audio recordings as well. For a detailed discussion of DV production, see Burn and Durran (2013). For details on the use of speech technologies in FL teaching and learning, see Pachler (2002).

Pitfalls and possible problems

Audio recordings lack the glamour of video recordings, and comprehension of the spoken word can be very demanding without access to the accompanying para-linguistic support of gestures, expressions and visual background/contextualisation. Dakin comments on the dangers of using recorded material purely for drill purposes.

The benefits are limited when learners use language as if there is 'an absence of meaning' (Dakin, 1976: 57). In order to be realistic, listening must take place in a context, so that the listener can place the language heard into a perceived situation, helping understanding of what the speaker means. The placing of a passage into a communicative context may well be a preliminary task, yet it is essential to do so in order to convey relevance and meaning of a passage. For a detailed discussion of the teaching of listening skills, see Chapter 9.

Audio material can be an effective tool in developing good linguistic habits. There is a place for repetition and drill exercises, for instance, through listening to songs and rhymes. Pronunciation can be focused on without necessarily fully comprehending the words. To attempt to place such an activity in a communicative context is worthy but may well lead to frustration. Pupils may opt out and resort to the 'tum te tum' effect described by Dakin (1976: 55), when pupils imitate the sounds without distinguishing the words. It is difficult to separate listening comprehension skills from memorising. Many pupils may need to hear a passage several times.

Many teachers view listening activities as 'settlers'. Use of recordings in whole-class situations requires silence, which you need to ensure before the listening activity commences. Frequently pupils disrupt listening activities with questions, which could have been answered in advance. Clear instructions often include a statement on how many times a passage will be heard, that pupils need to sit quietly throughout, that answers required are verbal or non-verbal, that answers are expected in the TL/L1 or in note form/full sentences and that questions do/don't follow the structure of the text.

As a whole-class activity, recorded material should be able to be heard by all and there should be no loose trailing wires that represent a health and safety hazard. Standing centre stage and needing to respond to pupils appearing to lose concentration, without making a noise, is demanding. It is during such activities that body language, gestures, eye contact, classroom scanning are essential. Pupils should be aware that any form of misbehaviour impinges on the quality of learning of others, and that misdemeanours will be noticed and dealt with afterwards. You should avoid disturbing the whole class for the sake of one miscreant, but must not allow this to prevent action being taken. An essential part of Kyriacou's concept of 'withitness' is the readiness on the part of the teacher to take action.

It is clear that the use of audio recordings is invaluable. However, you need to be confident in using them and selective in your choice of listening material. An awareness of what makes a passage difficult beyond the actual content facilitates the selection of 'texts'. Length of passage, speed of speech, local accents, background noise, number of speakers all contribute to the difficulty of a text. Activities need to be carefully structured to suit the learning process and the level of difficulty of tasks needs to be increased gradually. Support for less able listeners – for instance, in the form of differentiated listening tasks, is crucial. Visual aids in the form of clues and prompts can be used to provide such support. Pupils need to know the purpose of listening activities and, in order to prevent constant interruption, pupils should be informed in advance of how many times they will hear the passage.

Task 14.6 **USING RECORDED MATERIAL**

Listen to a range of recorded material from a variety of courses.

■ What do you notice about the different approaches?
■ Which type of passage lends itself to repetition, gist understanding, extraction of detail, rebuilding of language or stimulates language production?

THE CLASSROOM AS A SPACE FOR INFORMAL LEARNING

Within the context of a FLs lesson, informal learning can refer to those more open-ended contexts of learning in which learners have the opportunity to develop autonomy both with regard to their language learning behaviour and with regard to their TL use, the opportunity for incidental where noticing of items and patterns in the TL occurs in an unplanned way and on an individual basis for the learner. The role of the teacher is to manage this context, and to monitor and facilitate this process.

Pair work

Pair work needs very careful management. Kagan (1998, quoted in Bennett and Dunne, 1994: 166) points out that co-operative learning must be accompanied by effective classroom management, which includes paying attention to pupil behaviour and the structure and sequence of activities in a lesson. Bennett and Dunne (1994: 171) also quote the findings of the National Oracy Project, suggesting that pair work is a helpful preparation for group work and that younger pupils respond more positively to the smaller grouping.

Deciding on pairs is important. Quick practice (and this, of course, can be limited to *very* quick practice, e.g. 15 seconds to practise three new vocabulary items) is often best undertaken by friendship pairs or two pupils positioned side-by-side. This reduces unnecessary movement. Instructions need to be clear and noise is an important issue. Denscombe (1980, quoted in Kyriacou, 1991: 62) suggests that loudness does not necessarily equate to a loss of control. We concur with this observation; if interaction is purposeful, you should allow acceptable levels of noise.

The sequence and structure of a lesson are crucial. Pair work requires careful preparation and demonstration. The length of an activity needs to be spelled out clearly. During pair work you should circulate around the class, listening to pupils' oral work, making informal and formative assessments. This way, pupils know that an activity is important. To avoid the indignity of trying to shout louder than a classroom full of pupils speaking at once, you can circulate, giving advance warning that a pair work activity is due to end imminently. Pupils also need time to quieten down. Once warned that an activity is coming to an end, an effective strategy to achieve silence is to count backwards from ten to zero in the TL, encouraging pupils to join in the 'countdown' or have a distinctive timer or piece of digitally recorded music. Such a routine, once established, can be very effective. Another is to write 'silence' on the board slowly in the TL until all pupils fall quiet. Following pair work activities, you can reward good work by asking some pairs to demonstrate to the class. Transitions from one activity to another are always problematic and need to be planned for. Pair work, which can be hectic and exciting, is a relatively high-risk activity in this respect. You need to develop a bank of strategies to end 'stirrers' effectively and to continue with 'settlers'.

Task 14.7 **ENDING LIVELY ACTIVITIES**

Observe experienced teachers, including those in other subject areas such as music and drama, and note:

■   the ways lively activities are brought to a close;
■   the types of activities that follow lively activities.

Group work

In principle, managing group work is not so different from pair work. Group work, however, often takes longer and pupils perform different roles within the small group. Group work rarely requires only a single instruction. Projects demand discussion, negotiation, planning, redrafting and presentation. Pupils can be allocated tasks to fit these demands – scribe, researcher, presenter, actor, editor, etc. Clear instructions and briefing sheets in the TL are helpful. Pupils need to be aware of the need for teamwork and how they can interact with peers to inform their own contributions. This involves careful consideration of groupings – mixed ability, gender mix, ability groups, friendships, learning needs, etc. As Bennett and Dunne (1994: 167) note, the structure of lessons, where co-operative work takes place, is complex and pupils must be prepared to assume different roles from traditional teacher-led situations.

Research into the optimum size of groups (see Kagan, 1988) has come to no firm conclusions, but you should, nevertheless, be aware of some of the findings. Teams of four are suggested as the ideal, teams of three often result in two teaming up together and excluding the third. Teams of five can lead to cliques. On the other hand, the larger the number of pupils in a group, the greater the possible lines of communication. A final issue is the number of roles required by the task set. You should bear these issues in mind when planning for group work.

Pupils can be prepared for group tasks from the start of a lesson. As they enter the classroom, you should determine seating arrangements. You can place coloured or numbered cards on tables. On entering the classroom each pupil is given coloured or numbered slips of paper indicating which table to sit at. This prevents unnecessary movement during the lesson and also signals that you are in control. The mechanics of grouping pupils are relatively simple. However, the reasons for placing pupils in defined groups are often complex and requires your professional judgement.

Authentic material

When asked at interview how to make the learning of a FL interesting, many prospective FLs student teachers reply that they would appeal to pupils' interests. Authentic materials offer you the opportunity to expose pupils to material produced for 'real', out-of-classroom contexts and for specific purposes. With the arrival of the Internet, this task has become much easier for you.

Authentic materials can be one very effective resource. If used sensibly and sensitively they can motivate pupils, particularly if they are up to date and reflect the current context and culture(s) of the TL. Their use fits well within the aims and objectives underpinning communicative language teaching.

Authentic texts, either for listening, reading or viewing, are produced not with didactic-pedagogical objectives in mind but with the general intention of conveying information and/or ideas to speakers of the TL. The focus is on the message and tools other than language are used to help to communicate this message. The format and design, the style and, indeed, the content are moulded to suit a particular audience or readership. As a consequence, authentic material contains cultural information and overt clues to meaning. The level of language, therefore, need not be the sole determining factor for suitability. Learners can draw on their existing general knowledge to predict meaning.

In their book on learning languages from authentic texts, Little *et al.* (1989: 29–67) discuss a number of exercise types for working with authentic texts such as the use of comprehension questions, information extraction techniques, predictive activities, vocabulary organisation, productive exercise chains, rewriting texts or letter writing.

Use of authentic material serves several purposes. Simple props such as labels, packets, menus, timetables and advertisements can provide the bridge between the classroom and the real world. This bridge can reinforce your aim of demonstrating that what is taught and learned in the classroom is actually of real use. The very fact that the material is recognisably designed to fulfil a social function can be motivating.

Undoubtedly, material must be selected with care. Pupils need to be able to understand and interact with the content, and this is clearly not through word-for-word translation. Apart from drawing on existing skills and knowledge, pupils can develop particular strategies for comprehension. Focusing on headlines and titles, relating pictures to key phrases and understanding captions all contribute to gist understanding, which pupils need to develop.

Many authentic materials lend themselves to particular topics and you can be very creative in their use. Prices on posters and publicity sheets for supermarkets can support the reinforcement of numbers. Even the use of telephone directories can achieve this. The benefits in terms of developing pupils' cultural awareness are obvious. Menus, town plans and tourist guides contain language relevant to examination specifications but also to the realistic needs of pupils when visiting countries where the TL is spoken.

Authentic materials also provide excellent models for language production by pupils. Advertisements in particular can stimulate creative language use and can provide an appropriate context. When used sensitively, authentic materials offer a great deal (see Fawkes, 2001).

Kavanagh and Upton (1994: 12) draw attention to four important considerations, which are adapted here:

- the material must be interesting for pupils; the same text will probably not be of interest to all pupils in a class;
- the content must be accessible and objectives clearly defined and understood; this can guard against pupils feeling that they have to understand the meaning and grammatical function of every word;
- the task itself must appeal and *authentic material* should involve *authentic tasks*;
- the nature of the task should be varied and relevant to the original purpose of the text.

Pitfalls and possible problems

Above we considered it to be an advantage that authentic materials are not designed for use in the classroom. This can, however, also be a pitfall. No allowance is made for the learners' lack of knowledge of vocabulary, nor is the grammar used designed to support a particular stage of learning. Passages need to be placed in context. To expose a learner to authentic texts without prior preparation can be demotivating.

Consequently, efforts should be made to introduce the topic, present key phrases and even ideas expressed in the text in advance. The length of many passages is daunting. Pupils need to feel comfortable with a text before embarking on reading or listening to it. Tasks designed for particular texts can be graded. Activities involving the highlighting of key vocabulary, such as times, dates, addresses and prices do not require a detailed understanding. The identification of particular details can be achieved through non-verbal responses.

Mitchell and Swarbrick (1994: 2) stress the need to 'exploit pre-knowledge' to pre-empt learner alienation when faced with a lengthy authentic text. They include identifying known vocabulary or inferring meaning on the basis of headlines.

Another benefit of using authentic material can also lead to problems: the materials are *not* designed for the reader to focus on the *language* used *but* more to understand the *message*. The tasks designed for a text need to match this aim.

Working in groups with authentic material can be problematic. Often pupils may be distracted by the material being used by other groups. Access to reference material inevitably involves movement to other areas of the classroom. Pupils do not always work at the required pace and pupil absence can inhibit the work of others in a group.

Kyriacou (1991: 61) advises that teachers establish ground rules in advance:

- pupils should move from their seats for specified reasons only;
- only a pre-specified number of pupils should be out of their seats at any given time;
- pupils should be presented task in stages, with time limits on each stage;
- pupils should demonstrate completion of a stage to the teacher.

EXAMPLE OF GROUP TASK INVOLVING AUTHENTIC MATERIAL

The activity described here is designed to familiarise pupils with the format and content of newspapers without requiring an in-depth knowledge of the vocabulary of and background to particular articles.

Pupils are issued with newspapers, or given the opportunity to access newspapers online. They are asked to cut out five articles, which depict a happy event and five which depict a sad event. They then separate the headlines and pictures from each story. From the text they extract five key sentences, which serve as a summary of the events. The headlines, pictures and summary are exchanged with another group, whose task it is to reproduce the story. For support, a pupil from each group may read the entire story in private but she is only allowed to report back to her group without reference to the text.

In order to relate the content of lessons to pupils' 'real' needs and interests, the material selected could relate to a planned visit abroad. Pupils can be presented with brochures of all the places they are likely to visit. In groups they are asked to extract from the brochures details of opening times, cost of entries or accessibility and to draw up an itinerary. Again, this activity can be done online. In the event of the visit being to a partner school abroad, pupils from the partner institution could be approached to provide details of possible excursions. Recorded interviews and written surveys are useful this context. This way authentic material can be used to develop effective communication for real purposes.

Task 14.8 AUTHENTIC MATERIAL

1   Examine whether the use of authentic material is built into a unit of work currently in use in your school.
2   Devise an exercise appropriate for a beginners class you are currently teaching or observing around some authentic material. Then, with the same material, devise an activity for an intermediate class you are currently teaching or observing. Do any principles for the use of authentic material with pupils of different levels of linguistic skill emerge?
3   Seek out some authentic material and devise activities, which support the learning objectives of a unit of work of a specific class. Discuss the material and tasks with your tutor or a relevant class teacher; then adapt them as necessary. Ask your tutor or the class teacher if you can teach the activity.

LEARNING BEYOND THE CLASSROOM

Learning beyond the classroom encompasses both 'learning' and 'communicative' contexts for the learner, as the examples below indicate. While the role of the teacher and the control over the learning and language acquisition processes and procedures are reduced when outside the formal classroom, there is still a need to plan and monitor this experience in order to avoid it becoming directionless, ineffective and demotivating.

Homework

This is perhaps the most common way in which the FL learning experience extends beyond the temporal and spatial boundaries of the classroom. Most often, however, effective use of homework is enabled through clear linkage with the learning taking place in within lessons.

Homework can fulfil a number of different functions: it can supplement, extend and/or differentiate what happens in the FLs classroom; it can reinforce or consolidate linguistic items and structures; it allows pupils to work at their own pace and make use of reference material such as dictionaries. On occasion, tasks partially completed in class can be finished off at home. Homework can also yield valuable evidence for assessment purposes. The setting of homework also serves to reassure parents the focus and progress of study and to involve them in their children's FLs study.

It is very important to note that homework need not be confined to the skill of writing:

■ listening can be fostered by pupils listening to relevant role plays or other texts on an appropriate medium for them (via the Web, as a recording, etc.);
■ speaking can be encouraged by pupils recording pronunciation exercises, role plays or themselves reading aloud;
■ reading skills can be developed through reading for pleasure outside the classroom;
■ writing is often developed by way of completion of worksheets or exercises following on from oral or aural classroom work or scripting role plays. Drafting and redrafting with the help of digital technologies can also be meaningfully encouraged if pupils have access to a computer at home or at the school outside lesson time.

In addition to skill-specific tasks and activities, other areas such as cultural awareness, learning strategies and (inter)personal and research skills can be developed through homework. Prompted by some pictures with brief captions in the coursebook, pupils can be asked, individually or in small groups, to produce a leaflet on a region/country where the TL is spoken for a specific audience, e.g. a display for the school's open evening. You can either provide authentic resources such as leaflets for the task or pupils can be introduced to library resources, including material on an electronic encyclopaedia. Pupils can be asked to extract relevant information from source material in English or the TL, simplify and, where necessary, translate it.

From time to time the learning or revision of key linguistic items or structure might be an appropriate homework task. In order to enable pupils to gain most of such homework, they need to be taught some strategies how to learn new linguistic items and structures as well as revision techniques. Regular revision of some ten minutes or so a day can, for instance, be more effective than isolated longer revision sessions; simply reading words or texts again and again might be less effective than saying words aloud or using underlining or highlighting techniques; revision plans can help to prioritise and avoid omitting important information; mixing topics that are more appealing with ones that are (perceived to be) more challenging might avoid reluctance to revise; making revision notes may help as may making up mnemonics, acronyms such as 'UE': *Unión Europea* or word associations such as *tiempo: hacer calor, hacer frío, mal tiempo*. . . Hunt and Barnes (2003: 54) suggest the following creative ideas for homework:

- Pupils summarise a grammar point.
- Occasionally give pupils a choice for homework completion, e.g. (audio) record the presentation . . . or write it out or do it on PowerPoint, etc.
- Pupils list five ways they have used to memorise vocabulary.
- Review of a TV programme/book/film using a framework, where each pupil completes a term to be displayed.
- Look up a set of new words in the dictionary and record appropriately.
- Read a text and annotate it with words related to English/which they know/which they don't know, etc.
- Write in English the phrases they feel would be crucial in a particular context as preparation for a new topic.
- Submit homework as an email attachment.
- Memorise a short text or poem.
- Devise a mnemonic for a grammar rule or list of vocabulary.
- Language challenge, e.g. create as many words as possible from one target language phrase.
- Web-based activities/research.
- Logic puzzles, where reading and thinking are paramount rather than writing.
- Devise language puzzles and games for a different (perhaps younger) class.

With reference to learners of English as a FL in Germany, Kuty (2012: 320–321) states that homework offers many opportunities for individualised learning and suggests the following example of a short activity prepared for homework.

In order to maximise its benefits, homework needs to be planned into units of work and lessons, i.e. thought about carefully in advance.

Care needs to be taken that the departmental and school policies on homework are adhered to, for instance, in terms of homework days. Appropriateness and manageability are other important considerations when deciding on the quantity and nature of homework. For a discussion of homework, also see Hunt, 2014.

Homework activity: What would you like to show to your classmates? Bring it to school and tell your classmates about it. You will have 2 to 3 minutes' time.	
1 Introduction	You may use these phrases: Today, I'd like to talk about . . . a souvenir . . . a present . . . a hobby . . . a photo
2 What do you show? Describe it!	I (really) like it because . . . There is a story about it . . . I got it from . . .
3 Why do you show it?	This is a . . . It is (good) for . . . You can find it . . . It has . . . It can (do)

■ **Figure 14.4** An example of a homework activity

Instructions need to be clear and unambiguous and the use of the TL for setting homework needs to be thought through carefully. It is important to feed back to pupils regularly and preferably in the following lesson how well they have done and in class to go over some of the areas that caused problems to them. In providing feedback you need to adhere to the departmental and school marking policies, which will often specify a system of grades as well as the nature of TL to be used for feedback. The policy could, for instance, specify that pupils are given a list of grades in the L1 and the TL on a handout, which they stick into their exercise books for reference and which are used consistently across the department and/or school. For assessment for and of learning, see also Chapter 15.

Task 14.9 **GIVING WRITTEN FEEDBACK TO PUPILS**

1   Draw up two lists of comments in the TL you think are appropriate in giving written feedback to pupils about their homework, one list for beginners and one for intermediate-level learners. What sort of content might be included in these comments?

2   Next, ask your mentor or the class teacher for permission to collect in a set of books for various groups of learners in different year groups and note the comments your colleagues have made about pupils' work.

3   Then, compare your lists with the comments found in the exercise book and study the departmental marking policy.

4   Finally, discuss the findings with the teacher in question.

Task 14.10 **DESIGNING A GUIDE FOR PARENTS**

Devise a guide for parents with suggestions about how they can support their child's independent study and homework. Activities might include vocabulary testing, providing opportunities for listening to and reading the TL, researching holiday destinations.

Short stay study abroad

Perhaps the most intensive context of language immersion outside the classroom is that of the experience of 'study abroad', which when organised at school level takes the form of the school exchange visit. The communicative context of the residence abroad is evident both in the sense of the linguistic immersion in the TL and in the sense of engagement in interpersonal relations with native speakers. This is particularly the case if the pupils are hosted by the families of the exchange partners.

Studies indicate that there is a positive impact both on improvement in aspects of TL proficiency and on broader motivational and attitudinal dispositions. For instance, in their study of the impact of a French exchange visit by Y9 students of

French at three schools in England on gains in proficiency, Evans and Fisher (2005) found that there was a significant improvement in listening comprehension scores and in expressive use of language in writing tasks. The authors also found a correlation between proficiency gains and the students' reports of support from the host family in terms of communication in the TL and degree of help and correction of their use of French (p. 190). Similar findings were generated in a study of Spanish students on a study abroad visit in England by Llanes and Muñoz (2009: 362) who found 'even a stay abroad of 3–4 weeks produces significant gains in all areas studied: listening comprehension, oral fluency and accuracy'. Llanes (2012) compared the performance of two groups of 11-year-old Spanish students of English as a FL and found that the group that had completed the study abroad programme in Ireland, staying with Irish families, showed greater gains in the post tests (particularly in the oral skills) than the 'at home' group and that this comparative gain was still visible in a delayed post-test twelve months later.

SUMMARY

This chapter has outlined a perspective which provides ways to think about the languages classroom as a multidimensional learning environment. In particular we have stressed the importance of seeing your role as teacher as one of managing three dimensions of the learners' experience of the study of a foreign language – namely, through formal instruction, informal learning and language learning beyond the classroom. We have argued that it is important for you to recognise, in the first instance, the distinctive contributions that each of these contexts of learning offers the pupil and, second, to ensure that your lesson planning and teaching combines and integrates these three different kinds of experiences and learning opportunities within your approach.

FURTHER READING

Chambers, G. and Norman, N. (2003) Take six books. In *Language Learning Journal*, 28: 40–48.
This article compares and contrasts textbooks and advises on their use in the MFL classroom.

Evans, M. and Fisher, L. (2005) Measuring gains in pupils' foreign language competence as a result of participation in a school exchange visit: the case of Y9 pupils at three comprehensive schools in the UK. In *Language Teaching Research*, 9(2): 173–192.
This paper discussed the impact of an exchange visit by Year 9 pupils on language performance.

Hunt, M., Barnes, A. and Redford, J. (2009) MFL homework in Year 9 French: rising to the challenge. In *Language Learning Journal*, 37(1): 35–49.
This paper describes a homework project and evaluates its success and makes recommendations on how to increase the effectiveness of foreign languages homework.

Wright, T. (2005) *Classroom Management in Language Education*. Basingstoke and New York: Palgrave Macmillan.
This book provides a detailed examination of classroom management and provides useful summaries of the different theoretical perspectives as well as a discussion of practical issues.

CHAPTER 15

ASSESSMENT FOR AND OF LEARNING

INTRODUCTION

The fundamental question that we address in this chapter is: what is the role of assessment in helping pupils learn more effectively? We argue that assessment should be purposeful both for the learners in understanding the progress made and having it recognised, and for the teacher who needs to know what her students can or cannot do in order to move their learning on. The other audience for assessment is outside the classroom: school leadership and governors, parents, and government bodies who, through our reporting of results from internal testing and through the external validation of certificated examinations, can understand how a pupil and groups of pupils in this school and across the country are performing.

Assessment has been the subject of a lively educational and public debate in recent years. There has also been a substantial amount of research into assessment. This research has, and continues to be, directly informed by and to influence practice.

Work on assessment for learning, particularly by Black and Wiliam, has been very influential in the UK educational context (see Black *et al.*, 2002; Black and Wiliam, 2003; Gardner 2012). This work on assessment more generally has led to a linked specific research focus on FLs (see Black and Jones, 2006; Jones and Wiliam, 2008) as well as practical application of assessment for learning techniques and approaches (see Barnes and Hunt, 2003; Mutton, 2014).

In this chapter we consider two forms of assessment in relation to the implications for FL learning:

- *Assessment for learning (AfL)*, which has evolved from the term 'formative assessment' and is concerned with assessment practices and techniques that actively move the learner on to make progress and improve their understanding of how and why they are learning in the way they are;
- *Assessment of learning*, which is the broad equivalent of 'summative assessment' and involves the judging of the amount that has been learned usually through some form of testing and award of marks or grades.

While we contextualise our discussion in this chapter by way of the statutory requirements for England, and refer to the Common European Framework (see also Chapter 1), much of what is said about assessment issues is generic and, therefore, equally relevant to student teachers learning to teach in a variety of national contexts.

We begin the chapter by discussing briefly the purposes of and principles for assessment and offer definitions of key terms. We then focus on AfL and what it means for teachers of FLs, followed by a section on issues in summative assessment.

OBJECTIVES

By the end of this chapter you should:

- understand the key principles and some important purposes of assessing FLs learners, including assessment of and for learning;
- be familiar with key assessment terminology;
- understand the philosophy and values underpinning AfL and how it can be enacted in the FL classroom;
- be aware of important issues of and a range of activities for FL assessment;
- have an appreciation of internal and external assessment, including teacher assessment, pupil peer- or self-assessment and the GCSE examination.

PRINCIPLES, PURPOSES, TERMINOLOGY

What is assessment for?

In some ways it is easy to get tied up in the idea that assessment simply needs to be carried out, without really considering what the precise purpose for the assessment might be. There are numerous reasons why a teacher might assess her class, including the following:

- to generate information for pupils about their learning;
- to ensure that learning objectives have been reached;
- to motivate pupils;
- to gather data for reporting what pupils know, understand and/or can do;
- to select pupils (e.g. for groupings in school or for opportunities in later life);
- to identify strengths and weaknesses in pupils;
- to provide certification;
- to fulfil statutory requirements;
- to measure standards that will be used to hold teachers accountable.

Clearly, some of these are primarily for formative purposes, and some for summative assessment purposes. However, what needs to be borne in mind is that formative and summative assessments do not *describe* different forms of assessment but describe rather *how* the assessment is used. For example, if a teacher asks pupils to do a reading comprehension task with multiple-choice answers, it could serve to fulfil many of the functions listed above. It will only be formative if the teacher *uses* the results to carry learning forward in some way, such as to make adjustments to her teaching or to help learners to become aware of how they are achieving and to set goals. The main difference between summative and formative could be said to be that formative is built into the learning process and is central to pedagogy, whereas summative assessment comes at the end of a learning episode.

For most of the previous century, assessment was mainly carried for summative purposes, but a large-scale review of research published on the topic of research practices (Black and William, 1998) found the following:

■ teachers were setting tests that encouraged rote and superficial learning for tests;

■ marks and grades were overemphasised and offered to students with little advice on improvement;

■ lots of marks in markbooks that were quite meaningless in terms of individual learners' needs and there was little sharing of records from one year to the next;

■ a lack of sharing of practice across teachers and lack of analysis of whether tests actually measured what they set out to;

■ use of approaches comparing students' work with one another rather than against criteria. Students also then had a tendency to compare themselves to one another;

■ teachers, particularly in Primary schools, had a tendency to assess quantity/ presentation rather than quality and therefore criteria were not well laid out and being followed. This made for unreliable testing;

■ lack of knowledge of pupils and their learning needs, though teachers knew their level rather well.

How does your experience of assessment relate to any of what you have read? Task 15.1 asks you to reflect on the sorts of ways you were assessed in your own FL learning and to determine whether they were fit for purpose.

Task 15.1 PERSONAL ASSESSMENT EXPERIENCES

1 Think about a number of ways in which your FL learning has been assessed in the past. What were the purpose and the nature of the assessments?
2 Then, consider if the assessments were fit for purpose. List the strengths and weaknesses of the various assessments you undertook.

PRINCIPLES OF HOW TO ASSESS

From this we can collate some principles for assessment that are relevant to both assessment of and assessment for learning.

Assessment should:

- be an integral part of teaching and learning and follow from curricular objectives;
- be used to inform future teaching and learning which is adjusted in the light of information coming from ongoing as well as summative assessment;
- involve learner in the process, helping them to be aware of learning objectives and to evaluate their own and others' work against them;
- be used to motivate the learners and allow them to work towards their own goals;
- provide useful information about the progress, achievement and attainment of pupils that is shared with relevant parties;
- come at regular intervals to provide a critical mass of data to validate judgements;
- consist of a variety of methods to make data more reliable, such as criteria-referencing;
- be manageable for the teacher.

DEFINITION OF TERMS

We end this section with a glossary of terms in assessment practice (see Figure 15.1), where we define and explain some important terminology.

Term	Definition
Achievement	Progress made by pupils in relation to their past performance.
Attainment	Progress made by pupils in relation to the statutory framework.
Assessment for learning (AfL)	Assessment which focuses on the next steps to improve learning. This involves both feedback and feed forward assessment which describes/summarises what a learner has achieved/attained.
Assessment of learning	A snapshot of achievement. It also informs teachers how much of and how well a group of learners has progressed against the intended learning outcomes.
Assessment criteria	The criteria by which a piece of work of whatever type is assessed. These criteria need to be clear both to teachers and learners.
Criterion-referenced	Assessment which is judged according to the fulfilment of a description of a task, or a set of agreed criteria. If everyone fulfils the criteria, then everyone passes.
Diagnostic	Assessment opportunities aimed at identifying strengths and weaknesses in current performance and providing pointers for future work.

■ **Figure 15.1** Glossary of FLs assessment terminology

Term	Definition
Evaluative	To ascertain how well individual teachers or schools are performing.
External assessment	Assessment opportunities designed by outside agencies such as examination boards and other Awarding Bodies.
Fitness for purpose	The extent to which an assessment opportunity reflects the reasons for carrying out the assessment.
Formative/continuous assessment	Assessment opportunities, which are ongoing and an integral part of teaching. An ongoing process of gathering information on the processes of learning, the extent of learning, and on strengths and weaknesses, which provides learners and teachers with information for future planning to meet an individual pupil's needs; takes place during the course of teaching and is essentially used to feed back into the teaching/learning process.
Internal assessment	Assessment opportunities carried out by the teacher (teacher assessment) or pupils (self- and/or peer assessment); designed by the teacher or coursebook writers.
Norm-referenced	Assessment which measures all learners against each other and can place learners in rank order in relation to their peers. Marks are sometimes altered up or down if too many candidates succeed or fail, irrespective of the difficulty of the test or the ability of the candidates.
Peer assessment	Judgements made by one's peer(s) about one's own proficiency or achievement.
Predictive assessment	Using a range of data of prior attainment to provide indicators of future potential attainment and minimum target levels.
Proficiency	Level of linguistic skill and knowledge in relation to external criteria.
Reliability	The accuracy with which an assessment opportunity measures progress, attainment, achievement, proficiency, etc.
Self-assessment	Judgements made by the learner about his/her own proficiency or achievement.
Standardised assessment	Assessment opportunities devised and moderated by outside agencies, such as exam boards and other Awarding Bodies.
Summative assessment	Assessment opportunities coming at the end of a unit of work, term, year or course. These opportunities may be used to select learners for movement between classes, sets, streams or institutions. They are also used for certification purposes. Assessment which takes place at the end of a course of study or part of it and which measures learners' performance over that course or part of it; it provides information about how much learners have progressed and how well a course has worked.
Validity	The extent to which an assessment opportunity measures what has been taught and what pupils should have learnt.

■ **Figure 15.1** *continued*

ASSESSMENT FOR LEARNING: PRINCIPLES AND APPROACHES

Much research into AfL has shown it to be an effective tool for improving learning. The Assessment Reform Group (ARG), a team of researchers who came together to research ways in which assessment can aid learning, define AfL as: 'the process of seeking and interpreting evidence for use by learners and their teachers to decide where the learners are in their learning, where they need to go and how best to get there' (ARG, 2002). It is based on the principle that pupils' progress is optimal when they understand the aim of their learning, where they stand in relation to the aim of the learning and how they can achieve the aim (or close the gap between where they are now and where they need to be). It is not an 'add-on' or a project but rather it is central to effective teaching and learning.

As a result of their work, the ARG (2002) came up with ten research-based principles of AfL to guide classroom practice, which we list below:

Assessment for Learning:

■ is part of planning for effective learning;
■ focuses on how students learn;
■ is central to good classroom practice;
■ is a key professional skill;
■ is sensitive and constructive – assessment can have an emotional impact;
■ is a motivational tool;
■ helps learners to understand the learning goals and criteria for success;
■ helps learners know how to improve;
■ helps learners become self-reflective and self-managing;
■ should recognise the full range of achievement for all learners.

Applying AfL in the FLs classroom

In this section we offer some practical approaches and strategies for incorporating some of the principles of AfL listed above into FL teaching with reference to the following six themes:

1   sharing objectives for learning;
2   using questioning for learning;
3   using oral feedback for learning;
4   using marking for learning;
5   setting targets for learning;
6   self- and peer-assessment for learning.

Sharing objectives for learning

As we have already noted earlier in the book, what we should be assessing is driven by what we are teaching. If our lessons are objective-led, then we need to measure how successful they have been by looking for evidence of learning that helps us and pupils understand the extent to which the objectives have been met. The first point is to establish clear learning objectives and share them with the pupils. These need to be expressed in pupil-friendly language and in the early years especially, probably in the L1.

We need to be very careful to be sure that we are giving a *learning* objective and not listing things the students are going to do in the lesson, i.e. listing activities. Be specific about what the pupils will be able to do at the end of the lesson that they could not do at the beginning, for example: 'By the end of the lesson you will be able to understand someone giving opinions about their school subjects in German (Listening) and you'll be able to tell someone what you think about your subjects' (Speaking).

At this point it is also important to share the *success criteria* with the learners. This is about being really explicit about what we might expect in terms of outcome. What sort of communication are we expecting? Which grammar points do I need to get right to communicate well? What makes for a really good piece of work? The teacher will have thought about issues of differentiation and where appropriate may make some reference to this when discussing what the outcomes might look like.

It sounds fairly obvious but it is worth repeating that it is essential that built into the planning for the lesson is one or more activity that will actually provide an opportunity for pupils to demonstrate that they can meet the objective. For example, here, in order that the pupils can demonstrate that they can give opinions on their subjects, there will need to be some form of pair work or group work that allows pupils to express their views. Sometimes, though, it is only when teachers start to properly evaluate whether learning objectives have been met that they notice that they cannot judge, as they did not include activities that would give the information that they and the learners need. For example, a plenary activity where a few pupils give a sentence each tells us only what those few pupils can do. Careful thought needs to go into devising activities that provide good evidence.

Before starting to teach new material in a lesson, the teacher needs to check how much knowledge the pupils have already. Can they remember the school subjects from last lesson? How can this be checked? This needs to be built into the planning – e.g. a starter activity or some well thought-out questioning, as discussed in the next section.

Using questioning for learning

Question-and-answer work is an important teacher-led strategy, used often to draw on what was learned in previous lessons, to monitor what pupils can do at a point in the lesson before moving on, or to review the learning in a lesson. Questioning can provide a useful scaffold in moving from yes/no answers, which offer the most support, to questions requiring the pupil to repeat a word or phrase, to pupils' production of their own language (see Chapter 13 on differentiation also).

There are, however, a number of disadvantages of a traditional IRF (initiation–response–feedback) model of questioning. This takes the form of a teacher question: '*Qu' est-ce que c'est?*' to which the response might be '*C'est un chat*' to which the teacher responds and affirms '*Oui, c'est un chat*'. This is what Jones and Wiliam (2008: 8) describe as 'serial table tennis' between teacher and one pupil, and is in many ways more demanding on the teacher than the students. After all, in ten minutes of such questioning in class the teacher will have spoken much more

French than the pupils. Of course, the teacher may have a good rationale for using this form of questioning, but we can say that often, after initial modelling of new forms, there are probably better ways to involve all pupils in producing new language, e.g. via speaking in pair work which the teacher monitors.

The other drawback with IRF often means the teacher asking a question and calling on volunteers who put their hands up to answer it. However, it is often the same pupils volunteering again and again. Jones and Wiliam (2008) quote research that says that by conducting this form of questioning we are allowing the gap in achievement to increase, as those who answer are actively increasing their cognitive abilities (presuming we ask questions that challenge in some way) while the rest are not. The implication from this is that we need to explore ways of making *all* engage with questions.

One way is hands-down questioning. The teacher asks a question (and it is important to pose the question to the class *before* calling a pupil's name, which encourages everyone to think of an answer) and chooses either purposefully or at random. If using random selection there are a number of methods such as lollipop sticks with pupils' names on that are drawn from a jar, or www.classtools.net has a useful function for putting all names in and spinning a random selector. If the pupil selected cannot answer they can get support from others in class or the question can be reworded to offer more support.

Hands-down questioning has been widely adopted in schools. There may be some role for hands up too in the context of gathering evidence of learning. Rather than meaning 'I want to answer', as many pupils currently believe it to mean, the teacher needs to explain that hands up means 'I know the answer to this question' and that she needs this information from them so as to adapt the learning to suit what they can and cannot yet do. This sort of hands-up questioning may work better with factual or knowledge-based questions (direct comprehension, translation of a word, putting together a correct verb form).

This leads to the question as to whether in FL learning we ask enough 'higher-order' questions. These are questions that require, for example, hypothesising, explaining, exploring or evaluating, rather than 'lower-order' questions that are mainly about retrieval of information, e.g. gender of nouns, translation of words.

Developing more higher-order questions again needs building into planning, considering in advance how questions might be asked that extend thinking so that, for example, '*Qu'est-ce que tu as fait hier soir?*' is followed with questions to others '*Il a fait ça pourquoi?*' asking them to speculate and maybe relate to their own activities.

Higher-order questions often require some thinking time to formulate a response. Teachers can be uncomfortable with gaps or pauses in the 'action' – maybe FLs teachers in particular, where we feel the need to have speaking or listening of some sort at all times. However, research has shown (Black *et al.*, 2003) that when teachers pose a question and then do not expect an immediate answer but allow thinking time, there are the following benefits:

- longer answers;
- more students choose to answer;
- fewer refuse to answer;
- students comment on or elaborate other pupils' answers.

Allowing thinking time might look like this:

- teacher asks question;
- waits, modelling thinking (e.g. looking pensive, not making eye contact);
- pupils listen to question and get ready with an answer;
- if picked to respond they do and if not they listen carefully to classmate's answer and get ready to agree, disagree, develop it;
- teacher waits again after first pupil responds to allow the first pupil to elaborate or change something and others get ready to respond;
- teacher asks others to contribute.

Using oral feedback for learning

Some of the theoretical underpinning of the work on AfL comes from attribution theory in social psychology and from Dweck's growth theory of intelligence (Dweck, 2000). This suggests that what a pupil attributes his or her success to has a great influence on how she acts in the future when asked to do similar tasks. For example, there are two views of intelligence that a pupil might hold: she might believe that intelligence is 'fixed', i.e. you are either smart or you are not, or she might believe that it is 'incremental', i.e. you can get better at things by working harder on them. If the student has a 'fixed' intelligence mindset and she gets a bad result on a test while others seem to do better, then she may believe that she is simply not a good student (or not good at languages) and stop trying. On the other hand, if the student has an 'incremental' view of intelligence and does badly in a test she is more likely to view it as something she simply needs to work harder at. Dweck carried out a number of experiments in the 1990s which showed that teachers can help learners to develop 'incremental' views of intelligence. The result is that they become more concerned with mastery of the task than with performing well in relation to peers and can attribute success or lack of it in ways that are likely to help their learning not hinder it.

The main implications of this for giving feedback are as follows:

- avoid giving person-directed praise, e.g. 'you're good at this'; rather give process-directed praise such as 'that was a good way to work out what the reading passage meant' or 'you tried very hard to construct more complex sentences';
- give task-orientated praise, e.g. 'there are far fewer spelling mistakes this time' or 'you got your auxiliary verbs right' that focus on the criteria for success;
- in as far as is possible, make summative assessment more of a private than a public event, encouraging a pupil to think that she is not comparing herself to others but to her last performance in order to see how she is improving.

In Chapter 7 we discussed the idea of 'bookending', where the objectives are set at the beginning and revisited at the end of the lesson to allow the teacher and students to evaluate the extent to which they have been met. This is often, though does not have to be, in a final plenary. This sort of joint analysis of the outcomes of the lesson is useful for teacher planning and importantly to help the pupils make more realistic assessments of how well they did.

Often teachers ask students how confident they feel with the work they just did, using systems such as traffic light flashcards. All pupils hold up a card: green = I am confident I have met the objectives (e.g. I can tell someone what I think about my school subjects). Orange = I am fairly confident I can do this but I can only remember a couple of opinion words – I might need more practice. Red = I feel insecure on this and need more support. It must be remembered this is pupils' *perspectives*; it is not evidence of learning but rather an expression of pupil confidence with the material, which may or may not relate to what they can actually do.

Decisions as to whether such feedback is conducted in English or the TL needs to be taken within the context of the class's level and within the context of departmental practices. In line with our suggestions in Chapter 7 we suggest that TL is used wherever feasible.

Using marking for learning: focused and comment-only marking

Teachers are required to give written feedback on pupils' work. As discussed above, feedback should be used in a way that allows the learner to make progress as a result. This is likely to happen when we respond to their work following some of the key AfL principles – i.e. we should keep our feedback based on clear criteria (task-orientated), we should offer advice on how to improve and we should be careful about using data that might be interpreted in 'crude' ways – i.e. used to compare pupils.

In FL teaching and learning there are obviously a range of different types of mistakes (knowing a language form but misusing it) or errors (not knowing it yet) that a learner can make such as (see Beaton, 1990: 42–44):

■ grammatical errors, for instance, in the formation and structure of words (morphological), in the meaning of words (semantic), in the building of sentences (syntactic) or in spelling (orthographic) and punctuation;

■ failures in 'sociolinguistic competence': the inappropriate use of language in relation to the social context, e.g. use of the informal '*du*' form in a formal situation;

■ failures in 'strategic competence': e.g. lack of 'repair' strategies in the case of a breakdown in communication and lack of availability of alternative means of expression;

■ errors in the instrumental function of language: lack of success in transactional terms for a variety of reasons such as bad pronunciation.

All mistakes or errors in pupils' work are valuable insofar as they tell us where they are at this point with their learning. How much, then, should be corrected? A difficult area to find definitive answers is whether all mistakes need to be corrected all the time, which could be demotivating, or whether marking should focus solely on learning objectives that were being taught at that point. There are also issues with regard to assessing tasks where content and language are both focused upon, such as in content and language integrated learning (CLIL) work (see Morgan, 2006).

Obviously it is important for a student teacher to mark in accordance with the expectations of the department she is working in and the departmental handbook is a useful point of reference as it usually features a policy statement on marking. Marking policies should be in line with the overall school policy ensuring consistency across members of a department but also across school subjects for the benefit of the various 'audiences' of assessment such as pupils, parents, inspectors and the wider public. The departmental policy on marking might, for instance, include guidance on when and how to use grades, ticks and/or verbal comments. There might be reference to the use of the TL – i.e. when to use the TL and when to comment in the L1. If the departmental policy contains a list of phrases or a bank of comments in the TL to provide feedback on pupils' written work, you should use it.

If assessment criteria are clear, a short checklist on what has been done/not done can give more time and opportunity for constructive comments on the quality of the work.

Many teachers find it useful to mark written work with a coding system such as: Sp = spelling; T = tense; W.O.= word order, and so on, and students can then redraft their own work (see also self-assessment below).

Research into AfL has focused a great deal on comments and marks. Comments, particularly where they are specific (both linguistically and regarding content, structure, etc.), and where the advice can be implemented by the pupils to improve their learning are felt to be most useful, whereas simply giving marks or grades 'can have a negative effect as pupils will not read comments aimed at improving work as they will automatically look at the grade first' (Black *et al.*, 2002: 9). Giving marks and comments together seems to have the same effect as just giving marks; pupils pay attention to the marks only and disregard the comments. Attention is then focused on performance rather that mastery of the material. Comment-only marking, where pupils are advised as to strengths and weaknesses in the work, have a pedagogical purpose that marks are less likely to have.

Task 15.2 **DEPARTMENTAL MARKING POLICY**

■ Study the marking policy of the FLs department at your school.

■ Ask your mentor or a class teacher with whom you work closely if you can have a look at a set of books/some pieces of work she has marked to help you with the implementation of the departmental policy. Some FLs departments have statement banks with relevant comments, which help you in marking.

■ Ask your mentor or the class teacher for an opportunity to mark a set of books following the recommended procedures. Make a note of any queries, problems, insecurities or observations you have. Then, discuss your queries with your mentor or the class teacher and ask for her advice.

Setting targets for learning

To help pupils learn from their mistakes and for them to build on diagnostic feedback, pupils should be encouraged to re-examine marked pieces of work and correct certain mistakes, as well as implement advice. This should involve a two-way process. You may have written some excellent and helpful comments which, if followed, should help the learner make progress. This only happens if the learner engages with these comments. It could be an expectation in class that learners write a response to the comments, perhaps immediately (e.g. setting themselves what they see as an appropriate target arising from the comments) or on their next piece of work, indicating how the comments have been acted upon. This is known widely as *dialogic marking*.

Some schools have developed systems that have incorporated AfL into their marking schemes, using acronyms such as:

www = what went well . . . e.g. very accurate use of the future tense and additional vocabulary;

ebi = even better if . . . you would use more conversational Spanish that you know from last year.

Targets can be set by the teacher or by the pupil. Any target set should make the learner think about what he or she needs to do next to improve. This arises more naturally if a question is asked in the comments, such as 'Could you add more varied adjectives and use some subordinate clauses?' Often more open questions help the pupils to generate their own targets. A question such as 'Can you think of ways you could have extended this work?' can prompt pupils to think about what they might do next, though this needs to be monitored closely by the teacher; not all pupils can think of appropriate ways to progress and may need support.

It is important that targets are not simply set and ignored. Target setting and review is a *process* and it requires the teacher to remind the pupils to look at their targets before beginning the next piece of work. It is also important that the teacher makes reference to the target where possible in the next round of marking so as to build up pupils' sense of making progress towards their goals.

Our final theme of *self- and peer-assessment for learning* is considered in a separate section below.

SELF- AND PEER-ASSESSMENT FOR LEARNING

We want to start this section by stressing the importance of raising awareness in pupils about the differences between marking, assessing and evaluating. While the terms all refer to processes that are closely linked, they refer to different elements. Marking concerns judgements made by the teacher about individual pupil performances, frequently of specially designed assessment tasks against explicit criteria or rubrics, and according to particular marking schemes. Assessment concerns the systematic gathering of data about pupil achievement and attainment. And evaluation is about the efficacy with which particular objectives have been reached or judgements about how well particular interventions have worked. In order to be able to become effective partners in the assessment process, pupils need to be familiarised with relevant marking criteria, rubrics and schemes. Evaluation of their own performance or that of peers invariably will involve a diagnosis of the nature of the mistakes committed for which they require a high level of linguistic and metalinguistic knowledge and understanding.

Task 15.3 INVOLVING PUPILS IN THE ASSESSMENT PROCESS

Reflect on the distinction between marking, assessment and evaluation and devise ways of involving pupils by:

■ familiarising them with marking criteria, rubrics and schemes and how to apply them;
■ engaging them in devising assessment activities and tasks for peers; and
■ encouraging them to reflect critically on their own mistakes through self-regulation.

One important way of helping to involve pupils in the assessment process is through peer and self-assessment (see Stobart and Gipps, 1997; Morley and Truscott, 2006). A possible order for how learners might engage in assessment of their learning could be as follows:

1   self-assessment of work (using personalised checklist and the specific criteria for task);
2   peer-assessment (using the same criteria);
3   more self-assessment;
4   teacher assessment.

To be most profitable, this process should ideally focus on key pieces of work, although the principles above could apply to any task. Ideas and criteria need to be shared with the class and often the teacher might model how he/she would go about assessing a piece of work using an example (not work of a pupil in this group).

As discussed above, teacher-led plenaries where attention is explicitly drawn to the lesson objectives also have a vital role to play: how well have they, as individuals, met the lesson objectives? What needs to be done now? Many schools now have target sheets at the end of a week's work: what I've learned, what I need to do now, targets in all four skills. End-of-unit profiles or 'can-do' checklists allow pupils to evaluate themselves and set targets. These are increasingly included in coursebooks as 'Lernzielkontrollen' or 'bilans'. Again, use of the TL needs to be considered and strategies employed for optimising its use – for example, individuals or small groups might work with the foreign language assistant (FLA) on their 'can-do' checklists. In order to be able to assess themselves effectively, learners need:

■ to be aware of the specific objectives of a task/lesson/unit;
■ to be able to make meaningful comments on their own/their peers' performance in these areas.

These might include a wide range of elements, each of which needs to be clear to learners and each requires practice for them to be able to make comments which are useful and constructive. Such practice should also include examples of good responses, so they have a benchmark for what they are looking for. Individual items may include:

- pronunciation of new items;
- overall pronunciation (how French/German/Spanish did I/you sound?);
- communication of information;
- accuracy of language (e.g. tenses, adjectives, possessives, etc.);
- inclusion of all required 'bits' (i.e. did I/you make sure all elements of the task were complete?);
- range of language used (did you/I include different tenses, different sentence structures, etc.?).

To enable learners to be able to make real learning sense of assessment activities, many FLs teachers use simple checklists with certain key activities against which pupils can record their self-assessment or that of their peers. This may require a score or a comment or both.

How can pupils self-assess?

- self-checking activities;
- routinely testing themselves on vocabulary;
- carefully scrutinising their work/assignments before submitting them to the assessment of others (personal 'First Aid Kit', see Barnes and Hunt, 2003);
- checking achievement against 'can do' lists;
- developing ability to identify own weaknesses and difficulties (traffic light system);
- using benchmarks as a model for own work.

How can pupils peer-assess? Listed here are some practicalities as (based on Black, 2005):

- criteria need to be understood;
- modelling exercises are needed where task requirements are abstract;
- need for justifying WHY something is better/correct, etc. – encourage learners to discuss their own examples;
- need to learn to collaborate and listen to each other;
- in groups, give group members roles – one can be the 'challenger': whenever anyone comes up with something, the challenger says 'why?', etc.;
- teach learners to assess their progress keeping the aims and criteria in mind, to become independent;
- get pupils to look at tests and invent the mark scheme, get them to set questions for tests, so they can decide what makes a good question, why set it, etc.

If you've already modelled criteria quite well, then it should be a smaller step to get pupils to analyse their own work. First, self-assessment and/or peer assessment could take place using criteria you have supplied at the start of the task (e.g. simple tick sheets listing elements to be included such as hobby, day of the week, with whom, where, opinion, as well as broader issues such as accuracy of pronunciation). The class could then work out what would be an excellent response, given the criteria. Alternatively, an excellent response could be presented first as a model to be adapted. The approach should vary according to the stage of the learning:

■ how much support do the pupils need?
■ do certain pupils groups need support while others can work in a more open manner?

A plenary to this activity could consist of a discussion on what exactly makes an excellent response to this task and what now needs to be done to improve. Pupils can decide then on their own individual targets arising out of the activity. On some occasions pupils could link the activity and responses to level descriptions for each of the four skills and decide whether their response matches the criteria. Teachers might also start to make reference to the examination criteria in some of their self- and peer-assessment as pupils progress through the levels as a way of familiarising them with the requirements of external examinations.

SUMMATIVE ASSESSMENT AND EXTERNAL EXAMINATIONS

Teacher assessment

Teachers' professional judgement is essential in the assessment process. Learning to make valid and reliable judgements about pupils' progress in terms of the statutory requirements and/or the examination specifications as well as in relation to lesson and unit of work objectives is a necessary part of your programme of teacher preparation.

FLs teachers in England are currently required to report on pupils' attainment across the four skills of listening, speaking, reading and writing, and to report against criteria set out by the awarding body. Familiarity with the FLs department's specific practice and approaches to marking, assessment, recording and reporting which reflect the school's assessment policies is another prerequisite for developing competence in assessing pupils' achievement and attainment. A typical departmental policy on assessment might include information for staff on, for instance:

■ target setting with and for pupils;
■ the use of self- and peer-assessment;
■ marks/comments and feedback;
■ the nature of a departmental portfolio, including samples of annotated pupils' work (pieces of pupils' work, which are cross-referenced to the statutory requirements and have teacher comments attached explaining, for instance, how the work was completed) in order to reach a shared understanding and interpretation of the statutory requirements;
■ the overt use of assessment criteria clearly linked to teaching and learning objectives;
■ a mixture of both continuous and summative assessment activities covering all four skills across a range of different contexts/topics including a range of different task types;

■ the use of effective, multi-skill language activities for assessment;
■ the use of the TL for instructions and feedback on assessment tasks;
■ the use of resources, such as online dictionaries.

All types of summative assessment made by teachers concern issues of reliability and validity. Reliability is about the extent to which an assessment can be trusted to give consistent information on a pupil's progress; if two different markers used these same criteria and mark scheme they would come to the same results. Validity is about whether the assessment measures all that it might be felt important to measure – e.g. does asking pupils to complete a multiple choice on the listening exercise really tell you how much they have understood?

In many ways teachers are in the best place to judge a pupil's level of performance rather than external bodies as they can draw on a wide range of evidence. However, among the problems that can undermine confidence in teacher marking are standards being applied differently by different teachers and biased marking.

Assessment tends to fall into two categories: norm- or criterion-referenced. In criterion-referenced assessment there are clear elements that must be demonstrated for the award of marks. Under norm-referencing pupils are judged in relation to others who took the test, but does not necessarily let anyone else know *what* you can do. Another issue with norm-referenced assessment is that results vary depending on the cohort – i.e. I might be in the top 10 per cent one year but in another cohort taking the same test might no longer be in the top 10 per cent.

Task 15.4 **DEVISING SUMMATIVE TEACHER ASSESSMENT**

1   Devise an end-of-unit test for a class you are currently teaching. Clearly relate it to the unit objectives, base it on the principle of TL use, cover all four skill areas and match individual tasks to the statutory requirements.

2   Discuss your test with your mentor or the relevant class teacher and ask if you can administer the test to pupils. Then, mark the scripts. Note any queries, problems, insecurities, observations, etc. you have as a basis for a follow-up discussion with your mentor or the class teacher.

3   Also, speak to a couple of pupils immediately after they have taken the test. Ask them if they feel that the test allowed them to demonstrate what they think they *can do, understand* and *know*. Find out what they *liked* and *disliked* about the unit and the end-of-unit test.

ASSESSMENT FRAMEWORKS: THE COMMON EUROPEAN FRAMEWORK OF REFERENCE FOR LANGUAGES, THE NC AND GCSE

The Common European Framework of Reference (CEFR) www.coe.int/t/dg4/linguistic/Cadre1_en.asp, introduced in the early 2000s, is now published in nearly forty languages and is a criterion-referenced assessment system. The framework outlines what FLs learners 'can do' at a range of stages in their progress while learning. It was designed to provide a transparent, coherent and comprehensive basis for the elaboration of language syllabuses and curriculum guidelines, the design of teaching and learning materials, and the assessment of FL proficiency.

The General Certificate of Secondary Education (GCSE)

The GCSE is the dominant school-leaving qualification in England and an ostensibly criterion-referenced award, although there have been a number of controversial debates in the UK as to the extent to which it is fully criterion-referenced. Indeed, at the time of writing, the very future of the qualification is in doubt. The GCSE examination is externally set and administered by so-called Awarding Bodies who devise specifications that must adhere to the criteria laid down by Office of Qualifications and Examinations Regulation (Ofqual), formerly the Qualifications and Curriculum Authority (QCA). At the time of writing, schools can choose from the following Awarding Bodies: the Assessment and Qualifications Alliance (AQA, www.aqa.org.uk), the Edexcel Foundation (www.edexcel.org.uk) and Oxford, Cambridge and RSA Examinations (OCR; www.ocr.org.uk). Pupils can also study for Cambridge International Examinations' International GCSE, the IGCSE, (www.cie.org.uk/qualifications/academic/middlesec/igcse/subjects).

Task 15.5 **GCSE SPECIFICATIONS**

Familiarise yourself with the specific requirements of the GCSE specification used in your placement school. What do you perceive to be the strengths and weaknesses?

The GCSE is not without problems and critics. Lack of space does not allow for a detailed analysis but we raise a few points here:

■ The GCSE is ostensibly a terminal examination, testing the outcomes of five years of study, rather than an assessment of the learning process; it thereby militates against 'assessment motivation' and places a lot of emphasis on memorisation. This is especially true of the introduction of the controlled assessments.

■ The fitness for purpose of the examination is questionable: to what extent does it test what pupils should be taught in the context of the National Curriculum? For example, how well are pupils' cultural awareness or their ability to use reference material examined?

■ The examination appears to have a considerable backwash effect on teaching and learning, often leading to 'teaching to the test'. This can result in a narrow rote-learning approach, and has led to considerable emphasis being placed on the teaching of examination techniques and examination practice, for example in the form of so-called mock exams.

■ The skills-based approach (i.e. separate papers for listening, speaking, reading and writing) raises certain questions about the reliability and validity of the examination: how authentic are the tasks pupils are asked to perform, i.e. to what extent do they mirror real-life TL use? For example, to what extent are spontaneity and unpredictability of real-time language use reflected in the examination?

Pachler (2000: 30) argues that the methodology underpinning the GCSE is characterised by a narrow transactional-functional orientation in which pupils are prepared for the linguistic (and non-linguistic) needs of tourists, such as making travel arrangements, going to bars, restaurants, museums, booking into hotels, buying petrol for the car, etc., with the emphasis on 'getting by'. On one hand, this approach is characterised by a heavy emphasis on recall of often random lexical items and phrases derived from narrowly defined, idealised interactions and exchanges at the cost of the transfer of knowledge and skills across topics. On the other hand, it tends to ignore the teenage learner's communicative needs and does not allow her to engage in meaningful and realistic interaction, both supposedly central tenets of communicative methodology.

Below we discuss the criteria for the speaking exam for one of the awarding bodies, AQA, by way of exemplification of a criterion-referenced approach. Each of the two tasks is awarded a maximum of 30 marks based on how well a candidate does in communicating meaning, the range and accuracy of the language used, pronunciation and intonation and interaction with the teacher (e.g. answering questions (and fluency)). While we are aware of the dangers of 'backwash' from summative testing – i .e. where a teacher's classroom practice is heavily influenced by what will be tested later and may lead to the sidelining of things that will not be directly tested such as cultural understanding – it seems to us to make sense to use some of these criteria from early on in a pupil's language learning career. This allows for familiarisation with the criteria that will be used later and potentially for focused target-setting. Pupils can use these frameworks to self- and peer-assess, but the teacher needs to help the pupils to put 'meat on the bones', i.e. what does 'sufficient' look like in practice? The teacher can also add any other categories as she see fit for developing other competences (e.g. use of humour, clarity of speech, sociolinguistic competence – *tu*/*vous*, behaviours such as shaking hands) whether they will be tested in the examination or not.

Assessment criteria per task

Communication	10
Range and accuracy of language	10
Pronunciation and intonation	5
Interaction and fluency	5
Total	**30**

MARKS: COMMUNICATION

9–10 Very good: information, ideas and points of view are presented and explained with confidence. Can narrate events when appropriate.

7–8 Good: a good amount of information and points of view are conveyed and regularly developed.

5–6 Sufficient: a reasonable amount of information and points of view are conveyed and sometimes developed.

3–4 Limited: some simple information and opinions are conveyed.

1–2 Poor: few responses are developed. Little relevant information communicated. Very few appropriate responses are developed.

0 No relevant information conveyed. A zero score.

MARKS: RANGE AND ACCURACY OF LANGUAGE

9–10 A wide range of vocabulary, complex structures and a variety of verb tenses. Errors usually appear in more complex structures.

7–8 A range of vocabulary; some complex structures and a variety of verb tenses attempted, though not always well formed. Some errors occur but the message is clear.

5–6 Limited vocabulary; sentences generally simple but occasionally more complex. Errors are quite frequent, but the language is more accurate than inaccurate.

3–4 Very limited vocabulary; short, simple sentences. Errors very frequent.

1–2 Isolated words of vocabulary. Occasional short phrases. Errors often impede communication.

0 No language produced is worthy of credit.

MARKS: PRONUNCIATION AND INTONATION

5 Consistently good accent and intonation.

4 Generally good.

3 Generally accurate but some inconsistency.

2 Understandable, but comprehension is sometimes delayed.

1 Barely understandable, making comprehension difficult.

0 No language produced is worthy of credit.

MARKS: INTERACTION AND FLUENCY

5 Responds readily and shows initiative. Conversation sustained at a reasonable speed, language expressed fluently.

4 Answers without hesitation and extends responses beyond the minimum with some flow of language.

3 Ready responses; some evidence of an ability to sustain a conversation; little if any initiative.

2 Some reaction. Sometimes hesitant, little natural flow of language.

1 Little reaction. Very hesitant and disjointed.

0 No language produced is worthy of credit.

Task 15.6 **APPLYING ASSESSMENT CRITERIA**

Carry out some mock speaking examinations with a small number of pupils. Then, make a judgement about the pupils' performance using the AQA criteria. Finally, reflect on the process: what issues arise?

RECORDING JUDGEMENTS

Teachers need to record pupils' progress as accurately and fully as they can for a number of reasons. First, this can aid future planning. Teachers need to know how the individuals in their groups are progressing in key skill areas such as listening and speaking, etc., but also how they are using the language, their levels of contribution and confidence, whether they have missed key lessons, and so on. The mark book can be a place to record this sort of detail and is a useful tool in aiding future planning for learning. Recording in the mark book can take the form of marks and grades, where these have been generated through summative testing (for details, see Mutton, 2014), or comments generated from the teacher's professional understanding of how the learners are progressing.

Second, the mark book serves as a useful tool for ensuring effective progression for pupils at points of transition – e.g. when pupils pass from one teacher to another either at the end of or during the school year.

Finally, teachers' systematic records of pupils' achievements and attainments serve as evidence that can be reported to relevant parties, such as pupils, parents, school leadership, and so on. Currently, parents in England are entitled to one written report on their child's progress per academic year and a report in relation to the National Curriculum at the age of 14 prior to embarking on work more narrowly defined by the examination specifications.

In order to be able to identify pupils' progress, many FLs teachers keep a mark book either electronically or a paper version, often subdivided into sections that might include:

- name;
- Special Educational Needs;
- form group;
- listening;
- speaking;
- reading;
- writing;
- homework;
- use of TL;
- other comments.

The section on the TL allows the teacher to record, for example, spontaneous use of the TL in role play situations or pupils making a particular effort in using the TL in pupil–teacher and pupil–pupil interactions. In assessing pupils' spoken language, teachers can offer encouragement to pupils who make contributions to lessons and recording these in the mark book might provide an incentive to some pupils.

In another section, the individual term targets set for and by pupils could be recorded, as well as more formal targets and other data, e.g. schools now expect all pupils to have a target examination grade that is recorded and monitored.

The grading systems used to record FLs marks varies from school to school with some departments – for instance, awarding numbers out of ten, others using a system based on letters. Whichever system is used, there should be consistency between teachers, and the letters and numbers need to *equate to something*, otherwise they can be rather meaningless.

A key point to remember when considering what is recorded in the mark book is *usefulness*. There is little point in recording elaborate scores out of 37 for a reading comprehension if there is no information that will help you remember the sorts of skills the reading comprehension was testing, its level of difficulty, and so on: otherwise the only purpose the marks serve is to tell you how the learners did in relation to each other. This suggests that each piece of information logged should have some context included with it and teachers should be aware of why they think recording this information will be worthwhile.

Task 15.7 **WRITING A REPORT**

1   Find out about the school's policy for report writing and ask your mentor for some specimen report pro formas and sample reports. On the basis of your own records, your 'professional' opinion and the sample reports, write a report on a number of pupils of different abilities of a class you teach. Choose pupils your mentor also knows well.
2   Discuss the reports you have written with your mentor. Do they reflect what she thinks of the pupils? Did you have enough evidence to formulate objective judgements?

SUMMARY

Assessment serves many purposes but is integral to FL teaching and learning and not 'bolt-on'. AfL, aimed at gathering evidence of progress, sharing this with pupils and so using it to develop their knowledge and understanding, is at the heart of our assessment practice.

Pupil peer- and self-assessment is an important strand of AfL that allows pupils to better understand the criteria for success in language learning and to take responsibility for their learning.

Summative testing, including the use of professional judgement of the standards learners reach, serves to inform others of the progress made by the pupils in our classes. Teachers are required to work within the respective national statutory assessment framework and to prepare pupils for external assessment. Familiarity with the statutory requirements for internal and external assessment is, therefore, imperative. Summative assessment can be used formatively where teachers use the information it provides to adapt teaching and to help learners develop as a result.

FURTHER READING

Barnes, A. and Hunt, M. (2003) *Effective Assessment in Foreign Languages*. London: CILT.
    This book looks at all the main aspects of assessment in FL and has a number of practical activities and reflective tasks to enable you to develop a deeper understanding of the issues.

Black, P., Harrison, C., Lee, C., Marshall, B. and Dylan, W. (2003) *Assessment for Learning: Putting it into Practice*. London: Oxford University Press.
    A comprehensive guide to research and practice in this important area of teaching and learning.

Black, P. and Jones, J. (2006) Formative assessment and the learning and teaching of foreign languages: sharing the language learning road map with the learners. In *Language Learning Journal*, 34: 4–9.

An article jointly written by a foreign language teacher educator and an assessment researcher which brings together the generic aspects of assessment for learning with the subject specific requirements of foreign languages.

Jones, J. and Wiliam, D. (2008) *MFL inside the Black Box*. London: King's College London.

An issue of the 'black box' series on AfL with a foreign language focus.

REFERENCES

ACTFL (1998) *Program standards for the preparation of foreign language teachers.* Yonkers, NY: The American Council on the Teaching of Foreign Languages.

Ainslie, S. and Purcell, S. (2000) *Resource File 4: Mixed-ability Teaching in Language Learning.* London: CILT.

Alison, J. (1993) Are they being served? In *TES National Curriculum Update,* 10 February, p. 15.

Allen, J. (1983) General purpose language teaching: a variable focus approach. In Brumfit, C. (ed.) *General English Syllabus Design.* ELT Documents No. 118. London: Pergamon Press and the British Council.

Allford, D. (1999) Translation in the communicative classroom. In Pachler, N. (ed.) *Teaching Modern Foreign Languages at Advanced Level.* London: Routledge, pp. 230–250.

Allford, D. (2000) Pictorial images and language teaching. In *Language Learning Journal,* 22: 45–51.

Allford, D. and Pachler, N. (2007) *Language, Autonomy and the New Learning Environments.* Oxford: Peter Lang.

Amuzie, G. and Winke, P. (2009) Changes in language learning beliefs as a result of study abroad. In *System,* 37(3): 366–379.

Anderson, A. and Lynch, T. (1988) *Listening.* Oxford: Oxford University Press.

Anderson, J. (1995) *Cognitive Psychology and its Implications* (4th edn). New York: Freeman.

Anderson, N. (1999) *Exploring Second Language Reading: Issues and Strategies.* London: Heinle & Heinle.

Antón, M. (1999) The discourse of a learner-centred classroom: sociocultural perspectives on teacher-learner interaction in the second-language classroom. In *The Modern Language Journal,* 83(iii): 303–318.

Arthur, J., Davison, J. and Moss, J. (1998) *Subject Mentoring.* London: Routledge.

Assessment Reform Group (ARG) (2002) Assessment for learning: 10 principles. Available online at: www.nuffieldfoundation.org/assessment-reform-group

Atkinson, T. and Claxton, G. (eds) (2000) *The Intuitive Practitioner: On the Value of not Always Knowing What One is Doing.* Milton Keynes: Open University Press.

Bachmair, B. and Pachler, N. (2013) Composition and appropriation in a culture characterised by provisionality. In Böck, M. and Pachler, N. (eds) *Multimodality and Social Semiosis: Communication, Meaning-Making and Learning in the Work of Gunther Kress*. New York: Routledge, pp. 211–220.

Baddeley, A. D., Gathercole, S. E. and Papagno, C. (1998) The phonological loop as a language learning device. In *Psychological Review*, 105: 158–173.

Banks, F., Leach, J. and Moon, B. (1999) New understandings of teachers' pedagogic knowledge. In Leach, J. and Moon, R. (eds) *Learners and Pedagogy*. London: Paul Chapman Publishing, pp. 89–110.

Barcroft, J. (2004) Second language vocabulary acquisition: a lexical input processing approach. In *Foreign Language Annals*, 37(2): 200–208.

Barker, S., Brooks, V., March, K. and Swatton, P. (1996) *Initial Teacher Education in Secondary Schools: A Study of the Tangible and Intangible Costs and Benefits of Initial Teacher Education in Secondary Schools*. London: Association of Teachers and Lecturers.

Barnes, A. (1997) Buyer beware – evaluating MFL materials. In *German Teaching*, 16: 2–4.

Barnes, A. (2006) Confidence levels and concerns of beginning teachers of modern foreign languages. In *Language Learning Journal*, 34: 37–46.

Barnes, A. (2007) Communicative approaches to modern foreign language teaching and using the target language. In Pachler, N. and Redondo, A. (eds) *A Practical Guide to Teaching Modern Foreign Languages in the Secondary School*. London: Routledge, pp. 4–11.

Barnes, A. and Hunt, M. (2003) *Effective Assessment in MFL*. London: CILT.

Barrette, C., Paesani, K. and Vinall, K. (2010) Toward an integrated curriculum: maximising the use of TL literature. In *Foreign Language Annals*, 43(2): 216–230.

Barton, A. (2002a) Learning styles: the gender effect. In Swarbrick, A. (ed.) *Teaching Modern Foreign Languages in Secondary Schools: A Reader*. Buckingham: Open University Press, pp. 272–285.

Barton, A. (2002b) Teaching modern foreign languages to single-sex classes. In *Language Learning Journal*, 25: 8–14.

Bartrum, B. (2006) Attitudes to language learning: a comparative study of peer group influences. In *Language Learning Journal*, 33: 47–52.

Batstone, R. and Ellis, R. (2009) Principled grammar teaching. In *System*, 37:194–204.

Beaton, R. (1990) The many sorts of error. In Page, B. (ed.) *What Do You Mean it's Wrong?* London: CILT, pp. 38–47.

Becta (2003) What the research says about interactive whiteboards. Coventry. Available online at: www.dera.ioe.ac.uk/5318/1/wtrs_whiteboards.pdf

Beers, M. (2001) A media-based approach to developing ethnographic skills for second language teaching and learning. In *Zeitschrift für Interkulturellen Fremdsprachenunterricht*, 6(2). Available online at: http://.zif.spz.tu-darmstadt.de/jg-06–2/beitrag/beers2.htm

Bennett, J. (2008) On becoming a global soul. In Savicki, V. (ed.) *Developing Intercultural Competence and Transformation: Theory, Research and Application in International Education*. Stirling: Stylus, pp. 13–31.

Bennett, N. and Dunne, E. (1994) Managing groupwork. In Moon, B. and Shelton-Mayes, A. (eds) *Teaching and Learning in the Secondary School*. Milton Keynes: Open University Press, pp. 166–172.

Bernstein, B. (1971) *Class, Codes and Control: Theoretical Studies Towards a Sociology of Language*. London: Routledge & Kegan Paul.

Bialystok, E. and Hakuta, K. (1995) *In Other Words: The Science and Psychology of Second-language Acquisition*. London: Basic Books.

Black, P. (2005) How, and why, can assessment for learning be successful? Raising standards through formative assessment. Paper presented at Language World, University of Kent at Canterbury, 1 July.

Black, P. and Jones, J. (2006) Formative assessment and the learning and teaching of MFL: sharing the language learning road map with the learners. In *Language Learning Journal*, 34: 4–9.

Black, P. and Wiliam, D. (1998) Inside the black box: raising standards through classroom assessment. Phi Delta Kappa International. Available online at: www.measuredprogress.org/documents/10157/15653/InsideBlackBox.pdf

Black P. and Wiliam D. (2003) In praise of educational research: formative assessment. In *British Educational Research Journal*, 29: 623–638.

Black, P., Harrison, C., Lee, C., Marshall, B. and Wiliam, D. (2002) *Working Inside the Black Box: Assessment for Learning in the Classroom.* London: King's College London Department of Education and Professional Studies.

Black, P., Harrison, C., Lee, C., Marshall, B. and Wiliam, D. (2003) *Assessment for Learning: Putting it into Practice.* Maidenhead: Open University Press.

Booth, T., Ainscow, M., Black-Hawkins, K., Vaughan, M. and Shaw, L. (2000) *Index for Inclusion: Developing Learning and Participation in Schools.* Bristol: Centre for Studies on Inclusive Education in collaboration with the Centre for Educational Needs, University of Manchester and Centre for Educational Research, Canterbury Christ Church University College.

Borg, S. (1994) Language awareness as a methodology: implications for teachers and teacher training. In *Language Awareness*, 3(2): 61–71.

Borg, S. (2003) Teacher cognition in language teaching: a review of research on what language teachers think, know, believe and do. In *Language Teaching*, 36: 81–109.

Borg, S. (2010) Language teacher research engagement. In *Language Teaching*, 43(4): 391–429.

Bramall, G. (2002) How do you work that out? A comparison of two question types in the GCSE reading tests. In *Deutsch Lehren und Lernen*, 26:14–16.

Brandi, M. -L. and Strauss, D. (1985) *Training des Leseverstehens mit Hilfe von Sachtexten.* Munich: Goethe-Institut.

Broady, E. (2014) MFL teaching: understanding approaches, making choices. In Pachler, N. and Redondo, A. (eds) *A Practical Guide to Teaching Foreign Languages* (2nd edn). London: Routledge.

Brown, G. and Yule, G. (1983) *Teaching the Spoken Language.* Cambridge: Cambridge University Press.

Brown, H. D. (1986) Learning a second culture. In Valdes, J. M. (ed.) *Culture Bound: Bridging the Cultural Gaps in Language Teaching.* Cambridge: Cambridge University Press, pp. 33–48.

Bruner, J. (1996) *The Culture of Education.* Cambridge, MA: Harvard University Press.

Bruton, A. (2005) Task-based language teaching: for the state secondary FL classroom? In *Language Learning Journal*, 31(1): 55–68.

Bruton, A. (2011) Is CLIL so beneficial, or just selective? Re-evaluating some of the Research. In *System*, 39: 523–532.

Bruton, A., Lopez, M. and Mesa, R. (2011) Incidental L2 vocabulary learning: an impracticable term? In *TESOL Quarterly*, 45(4): 759–768.

Buckby, M. (1980) *Action 1. Teacher's Book.* Walton-on-Thames: Nelson Thornes.

Burn, A. and Durran, J. (2013) Making the moving image: teaching and learning with digital video production. In Leask, M. and Pachler, N. (eds) *Learning to Teach using ICT in the Secondary School* (3rd edn). London: Routledge.

Burns, A. (2001) Analysing spoken discourse: implications for TESOL. In Burns, A. and Coffin, C. (eds) *Analysing English in a Global Context: A Reader.* London: Routledge, pp. 123–148.

Burns, A., Gollin, S. and Joyce, H. (1997) Authentic spoken texts in the language classroom. In *Prospect*, 12: 72–86.

Butler, M. and Kelly, P. (1999) Videoconferencing. In Leask, M. and Pachler, N. (eds) *Learning to Teach using ICT in the Secondary School*. London: Routledge, pp. 95–108.

Butzkamm, W. (2003) We only learn language once. The role of the mother tongue in FL classrooms: death of a dogma. In *Language Learning Journal*, 28: 29–39.

Bygate, M. (1987) *Speaking*. Oxford: Oxford University Press.

Byram, M. (1989) *Cultural Studies in Foreign Language Education*. Clevedon: Multilingual Matters.

Byram, M. (1997) *Teaching and Assessing Intercultural Communicative Competence*. Clevedon: Multilingual Matters.

Byram, M. (2010) Linguistic and cultural education for Bildung and citizenship. In *The Modern Language Journal*, 94(ii): 317–321.

Byram, M. and Feng, A. (2004) Culture and language learning: teaching, research and scholarship. In *Language Teaching*, 37: 149–168.

Byram, M. and Risager, K. (2002) Stereotypes, prejudice and tolerance. In Swarbrick, A. (ed.) *Teaching Modern Foreign Languages in Secondary Schools: A Reader*. London: Routledge, pp. 81–94.

Byram, M., Morgan, C. *et al.* (1994) *Teaching-and-Learning Language-and-Culture*. Clevedon: Multilingual Matters.

Cable, C., Driscoll, P., Mitchell, R., Sing, S., Cremin, T., Earl, J., Eyres, I., Holmes, B., Martin, C. and Heins, B. (2010) Languages learning at Key Stage 2. A longitudinal study. Final report. London: DCSF. Available online at: www.eprints.soton.ac.uk/143157/1/DCSF-RR198.pdf

Cajkler, W. and Addelman, R. (2000) *The Practice of Foreign Language Teaching* (2nd edn). London: David Fulton.

Calvert, M. (2014) Reflective practice through teacher research. In Pachler, N. and Redondo, A. (eds) *Teaching Foreign Languages in the Secondary School – A Practical Guide* (2nd edn). London: Routledge.

Campbell, A. (2005) Weblog applications for EFL/ESL classroom blogging: a comparative review. In *TESL-EL*, 9(3). Available online at: www.tesl-ej.org/ej35/m1.html

Canale, M. and Swain, M. (1980) Theoretical bases of communicative approaches to second language teaching and testing. In *Applied Linguistics*, 1(1): 1–47.

Carter, R. (1987) Vocabulary and second/foreign language learning. In *Language Teaching*, 20(1): 3–16.

Carter, R. (1997) *Investigating English Discourse*. London: Routledge.

Carter, R. and Long, M. (1991) *Teaching Literature*. Harlow: Longman.

CCSSO (2011) In TASC model core teaching standards: a resource for State dialogue. Council of Chief State School Officers. Washington, DC. Available online at: www.ccsso.org/documents/2011/intasc_model_core_teaching_standards_2011.pdf

Celce-Murcia, M. (1991) Grammar pedagogy in second and foreign language teaching. In *TESOL Quarterly*, 25(3): 459–480.

Chambers, G. (1996) Listening, Why? How? In *Language Learning Journal*, 7: 13–16.

Chambers, G. (1999) *Motivating Language Learners*. Clevedon: Multilingual Matters.

Chambers, G. (2014) Developing listening skills in the modern foreign language. In Pachler, N. and Redondo, A. (eds) *Teaching Foreign Languages in the Secondary School: A Practical Guide*. London: Routledge.

Chamot, A. (2005) Language learning strategy instruction: current issues and research. In *Annual Review of Applied Linguistics*, 25:112–130.

Chapelle, C. (1998) Multimedia CALL: lessons to be learnt from research on instructed SLA. In *Language Learning & Technology*, 2(1): 21–39. Available online at: www.llt.msu.edu/vol2num1/article1

Clark, A. and Trafford, J. (1996) Return to gender: boys' and girls' attitudes and achievements. In *Language Learning Journal*, 14: 40–49.

Cohen, A. and Macaro, E. (2007) (eds) *Language Learning Strategies: 30 Years of Research and Practice*. Oxford: Oxford University Press.

Convery, A. and Coyle, D. (1993) *Differentiation – Initiative*. London: CILT.

Cook, G. (2010) *Translation in Language Teaching*. Oxford: Oxford University Press.

Coonan, C. (2007) Insider views of the CLIL class through teacher self-observation-introspection. In *The International Journal of Bilingual Education and Bilingualism*, 10: 625–646.

Cornell, A. (1996) Grammar – grinding or grounding? In *German Teaching*,13: 26–29.

Council of Europe (2001) Common European framework of reference for languages: learning, teaching, assessment. Strasbourg: Council of Europe and Cambridge: Cambridge University Press. Available online at: www.coe.int/t/dg4/linguistic/ source/framework_en.pdf

Council of Europe (2006) Plurilingual education in Europe. 50 years of international co-operation. Strasbourg: Language Policy Division. Available online at: www. coe.int/t/dg4/linguistic/Source/PlurinlingalEducation_En.pdf

Cox, M. and Webb, M. (eds) (2004) *An Investigation of the Research Evidence Relating to ICT Pedagogy. Version 1*. Coventry: Becta, p. 123. A revised version entitled *ICT and Pedagogy: A Review of the Research Literature*. A report to the DfES. ICT in Schools Research and Evaluation Series 18.

Coyle, D., Holmes, B. and King, L. (2009) *Towards an Integrated Curriculum: CLIL National Statement and Guidelines*. Lancaster: The Languages Company.

Coyle, D., Hood, P. and Marsh, D. (2010) *CLIL: Content and Language Integrated Learning*. Cambridge: Cambridge University Press.

Crozier, M., Gidley, R., Lertoria, T., Murphy, D., Slater, S. and Wardle, M. (2003) Starters and plenaries – a practical resource. In *Deutsch: Lehren und Lernen*, 28:11–14.

Crystal, D. (2003) *The Cambridge Encyclopedia of Language* (2nd edn). Cambridge: Cambridge University Press.

Cunningsworth, A. (1995) *Choosing your Coursebook*. Oxford: Heinemann.

Dakin, J. (1976) *The Language Laboratory and Language Learning*. Harlow: Longman.

Dalton-Puffer, C. (2011) Content and language integrated learning: from practice to principles. In *Annual Review of Applied Linguistic*, 31: 182–204.

Dam, L. (1990) Learner autonomy in practice. In Gathercole, I. (ed.) *Autonomy in Language Learning*. London: CILT, pp. 16–37.

Dam, L. (1995) *Learner Autonomy 3: From Theory to Classroom Practice*. Dublin: Authentik.

Davies, H., Nutley, S. and Smith, P. (eds) (2000) *What Works? Evidence-based Policy and Practice in Public Services*. Bristol: The Policy Press.

Davison, J. (2000) Managing classroom behaviour. In Capel, S., Leask, M. and Turner, T. (eds) *Learning to Teach in the Secondary School* (2nd edn). London: Routledge, pp. 120–132.

DCSF (2009) Developing language in the primary school: literacy and primary languages. London: DCSF. Available online at: www.dera.ioe.ac.uk/2389/1/mfl_ pri_gd_del_lang_full.pdf

Deane, M. (1992) Teaching modern languages to pupils with special educational needs? With pleasure! In *Language Learning Journal*, 6: 43–47.

DeKeyser, R. (2005) What makes learning second-language grammar difficult? A review of issues. In *Language Learning*, 55(1): 1–25.

Delaney, Y. (2012) Research on mentoring language teachers: its role in language education. In *Foreign Language Annals*, 45(1): 184–202.

Denscombe, M. (1980) Keeping 'em quiet: the significance of noise for the practical activity of teaching. In Woods, P. (ed.) *Teacher Strategies*. London: Croom Helm.

Denscombe, M. (2007) *Good Research Guide: For Small Scale Social Research Projects*, Maidenhead: Oxford University Press.

Denton, C. and Postlethwaite, K. (1985) *Able Children: Identifying Them in the Classroom*. Windsor: NFER-Nelson.

Derwing, T. and Munro, M. (2005) Second language accent and pronunciation: a research-based approach. In *TESOL Quarterly*, 39(3): 379–397.

DES/Welsh Office (1990) *Modern Foreign Languages for Ages 11–16*. London: HSMO.

DES/Welsh Office (1991) *Modern Foreign Languages in the National Curriculum*. London: HMSO.

DfE (2010) *The Importance of Teaching. The Schools White Paper 2010*. Available online at: www.education.gov.uk/publications/eOrderingDownload/CM-7980.pdf

DfE (2011a) *Review of the National Curriculum in England. Report on subject breadth in international jurisdictions. DFE-RR178a*. Available online at: www.education.gov.uk/publications/eOrderingDownload/DFE-RR178a.pdf

DfE (2011b) *The Framework for the National Curriculum*. London: DfE. Available online at: www.education.gov.uk/publications/eOrderingDownload/NCR-Expert%20Panel%20Report.pdf

DfE (2012) *Teachers' Standards*. London. Available online at: www.education.gov.uk/publications/eOrderingDownload/teachers%20standards.pdf

DfE (2013) *The National Curriculum in England. Framework Document for Consultation*. London: HMSO. Available online at www.education.gov.uk/national curriculum

DfE/Welsh Office (1994) *Code of Practice on the Identification and Assessment of Special Educational Needs*. London: HMSO.

DfEE/QCA (1999) *Modern Foreign Languages: The National Curriculum for England*. London.

DfES (2002) *Key Stage 3 Strategy – Framework for teaching MFL*. London: DfES.

DfES (2004) *Use of Interactive Whiteboards in Modern Foreign Languages. Embedding ICT @ Secondary*. London: DfES.

DfES (2005a) *Key Stage 2 Framework for Languages, Parts 1 and 2*. Nottingham: DfES Publications. Available online at: www.education.gov.uk/publications/standard/publicationDetail/Page1/DFES%20201721%202005#downloadableparts

DfES (2005b) *Key Stage 2 to Key Stage 3 Transition Project*. London: DfES. Available online at: www.trevorfolley.com/wp-content/uploads/2011/09/KS2-to-KS3-Transition-Report-Mouchel-.pdf

DfES (2005c) *Developing the Global Dimension in the School Curriculum*. London: DfES. Available online at: www.dfid.gov.uk/pubs/files/dev-global-dim.pdf

Dickson, P. (1996) *Using the Target Language: A View from the Classroom*. Slough: NFER.

Dörnyei, Z. (2001) *Teaching and Researching Motivation*. London: Longman.

Dörnyei, Z. and Csizér, K. (1998) Ten commandments for motivating language learners: results of an empirical study. In *Language Teaching Research*, 2(3): 203–229.

Dörnyei, Z. and Skehan, P. (2003) Individual differences in second language learning. In Doughty, C. and Long, M. (eds) *The Handbook of Second Language Acquisition*. Oxford: Blackwell, pp. 589–630.

Dörnyei, Z. and Thurrell, S. (1994) Teaching conversational skills intensively: course content and rationale. In *ELT Journal*, 48: 40–49.

Doyé, P. (1999) *The Intercultural Dimension: Foreign Language Education in the Primary School*. Berlin: Cornelsen.

Duff, A. (1989) *Translation*. Oxford: Oxford University Press.

Dunne, E. (1993) Theory into practice. In Bennett, N. and Carré, C. (eds) *Learning to Teach*. London: Routledge, pp. 105–119.

Dweck, C. (2000) *Self-Theories: Their Role in Motivation, Personality, and Development*. Philadelphia, PA: The Psychology Press.

Ellis, G. and Sinclair, B. (1989) *Learning to Learn English: A Course in Learner Training*. Cambridge: Cambridge University Press.

Ellis, R. (1994) *The Study of Second Language Acquisition*. Oxford: Oxford University Press.

Ellis, R. (2000) Task-based research and language pedagogy. *Language Teaching Research*, 4(3):193–220.

Ellis, R. (2003) *Task-based Language Learning and Teaching*. Oxford: Oxford University Press.

Ellis, R. (2005) Principles of instructed language learning. In *System, 33*: 209–224.

Ellis, R. (2006) Issues in the teaching of grammar: an SLA perspective. In *TESOL Quarterly*, 40(1): 83–107.

Ellis, R. (2012) *Language Teaching Research and Language Pedagogy*. Oxford: Wiley-Blackwell.

Erler, L. (2004) Near-beginner learners of French are reading at a disability level. In *Francophonie*, 30: 9–15.

European Commission (2003) Promoting language learning and linguistic diversity: an action plan 2004–2006. Available online at: www.eur-lex.europa.eu/LexUriServ/ LexUriServ.do?uri=COM:2003:0449:FIN:EN:pdf

Evans, M. and Fisher, L. (2005) Measuring gains in pupils' foreign language competence as a result of participation in a school exchange visit: the case of Y9 pupils at three comprehensive schools in the UK. In *Language Teaching Research*, 9(2): 173–192.

Evans, M. and Fisher, L. (2009) Language learning at Key Stage 3: the impact of the Key Stage 3 modern foreign language framework and changes to the curriculum on provision and practice. London: DCSF. Available online at: www.dera.ioe. ac.uk/11170/1/DCSF-RR091.pdf

Evans, M. and Fisher, L. (2012) Emergent communities of practice: secondary schools' interaction with primary school foreign language teaching and learning. In *Language Learning Journal*, 40(2): 157–173.

Everett, V. (2005) You can get the grammar needed for GCSE on to one side of A4 . . . but it takes two years to get good at using it. In *Language Learning Journal*, 32: 68–73.

Fawkes, S. (2001) *CILT Briefings 1: Using Authentic Materials in Key Stages 3 and 4*. London: CILT.

Fernández-Toro, M. (2005) The role of paired listening in L2 Listening instruction. In *Language Learning Journal*, 31: 3–8.

Fernheimer, J. and Nelson, T. (2005) Bridging the composition divide: blog pedagogy and the potential for agonistic classrooms. In *Currents in Electronic Literacy* 9. Available online at: www.cwrl.utexas.edu/current/fall05/fernheimernelson.html

Field, J. (2008) *Listening in the Language Classroom*. Cambridge: Cambridge University Press.

Field, K. (1999) GCSE and A/AS level teaching: similarities and differences. In Pachler, N. (ed.) *Teaching Modern Foreign Languages at Advanced level*. London: Routledge, pp. 33–59.

Field, K. (2000) Why are girls better at modern foreign languages than boys? In Field, K. (ed.) *Issues in the Teaching of Modern Foreign Languages*. London: Routledge, pp. 134–145.

Field, K., Holden, P. and Lawlor, H. (2000) *Effective Subject Leadership*. London: Routledge.

Field, S. (2014) Presenting new vocabulary and structures. In Pachler, N. and Redondo, A. (eds) *A Practical Guide to Teaching Foreign Languages* (2nd edn). London: Routledge.

Figueras, N. (2012) The impact of the CEFR. In *ELT Journal*, 66(4): 477–485.

Fisher, L. and Evans, M. (2000) The school exchange visit: effects on attitudes and proficiency in language learning. In *Language Learning Journal*, 22: 11–16.

Fleming, F. and Walls, G. (1998) What pupils do: the role of strategic planning in modern foreign language learning. In *Language Learning Journal*, 18: 1–21.

Foote, J., Trofimovich, P., Collins, L. and Uruzua, F. (2013) Pronunciation teaching practices in communicative second language classes. In *The Language Learning Journal*. FirstView. DOI:10.1080/09571736.2013.784345

Forth, I. and Naysmith, J. (1995) 'The good the bad and the ugly': some problems with grammar rules. In *Language Learning Journal*, 11: 78–81.

Freeman, D. (2002) The hidden side of the work: teacher knowledge and learning to teach. A perspective from North American educational research on teacher education in English language teaching. In *Language Teaching*, 35: 1–13.

Furlong, J. and Maynard, T. (1995) *Mentoring Student Teachers: The Growth of Professional Knowledge*. London: Routledge.

Furlong, J., Whitty, G., Miles, S., Barton, L. and Barrett, E. (1996) From integration to partnership: changing structures in initial teacher education. In McBride, R. (ed.) *Teacher Education Policy: Some Issues Arising from Research and Practice*. London: Falmer Press, pp. 22–35.

Furstenberg, G., Levet, S., English, K. and Maillet, K. (2001) Giving a virtual voice to the silent language of culture: The Cultura project. In *Language Learning & Technology*, 5(1): 55–102. Available online at: www.llt.msu.edu/vol5num1/furstenberg/default.pdf

Ganschow, L. and Sparks, R. (2000) Reflections on foreign language study for students with language learning problems: research, issues and challenges. In *Dyslexia*, 6(2), pp. 87–100.

Gardner, H. (1983) *Frames of Mind*. New York: Basic Books.

Gardner, J. (2012) *Assessment and Learning*. London: Sage.

Gee, P. (2010) *How to do Discourse Analysis: A Toolkit*. London: Routledge.

General Teaching Council for Northern Ireland (GTCNI) (2011) Teaching: the reflective profession. Available online at: www.epublishbyus.com/the_reflective_profession/10020354

General Teaching Council for Scotland (GTCS) (2012) The Standards for Registration. Draft. August. Available online at: www.gtcs.org.uk/web/FILES/about-gtcs/standards-for-registration-draft-august-2012.pdf

George, D. (1993) Meeting the challenge of the able child. In *Topic 10*. Windsor: NFER-Nelson.

George, P. (2005) A rationale for differentiating instruction in the regular classroom. In *Theory into Practice*, 44(3): 185–193.

Gibson, S. (2008) Reading aloud: a useful learning tool? In *ELT Journal*, 62(1): 29–36.

Gilmore, A. (2007) Authentic materials and authenticity in foreign language learning. In *Language Teaching*, 40(2): 97–118.

Godwin-Jones, R. (2006) Tag clouds in the blogsphere: electronic literacy and social networking. In *Language Learning & Technology*, 10(2): 8–15. Available online at: www.llt.msu.edu/vol10num2/emerging/default.html

Godwin-Jones, R. (2007) Digital video update: YouTube, Flash, High-Definition. In *Language Learning & Technology*, 11(1): 16–21. Available online at: www.llt.msu.edu/vol11num1/default.html

Goleman, D. (1996) *Emotional Intelligence: Why it Can Matter More Than IQ.* London: Bloomsbury.

González Davies, M. (2004) *Multiple Voices in the Translation Classroom: Activities, Tasks and Projects.* Amsterdam: John Benjamins.

Grabe, W. (2004) Research on teaching reading. In *Annual Review of Applied Linguistics,* 24: 44–69.

Graham, S. (1997) *Effective Language Learning: Positive Strategies for Advanced Level Language Learning.* Clevedon: Multilingual Matters.

Graham, S. (2003) Learner strategies and advanced level listening comprehension. In *Language Learning Journal,* 28: 64–69.

Graham, S. (2004) Giving up on Modern Foreign Languages? Students' perceptions of learning French. In *The Modern Language Journal,* 88(2): 171–191.

Graham, S. (2006) Listening comprehension: the learners' perspective. In *System,* 34: 165–182.

Graham, S. (2014) Developing speaking skills in the modern foreign language. In Pachler, N. and Redondo, A. (eds) *Teaching Foreign Languages in the Secondary School: A Practical Guide.* London: Routledge, pp. 58–66.

Grauberg, W. (1997) *The Elements of Foreign Language Teaching.* Clevedon: Multilingual Matters.

Graves, K. (2008) The language curriculum: a social contextual perspective. In *Language Teaching,* 41(2): 147–181.

Green, P. and Hecht, K. (1992) Implicit and explicit grammar: an empirical study. In *Applied Linguistics,* 13: 168–184.

Grell, J. and Grell, M. (1985) *Unterrichtsrezepte.* Weinheim and Basel: Beltz Verlag.

Grenfell, M. (1998) *Training Teachers in Practice.* Clevedon: Multilingual Matters.

Grenfell, M. and Harris, V. (2013) Making a difference in language learning: the role of sociocultural factors and of learner strategy instruction. In *Curriculum Journal,* 24(1): 121–152.

Griffith, N. (2007) *100+ Ideas for Teaching Languages.* London: Continuum.

Griffiths, C. (2008) *Lessons from Good Language Learners.* Cambridge: Cambridge University Press.

Groot, P. (2000) Computer assisted second language vocabulary acquisition. In *Language Learning & Technology,* 4(1): 60–81. Available online at: www.llt.msu.edu/vol4num1/groot/default.html

Grossman, P. and McDonald, M. (2008) Back to the future: directions for research in teaching and teacher education. In *American Educational Research Journal,* 45(1): 184–205.

Grossman, P., Hammerness, K. and McDonald, M. (2009) Redefining teaching, re-imagining teacher education. In *Teachers and Teaching,* 15(2): 273–289.

Guichon, N. and McLornan, S. (2008) The effects of multimodality on L2 learners: implications for CALL resource design. In *System,* 36:85–93.

Hall, J. (2004) 'Practicing speaking' in Spanish: lessons from a high school foreign language classroom. In Boxer, D. and Cohen, A. (eds) *Studying Speaking to Inform Second Language Learning.* Clevedon: Multilingual Matters, pp. 68–87.

Hall, J. (2011) *Teaching and Researching: Language and Culture* (2nd edn). Pearson Education.

Hallam, S. and Deathe, K. (2002) Ability grouping: year group differences in self-concept and attitudes of secondary school pupils. In *Westminster Studies in Education,* 25(1): 7–17.

Halliday, M. A. K. (1976) Anti-Languages. In *American Anthropologist,* 78(3): 570–584.

Halliwell, S. (1991) *Yes – But will they Behave? Managing the Interactive Classroom.* London: CILT.

REFERENCES ▨ ▨ ■ ■

Halliwell, S. (1993) *Grammar Matters*. London: CILT.

Hamilton, M. (2013) *Autonomy and Foreign Language Learning in a Virtual Learning Environment*. London: Bloomsbury.

Hanauer, D. (2012) Meaningful literacy: writing poetry in the language classroom. In *Language Teaching*, 45(1): 105–115.

Harris, D. (1994) Learning from experience. In *Languages Forum* (2/3): 33–35.

Harris, V. (1997) *Teaching Learners How to Learn: Training in the ML Classroom*. London: CILT.

Harris, V. (2002) Treading a tightrope: supporting boys to achieve in MFL. In Swarbrick, A. (ed.) *Teaching Modern Foreign Languages in Secondary Schools: A Reader*. London: RoutledgeFalmer, pp. 187–202.

Hassan, X., Macaro, E., Mason, D., Nye, G., Smith, P., Vanderplank, R. (2005) Strategy training in language learning – a systematic review of available research. In *Research Evidence in Education Library*. London: EPPI-Centre, Social.

Hatch, E. (1978) Apply with caution. In *Studies in Second Language Acquisition*, 2: 123–143.

Hawkes, R. (2012) Learning to talk and talking to learn: how can spontaneous teacher-learner interaction in the secondary foreign languages classroom provide greater opportunities for L2 learning? Unpublished PhD, University of Cambridge. Available online at: www.rachelhawkes.com/RHawkes_FinalThesis.pdf

Hawkins, E. (1984) *Awareness of Language*. Cambridge: Cambridge University Press.

Hawkins, E. (1987) *Modern Languages in the Curriculum* (revised edn). Cambridge: Cambridge University Press.

Heafford, M. (1995) The quest for fluency and accuracy. In *German Teaching*, 11: 9–13.

Heilenman, L. (1991) Writing in foreign language classrooms: processes and reality. In Alatis, J. (ed.) *Georgetown University Round Table on Languages and Linguistics*. Washington, DC: Georgetown University Press, pp. 273–288.

Hewer, S. (1997) *Text Manipulation: Computer-based Activities to Improve Knowledge and Use of the Target Language*. London: CILT.

Hewings, M. (2004) *Pronunciation Practice Activities: A Resource Book for Teaching English Pronunciation*. Cambridge: Cambridge University Press.

Hill, B. (1989) *Making the Most of Video*. London: CILT.

Hill, J. (2004) Developing reading skills during Key Stage 3. In *Deutsch Lehren und Lernen*, 30: 12–14.

HMI (1992) *Special Needs Issues: A Survey by HMI*. London: HMSO.

Holmes, P. (2014) The (inter)cultural turn in foreign language teaching. In Pachler, N. and Redondo, A. (eds) *Teaching Foreign Languages in the Secondary School: A Practical Guide* (2nd edn). London: Routledge.

Howatt, A. (1984) *A History of English Language Teaching*. Oxford: Oxford University Press.

Hulstijn, J. H. (2001) Intentional and incidental second language vocabulary learning: a reappraisal of elaboration, rehearsal and automaticity. In Robinson, P. (ed.) *Cognition and Second Language Instruction*. Cambridge: Cambridge University Press, pp. 258–286.

Hulstijn, J. (2003) Connectionist models of language processing and the training of listening skills with the aid of multimedia software. In *Computer Assisted Language Learning*, 16: 413–425.

Hunt, A. and Beglar, D. (1998) Current research and practice in teaching vocabulary. In *The Language Teacher*, 22(1). Available online at: www.jalt-publications.org/tlt/articles/1914-current-research-and-practice-teaching-vocabulary

Hunt, M. (2014) Supporting foreign language learning through homework. In Pachler, N. and Redondo, A. (eds) *A Practical Guide to Teaching Modern Foreign Languages in the Secondary School* (2nd edn). London: Routledge.

Hunt, M. and Barnes, A. (2003) *Effective Assessment in MFL*. London: CILT.

Hurren, C. (1992) *Departmental Planning and Schemes of Work*. London: CILT.

Hymes, D. (1971) *On Communicative Competence*. Philadelphia, PA: University of Pennsylvania Press.

Ioannou Georgiou, S. (2012) Reviewing the puzzle of CLIL. In *ELT Journal*, 66(4): 495–504.

Jackson, J. (2002) Critical incidents across cultures. Available online at: www.llas.ac.uk/resources/paper/1426#ref11

James, C. and Garrett, P. (1991) (eds) *Language Awareness in the Classroom*. London: Longman.

Jenkins, J. (2000) *The Phonology of English as an International Language*. Cambridge: Cambridge University Press.

Jenkins, J. (2004) Research in teaching pronunciation and intonation. In *Annual Review of Applied Linguistics*, 24: 109–125.

Jones, B. (1995) *Exploring Otherness: An Approach to Cultural Awareness*. London: CILT.

Jones, B. (2000) Developing cultural awareness. In Field, K. (ed.) *Issues in Modern Foreign Languages teaching*. Routledge: London, pp. 158–170.

Jones, B. and Jones, G. (2000) *Boys' performance in modern foreign languages: Listening to Learners*. Cambridge: CILT/QCA/Homerton College.

Jones, J. (2000a) Teaching and learning modern foreign languages and able pupils. In Field, K. (ed.) *Issues in the Teaching of Modern Foreign Languages*. London: Routledge, pp. 105–121.

Jones, J. (2000b) Teaching grammar in the MFL classroom. In Field, K. (ed.) *Issues in Modern Foreign Language Teaching*. London: Routledge, pp. 146–161.

Jones, J. and Coffey, S. (2006) *Modern Foreign Languages 5–11: A Guide for Teachers*. London: David Fulton.

Jones, J. and McLachlan, A. (2009) *Primary Languages in Practice*. Maidenhead: Open University Press.

Jones, J. and Wiliam, D. (2008) *MFL Inside the Black Box*. London: King's College London.

Kagan, S. (1998) *Co-operative Learning: Resources for Teachers*. Riverside: University of California.

Kasper, G. (2001) Four perspectives on L2 pragmatic development. In *Applied Linguistics*, 22: 502–530.

Kast, B. (1985) Von der Last des Lernens, der Lust des Lesens und der Lust der Didaktik. Literarische Texte für Anfänger im kommunikativen Fremdsprachenunterricht. In Heid, M. (ed.) *Literarische Texte im kommunikativen Fremdsprachenunterricht. New Yorker Werkheft*. Munich: Goethe-Institut, pp. 132–154.

Kasten, J. (1995) Eine Insel in der Hauptstadt. In *Education Guardian*, March, 21: 15.

Kavanagh, B. and Upton, L. (1994) *Creative Use of Texts*. London: CILT.

Kay, J. (1978) *Un kilo de chansons*. Cheltenham: Mary Glasgow Publications.

Kern, R. (1994) The role of mental translation in Second Language Reading. In *Studies in Second Language Acquisition*, 16(4): 441–461.

Kern, R. (2000) *Literacy and Language Teaching*. Oxford: Oxford University Press.

Kern, R. (2002) Reconciling the language-literature split through literacy. In *ADFL Bulletin*, 33(3): 20–24.

Kern, R. (2003) Literacy as a new organising principle for foreign language education. In Patrikis, P. (ed.) *Reading Between the Lines: Perspectives on Foreign Language Literacy*. New Haven, NJ: Yale University Press, pp. 40–59.

Kern, R., Ware, P. and Warschauer, M. (2004) Crossing frontiers: new directions in online pedagogy and research. In *Annual Review of Applied Linguistics*, 24: 243–260.

Kilianska-Przybylo, G. (2009) The analysis of 'critical incidents' as a way to enhance intercultural competence. In *Humanising Language Teaching*, 11(3). Available online at: www.hltmag.co.uk/jun09/sart09.htm

Kingman, J. (1988) *Report on the Committee of Enquiry into the Teaching of English Language.* London: HMSO.

Klapper, J. (1997) Language learning at school and university: the great grammar debate continues. In *Language Learning Journal*, 16: 22–27.

Klapper, J. (2003) Taking communication to task? A critical view of recent trends in language teaching. In *Language Learning Journal*, 27: 33–42.

Kolb, D., Rubin, I. and McIntyre, J. (1974) *Organisational Psychology: An Experiential Approach.* Hemel Hempstead: Prentice Hall.

Kramsch, C. (2006) From communicative competence to symbolic competence. In *Modern Language Journal*, 90(ii): 249–252.

Kramsch, C. and Thorne, S. (2002) Foreign language learning as global communicative practice. In Block, D. and Cameron, D. (eds) *Globalization and Language Teaching.* London: Routledge, pp. 83–100.

Krashen, S. (1982) *Principles and Practice in Second Language Acquisition.* Oxford: Pergamon Press.

Krashen, S. (2013) Free reading: still a great idea. In Bland, J. and Lütge, C. (eds) *Children's Literature in Second Language Education.* London: Bloomsbury, pp. 15–24.

Kress, G. (2010a) *Multimodality: A Social Semiotic Approach to Contemporary Communication.* London: Routledge.

Kress, G. (2010b) The profound shift of digital literacies. In Gillen, J. and Barton, D. *Digital Literacies: A Research Briefing by the Technology Enhanced Learning Phase of the Teaching and Learning Research Programme.* London: TLRP.

Kuty, M. (2012) Learner autonomy and individualisation. In Eisenmann, M. and Summer, T. (eds) *Basic Issues in EFL Teaching and Learning.* Heidelberg: Universitätsverlag Winter, pp. 313–326.

Kyriacou, C. (1986) *Effective Teaching in Schools.* Hemel Hempstead: Basil Blackwell.

Kyriacou, C. (1991) *Essential Teaching Skills.* Hemel Hempstead: Basil Blackwell.

Ladson-Billings, G. (1994) *The Dreamkeepers: Successful Teaching for African-American Students.* San Francisco, CA: Jossey-Bass.

Lamb, T. and Simpson, M. (2003) Escaping from the treadmill: practitioner research and professional autonomy. In *Language Learning Journal*, 28: 55–63.

Langran, J. and Purcell, S. (1994) *Language Games and Activities.* London: CILT.

Languages and Cultures in Europe (LACE) (2007) The intercultural competences developed in compulsory foreign language education in the European Union. Available online at: www.ec.europa.eu/education/languages/archive/doc/lace_en.pdf

Lantolf, J. (1999) Second culture acquisition. Cognitive considerations. In Hinkel, E. (ed.) *Culture in Second Language Teaching.* Cambridge: Cambridge University Press.

Larsen-Freeman, D. (2003) *Teaching Language: From Grammar to Grammaring.* Boston: Heinle & Heinle.

Lasagabaster, D. and Sierra J. M. (2009) Language attitudes in CLIL and traditional EFL classes. In *International CLIL Research Journal*, 1(2): 4–17.

Lasagabaster, D. and Sierra, J. M. (2010) Immersion and CLIL in English: more differences than similarities. In *ELT Journal*, 64(4): 367–375.

Laufer, B. (2009) Second language vocabulary acquisition from language input and from form-focused activities. In *Language Teaching*, 42(3): 341–354.

Leach, J. and Moon, B. (2008) *The Power of Pedagogy*. London: Sage.

Lenneberg, E. (1967) *Biological Foundations of Language*. New York: Wiley.

Leons, E., Herbert, C. and Gobbo, K. (2009) Students with learning disabilities and AD/HD in the foreign language classroom: supporting students and instructors. In *Foreign Language Annals*, 42(1): 42–54.

Levy, M. (2007) Culture, culture learning and new technologies: towards a pedagogical framework. In *Language Learning & Technology*, 11(2): 104–127. Available online at: www.llt.msu.edu/vol11num2/pdf/levy.pdf

Lewis, C., Perry, R., Friedkin, S. and Roth, J. (2012) Improving teaching does improve teachers: evidence from lesson study. In *Journal of Teacher Education*, 63(5): 368–375.

Liamkina, O. and Ryshina-Pankova, M. (2012) Grammar dilemma: teaching grammar as a resource for meaning making. In *The Modern Language Journal*, 96(ii): 270–289.

Liddicoat, A., Papademetre, L., Scarino, A. and Kohler, M. (2003) Report on intercultural language learning. Prepared by Griffith University for the Australian Government Department of Education, Science and Training. Available online at: www1.curriculum.edu.au/nalsas/pdf/intercultural.pdf

Lightbown, P. (2003) SLA research in the classroom/SLA research for the classroom. In *Language Learning Journal*, 28: 4–13.

Lightbown, P. and Spada, N. (2013 [1993]) *How Languages are Learnt* (4th edn). Oxford: Oxford University Press.

Lin, M. and Mackay, C. (2003) *Thinking through Modern Foreign Languages*. London: Chris Kington Publications.

Little, D., Devitt, S. and Singleton, D. (1989) *Learning Foreign Languages from Authentic Texts*. Dublin: Authentik.

Littlewood, W. (1981) *Communicative Language Teaching*. Cambridge: Cambridge University Press.

Littlewood, W. (2004) The task-based approach: some questions and suggestions. In *ELT Journal*, 58(4): 319–326.

Llanes, A. (2012) The short- and long-term effects of a short study abroad experience: the case of children. In *System*, 40:179–190.

Llanes, A. and Muñoz, C. (2009) A short stay abroad: does it make a difference? In *System*, 37(3): 353–365.

Long, M. (1981) Input, interaction and foreign language acquisition. In Winitz, H. (ed.) *Native Language and Foreign Language Acquisition. Annals of the New York Academy of Sciences*, 379: 259–278.

Long, M. and Crookes, G. (1993) Units of analysis in syllabus design: the case for the task. In Crookes, G. and Gass, S. (eds) *Tasks in a Pedagogical Context*. Clevedon: Multilingual Matters, pp. 9–68.

Long, M. and Norris, J. (2000) Task-based language teaching and assessment. In Bryam, M. (ed.) *Encyclopedia of Language Teaching*. London: Routledge, pp. 597–603.

Lund, R. (1991) A comparison of second language listening and reading comprehension. In *Modern Language Journal*, 75(2): 196–204.

Lustig, M. and Koester, J. (2006) *Intercultural Competence: International Communication Across Cultures* (5th edn). Boston, MA: Pearson.

Lwo, L. and Chia-Tzu Lin, M. (2012) The effects of captions in teenagers' multimedia L2 learning. In *ReCALL*, 2:188–208.

REFERENCES ■ ■ ■ ■

Lynch, T. (1997) Nudge, nudge: teacher interventions in task-based learner talk. In *ELT Journal*, 51(4): 317–325.

Lyster, R. and Ballinger, S. (2011) Content-based language teaching: convergent concerns across divergent contexts. In *Language Teaching Research*, 15(3): 279–288

Macaro, E. (1997) *Target Language, Collaborative Learning and Autonomy*. Clevedon: Multilingual Matters.

Macaro, E. (2000) Issues in target language teaching. In Field, K. (ed.) *Issues in Modern Foreign Languages Teaching*. London: Routledge, pp. 175–193.

Macaro, E. (2003a) Second language teachers as second language researchers. In *Language Learning Journal*, 27: 43–51.

Macaro, E. (2003b) *Teaching and Learning a Second Language: A Guide to Recent Research and its Applications*. London: Continuum.

Macaro, E. (2006) Strategies for language learning and for language use: revising the theoretical framework. In *The Modern Language Journal*, 90(3): 320–337.

Macaro, E., Vanderplank, R. and Graham, S. (2005) A systematic review of the role of prior knowledge in unidirectional listening comprehension. In *Research Evidence in Education Library*. London: EPPI-Centre, Social Science Research Unit, Institute of Education, University of London. Available online at: www.eppi. ioe.ac.uk/EPPIWebContent/reel/review_groups/MFL/mfl_rv2/MFL_rv2.pdf

MacDonald, C. (1993) *Using the Target Language*. Cheltenham: MGP/ALL.

Martïnez-Flor, A. and Usó-Juan, E. (2006) A comprehensive pedagogical framework to develop pragmatics in the foreign language classroom: The 6Rs approach. In *Applied Language Learning*, (16): 39–64.

Maxim, H. (2002) A study into the feasibility and effects of reading extended authentic discourse in the beginning German language classroom. In *The Modern Language Journal*, 90(1):19–32.

Mayer, R. E. (2001) *Multimedia Learning*. Cambridge: Cambridge University Press.

McCarten, J. (2007) *Teaching Vocabulary: Lessons from the Corpus. Lessons for the Classroom*. Cambridge: Cambridge University Press.

McCarthy, M. and O'Keeffe, A. (2004) Research in the teaching of speaking. In *Annual Review of Applied Linguistics*, 24: 26–43.

McFarlane, A. (1996) Blessings in disguise. In *TES Computers Update*, June, 28: 4.

McKeown, S. (2004) *Meeting SEN in the Curriculum: Modern Foreign Languages*. London: David Fulton.

McLachlan, A. (2002) *New Pathfinder 1. Raising the Standard: Addressing the Needs of Gifted and Talented Pupils*. London: CILT.

Mcrory, G. (2000) Learning to teach grammar in the modern foreign languages classroom. Some implications for initial teacher education. In *Research in Education*, 64: 1–11.

Medgyes, P. (2001) When the teacher is a non-native speaker. In Celce-Murcia, M. (ed.) *Teaching English as a Second or Foreign Language*. Boston, MA: Heinle & Heinle, pp. 429–442.

Meijer, D. with Jenkins, E. -M. (1998) Landeskundliche Inhalte – die Qual der Wahl? Kriterienkatalog zur Beurteilung von Lehrwerken. In *Fremdsprache Deustch*, 18 (1): 18–25. Klett Verlag: Stuttgart.

Mercer, N. (2000) *Words and Minds: How We Use Language to Together*. London: Routledge.

Mercer, N. (2004) Sociocultural discourse analysis: analysing classroom talk as a social mode of thinking. In *Journal of Applied Linguistics* 1: 137–168.

Mercer, S. (2008) Learner self-beliefs. In *ELT Journal*, 62(2): 182–183.

Miller, A. (1995) *Creativity*. Cheltenham: Mary Glasgow Publications and Association for Language Learning.

Miller, A. (2002) Communicative grammar teaching. In Swarbrick, A. (ed.) *Teaching Modern Foreign Languages in Secondary Schools: A Reader*. Open University/ Routledge Falmer, pp. 141–155.

Milton, J. (2006) Language lite: learning French vocabulary in school. In *Journal of French Language Studies*, 16:187–205.

Milton, J. and Meara, P. (1998) Are the British really bad at learning foreign languages? In *Language Learning Journal*, 18: 68–76.

Ministère d'Education (2011) *Dossier de rentrée. Année scolaire 2011–12*. Paris: spresse. Available online at: www.media.education.gouv.fr/file/Rentree_scolaire/ 59/5/Rentree-scolaire-2011_190595.pdf

Mitchell, I. and Swarbrick, A. (1994) *Developing Skills for Independent Reading*. London: CILT.

Mitchell, R. (1988) *Communicative Language Teaching in Practice*. London: CILT.

Mitchell, R. (1994) The communicative approach to language teaching: an introduction. In Swarbrick, A. (ed.) *Teaching Modern Languages*. London: Routledge, pp. 33–42.

Mitchell, R. (2000) *Applied linguistics and evidence-based classroom practice: the case of foreign language grammar pedagogy*. In *Applied Linguistics*, 21(3): 281–303.

Mittergeber, M. (2004) Interessante WebQuests – Lernabenteuer im Internet. In *TEL & CAL*, 01/04: 44–49. Available online at: www.eduhi.at/dl/0812.pdf

Mochizuki, N. and Ortega, L. (2008) Balancing communication and grammar in beginning-level foreign language classrooms: a study of guided planning and relativization. In *Language Teaching Research*, 12(1): 11–37.

Modern Language Association of America (MLA) (2007) Foreign languages and higher education: new structures for a changed world. Available online at: www.mla.org/pdf/forlang_news_pdf.pdf

Morgan, C. (2006) Appropriate language assessment in content and language integrated learning. In *Language Learning Journal*, 33: 59–67.

Morgan, C. and Neil. P. (2001) *Teaching Modern Foreign Languages*. London: Kogan Page.

Morley, J. and Truscott, S. (2006) Incorporating peer assessment in to tandem learning. *Language Learning Journal*, 33: 53–58.

Moss, G., Jewitt, C., Levacic, R., Armstrong, V., Cardini, A. and Castle, F. (2007) The interactive whiteboards, pedagogy and pupil performance evaluation: an evaluation of the Schools Whiteboard Expansion (SWE) project: London Challenge. London. DfES Research report 816. Available online at: www.eprints.ioe.ac.uk/ 905/1/Moss2007whiteboardsRR816.pdf

Muñoz, C. (2006) The effects of age on foreign language learning: The BAF project. In Muñoz, C. (ed.) *Age and the Rate of Foreign Language Learning*. Clevedon: Multilingual Matters, pp. 1–40.

Muñoz, C. (2010) On how age affects foreign language learning. In *Advances in Research on Language Acquisition and Teaching*. Selected papers. Available online at: www.enl.auth.gr/gala/14th/Papers/Invited%20Speakers/Munoz.pdf

Mutton, T. (2014) Developing modern foreign language skills through formative assessment. In Pachler, N. and Redondo, A. (eds) *A Practical Guide to Teaching Modern Foreign Languages in the Secondary School* (2nd edn). London: Routledge.

Myles, F. *et al.* (2012) Learning French from ages 5, 7, and 11: an investigation into starting ages, rates and routes of learning amongst early foreign language learners. ESRC End of Award Report, RES-062–23–1545. Swindon: ESRC. Available online at: www.esrc.ac.uk/my-esrc/grants/RES-062–23–1545/outputs/Download/ 22d46b55–42c5–419c-8b51-be582865e6d6

Myles, F., Hooper, J. and Mitchell, R. (1998) Rote or rule? Exploring the role of formulaic language in classroom foreign language learning. In *Language Learning*, 48(3): 323–363.

NALA and Central Bureau (1992) *The Foreign Language Assistant: A Guide to Good Practice*. London: Central Bureau.

Nassaji, H. and Fotos, S. (2004) Current developments in research on the teaching of grammar. In *Annual Review of Applied Linguistics*, 24: 126–145.

Nation, I. (2001) *Teaching and Learning Vocabulary*. New York: Newbury House.

National Reading Panel (2000) Teaching children to read: an evidence-based assessment of the scientific research literature on reading and its implications for reading instruction. Reports of the subgroups. National Institute of Child Health and Human Development/National Institute for Literacy/U.S. Department for Education. Available online at: www.nichd.nih.gov/publications/pubs/nrp/ Documents/report.pdf

NCC (1989) *Special Educational Needs in the National Curriculum*. York: NCC.

NCC (1992) *Modern Foreign Languages Non-statutory Foreign Languages and Special Educational Needs: A New Commitment*. York: NCC.

Neil, P. (1997) *Reflections on the Target Language*. London: CILT.

Neuner, G. and Hunfeld, H. (1993) *Methoden des fremdsprachlichen Deutschunterrichts. Eine Einführung*. Berlin: Langenscheidt.

Nicol, D. (2007) Principles of good assessment and feedback: theory and practice. Keynote paper at Assessment Design for Learning Responsibility, 29–31, May. Available online at: www.york.ac.uk/media/staffhome/learningandteaching/ documents/keyfactors/Principles_of_good_assessment_and_feedback.pdf

Niño, A. (2009) Machine translation in foreign language learning: language learners' and tutors' perceptions of its advantages and disadvantages. In *CALL*, 21(2): 241–258.

Norris, J. (2011) Task-based teaching and testing. In Long, M. and Doughty, C. (eds) *The Handbook of Language Teaching*. Chichester: Wiley-Blackwell, pp. 578–594.

Nunan, D. (1989) *Designing Tasks for the Communicative Classroom*. Cambridge: Cambridge University Press.

Nunan, D. and Lamb, C. (1996) *The Self-directed Teacher: Managing the Learning Process*. Cambridge: Cambridge University Press.

Oates, T. (2012) Could do better: using international comparisons to refine the National Curriculum in England. In *The Curriculum Journal*, 22(2): 121–150.

O'Brien, T. (2004) Writing in a foreign language: teaching and learning. In *Language Teaching*, 37: 1–28.

O'Dowd, R. (2007) (ed.) *Online Intercultural Exchange: An Introduction for Foreign Language Teachers*. Clevedon: Multilingual Matters.

Ofqual (2011) GCSE subject criteria for modern foreign languages. London. Available online at: www.rewardinglearning.org.uk/docs/regulation/gcse_criteria/nov11/ gcse-subject-criteria-modern-foreign-languages.pdf

Ofsted (2005) Implementing languages entitlement in primary schools: an evaluation of progress in 10 Pathfinder LEAs. London. HMI 2476: Available online at: www. dera.ioe.ac.uk/5386/1/Implementing%20languages%20entitlement%20in%20 primary%20schools%20%28PDF%20format%29.pdf

Ofsted (2008) The changing landscape of languages – an evaluation of language learning. London. Available online at: www.ofsted.gov.uk/resources/changing-landscape- of-languages

Ofsted (2011) Modern languages: achievement and challenge 2007–2010. London. Available online at: www.ofsted.gov.uk/resources/modern-languages-achievement-and-challenge-2007-2010

O'Malley, J., Chamot, A., Stewner-Manzanares, G., Kupper, L. and Russo, R. (1985) Learning strategies used by beginning and intermediate ESL students. In *Language Learning*, 35(1): 21–46.

Ortega, L. (2009) *Understanding Second Language Acquisition*. London: Hodder Education.

Oxford, R. (1987) *Language Learning Strategies: What Every Teacher Should Know*. Boston: Heinle & Heinle.

Oxford, R. (2011) *Teaching and Researching Language Learning Strategies*. Harlow: Pearson Longman.

Pachler, N. (ed.) (1999a) *Teaching Modern Foreign Languages at Advanced Level*. London: Routledge.

Pachler, N. (1999b) Teaching and learning culture. In Pachler, N. (ed.) *Teaching Modern Foreign Languages at Advanced Level*. London: Routledge, pp.76–92.

Pachler, N. (1999c) Teaching and learning grammar. In Pachler, N. (ed.) *Teaching Modern Foreign Languages at Advanced Level*. London: Routledge, pp. 93–115.

Pachler, N. (2000) Re-examining communicative language teaching. In Field, K. (ed.) *Issues in Modern Foreign Language Teaching*. London: RoutledgeFalmer, pp. 26–41.

Pachler, N. (2001) Electronic reference tools for foreign language learners, teachers and users: off line vocabulary look-up programs. In *Language Learning Journal*, 24: 24–29.

Pachler, N. (2002) Speech technologies and foreign language teaching and learning. In *Language Learning Journal*, 26: 54–61. Rugby: ALL.

Pachler, N. (2003) Foreign language teaching as an evidence-based profession? In *Language Learning Journal*, 27: 4–14. Rugby: ALL.

Pachler, N. (2007) Internet-based approaches to modern foreign language teaching and learning. In Pachler, N. and Redondo, A. (eds) *Teaching Modern Foreign Languages in the Secondary School: A Practical Guide*. London: Routledge, pp. 93–99.

Pachler, N. and Allford, D. (2000) Literature in the communicative classroom. In Field, K. (ed.) *Issues in Modern Foreign Languages Teaching*. London: Routledge, pp. 228–244.

Pachler, N. and Field, K. (1999) Learner independence. In Pachler, N. (ed.) *Teaching Modern Foreign Languages at Advanced Level*. London: Routledge, pp. 60–75.

Pachler, N. and Redondo, A. (eds) (2005) Support for learning: special issue on inclusive approaches to teaching foreign languages. *British Journal of Learning Support*, 20(3). NASEN.

Pachler, N. and Redondo, A. (2012) Secondary education. In Byram, M. (ed.) *Encyclopedia of Language Teaching and Learning*. London: Routledge.

Pachler, N. with Reimann, T. (1999) Reaching beyond the classroom. In Pachler, N. (ed.) *Teaching Modern Foreign Languages at Advanced level*. London: Routledge, pp. 282–297.

Pachler, N., Bachmair, B. and Cook, J. (2010) *Mobile Learning: Structures, Agency, Practices*. New York: Springer.

Pachler, N., Evans, M. and Lawes, S. (2007) *Modern Foreign Languages: Teaching School Subjects 11–19*. London: Routledge.

Pachler, N., Makoe, P., Burns, M. and Blommaert, J. (2008) The things (we think) we (ought to) do: ideological processes and practices in teaching. In *Teaching and Teacher Education*, 24(2): 437–450.

Page, R. (1997) *Working with Your Foreign Language Assistant.* Cheltenham: Mary Glasgow Publications/Association for Language Learning.

Paige, M., Jorstad, H., Siaya, L., Klein, F. and Colby, J. (2000) Culture learning in language education: a review of the literature. St Paul, MN: Centre for Advanced Research in Language Acquisition (CARLA), University of Minnesota. Available online at: www.education.umn.edu/EdPA/People/paigCV.pdf

Paribakht, T. and Wesche, M. (1993) Reading comprehension and second language development in a comprehension-based ESL programme. In *TESL Canada Journal*, 11: 9–27.

Parkinson, B. (1992) Observing foreign language lessons. In *Language Learning Journal*, 5, pp. 20–24.

Peacey, N. (2013) An introduction to inclusion, special educational needs and disability. In Capel, S., Leask, M. and Turner, T. (eds) *Learning to Teach in the Secondary School: A Companion to School Experience* (6th edn). London: Routledge, pp. 285–304.

Perry, L. and Southwell, L. (2011) Developing intercultural understanding and skills models and approaches. In *Intercultural Education*, 22(6): 453–466.

Pickering, J., Daly, C. and Pachler, N. (2007) Introduction. In Pickering, J., Daly, C. and Pachler, N. (eds) *New Designs for Teachers' Professional Learning*. Bedford Way Papers. London: Institute of Education, pp. 1–22.

Porto, M. (2010) Culturally responsive L2 education: an awareness-raising proposal. In *ELT Journal*, 64(1): 45–53.

Porto, M. (2013) Language and intercultural education: an interview with Michael Byram. In *Pedagogies: An International Journal*. DOI:10.1080/1554480X.2013. 769196

Powell, B. (1999) Developing receptive language skills – listening and reading. In Pachler, N. (ed.) *Teaching Modern Foreign Languages at Advanced Level*. London: Routledge, pp. 160–183.

Powell, B. and Barnes, A. (1996) *Developing Advanced Skills*. Cheltenham: MGP/ Stanley Thornes.

Prabhu, N. (1987) *Second Language Pedagogy*. Oxford: Oxford University Press.

QCA (2000) GCSE criteria for modern foreign languages. London.

Rampillon, U. (1994) *Lerntechniken im Fremdsprachenunterricht* (2nd edn). Munich: Hueber.

Read, J. (2004) Research in teaching vocabulary. In *Annual Review of Applied Linguistics*, 24: 146–161.

Redman, J. (2005) Stationenlernen: a student-centred approach to working with foreign language texts. In Die Unterrichtspraxis/Teaching German 38(2): 135–142.

Redondo, A. (2000) Mixed ability grouping in modern foreign languages teaching. In Field, K. (ed.) *Issues in Modern Foreign Languages Teaching*. London: Routledge, pp. 122–133.

Redondo, A. (2014) Working with other adults. In Pachler, N. and Redondo, A. (eds) *A Practical Guide to Teaching Foreign Languages in the Secondary School* (2nd edn). London: Routledge.

Reichelt, M., Lefkowitz, N., Rinnert, C. and Schultz, J. (2012) Key issues in foreign language writing. In *Foreign Language Annals*, 45(1): 22–41.

Richards, J. (1998) What's the use of lesson plans? In Richards, J. (ed.) *Beyond Training*. Cambridge: Cambridge University Press, pp. 103–121.

Richards, J. (2013) Curriculum approaches in language teaching: forward, central, and backward design. In *RELC Journal*, 44(5): 5–33.

Richards, J. and Rodgers, T. (2001) *Approaches and Methods in Language Teaching* (2nd edn). Cambridge: Cambridge University Press.

Richards, K. (2006) 'Being the teacher': identity and classroom conversation. In *Applied Linguistics*, 27(1): 51–77.

Riener, C. and Willingham, D. (2010) The myth of learning styles. In *Change: The Magazine of Higher Learning*, 42(5): 32–35.

Roberts, C., Byram, N., Barro, A., Jordan, S., and Street, B. (2000) *Language Learners as Ethnographers*. Clevedon: Multilingual Matters.

Roberts, J. (1998) *Language Teacher Education*. London: Arnold.

Roberts, T. (1992) *Towards a Learning Theory in Modern Languages*. Occasional Paper No. 2. London: Institute of Education.

Robertson, J. (1989) *Effective Classroom Control: Understanding Pupil/Teacher Relationships*. London: Hodder & Stoughton.

Rojas-Drummond, S. and Mercer, N. (2003) Scaffolding the development of effective collaboration and learning. In *International Journal of Educational Research*, 39(2): 99–111.

Rose, J. (2009) Independent review of the primary curriculum. Final report. Available online at: www.education.gov.uk/publications/eOrderingDownload/Primary_curriculum_Report.pdf

Rowles, D., Carty, M. and McLachlan, A. (1998) *The Foreign Language Assistant: A Guide to Good Practice*. London: CILT.

Rubin, J. (1975) What the 'good language learner' can teach us. In *TESOL Quarterly*, 9(1): 41–51.

Rumley, G. and Sharpe, K. (1993) Generalisable game activities in modern language learning. In *Language Learning Journal*, 8: 35–38.

Rutherford, W. (1987) *Second Language Grammar: Learning and Teaching*. London: Longman.

Scarino, A. (2010) Assessing intercultural capability in learning languages: a renewed understanding of language, culture, learning, and the nature of assessment. In *The Modern Language Journal*, 94(ii): 324–329.

Schmidt, R. (2001) Attention. In Robinson, P. (ed.) *Cognition and Second Language Instruction*. Cambridge: Cambridge University Press.

Schmitt, N. (2008) Instructed second language vocabulary learning. In *Language Teaching Research*, 12(3): 329–363.

Schneider, E. and Evers, T. (2009) Linguistic intervention techniques for at-risk English language learners. In *Foreign Language Annals*, 42(1): 55–76.

Seipold, J., Pachler, N., Bachmair, B. and Döbeli, B. (2014) Mobile learning – strategies for planning and implementing learning with mobile devices in Secondary school contexts. In Leask, M. and Pachler, N. (eds) *Learning to Teach using ICT in the Secondary school*. London: Routledge.

Setter, J. and Jenkins, J. (2005) Pronunciation. In *Language Teaching*, 38: 1–17.

Shaw, P. (1994) Reluctant learners – you can do it! In McLagan, P. (ed.) *Steps to Learning: Modern Languages for Pupils with Special Educational Needs*. London: CILT, pp. 35–39.

Shively, R. (2010) From the virtual world to the real world: a model of pragmatics instruction for study abroad. In *Foreign Language Annals*, 43(1): 105–137.

Shulman, L. (1987) Knowledge and teaching: foundations of the New Reform. In *Harvard Educational Review*, 57(1): 1–21.

Sinclair, J. and Coulthard, M. (1975) *Towards an Analysis of Discourse: The English Used by Teachers and Pupils*. London: Oxford University Press.

Singleton, D. and Muñoz, C. (2011) Around and beyond the critical period hypothesis. In Hinkel, E. (ed.) *Handbook of Research in Second Language Teaching and Learning*, Vol II. London: Routledge, pp. 407–425.

Skehan, P. (1996) A framework for the implementation of task-based instruction. In *Applied Linguistics*, 17(1): 38–62.

Skehan, P. (2003) Task-based instruction. In *Language Teaching*, 36: 1–14.

Skehan, P. and Foster, P. (1997) Task type and task processing conditions as influences on foreign language performance. In *Language Teaching Research*, 1:185–211.

Slade, D. (1997) Stories and gossip in English: the macro-structure of casual talk. In *Prospect*,12: 72–86.

Snow, D. and Byram, M. (1997) *Crossing frontiers: The School Study Visit Abroad*. London: CILT.

Spada, N. (2007) Communicative Language Teaching: current status and future prospects. In Cummins, J. and Davison, C. (eds) *International Handbook of English Language Teaching. Part 1*. New York: Springer, pp. 271–288.

Spenader, A. (2011) Language learning and acculturation: lessons from high school and gap-year exchange students. In *Foreign Language Annals* 44(2): 381–398.

Stern, H. (1985) Literature teaching and the communicative approach. In Heid, M. (ed.) *Literarische Texte im kommunikativen Fremdsprachenunterricht. New Yorker Werkheft*. Munich: Goethe-Institut, pp. 6–46.

Stobart, G. and Gipps, C. (1997) *Assessment: A Teacher's Guide to the Issues* (3rd edn). London: Hodder & Stoughton.

Strasser, T. and Pachler, N. (2014) Digital technologies in foreign language teaching and learning. In Pachler, N. and Redondo, A. (eds) *Teaching Modern Foreign Languages in the Secondary School: A Practical Guide* (2nd edn). London: Routledge.

Stubbs, M. (1986) Lexical density: a technique and some findings. In Coulthard, D. (ed.) *Talking about Text: Studies Presented to David Brazil on his Retirement*. Discourse Analysis Monograph 13. Birmingham: English Language Research, pp. 27–42.

Summer, T. (2012) Introduction: from method to post-method. In M. Eisenmann and T. Summer (eds) *Basic Issues in EFL Teaching and Learning*. Heidelberg: Universitaetsverlag Winter, pp. 1–15.

Svalberg, A. (2007) Language awareness and language learning. In *Language Teaching*, 40(4): 287–308.

Swaffar, J. and Vlatten, A. (1997) A sequential model for video viewing in the foreign language curriculum. In *The Modern Language Journal*, 81(ii): 175–184.

Swan, M. (2006) Two out of three ain't enough: the essential ingredients of a language course. Keynote at IATEFL Harrogate. Available online at: www.mikeswan.co.uk/elt-applied-linguistics/Two-out-of-three-aint-enough-the-essential-ingredients-of-a-language-course

Swarbrick, A. (1998) *More Reading for Pleasure in a Foreign Language*. London: CILT.

Sygmund, D. and Smith, B. (n.d.) *Transition between Primary and Secondary Education: State of the Art*. Report produced as part of the EU-funded Comenius project PRI-SEC-CO: Primary and Secondary Continuity in Foreign Language Teaching 2007–2009. Pädagogische Hochschule Freiburg.

Taber, K. (2007) *Classroom-based Research and Evidence-based Practice*. London: Sage.

Taylor, W. (1994) Classroom variables. In Moon, B. and Shelton-Mayes, A. (eds) *Teaching and Learning in the Secondary School*. Milton Keynes: Open University Press, pp. 161–165.

Taylor, H. and Sorenson, J. (1961) Culture capsules. In *The Modern Language Journal*, 45(8): 350–354.

Thomas, J. (2012) Classroom discourse in foreign language classrooms: a review of the literature. In *Foreign Language Annals*, 45(1): 8–27.

Thorne, S. (2003) Artifacts and cultures-of-use in intercultural communication. In *Language Learning & Technology* 7(2): 38–67. Available online at: www.llt.msu. edu/vol7num2/pdf/thorne.pdf

Ting, Y. (2011) CLIL . . . not only not immersion but also more than the sum of its parts. In *ELT Journal*, 65(3): 314–317.

Tinsley,T. (2013) Languages: the state of the nation. Demand and supply of language skills. London: British Academy. Available online at: www.britac.ac.uk/policy/ State_of_the_Nation_2013.cfm

Toddhunter, S. (2007) Instructional Conversations in a High School Spanish Class. In *Foreign Language Annals*, 40(4): 604–621.

Turner, J. (2001) Breaking the ice on exchanges: a tried and tested exercise to bring German and English exchange partners together. In *Deutsch Lehren und Lernen*, 23: 3–6.

Turner, K. (1996) The National Curriculum and syllabus design. In *Language Learning Journal*, 14: 14–18.

Turner, T. with Field, K. and Arthur, J. (1997) Working with your mentor. In Capel, S., Leask, M. and Turner, T. (eds) *Starting to Teach in the Secondary School: A Companion for the Newly Qualified Teacher*. London: Routledge, pp. 26–39.

ufi/learndirect and kineo (2007) *Podcasting reviewed*. Available online at: www.kineo. com/ufi/learndirect-kineo-guides/good-practice-guides-with-ufilearndirect.html

Ushioda, E. (2011) Language learning motivation, self and identity: current theoretical perspectives. In *Computer Assisted Language Learning*, 24(3): 199–210.

Vandergrift, L. (2004) Listening to learn or learning to listen? In *Annual Review of Applied Linguistics*, *24*: 3–25.

Vandergrift, L. (2007) Recent developments in second and foreign language listening comprehension research. In *Language Teaching*, 40(3): 191–210.

van den Branden, K. (2009) Mediating between predetermined order and chaos: the role of the teacher in task-based language education. In *International Journal of Applied Linguistics*, 19(3): 247–285.

van Leeuwen, L. (2009) Discourses of identity. In *Language Teaching*, 42(2): 212–221.

van Lier, L. (2007) Action-based teaching, autonomy and identity. In *Innovation in Language Learning and Teaching*, 1(1): 46–65.

van Lier, L. (2010) Ecological-semiotic perspectives on educational linguistics. In Spolsky, B. and Hult, F. M. (eds) *The Handbook of Educational Linguistics*. Malden and Oxford: Wiley-Blackwell, pp. 598–605.

van Lier, L. (2011) Language learning: an ecological-semiotic approach. In Hinkel, E. (ed.) *Handbook of Research in Second Language Teaching and Learning*, Vol. II, New York and Abingdon: Routledge, pp. 383–394.

Wade, P., Marshall, H. and O'Donnell, S. (2009) Primary modern foreign languages: longitudinal survey of implementation of national Entitlement to Language Learning at Key Stage 2. Final report. London: DCSF. Available online at: www. education.gov.uk/publications/eOrderingDownload/DCSF-RR127A.pdf

Wajnryb, R. (1992) *Classroom Observation Tasks: A Resource Book for Language Teachers and Trainers*. Cambridge: Cambridge University Press.

Walsh, S. (2002) Construction and obstruction: talk and learner involvement in the EFL classroom. In *Language Teaching Research*, 6(1): 3–24.

Wang, C. (2010) Towards a second language socialization perspective: issues in study abroad research. In *Foreign Language Annals*, 43(1): 50–63.

Waring, H. (2009) Moving out of IRF(initiation-response-feedback): a single case analysis. In *Language Learning*, 59: 796–824.

Warnock, M. (1978) *Report on the Committee of Enquiry into the Education of Handicapped Children and Young People.* London: HMSO.

Way, D., Joiner, E. and Seaman, M. (2000) Writing in the secondary foreign language classroom: the effects of prompts and tasks on novice learners of French. In *The Modern Language Journal*, 84(ii): 171–184.

Wells, G. (1993) Reevaluating the IRF sequence: a proposal for the articulation of theories of activity and discourse for the analysis of teaching and learning in the classroom. In *Linguistics in Education*, 5: 1–37.

Wenger, E. (1998) *Communities of Practice: Learning, Meaning and Identity.* Cambridge: Cambridge University Press.

White, J. (2005) Howard Gardner: the myth of multiple intelligences. *Viewpoint 16.* Institute of Education, University of London. Available online at: http://.eprints. ioe.ac.uk/1263/1/WhiteJ2005HowardGardner1.pdf

Whong, M. (2011) *Language Teaching: Linguistic Theory in Practice.* Edinburgh: Edinburgh University Press.

Widdowson, H. (1998) Skills, abilities, an contexts of reality. In *Annual Review of Applied Linguistics*, 18: 323–333.

Williams, E. (1982) The 'witness' activity: group interaction through video. In Geddes, M. and Sturtridge, G. (eds) *Video in the Language Classroom.* London: Heinemann, pp. 69–73.

Williams, K. (1991) Modern languages in the school curriculum: a philosophical view. In *Journal of Philosophy of Education*, 25(2): 247–258.

Williams, M., Burden, R. and Lanvers, U. (2002) 'French is the Language of Love and Stuff': student perceptions of issues related to motivation in learning a foreign language. In *British Educational Research Journal*, 28(4): 503–528.

Williams, M., Burden, R., Poulet, G. and Maun, I. (2004) Learners' perceptions of their successes and failures in foreign language learning. In *Language Learning Journal*, 30: 19–29.

Wilson, E. (ed.) (2012) *School-based Research: A Guide for Education Students* (2nd edn). London: Sage.

Wintergerst, A. and McVeigh, J. (2010) *Tips for Teaching Culture: Practical Approaches to Intercultural Communications.* White Plains, NY: Pearson Education.

Wong, L. -H. and Looi, C. -K. (2010) Vocabulary learning by mobile-assisted authentic content creation and social meaning-making: two case studies. In *Journal of Computer Assisted Learning*, 26(5): 421–433.

Wood, D., Bruner, J. and Ross, G. (1976) The role of tutoring in problem solving. In *Journal of Child Psychology & Psychiatry & Allied Disciplines*, 17: 89–100.

Woore, R. (2009) Beginners' progress in decoding L2 French: some longitudinal evidence from English Modern Foreign Languages classrooms. In *Language Learning Journal*, 37(1): 3–18.

Wragg, T. (ed.) (1984) *Classroom Teaching Skills.* London: Croom Helm.

Wray, D. and Lewis, M. (1998) An approach to scaffolding children's non-fiction writing: the use of writing frames. In Shiel, G. and Dhalaigh, N. (eds) *Developing Language and Literacy: The Role of the Teacher.* Dublin: Reading Association of Ireland. Also available online at: www2.warwick.ac.uk/fac/soc/wie/research-new/teachingandlearning/publications/framesrai.pdf

Wray, D. and Lewis, M. (2000) Developing non-fiction writing: beyond writing frames. In Evans, J. (eds) *The Writing Classroom.* London: David Fulton, pp. 108–115.

Also available online at: www2.warwick.ac.uk/fac/soc/wie/research-new/teaching andlearning/publications/framesevans.pdf

Wright, M. and Brown, P. (2006) Reading in a modern foreign language: exploring the potential benefits of reading strategy instruction. In *Language Learning Journal*, 33: 22–33.

Wright, T. (2005) *Classroom Management in Language Education*. Basingstoke and New York: Palgrave Macmillan.

Wringe, C. (1989) *The Effective Teaching of Modern Languages*. London: Longman.

Wringe, C. (1994) Ineffective lessons – reasons and remedies: jottings from the tutor's notepad. In *Language Learning Journal*, 10: 11–14.

Yaxley, B. (1994) *Developing Teachers' Theories of Teaching: A Touchstone Approach*. Brighton: Falmer Press.

Zeichner, K. and Liston, D. (1996) *Reflective Teaching: An Introduction*. Mahwah, NJ: Lawrence Erlbaum Associates.

Zhang, S. and Cheng, Q. (2011) Learning to teach through a practicum-based micro-teaching model. In *Action in Teacher Education*, 33(4): 343–358.

Zimmer, B. (2010) Chunking. Available online at: www.nytimes.com/2010/09/19/magazine/19FOB-OnLanguage-Zimmer.html?ref=onlanguage&pagewanted=print

INDEX